MW00981972

The

London

Jobhunter's
Guide

2003/2004

Books to make you better

Books to make you better. To make you *be* better, *do* better, *feel* better. Whether you want to upgrade your personal skills or change your job, whether you want to improve your managerial style, become a more powerful communicator, or be stimulated and inspired as you work.

Prentice Hall Business is leading the field with a new breed of skills, careers and development books. Books that are a cut above the mainstream – in topic, content and delivery – with an edge and verve that will make you better, with less effort.

Books that are as sharp and smart as you are.

Prentice Hall Business.
We work harder – so you don't have to.

For more details on products, and to contact us, visit
www.business-minds.com
www.yourmomentum.com

The

London

Jobhunter's
Guide

2003/2004

All the information you
need to get the **right job**
with the **least stress**

Tim Gough
Shamus Fitzsimons

An imprint of Pearson Education

London ■ New York ■ Toronto ■ Sydney ■ Tokyo ■ Singapore ■ Hong Kong ■ Cape Town
New Delhi ■ Madrid ■ Paris ■ Amsterdam ■ Munich ■ Milan ■ Stockholm

PEARSON EDUCATION LIMITED

Head Office:
Edinburgh Gate
Harlow CM20 2JE
Tel: +44 (0)1279 623623
Fax: +44 (0)1279 431059

London Office:
128 Long Acre, London WC2E 9AN
Tel: +44 (0)20 447 2000
Fax: +44 (0)20 447 2170
Website: www.business-minds.com

First published in Great Britain in 2003
Pages 3–27, 38–56, 68–114, 119–180, 188–219 and 227–270 © S C Fitzsimons 2003
Pages 115–118 © Deloitte & Touche 2003
Remainder © Pearson Education Limited 2003

ISBN 0 273 65934 0

The right of Tim Gough and Shamus Fitzsimons to be identified as
authors of this work has been asserted by them in accordance
with the Copyright, Designs and Patents Act 1988.

British Library Cataloguing in Publication Data
A CIP catalogue record for the print version of this book can be obtained from the British Library.

10 9 8 7 6 5 4 3 2 1

Typeset in house by Pearson Education Limited
Printed and bound in Great Britain by Biddles Ltd of Guildford and King's Lynn

The Publishers' policy is to use paper manufactured from sustainable forests.

Contents

Introduction

by Tim Gough and Shamus Fitzsimons

Finding the job you want in London might not be as easy as you think. There is a wealth of information and help available to you, but do you know where to go for this help or how to get the help you need?

Where are you going to start the hunt for your new job? Employment agencies, advertisements from newspapers, the internet, word of mouth, or by going straight to the employer? The London Jobhunter's Guide 2003/2004 will prepare you for whichever route you choose to take.

Before you apply for the job you're going to have to do some serious preparation. How good is your CV? When did you last update it? What does an employer want to see on your CV anyway? Maybe you could do with some help to get your CV up to standard? Maybe you need to update your computer skills before you apply for the new office job? This book lists organisations that can help you: professional CV writers and computer training providers.

Hopefully you'll now get the interview. When did you have your last one? When did someone last sit you down and fire questions at you? What are your strengths and weaknesses? What are you looking for in an employer? Where do you see yourself in five years' time? This book will help you prepare for those first and second interviews, and tell you what to expect from interviews and assessments.

Many people in London take advantage of one of the thousands of employment agencies that are always offering to get you the job you want. How are you going to find the employment agency that has the work you want? What will happen when you go to see them? What is their registration process? Who are *they* looking for? The listings in this book will tell you everything you need to know about these agencies, and will save you the time, expense and frustration of contacting unsuitable agencies. Each listing provides full contact details and information on what they do, how to apply and what the agency is looking for.

This book includes an article from one of the industry's experts and excerpts from previously published books on topics such as CVs, interviews, the internet and graduate recruitment. Together with the help of employment agencies, CV writers, training providers and image consultants, you'll soon be on the way to finding the right job, with the least stress.

About the Directory Sections

The directory sections of this book include details of recruitment agencies operating within the London 0207 dialling code area. For this edition we have only included details of agencies who have an active website address and, in most cases, a contactable e-mail address for ease of use by our readers. Some organisations are listed as 'apply directly on line' when the e-mail address is not given on the main website.

All agencies listed have a main entry in the directory section that deals with their primary market sector. Where an agency has a second major market sector, a smaller entry is included in the appropriate directory section with a cross-reference to the agency's full details in their main entry.

Within the directory section dealing with each business category, agencies are listed alphabetically. All the agencies listed in the directory sections appear in the full alphabetical index at the back of the book.

Authors' Note

The London Jobhunter's Guide 2003/2004 has been compiled by researching data available in the public domain. This includes the Brief Description supplied for each agency and it is recommended that readers verify any information independently prior to making any decisions based on this data.

As part of the recruitment agency listings we indicate whether an agency is a member of the Recruitment and Employment Confederation (REC). The REC promotes high standards, including a strict code of practice and adherence to all relevant legislation. It is not however a guarantee by us that the agency will offer you a better service than a non-member. For further information on the REC, visit their website at www.rec.uk.com

Whilst every effort has been made to obtain and verify accurate information, occasional errors are inevitable due to the magnitude of the database. Should you discover an error, or if a company has been omitted, please send an e-mail to Shamus at **LJG@pearsoned-ema.com** so that we may update future editions and consider nominations for new entries.

Recruitment Agencies

Accountancy and Banking

AA Appointments
See **Secretarial, page 227**

Absolute Recruitment Ltd
See **Legal, page 188**

Accountancy Additions Ltd

Head Office   ✉ Page House, 39–41 Parker St, WC2B 5LN
  ℂ T 020 7831 2000   F 020 7404 5557

  ✉ 67–71 Oxford St, W1R 1RB
  ⊖ Tottenham Court Rd
  ▤ Euston
  ℂ T 020 7255 9250   F 020 7255 9269
  @ westendcentral@accountancyadditions.com
Market areas   Accountancy and Finance

  ✉ Victoria Station House, 191 Victoria St, SW1E 5NE
  ⊖ Victoria
  ▤ Victoria
  ℂ T 020 7233 5973   F 020 7233 7938
  @ victoria@accountancyadditions.com
Market areas   Accountancy and Finance

  ✉ Devonshire House, 146 Bishopsgate, EC2M 4JX
  ⊖ Moorgate
  ▤ Moorgate
  ℂ T 020 7375 3749   F 020 7377 9884
  @ city@accountancyadditions.com,
  docklands@accountancyadditions.com
Market areas   Accountancy and Finance

  ✉ Centric House, 390–391 The Strand, WC2R 0LT
  ⊖ Charing Cross
  ▤ Charing Cross
  ℂ T 020 7379 5333   F 020 7836 0655
  @ strand@accountancyadditions.com
Market areas   Accountancy and Finance

  ✉ Bridge House, 4 Borough High St, SE1 9QW
  ⊖ London Bridge
  ▤ London Bridge
  ℂ T 020 7939 7560   F 020 7403 3937
  @ londonbridge@accountancyadditions.com,
  publicsector@accountancyadditions.com
Market areas   Accountancy and Finance, Public Practice

Website www.accountancyadditions.com
UK Offices 27
REC Member No

Brief Description Accountancy Additions are a division of Michael Page International, specialising in the recruitment of permanent and temporary staff from Junior Accounts Staff to Part Qualified Accountants across all areas of Industry, Commerce and Public Practice. With 26 offices strategically positioned throughout the UK, Accountancy Additions are committed to providing a high-quality individualised recruitment service for every client and candidate, focusing on the development of long term relationships.

Preferred method of contact Interviews are by appointment only – please make initial contact by telephone or email
Minimum requirements None
Type of business Contract, Temporary and Permanent
Grade/Level of Appointments Junior Accounts Staff to Part Qualified level

Accountancy Careers

Head Office   ✉ New Penderel House, 283–288 High Holborn, WC1V 7HF
  ⊖ Chancery Lane
  ▤ City Thameslink
  ℂ T 020 7242 4230   F 020 7242 4620
  @ natalie.ac@abbatt.co.uk
Market areas   Accountancy and Finance

Website www.abbatt.co.uk
UK Offices 1
REC Member No
Brief Description Accountancy Careers are part of the Abbatt Group specialising in all levels of Accountancy recruitment.

Preferred method of contact Interviews are by appointment only – please make initial contact by telephone or email
Minimum requirements None
Type of business Contract, Temporary and Permanent
Grade/Level of Appointments Junior Accounts Staff to Qualified

Accountancy Connections

Head Office   ✉ 43 Eagle St, WC1R 4AP
  ⊖ Holborn
  ▤ City Thameslink
  ℂ T 020 7304 6400   F 020 7304 6422
  @ howard.foster@executiveconnections.co.uk
Market areas   Accountancy, Finance and Banking

Website www.accountancy-connections.co.uk
UK Offices 1
REC Member No

Brief Description Accountancy Connections is part of the Executive Connections Group, dealing with the recruitment of part-qualified and non-qualified Finance staff. Specialising in permanent and temporary appointments, their client database includes most of the large 'blue chip' multinationals FTSE 100 and Fortune 500 companies. Their consultants are equally experienced in managing the recruitment needs of small entrepreneurial businesses within niche market sectors.

Preferred method of contact Interviews are by appointment only – please make initial contact by telephone or email

Minimum requirements None

Type of business Contract, Temporary and Permanent

Grade/Level of Appointments Junior Accounts Staff to Part Qualified level

---

The Accountancy Task Force Group Ltd

Head Office ✉ 75 Watling St, EC4M 9BJ
🚇 Mansion House
🚊 Cannon St
☎ T 020 7329 3923 F 020 7329 4992
@ atf@globalnet.co.uk
Market areas Accountancy

Website www.users.globalnet.co.uk/~atf
UK Offices 1
REC Member No

Brief Description Accountancy Task Force (ATF) have been established for over 25 years, providing a specialist recruitment service to Commerce and Industry in the selection of permanent and temporary Accountancy Staff, with clients ranging from Manufacturing, Service and Distribution to Advertising and Media.

Preferred method of contact Interviews are by appointment only – please make initial contact by telephone or email

Minimum requirements None

Type of business Contract, Temporary and Permanent

Grade/Level of Appointments 1st Jobbers to Accountants, Finance Director

---

Accountants on Call (AOC)

✉ 6 Newman St, London
🚇 Tottenham Court Rd
🚊 Euston
☎ T 020 7440 3670 F 020 7440 3680
@ londonwestend@aocuk.com
Market areas Accountancy and Finance

✉ 34 London Wall,
🚇 Moorgate
🚊 Moorgate
☎ T 020 7329 7700 F 020 7329 7711
@ londoncity@aocuk.com
Market areas Accountancy and Finance

Website www.aocnetuk.com
UK Offices 9
REC Member No
Head Office Richmond Office

Brief Description Part of the Adecco group, AOC is one of the largest and fastest-growing financial staffing and recruiting specialists in the world. The global AOC brand provides a wide range of Accounting and Financial Specialists through more than 125 offices in the UK, Canada, USA, Ireland, France, Portugal, Spain, Belgium and Italy.

Preferred method of contact Interviews are by appointment only – please make initial contact by telephone or email

Minimum requirements None

Type of business Contract, Temporary and Permanent

Grade/Level of Appointments Junior Accounts Staff to Qualified level

---

Accountemps

Head Office ✉ Walter House, 48 Strand, WC2R 0PT
☎ T 020 7395 9600 F 020 7836 4942

✉ Rex House, 10 Regent St, SW1Y 4PE
🚇 Piccadilly Circus
🚊 Charing Cross
☎ T 020 7389 6900 F 020 7389 6999
@ westend@accountemps.co.uk
Market areas Accountancy, Finance and Banking

Website www.accountemps.net
UK Offices 15
REC Member No

Brief Description Accountemps, A Robert Half International Company. Founded in 1948, the company pioneered specialised staffing services and today leads the world in the field. With more than 330 locations throughout UK, Europe, Australia, New Zealand and United States, the company is traded on the New York Stock Exchange and operates five separate divisions, each serving different markets. These are Robert Half, which specialises in placing permanent Accounting and Finance Professionals, Accountemps – temporary Accounting, Banking and Finance Support Personnel, RHI Management Resources – Senior-level Accounting and Finance Management on an individual or project-team basis, Office Team – temporary Administrative and Office Support Personnel, RHI Consulting – permanent and contract IT Specialists.

Preferred method of contact Interviews are by appointment only – please make initial contact by telephone or email

Type of business Temporary and Contract

Grade/Level of Appointments All levels

Acme Appointments

Head Office ✉ 315–317 Oxford St, W1R 2HH
⊖ Oxford Circus
🚆 Charing Cross
📞 T 020 7493 4000   F 020 7493 4383
@ info@acme-appointments.co.uk
Market areas Accountancy and Finance, Secretarial, Desktop Publishing and Property Management

✉ 88 Cannon St, EC4M 6HT
⊖ Cannon St
🚆 Cannon St
📞 T 020 7623 3883   F 020 7283 3427
@ info@acme-appointments.co.uk
Market areas Accountancy and Finance, Secretarial and Desktop Publishing

✉ 122 Middlesex St, E1 7HY
⊖ Liverpool St
🚆 Liverpool St
📞 T 020 7377 9923   F 020 7375 2948
@ info@acme-appointments.co.uk
Market areas Accountancy and Finance, Secretarial and Desktop Publishing

Website www.acme-appointments.co.uk

UK Offices 3

REC Member No

Brief Description Acme Appointments is divided into three distinct areas of business covering Accountancy recruitment across all levels, General Secretarial and Desktop Publishing, particularly Powerpoint and Quark Xpress

Preferred method of contact Interviews are by appointment only – please make initial contact by telephone or email

Type of business Contract, Temporary and Permanent

Grade/Level of Appointments All levels

Alexander Mann Group

See **IT and Telecoms, page 153**

Alexander McCann Ltd

Head Office ✉ Davena House, 137–149 Goswell Rd, EC1V 7ET
⊖ Angel
🚆 Kings Cross
📞 T 020 7553 7900   F 020 7553 7901
@ mail@alexandermann.co.uk
Market areas IT, Banking, Finance, Scientific, New Technology

Website www.alexandermccann.com

UK Offices 1

REC Member No

Brief Description Whether you are seeking permanent or contract work, the aim of Alexander McCann is to find the role that best suits your financial and career aspirations using their many close relationships with clients in many industry sectors.

Preferred method of contact Telephone for appointment

Minimum requirements None

Type of business Contract and Permanent

Grade/Level of Appointments Graduate to Management level

Allegro Solutions Ltd

See **Legal, page 188**

Amery Cooper Financial Recruitment Consultants

Head Office ✉ Chesham House, 150 Regent St, W1B 5SJ
⊖ Piccadilly Circus
🚆 Charing Cross
📞 T 020 7494 2224   F 020 7432 0516
@ info@amerycooper.co.uk
Market areas Investment Banking, Financial Services

Website www.amerycooper.com

UK Offices 1

REC Member Yes

Brief Description Amery Cooper is a financial recruitment consultancy which specialises exclusively in selecting qualified professionals for Investment Banks, Financial Services Organisations and Major Multi-national Companies. They concentrate on only introducing candidates with high academic achievements and proven success records into the most prestigious City and International Finance careers. In particular, they are retained by a number of Investment Banks to advise newly qualified Chartered Accountants considering moving from a 'big five' firm, notably to opportunities within Corporate Finance, Equity Research and Structured and Project Finance.

Preferred method of contact Apply on line or telephone for appointment

Minimum requirements Newly qualified Accountant, Banking professionals

Type of business Permanent

Grade/Level of Appointments Debt Advisory Executive/Equity Analyst to Corporate Finance Executive

Andersen Leigh Associates Plc

Head Office ✉ 32–36 Great Portland St, W1W 8QX
⊖ Oxford Circus
🚆 Charing Cross
📞 T 020 7307 6500   F 020 7307 6555

@ recruit@andersonleigh.com
Market areas Accountancy, Secretarial

Website www.andersenleigh.com

UK Offices 1

REC Member Yes

Brief Description Andersen Leigh Associates Plc is a full service Human Resource Management group which specialises in the placement of temporary and permanent Accountancy and Secretarial/Support Staff.

Preferred method of contact Telephone for appointment

Minimum requirements None

Type of business Temporary and Permanent

Grade/Level of Appointments Juniors/Graduates to Qualified Accountants/Office Managers

Andersons (UK) Ltd

Head Office ✉ 61 Cheapside, EC2V 6BU
　　　　　　 ⊖ St Pauls
　　　　　　 🚇 Cannon St
　　　　　　 ☎ T 020 7466 0666　F 020 7466 0667
　　　　　　 @ info@andersons-uk.co.uk
Market areas Banking and Financial Services

Website www.andersons-uk.co.uk

UK Offices 1

REC Member No

Brief Description Andersons is a specialist recruitment company working in the Financial Markets, with offices in the City of London, Frankfurt and Geneva. Consultants have experience spanning virtually every area of Investment and Commercial Banking, Securities, Fund Management, Leasing/Asset Finance and other Financial Services companies.

Preferred method of contact Telephone for appointment

Minimum requirements None

Type of business Temporary, Permanent and Contract

Grade/Level of Appointments Junior to Senior Executive Management

Antal International

Head Office ✉ 2nd Floor, 90 Tottenham Ct Rd, W1T 4AN
　　　　　　 ⊖ Tottenham Court Rd
　　　　　　 🚇 Euston
　　　　　　 ☎ T 020 7637 2001　F 020 7638 0949
　　　　　　 @ uk@antal.com
Market areas IT, Accountancy and Finance, Sales and Marketing, HR, Executive Search

Website www.antal.com

UK Offices 1

REC Member No

Brief Description Antal International was established in 1993 and today employs over 300 staff within a fully integrated network of 15 offices in 13 countries.

Preferred method of contact Telephone for appointment

Minimum requirements None

Type of business Permanent and Contract

Grade/Level of Appointments All levels

ARC Recruitment

See **IT and Telecoms, page 153**

Aston Carter

See **IT and Telecoms, page 154**

Audit Professionals

Head Office ✉ 26–28 Bedford Row, WC1R 4HE
　　　　　　 ⊖ Chancery Lane
　　　　　　 🚇 City Thameslink
　　　　　　 ☎ T 020 7845 4200　F 020 7845 4249
　　　　　　 @ cvregistration@financeprofessionals.com
Market areas Audit and Risk Management

Website www.pro-rec-org.com

UK Offices 2

REC Member No

Brief Description Audit Professionals is one of the specialist divisions of the Professional Recruitment Organisation (PRO). This division concentrates on promoting the role of Internal Audit and Risk Management to the finance market to generate existing or potential Auditors for client requirements.

Preferred method of contact Apply on line or telephone for appointment

Minimum requirements Previous professional experience

Type of business Temporary, Permanent and Contract

Grade/Level of Appointments Systems Auditor to Director of Audit

Austen Smythe

See **Secretarial, page 230**

Badenoch & Clark

Head Office ✉ 16–18 New Bridge St, EC4V 6HU
　　　　　　 ⊖ Blackfriars
　　　　　　 🚇 Blackfriars

(T 020 7583 0073   F 020 7353 3908
@ corp.comms@badenochandclark.com
Market areas   Accountancy and Finance, IT, Legal, Banking

Website www.badenochandclark.com
UK Offices 13
REC Member No

Brief Description   Established in 1980, Badenoch & Clark specialises in Accountancy, Legal, Banking, IT, Public Sector, Surveying and Personnel markets. Part of the MPS Group, the company now have 13 offices across the UK.

Preferred method of contact Telephone for appointment
Minimum requirements None
Type of business Permanent, Temporary and Contract
Grade/Level of Appointments Graduate/Junior to Director

Banking Additions

Head Office ✉ Devonshire House, 146 Bishopsgate, EC2M 4JX
⊖ Liverpool St
🚇 Liverpool St
(T 020 7247 6113   F 020 7377 6993
@ bankingoperations@bankingadditions.com, temps@bankingadditions.com, finance@bankingadditions.com, fundmanagement@bankingadditions.com
Market areas Investment Banking, Fund Management, Global Custody, Finance and Accountancy

Website www.bankingadditions.com
UK Offices 1
REC Member No

Brief Description   Established in 1996, Banking Additions is a division of Michael Page International, specialising in the recruitment of permanent and temporary staff within Finance, Operations and Support for London's Financial Services Industry, recruiting on behalf of a wide range of organisations from premier Investment Banking institutions to smaller firms.

Preferred method of contact Telephone for appointment
Minimum requirements None
Type of business Permanent, Temporary and Contract
Grade/Level of Appointments Junior to Management level

Barbara Houghton Associates Ltd

Head Office ✉ City Business Centre, 2 London Wall Buildings, EC2M 5PP
⊖ Moorgate
🚇 Moorgate
(T 020 7417 0070   F 020 7972 9461
@ cvs@bhal.co.uk
Market areas Banking and Financial

Website www.bhal.co.uk
UK Offices 1
REC Member No

Brief Description   Established in 1988, Barbara Houghton Group provides high calibre permanent, contract and temporary personnel to a wide selection of clients including UK and International Banking and Financial institutions.

Preferred method of contact Telephone for appointment
Minimum requirements None
Type of business Permanent and Temporary
Grade/Level of Appointments All levels

Barclay Simpson

Head Office ✉ Hamilton House, 1 Temple Avenue, EC4Y 0HA
⊖ Blackfriars
🚇 Blackfriars
(T 020 7936 2601   F 020 7936 2655
@ bs@barclaysimpson.com
Market areas Risk Management, Internal and Computer Auditors

Website www.barclaysimpson.com
UK Offices 1
REC Member No

Brief Description   Barclay Simpson specialises in the recruitment of Internal and Computer Auditors, Risk Management and Information Security professionals covering all business sectors such as Banking, Financial Services, Retail and Commerce.

Preferred method of contact Telephone for appointment
Minimum requirements None
Type of business Permanent, Contract and Temporary
Grade/Level of Appointments All levels

Bermingham Power Ltd

Head Office ✉ 127 Cheapside, EC2V 6DT
⊖ Bank
🚇 Cannon St
(T 020 7600 0444   F 020 7600 4084
@ info@berminghampower.demon.co.uk
Market areas Public Practice, Banking, Finance and Accountancy, Executive Search

Website www.hrgo.co.uk
UK Offices 1
REC Member No

Brief Description   Bermingham Power, a division of the Human Resources Group plc, has been established since 1995 recruiting personnel from Finance disciplines for diverse business sectors. Over the years their committed approach has led to the development of strong relationships with clients within Banking, Finance, Commerce and Industry and Public Practice.

7

Preferred method of contact Telephone for appointment

Minimum requirements Previous experience within market sectors

Type of business Permanent, Temporary and Contract

Grade/Level of Appointments All levels

Bond Accountancy

Head Office ✉ 22 Henrietta St, WC2E 8ND
⊖ Covent Garden
🚃 Charing Cross
☎ T 020 7420 3960   F 020 7240 9431
@ enq@bondaccountancy.co.uk
Market areas Accountancy, Media

Website www.bondaccountancy.co.uk

UK Offices 1

REC Member Yes

Brief Description Part of the Madsen Clark Group, Bond Accountancy was established in 1988 and recruits both permanent and temporary Finance and Media professionals for clients across the London market ranging from Financial Services, Retail, Public Sector, to Leisure and IT.

Preferred method of contact Apply on line or telephone for appointment

Minimum requirements None

Type of business Temporary, Permanent and Contract

Grade/Level of Appointments Administration/1st Jobber to Finance Director

Brian Durham

Head Office ✉ Rooms 459–464, 2nd Floor, Salisbury House, London Wall, EC2M 5QQ
⊖ Moorgate
🚃 Moorgate
☎ T 020 7628 4450   F 020 7628 4451
@ perms@briandurham.com
Market areas Banking

Website www.briandurham.com

UK Offices 1

REC Member No

Brief Description Established in 1980, Brian Durham Recruitment Services has now become synonymous with supplying high calibre banking personnel to major financial institutions in London.

Preferred method of contact Telephone for appointment

Minimum requirements Previous professional experience

Type of business Permanent

Grade/Level of Appointments All levels

Campion Computer Recruitment Ltd

See **IT and Telecoms, page 155**

Capital Market Appointments

Head Office ✉ 109 Salisbury House, London Wall, EC2M 5QQ
⊖ Moorgate
🚃 Moorgate
☎ T 020 7638 5995   F 020 7638 5424
@ recruitment@cma-uk.com
Market areas Retail and International Banking

Website www.cma-uk.com

UK Offices 1

REC Member No

Brief Description Capital Market Appointments specialises in Banking recruitment for the International Capital and Derivative markets and the Banking, IT industry including Treasury, Emerging Markets, Middle Office, Compliance, Money Markets, Analytical, Risk and Economic sectors.

Preferred method of contact Apply on line or telephone for appointment

Minimum requirements Previous professional experience

Type of business Permanent

Grade/Level of Appointments Trainers/Help Desk Assistants to Project Managers/Business Analysts

Carr-Lyons Search & Selection Ltd

Head Office ✉ Warnford Ct,29 Throgmorton St, EC2N 2AT
⊖ Bank
🚃 Cannon St
☎ T 020 7588 3322   F 020 7628 2400
@ info@carr-lyons.com
Market areas Banking, Finance, HR

Website www.carr-lyons.co.uk

UK Offices 2

REC Member No

Brief Description Carr-Lyons provides a professional recruitment service specialising in Banking, Finance, Human Resources and Asset Management, with opportunities within Project Finance, Credit Risk, Fund Management, Financial Services, Private Banks, Stockbrokers, Commerce and Industry.

Preferred method of contact Telephone for appointment

Minimum requirements None

Type of business Permanent and Contract

Grade/Level of Appointments Graduate/1st Jobbers to Director level/Fund Managers

Central London Services

Head Office ✉ 5th Floor, 13–14 Hanover St, W1S 1YH
⊖ Oxford Circus
🚊 Charing Cross
☎ T 020 7629 4909   F 020 7409 3373
@ mail@cls-recruitment.co.uk
Market areas Banking, IT

Website www.cls-recruitment.co.uk

UK Offices 1

REC Member No

Brief Description Established in 1993, Central London Services Ltd are a specialist agency in the fields of Banking and IT for clients in London and across the UK.

Preferred method of contact Apply on line or telephone for appointment

Minimum requirements None

Type of business Permanent, Temporary and Contract

Grade/Level of Appointments Graduate/Receptionist to Account Manager/Operations Services Architect

Charterfield

Head Office ✉ 10 Lindsey St, EC1A 9HP
⊖ Barbican
🚊 Barbican
☎ T 020 7959 5800   F 020 7959 5801
@ london@charterfieldexec.com
Market areas Leasing, Global Markets, Retail, Technology

Website www.charterfieldexec.com

UK Offices 1

REC Member No

Brief Description In 1991 Morgan Chase (now Charterfield) was a small recruitment consultancy formed from the passionate belief that specialisation would provide excellence. Today they operate five specialist divisions - Leasing, Global Markets, Retail, Technology and Eastern Europe from offices in London, Amsterdam, Moscow and Dallas comprising a client base of some of the world's leading organisations.

Preferred method of contact Apply on line or telephone for an appointment

Minimum requirements Relevant industry exposure

Type of business Permanent

Grade/Level of Appointments All levels

Chase Moulande

Head Office ✉ Axe and Bottle Ct, 70 Newcomen St, SE1 1YT
⊖ London Bridge
🚊 London Bridge
☎ T 020 7940 4800   F 020 7357 6969
@ payroll@chasemoulande.com
Market areas Payroll and Regeneration

Website www.chasemoulande.com

UK Offices 1

REC Member No

Brief Description Launched in 1995, Chase Moulande employs over 30 staff with an annual turnover exceeding £2 million. The core business focus for the company is the provision of temporary, contract and permanent staff to both Public and Private Sector organisations throughout the UK. The two areas of specialist recruitment are for the Payroll Industry and the Regeneration Sector.

Preferred method of contact Apply on line or telephone for an appointment

Minimum requirements None

Type of business Temporary and Permanent

Grade/Level of Appointments All levels

Citielite Resources Ltd

Head Office ✉ 1 Groveland Ct, Bow Lane, EC4M 9EH
⊖ Mansion House
🚊 City Thameslink
☎ T 020 7236 4299   F 020 7236 4277
@ research@citielite.co.uk
Market areas Banking

Website www.citielite.co.uk

UK Offices 1

REC Member No

Brief Description Citielite Resources and Parallel International are respectively a combined contract and permanent hire recruiter for Investment Banking, Stockbroking and various professional services organisations focusing on IT, Operations and Finance within the City of London and major European financial cities.

Preferred method of contact Apply on line or telephone for an appointment

Minimum requirements None

Type of business Contract and Permanent

Grade/Level of Appointments All levels

Citifocus

Head Office ✉ 1 College Hill, EC4R 2RA
⊖ Mansion House
🚊 City Thameslink
☎ T 020 7329 3973   F 020 7329 3986
@ recruitment@citifocus.co.uk
Market areas Banking

Website www.citifocus.co.uk

UK Offices 1

REC Member Yes

Brief Description Established in 1991, Citifocus is one of the city's leading recruitment specialists for the Investment/International Banking, Asset Management, Global Custody and Stockbroking sectors, placing permanent and temporary staff within Front Office, Middle Office and Operations positions.

Preferred method of contact Apply on line or telephone for appointment

Minimum requirements None

Type of business Temporary and Permanent

Grade/Level of Appointments Graduate to Management level

City Consultants Ltd

⊠ 17–29 Sun St, EC2M 2PT
⊖ Liverpool St
🚇 Liverpool St
☎ T 020 7422 1900   F 020 7422 1999
@ marketing@cityconsultants.com
Market areas Banking, Securities

Website www.cityconsultants.com

REC Member Yes

Head Office France

Brief Description Part of the Altram Group, City Consultants was established in 1988 to meet the market requirement for a management consultancy to specialise in the Securities and Finance industries with opportunities ranging from Project Management, Systems Analysis, Operational Accounting to Business Analysis.

Preferred method of contact Telephone for appointment

Minimum requirements Previous professional experience

Type of business Contract

Grade/Level of Appointments All levels

City Executive Consultants Ltd

Head Office ⊠ 69 King William St, EC4N 7HR
⊖ Monument
🚇 Cannon St
☎ T 020 7929 6900   F 020 7929 6901
@ cec@cityexec.co.uk
Market areas Financial Services

Website www.cityexec.co.uk

UK Offices 1

REC Member No

Brief Description City Executive Consultants (City Exec) recruits for the Financial Services sector in London and across Europe, specialising in providing candidates for Investment Banking, Securities and Fund

Management with opportunities from Senior Derivatives. Fixed Income to Fund Manager and Managing Director.

Preferred method of contact Telephone for appointment

Minimum requirements Previous professional experience

Type of business Permanent

Grade/Level of Appointments Graduate and above

City Quest Recruitment Ltd

⊠ 12th Floor, Cannon Centre, 78 Cannon St, EC4M 6HH
⊖ Cannon St
🚇 Cannon St
☎ T 020 7623 9933   F 020 7623 9911
@ positions@quest-recruitment.co.uk
Market areas Secretarial, Banking

Website www.quest-recruitment.co.uk

UK Offices 1

REC Member Yes

Head Office Tokyo

Brief Description Part of the JAC Group, City Quest Recruitment specialises in international trade personnel for a wide range of industry sectors including Administration, Customer Services and Accounting with opportunities for Graduates to Senior Management level.

Preferred method of contact Apply on line or telephone for appointment

Minimum requirements None

Type of business Temporary, Permanent and Contract

Grade/Level of Appointments Graduate to Senior Management level

Contact Recruitment Ltd

Head Office ⊠ 66–67 Cornhill, EC3V 3NB
⊖ Bank
🚇 Cannon St
☎ T 020 7280 9400   F 020 7280 9430
@ contact@contact-recruitment.co.uk
Market areas Banking, Asset Management, Securities

Website www.contact-recruitment.com

UK Offices 1

REC Member Yes

Brief Description Established in 1979, Contact Recruitment is based in the heart of the City and is a specialist consultancy supplying permanent, temporary and contract staff across Operations and Finance within the Investment Banking, Asset Management and Securities industries.

Preferred method of contact Telephone for appointment

Minimum requirements None

Type of business Temporary, Permanent and Contract

Grade/Level of Appointments All levels from Accounts Assistant to Business Manager

David Chorley Associates

Head Office ✉ Hanover House, 73–74 High Holborn, WC1V 6LR
      ⊖ Holborn
      🚋 City Thameslink
      ✆ T 020 7242 0509   F 020 7831 4872
      @ holborn@davidchorley.co.uk
Market areas Accountancy and Finance, Banking

Website www.davidchorley.co.uk

UK Offices 4

REC Member No

Brief Description Part of TRS Management Resources, David Chorley International (DCI) is an established international consultancy with over 18 years experience in the Banking, Financial and Accountancy recruitment sectors. DCI build strong working relationships with both candidates and clients alike to ensure that successful, long-term partnerships are forged.

Preferred method of contact Apply on line or telephone for appointment

Minimum requirements None

Type of business Temporary, Permanent and Contract

Grade/Level of Appointments Accounts Clerk/Legal Cashier to Finance Director/Business Analyst

Davies Kidd

See Financial Services and Insurance, page 121

Diamond Resourcing – Accountancy/IT/ Sales/Banking

Head Office ✉ 62–74 Leadenhall Market, EC3V 1LT
      ⊖ Bank
      🚋 Cannon St
      ✆ T 020 7929 2975   F 020 7929 2973
      @ info@diamondresourcing.com
Market areas IT, Banking, Accountancy and Finance, Secretarial, Sales and Insurance

Website www.diamondresourcing.com

UK Offices 3

REC Member Yes

Brief Description Established in 1988, Diamond Resourcing is located in the heart of the City of London. Their broad client base ranges from many small and medium business enterprises to large and well known blue chip organisations throughout the UK and

Europe. They have a proven track record in the placement of key personnel in IT, Accountancy, Secretarial, Banking/Finance, Insurance, Telecoms and Sales. Each division is an independent business ensuring that their consultants have the extensive expertise that their clients and candidates expect from a leading recruitment consultancy.

Preferred method of contact Apply on line or telephone for appointment

Minimum requirements None

Type of business Temporary, Permanent and Contract

Grade/Level of Appointments Office Junior to Finance Director/ Analyst

Dunlop & Badenoch Ltd

Head Office ✉ 60 Mark Lane, EC3R 7ND
      ⊖ Tower Hill
      🚋 Fenchurch St
      ✆ T 020 7265 0377   F 020 7480 6207
      @ recruit@dunlopbadenoch.co.uk
Market areas Accountancy and Banking

Website www.dbrecruitment.com

UK Offices 1

REC Member Yes

Brief Description Part of the Virtual Purple Group, Dunlop & Badenoch have gained the reputation of providing a personal service to both client and candidates alike. Building on this, they have become the preferred supplier to a number of blue chip companies and banking institutions by specialising in placing both temporary and permanent staff in Accountancy and Investment Banking.

Preferred method of contact Apply on line or telephone for appointment

Minimum requirements None

Type of business Temporary and Permanent

Grade/Level of Appointments All levels

Edge Recruitment

Head Office ✉ 15 Southampton Place, WC1A 2AJ
      ⊖ Holborn
      🚋 City Thameslink
      ✆ T 020 7430 9898   F 020 7430 9696
      @ info@edge-recruit.com
Market areas Accountancy, Legal, Taxation

Website www.edge-recruit.com

UK Offices 2

REC Member No

Brief Description Established in 1997 as Edgebaston Associates and incorporated as Edge Recruitment in 2001, they operate from offices in Birmingham and London. Edge Recruitment is an independent and expanding recruitment consultancy focused on the appointment of Accountants, Taxations Specialists and Lawyers to positions within the Accountancy and Legal professions and Industry and Commerce.

Preferred method of contact Telephone for appointment

Minimum requirements Previous professional experience

Type of business Permanent

Grade/Level of Appointments Accountants/Lawyers/Auditors to Partner level

Elan Recruitment

See **Secretarial, page 237**

Exchange Consulting Group

Head Office	✉	13 St Swithins Lane, EC4N 8AL
	🚇	Bank
	🚊	Cannon St
	☎	T 020 7929 2383 F 020 7929 2805
	@	info@exchangeconsulting.com
Market areas		Commodities, Power, Capital Markets, Private Banking

Website www.ecg.informage.co.uk

UK Offices 1

REC Member No

Brief Description Established in 1988, Exchange Consulting Group's ex-market practitioners have become the industry's first choice for both candidates and employers seeking advice across a broad range of recruitment disciplines. The heart of Exchange Consulting Group's approach is a blend of market knowledge and the recruitment intelligence that has won industry awards for excellence in Financial Services and Commodity recruitment.

Preferred method of contact Apply on line or telephone for appointment

Minimum requirements Previous professional experience

Type of business Permanent

Grade/Level of Appointments All levels

Executive Connections

Head Office	✉	43 Eagle St, WC1R 4AP
	🚇	Holborn
	🚊	City Thameslink
	☎	T 020 7304 9000 F 020 7304 9001
	@	response@executive-connections.co.uk
Market areas		Accountancy and Finance

Website www.executive-connections.co.uk

UK Offices 1

REC Member No

Brief Description Established in 1984, Executive Connections is a recruitment consultancy specialising in the recruitment of Accountancy and Finance professionals. Their client list continues to expand, as does the number of assignments their existing clients give them. In addition, the services they offer have expanded to include Management Consultancy and Banking Operations, amongst others, in response to client demands.

Preferred method of contact Apply on line or telephone for appointment

Minimum requirements None

Type of business Temporary, Permanent and Contract

Grade/Level of Appointments All levels

Finance Professionals

Head Office	✉	26–28 Bedford Row, WC1R 4HE
	🚇	Chancery Lane
	🚊	City Thameslink
	☎	T 020 7845 4200 F 020 7845 4249
	@	admin @financeprofessionals.com
Market areas		Accountancy and Finance

Website www.pro-rec-org.com

UK Offices 2

REC Member No

Brief Description Finance Professionals was the first division of the Professional Recruitment Organisation and has grown exponentially since formation in 1997. Since then Finance Professionals has been setting new standards in the recruitment industry in terms of the professional and effective service that they offer both their candidates and clients. In a short space of time they have established themselves as major players within the following sectors: Investment Banking, Industry and Commerce, Practice and Management Consultancy.

Preferred method of contact Apply on line or telephone for appointment

Minimum requirements Previous professional experience

Type of business Temporary, Permanent and Contract

Grade/Level of Appointments Part Qualified Accountant to Corporate Finance Director

Firth Ross Martin

See **Executive Search, page 87**

Fleet Search and Selection

See **Executive Search, page 87**

FSS

Head Office	✉	Charlotte House, 14 Windmill St, W1T 2DY
	⊖	Tottenham Court Rd
	⊠	Euston
	☎	T 020 7209 1000 F 020 7209 0001
	@	info@fss.co.uk
Market areas		Accountancy and Banking, Financial Services, Sales and Marketing, General Management

Website www.fss.co.uk

UK Offices 4

REC Member No

Brief Description FSS, a Spherion company, is an international recruitment consultancy specialising in the provision of talent at all levels and across a wide spectrum including Accounting and Finance, Banking and Financial Services, Human Resources, Sales and Marketing and General Management. FSS was founded in 1983, and currently has offices in London, Windsor, Milton Keynes, Sydney and Melbourne. FSS comprises of four specialist divisions: Financial, Foundations, City, International.

Preferred method of contact Apply on line or telephone for appointment

Minimum requirements None

Type of business Temporary and Permanent

Grade/Level of Appointments All levels

G Solution

Head Office	✉	90 Long Acre, WC2E 9RZ
	⊖	Covent Garden
	⊠	Charing Cross
	☎	T 020 7849 3011 F 020 7849 3200
	@	information@g4solution.com
Market areas		Finance

Website www.g4solution.com

UK Offices 1

REC Member No

Brief Description G Solution specialises in the appointment of finance executives within the Media sector. Their client portfolio is extensive and boasts many of the leading international Entertainment and, more recently, New Media companies. They pride themselves on their client and candidate care, recognising that today's candidate is tomorrow's client and deliver the same service to all.

Preferred method of contact Telephone for appointment

Minimum requirements Previous professional experience

Type of business Permanent and Contract

Grade/Level of Appointments Accounts Assistant to Director

Gel Appointments
See **Secretarial, page 238**

Global Markets Recruitment Ltd
See **Executive Search, page 89**

Goodman Mason Ltd

Head Office	✉	4th Floor, 120 Aldersgate St, EC1A 4JQ
	⊖	Barbican
	⊠	Barbican
	☎	T 020 7336 7711 F 020 7336 7722
	@	recruit@goodmanmasson.com
Market areas		Accountancy and Finance

Website www.goodmanmasson.com

UK Offices 1

REC Member No

Brief Description Goodman Masson offer unrivalled finance and accountancy opportunities in Commerce and Industry, Banking and Financial Services, Public Practice, Management Consultancy and the Public Not for Profit sector. They aim to provide advice and assistance of the highest quality for all candidates. To achieve this they utilise their detailed knowledge of the Accountancy recruitment market combined with an informal, friendly and highly professional approach.

Preferred method of contact Apply on line or telephone for appointment

Minimum requirements None

Type of business Temporary and Permanent

Grade/Level of Appointments All levels

Gray & Associates
See **Secretarial, page 239**

Greythorn Plc
See **IT and Telecoms, page 162**

Guardian Appointments Ltd
See **IT and Telecoms, page 162**

Hanbury Financial Ltd

Head Office	✉	127 Bishopsgate, EC2M 4NQ
	⊖	Liverpool St
	⊠	Liverpool St

C T 020 7626 1330   F 020 7626 1291
@ innovation@hanbury.com
Market areas Banking, Investment Banking

Website www.hanburyfinancial.com

UK Offices 1

REC Member Yes

Brief Description Based in the City, Hanbury Financial specialise in all areas of Banking/Investment Banking/Financial Services for a variety of clients across the London market.

Preferred method of contact Apply on line or telephone for appointment

Minimum requirements None

Type of business Permanent

Grade/Level of Appointments Support Staff/Secretary to Senior Management

Hanover Search & Selection

Head Office ✉ 46 Cannon St, EC4N 6JJ
⊖ Cannon St
🚆 Cannon St
C T 020 7248 2244   F 020 7248 2131
@ info@hanover-search.com
Market areas Actuarial, Banking, Asset Management, Insurance, Financial Services

✉ 75 Cannon St, EC4N 5BN
⊖ Cannon St
🚆 Cannon St
C T 020 7556 7042   F 020 7556 7454
@ info@hanover-search.com
Market areas Actuarial, Banking, Asset Management, Insurance, Financial Services

✉ 10 Stratton St, W1 8LG
⊖ Green Park
🚆 Victoria
C T 020 7546 8569   F 020 7546 8568
@ info@hanover-search.com
Market areas Actuarial, Banking, Asset Management, Insurance, Financial Services

Website www.hanover-search.com

UK Offices 4

REC Member No

Brief Description Established in 1996 with headquarters in the heart of London's square mile. Hanover Search & Selection is privately owned by four directors who employ 60 staff from four main UK offices and three subsidiaries.

Preferred method of contact Apply on line or telephone for an appointment

Minimum requirements Previous professional experience

Type of business Permanent

Grade/Level of Appointments Account Manager to Operations Director

Hardy Financial

See **Executive Search, page 90**

Harpur Accountancy Recruitment Ltd

Head Office ✉ Linen Hall, 162 Regent St, W1R 5TB
⊖ Piccadilly Circus
🚆 Charing Cross
C T 020 7437 4567   F 020 7734 1884
@ mail@harpur.co.uk
Market areas Accountancy

Website www.harpur.co.uk

UK Offices 1

REC Member Yes

Brief Description Harpur Accountancy have formed effective working relationships with a well established client base over the past 10 years, covering a variety of sectors including many blue chip concerns. They specialise in Accountancy, recruiting both temporary and permanent staff covering a full range of accounts staff from Accounts Assistant to Financial Director level.

Preferred method of contact Telephone for appointment

Minimum requirements None

Type of business Temporary, Permanent and Contract

Grade/Level of Appointments Accounts Clerks to Finance Directors

Harvey Sutton Ltd

Head Office ✉ Holborn Gate,330 High Holborn, WC1V 7QT
⊖ Holborn
🚆 City Thameslink
C T 020 7203 8422   F 020 7203 6701
@ bjackson@harveysutton.co.uk
Market areas Legal and Accountancy

Website www.harveysutton.co.uk

UK Offices 1

REC Member No

Brief Description Harvey Sutton has provided a recruitment service for the Legal and Accountancy professions for over a decade. They aim to forge an intimate, ongoing relationship with their clients and candidates, and do their utmost to ensure that both parties are well matched. Their clients include 'magic circle' firms, as well as the full spectrum of small, medium-sized, niche, MDPs and overseas firms.

Preferred method of contact Telephone for appointment

Minimum requirements Previous professional experience

Type of business Permanent

Grade/Level of Appointments All levels

Hays Accountancy Personnel

Head Office ✉ 141 Moorgate, EC2M 6TX
      🚇 Moorgate
      🚆 Moorgate
      ☎ T 020 7638 3955   F 020 7588 6448
      @ moorgate@hays-ap.co.uk

Market areas Accountancy and Finance

      ✉ 14 Great Castle St, W1N 7AD
      🚇 Oxford Circus
      🚆 Charing Cross
      ☎ T 020 7580 9186   F 020 7436 2064
      @ west-end@hays-ap.co.uk

Market areas Accountancy and Finance

      ✉ 4th Floor, 1 Wilton St, SW1V 1AB
      🚇 Victoria
      🚆 Victoria
      ☎ T 020 7828 7555   F 020 7828 7059
      @ victoria@hays-ap.co.uk

Market areas Accountancy and Finance

      ✉ 2nd Floor, 14 Great Castle St, W1N 7AD
      🚇 Oxford Circus
      🚆 Charing Cross
      ☎ T 020 7287 2873   F 020 7734 3877
      @ tcr@hays-ap.co.uk

Market areas Accountancy and Finance

      ✉ 1st Floor, 1 Southampton St, WC2R 0LR
      🚇 Covent Garden
      🚆 Charing Cross
      ☎ T 020 7520 5983
      @ strand@hays-ap.co.uk

Market areas Accountancy and Finance

      ✉ 73 New Bond St, W1Y 9DD
      🚇 Bond St
      🚆 Paddington
      ☎ T 020 7493 3813   F 020 7495 0117
      @ new-bond-street@hays-ap.co.uk

Market areas Accountancy and Finance

      ✉ 61 Brompton Rd, SW3 1DB
      🚇 Knightsbridge
      🚆 Victoria
      ☎ T 020 7581 5021   F 020 7584 0974
      @ knightsbridge@hays-ap.co.uk

Market areas Accountancy and Finance

      ✉ 307–8 High Holborn, WC1V 7LR
      🚇 Holborn
      🚆 City Thameslink
      ☎ T 020 7404 4561   F 020 7831 3936
      @ holborn@hays-ap.co.uk

Market areas Accountancy and Finance

      ✉ 104 Baker St, W1M 1LA
      🚇 Baker St
      🚆 Marylebone
      ☎ T 020 7935 1493   F 020 7487 4362
      @ baker-street@hays-ap.co.uk

Market areas Accountancy and Finance

Website www.haysworks.com

UK Offices 125

REC Member No

Brief Description Hays Personnel Services is a division of Hays plc, the business services group listed in the FTSE 100. Hays Personnel Services is Europe's leading specialist professional recruitment group. Hays Accountancy Personnel is the largest specialist Finance recruitment consultancy in the UK and Ireland. With 125 offices, they've got the nation covered. They place temporary, permanent and contract Accountants and Accounts Staff, with an emphasis on speed of service without compromising on quality.

Preferred method of contact Apply on line or telephone for an appointment

Minimum requirements None

Type of business Temporary and Permanent

Grade/Level of Appointments All levels

Hays Banking Personnel

Head Office ✉ 141 Moorgate, EC2M 6TX
      ☎ T 020 7628 9999   F 020 7628 4698

      ✉ 41–42 London Wall, EC2M 5TB
      🚇 Moorgate
      🚆 Moorgate
      ☎ T 020 7638 7003   F 020 7628 5057
      @ london-wall.secs@hays-banking.co.uk

Market areas Secretarial

      ✉ 41–42 London Wall, EC2M 5TB
      🚇 Moorgate
      🚆 Moorgate
      ☎ T 020 7588 0781   F 020 7562 9395
      @ london-wall.temp@hays-banking.co.uk

Market areas Banking

      ✉ 41–42 London Wall, EC2M 5TB
      🚇 Moorgate
      🚆 Moorgate
      ☎ T 020 7256 5866   F 020 7856 5804
      @ london-wall.perm@hays-banking.co.uk

Market areas Banking

      ✉ 1st Floor, 30 Marsh Wall, E14 9TP
      🚇 South Quay
      🚆 Limehouse
      ☎ T 020 7538 1473   F 020 7531 3591
      @ docklands@hays-banking.co.uk

Market areas Banking

Website www.haysworks.com

UK Offices 4

REC Member No

Brief Description Hays Personnel Services is a division of Hays plc, the business services group listed in the FTSE 100. Hays Personnel Services is Europe's leading specialist professional recruitment group. Hays Banking Personnel offers a market leading range of services, providing temporary and permanent staff to Merchant and International Banks, from offices in the City, Docklands and Edinburgh. A dedicated division provides Secretarial, Clerical and Administrative recruitment services to the Financial sector.

Preferred method of contact Apply on line or telephone for an appointment

Minimum requirements None

Type of business Temporary and Permanent

Grade/Level of Appointments All levels

Hays City

See Executive Search, page 91

Healy Hunt

Head Office ✉ 2–3 Philpott Lane, EC3M 8AN

⊖ Monument

🚇 Cannon St

☎ T 020 7398 3322   F 207 929 0327

@ search@healyhunt.com

Market areas Banking

Website www.healyhunt.com

UK Offices 1

REC Member No

Brief Description Healy Hunt Banking Recruitment focuses exclusively on providing professional recruitment services to Corporate and Investment Banking sectors. A successful placement track record has been achieved through the knowledge and intuition of their consultants, combined with their extensive personal experience of this specialist market as senior bankers.

Preferred method of contact Apply on line or telephone for an appointment

Minimum requirements Previous professional experience

Type of business Permanent

Grade/Level of Appointments All levels

Hogarth Davies Lloyd

See Executive Search, page 93

Hudson Shribman - Accountancy Division

Head Office ✉ Vernon House, Sicilian Avenue, WC1A 2QH

⊖ Holborn

🚇 City Thameslink

☎ T 020 7831 2323   F 020 7404 5773

@ info@hudson-shribman.co.uk

Market areas Accountancy and Finance

Website www.hudson-shribman.co.uk

UK Offices 2

REC Member No

Brief Description Established in 1977, Hudson Shribman has firmly held the belief since its inception that the human resource is the most critical factor in determining the health and success of any organisation. Hudson Shribman Financial Recruitment is solely dedicated to the discipline of Accountancy. Based in London, the company operates throughout the UK supplying quality Financial personnel to Industrial, Commercial, Public Sector and Professional organisations.

Preferred method of contact Apply on line or telephone for an appointment

Minimum requirements None

Type of business Temporary, Permanent and Contract

Grade/Level of Appointments Student to Board level appointments

Hudson York Farrell

See Secretarial, page 241

Hunter Campbell

Head Office ✉ 1 Prince of Wales Passage, 117 Hampstead Rd, NW1 3EE

⊖ Euston Sq

🚇 Euston

☎ T 020 7383 3553   F 020 7383 2795

@ info@hunter-campbell.co.uk

Market areas Banking and Compliance

Website www.hunter-campbell.co.uk

UK Offices 1

REC Member No

Brief Description The Hunter Campbell Recruitment Consultancy was set up in 1991, specialising in the provision of a recruitment service targeted towards the Financial Services industry, specifically all areas of Banking and Finance. Their clients range from major blue chip organisations to small start-ups.

Preferred method of contact Apply on line or telephone for an appointment

Minimum requirements Previous professional experience

Type of business Permanent

Grade/Level of Appointments All levels

Huxley Associates

See IT and Telecoms, page 163

IMR Recruitment

Head Office ✉ Walbrook House, 23–29 Walbrook, EC4N 8LD

         ⊖ Cannon St

         🚇 Cannon St

         ☎ T 020 7477 6500   F 020 7477 6768

Market areas Banking, Financial Services

Website www.imr.uk.com

UK Offices 1

REC Member No

Brief Description IMR has specialised in the recruitment of professionals for the Banking and Financial Services industry since 1991, and has many top quality clients. They deal with all aspects of the investment process, including Fund Management, Stockbroking, Trading, Risk Management, Compliance, Settlements and Trading.

Preferred method of contact Apply on line or telephone for an appointment

Minimum requirements None

Type of business Permanent

Grade/Level of Appointments Graduates to Senior Management level

Indigo Selection – Banking and Finance Division

Head Office ✉ 5th Floor, New Zealand House, 80 Haymarket, SW1Y 4HU

         ☎ T 020 7930 9066   F 020 7839 5457

         ✉ 2nd Floor, 40 Lime St, EC3M 7AW

         ⊖ bank

         🚇 Cannon St

         ☎ T 020 7220 7777   F 020 7339 7599

Market areas Accountancy and Finance

Website www.indigoselection.com

UK Offices 2

REC Member No

Brief Description The Indigo Selection Banking team was established in 1994 and specialises in the recruitment of Back and Middle Office positions at all levels for a large number of Banking, Finance and Fund Management institutions in the City. The Accountancy and Finance Division recruits at all levels from Accounts Clerk to Financial Director across various sectors including Investment

Banks, other Financial Services organisations and blue chip Commercial companies.

Preferred method of contact Apply on line or telephone for an appointment

Minimum requirements None

Type of business Temporary and Permanent

Grade/Level of Appointments All levels

Indigo Selection – Commerce and Accounting Division

Head Office ✉ 5th Floor, New Zealand House, 80 Haymarket, SW1Y 4HU

         ⊖ Piccadilly Circus

         🚇 Charing Cross

         ☎ T 020 7930 9066   F 020 7839 5457

Market areas Accountancy, Insurance

Website www.indigoselection.com

UK Offices 2

REC Member No

Brief Description The Indigo Selection Banking team was established in 1994 and specialises in the recruitment of Back and Middle Office positions at all levels for a large number of Banking, Finance and Fund Management institutions in the City. The Accountancy and Finance Division recruits at all levels from Accounts Clerk to Financial Director across various sectors including Investment Banks, other Financial Services organisations and blue chip Commercial companies.

Preferred method of contact Apply on line or telephone for an appointment

Minimum requirements None

Type of business Temporary and Permanent

Grade/Level of Appointments All levels

Intelect Recruitment Ltd

See IT and Telecoms, page 164

JH Consulting Ltd

Head Office ✉ 4th Floor, 4–5 Castle Ct, EC3V 9DL

         ⊖ Bank

         🚇 Cannon St

         ☎ T 020 7623 3300   F 020 7220 7605

         @ info@jhcl.co.uk

Market areas Financial Services

Website www.jhcl.co.uk

UK Offices 1

REC Member No

Brief Description JH Consulting are a small, privately owned recruitment consultancy providing permanent, temporary and contract staff to some of the most prestigious International Banking and Finance institutions in the City. They offer their candidates a broad range of career opportunities, as well as providing a practical, professional and confidential approach to recruitment.

Preferred method of contact Apply on line or telephone for an appointment

Minimum requirements None

Type of business Temporary and Permanent

Grade/Level of Appointments All levels

JHW Ltd

Head Office   ✉   10 Bow Lane, EC4M 9AL
  ⊖   Mansion House
  🚊   Cannon St
  ☏ T 020 7248 5488   F 020 7329 1525
  @   enquiries@jhw.co.uk
Market areas   Banking, Asset Management, Secretarial

Website www.jhw.co.uk

UK Offices 1

REC Member No

Brief Description JHW was formed in 1999 by Sarah Jones and Colin Wilson. Both have held directorships in other city recruitment companies and they offer experience of London's permanent and temporary recruitment markets that is second to none.

Preferred method of contact Apply on line or telephone for an appointment

Minimum requirements None

Type of business Temporary and Permanent

Grade/Level of Appointments All levels

Jonathan Wren

Head Office   ✉   34 London Wall, EC2M 5RU
  ⊖   Moorgate
  🚊   Moorgate
  ☏ T 020 7309 3550   F 020 7309 3552
  @   career@jwren.com
Market areas   Banking, Financial Services

Website www.jwren.com

UK Offices 1

REC Member No

Brief Description Jonathan Wren was founded in the City of London over 30 years ago, specifically to provide recruitment services to the Banking and Investment sector. The company was acquired by Adia (now Adecco) in 1986, but retains its autonomy by virtue of its

history and niche positioning in Financial Markets. Their main divisions recruit many experienced personnel on behalf of clients into Investment Banking (both temporary and permanent, Front and Back Office), Technology, Accounting and Finance, Secretarial and Life and Pensions. Within these divisions are consultants who specialise in key areas such as Operations and Support, Multi-lingual skills, Risk, Compliance, Asset and Fund Management, Equities, Derivatives and Fixed Income sales and research, e-Commerce, Accountancy and so on.

Preferred method of contact Apply on line or telephone for an appointment

Minimum requirements None

Type of business Temporary and Permanent

Grade/Level of Appointments All levels

Joslin Rowe

Head Office   ✉   Bell Ct House, 11 Blomfield St, EC2M 7AY
  ⊖   Moorgate
  🚊   Moorgate
  ☏ T 020 7786 6900   F 020 7786 6451
Market areas   Accountancy and Banking, Telecoms, Life and Pensions

Website www.joslinrowe.com

UK Offices 5

REC Member No

Brief Description Part of the Blomfield Group, operating out of three office locations in the City of London, Joslin Rowe specialises in the recruitment of both Finance and Marketing professionals and Infrastructure staff for: Investment Banking and Securities, Investment Management, Finance and Accountancy, Insurance, Life and Pensions, Telecommunications, Risk Management and Professional Services sectors. Joslin Rowe places professionals at all levels, from junior to senior management level into temporary, contract and permanent roles.

Preferred method of contact Apply on line or telephone for an appointment

Minimum requirements None

Type of business Temporary, Permanent and Contract

Grade/Level of Appointments Junior to Senior Management level

Lancaster Associates

See **Secretarial, page 245**

Lindsey Morgan Associates

See **Secretarial, page 247**

LJC Banking

Head Office ✉ Devonshire House, 146 Bishopsgate, EC2M 4JX
⊖ Bank
🚊 Cannon St
☎ T 020 7377 5040   F 020 7375 1950
@ banking@ljcgroup.co.uk
Market areas Banking

Website www.ljcgroup.co.uk
UK Offices 2
REC Member Yes
Brief Description LJC Group is split into two separate companies: LJC Banking specialising in Back and Middle Office operations, including Risk, Treasury, Derivatives, Trade Finance and Securities; and Secretaries Plus which deals with permanent, temporary and contract Secretarial and Support staff for a range of clients.
Preferred method of contact Apply on line or telephone for an appointment
Minimum requirements None
Type of business Temporary, Permanent and Contract
Grade/Level of Appointments 1st Jobber to Management level

Management Selection Consultants

Head Office ✉ 12 Park Place, SW1A 1LP
⊖ Green Park
🚊 Victoria
☎ T 020 7491 2300   F 020 7629 2014
@ msc@msc-group.co.uk
Market areas Banking, IT, PR, Marketing

Website www.msc-group.co.uk
UK Offices 1
REC Member No
Brief Description MSC Group specialises in providing staff encompassing all levels of employment for the Banking, Commerce, IT, Public Relations and Marketing Communications sector.
Preferred method of contact Telephone for appointment
Minimum requirements None
Type of business Permanent
Grade/Level of Appointments Junior to Executive level appointments

Manorsearch

Head Office ✉ Georgian House, 63 Coleman St, EC2R 5BB
⊖ Bank
🚊 Cannon St
☎ T 020 7920 9100   F 020 7496 0455
@ enquiries@manorsearch.com
Market areas Banking

Website www.manorsearch.com
UK Offices 1
REC Member No
Brief Description Manorsearch is an established company within the highly competitive Global Financial recruitment sector. Their areas of expertise are Front, Middle and Back Office roles in Equities, Foreign Exchange and Eurobonds, i.e. Analysts, Risk Managers, Traders, Sales and Marketers. Their database is constantly networking and growing. With 25 years of International Banking experience they have accumulated a wide range of excellent contacts and information sources.
Preferred method of contact Apply on line or telephone for an appointment
Minimum requirements Relevant Banking exposure
Type of business Permanent
Grade/Level of Appointments Junior Bond Sales to Senior Broker

Marks Sattin

Head Office ✉ 1st Floor, 32 Haymarket, SW1Y 4TP
⊖ Piccadilly Circus
🚊 Charing Cross
☎ T 020 7321 5000   F 020 7930 1596
@ info@markssattin.co.uk
Market areas Accountancy and Finance

Website www.markssattin.co.uk
UK Offices 1
REC Member No
Brief Description Marks Sattin was established in 1988 in order to provide both a comprehensive and focused recruitment service for Finance and Accountancy professionals on a permanent and contract/temporary basis. Their clients include 75 of the top 100 companies as ranked by the FTSE 100 and 45 of the companies as ranked by the Fortune 500. Their office is conveniently located in the West End, with their core business in London and the South East of England ranging from Cambridge in the North, to the South Coast and to Oxford in the West. They also handle overseas recruitment on behalf of clients elsewhere in the UK on a more specialised basis.
Preferred method of contact Apply on line or telephone for an appointment
Minimum requirements None
Type of business Temporary, Permanent and Contract
Grade/Level of Appointments Graduates/Part Qualified to Finance Director/Qualified level

Martin Ward Anderson

Head Office ✉ 7 Savoy Ct, Strand, WC2R 0EL
⊖ Temple
🚊 Blackfriars
☎ T 020 7240 2233   F 020 7240 8818

@ london@martinwardanderson.com

Market areas Accountancy and Finance

Website www.martinwardanderson.com

UK Offices 6

REC Member No

Brief Description Martin Ward Anderson is a leading international recruiter with a network of offices in the UK and the Netherlands. MWA also have alliances and partnerships in Australia, New Zealand and South Africa.

Preferred method of contact Apply on line or telephone for an appointment

Minimum requirements Relevant sector exposure

Type of business Temporary, Permanent and Contract

Grade/Level of Appointments Part Qualified/Ledger Controller to Qualified/Finance Director

Michael Page

✉ Savannah House, 11–12 Charles II St, SW1Y 4QZ
⊖ Piccadilly Circus
🚊 Charing Cross
☎ T 020 7831 2000

Market areas Accountancy and Finance, Banking and Financial Markets, Marketing, Sales, Retail, Legal, Technology

✉ 50 Cannon St, EC4N 6JJ
⊖ Cannon St
🚊 Cannon St
☎ T 020 7831 2000

Market areas Accountancy and Finance, Banking and Financial Markets, Marketing, Sales, Retail, Legal, Technology

✉ Page House, 39–41 Parker St, WC2B 5LN
⊖ Holborn
🚊 City Thameslink
☎ T 020 7831 2000

Market areas Accountancy and Finance, Banking and Financial Markets, Marketing, Sales, Retail, Legal, Technology

Website www.michaelpage.co.uk

UK Offices 22

REC Member No

Head Office Corporate Office, 8 Bath Rd, Slough, Berkshire, SL1 3SA

Brief Description Michael Page is one of the world's leading professional recruitment consultancies, specialising in the placement of candidates in permanent, contract, temporary and interim positions with clients around the world. The group has operations in the UK, Continental Europe, Asia-Pacific and the Americas and focuses on the areas of Accounting and Finance, Banking and Financial Markets, Marketing, Retail, Sales, Legal, Technology, Human Resources, Engineering, Taxation, Corporate Treasury and Consultancy.

Preferred method of contact Apply on line or telephone for an appointment

Minimum requirements Relevant industry exposure

Type of business Temporary, Permanent and Contract

Grade/Level of Appointments Part Qualified to Senior level appointments

Millar Associates

Head Office ✉ 1 Glynde Mews, SW3 1SB
⊖ Knightsbridge
🚊 Victoria
☎ T 020 7589 8000   F 020 7589 5010
@ info@millarassociates.com

Market areas Banking

Website www.millarassociates.com

UK Offices 1

REC Member No

Brief Description Millar Associates specialise in placing high calibre professionals within the Banking and Finance sector, ranging from Risk Analyst to Senior Derivatives Specialist.

Preferred method of contact Apply on line or telephone for an appointment

Minimum requirements Relevant industry exposure

Type of business Permanent

Grade/Level of Appointments Middle to Senior Management level

Mison Recruitment

See **Secretarial, page 248**

Monument Recruitment

See **Secretarial, page 249**

Morgan Hunt

See **Executive Search, page 100**

Newlands Resourcing

Head Office ✉ 5th Floor, 15 Wilton Rd, SW1V 1LT
⊖ Victoria
🚊 Victoria
☎ T 020 7834 8585   F 020 7834 2670
@ info@newlandsresourcing.co.uk

Market areas Accountancy and Banking

Website www.newlandsresourcing.co.uk

UK Offices 1

REC Member No

Brief Description Newlands Resourcing is a dynamic new company created to provide bespoke recruitment solutions for the Financial Services industry. Newlands Resourcing specialises in providing candidates to Investment Banks, Asset Management companies, Internet start-ups and Accountancy Practices across London. They provide Middle and Back Office staff at all levels from Settlements Clerks to Finance Directors. They find candidates for temporary, contract and permanent vacancies

Preferred method of contact Apply on line or telephone for an appointment

Minimum requirements Ideally, relevant industry exposure

Type of business Temporary, Permanent and Contract

Grade/Level of Appointments All levels

Nicholas Andrews & Temps Financial

⌧ 4th Floor, Elan House, 5–11 Fetter Lane, EC4A 1EB
⊖ Chancery Lane
🚊 City Thameslink
☎ T 020 7830 1410   F 020 7830 1449

Market areas Accountancy, Secretarial

Website www.natf.co.uk

UK Offices 16

REC Member No

Head Office 126 Colmore Row, Birmingham, B3 3AP

Brief Description Established in 1987, Nicholas Andrews & Temps Financial is now rapidly becoming the UK's leading specialist financial recruitment consultancy. Their national network of offices are strategically located, serving the needs of clients and candidates alike. A full range of recruitment solutions spans all industry sectors from High Street to High Tech and covers all levels of appointment from Accounting Support Staff through to Board positions. They work as strategic recruitment partners with companies throughout the UK. Their client base includes national and international accountancy practices, blue chip corporations and private businesses.

Preferred method of contact Apply on line or telephone for an appointment

Minimum requirements None

Type of business Temporary and Permanent

Grade/Level of Appointments All levels

Nigel Lynn Associates

⌧ 5th Floor, 16 High Holborn, WC1N 6BX
⊖ Chancery Lane
🚊 City Thameslink
☎ T 020 7269 5850   F 020 7269 5855
@ london@nigel-lynn.com

Market areas Accountancy and Banking

Website www.nigel-lynn.com

UK Offices 17

REC Member No

Head Office Basingstoke

Brief Description Nigel Lynn Associates are a market leading independent recruitment consultancy, specialising in permanent, temporary and contract recruitment for all levels of Accountancy, International and Investment Banking Staff.

Preferred method of contact Apply on line or telephone for an appointment

Minimum requirements None

Type of business Temporary, Permanent and Contract

Grade/Level of Appointments All levels

OTC Computing Ltd

See **IT and Telecoms**, page 171

Parker Bridge

Head Office ⌧ Malborough Ct, 14–18 Holborn, EC1N 2LE
⊖ Chancery Lane
🚊 City Thameslink
☎ T 020 7464 1550   F 020 7464 1999
@ info@parkerbridge.co.uk

Market areas Banking, Accountancy

Website www.parkerbridge.com

UK Offices 1

REC Member Yes

Brief Description Parker Bridge recruits temporary and permanent Finance staff at all levels in the Banking, Commerce and Industry and Communications sectors. Parker Bridge was established in 1989 and through concentrating on specialised areas they have gained an in-depth knowledge of their core markets enabling them to deliver an unrivalled service. Parker Bridge Investment Banking division specialises in the recruitment of staff within Finance and Operations and the placement of qualified and part qualified Accountants and manages a variety of roles including Compliance, Systems Accounting, Credit Analysis, Risk and Tax. The Operations team recruits within Settlements, Corporate Actions, Trade Support, Fund Administration and Client Service areas.

Preferred method of contact Apply on line or telephone for an appointment

Minimum requirements None

Type of business Temporary and Permanent

Grade/Level of Appointments Part Qualified to Senior level appointments

---

PAYTemps

Head Office ✉ Axe and Bottle Ct, 70 Newcomen St, SE1 1YT
⊖ London Bridge
🚊 London Bridge
☎ T 020 7940 4844   F 020 7940 4843
@ information@chasemoulande.com
Market areas Payroll and Regeneration

Website www.chasemoulande.com

UK Offices 1

REC Member No

Brief Description Part of Chase Moulande, 2000 saw the launch of PAYTemps (a sister company to Chase Moulande), offering both temps and clients a more structured and responsive temporary service across the UK. PAYTemps provide Payroll training to temporary workers plus a range of incentives and workshops for which PAYTemps won the Best Support/Service Award to the Payroll Industry at Pay Magazine's Annual Payroll Awards in September 2000. This was an accolade never before given to a recruitment company.

Preferred method of contact Apply on line or telephone for an appointment

Minimum requirements None

Type of business Temporary and Permanent

Grade/Level of Appointments All levels

Portfolio Payroll

Head Office ✉ 228 Shoreditch High St, E1 6PJ
⊖ Liverpool St
🚊 Liverpool St
☎ T 020 7247 9455   F 020 7247 9673
Market areas Payroll

Website www.portfoliopersonnel.com

UK Offices 1

REC Member Yes

Brief Description The team at Portfolio Payroll have over 50 years of recruitment experience, the majority of which is within the Payroll field. Many of their consultants have been with Portfolio Payroll for several years and take pride in the fast, professional service they provide. Portfolio Payroll provide permanent, contract and temporary Payroll staff of all levels throughout the UK.

Preferred method of contact Apply on line or telephone for an appointment

Minimum requirements Previous professional experience

Type of business Temporary and Permanent

Grade/Level of Appointments All levels

Prime Accountancy

Head Office ✉ 11 Blomfield St, EC2M 7AY
⊖ Holborn
🚊 City Thameslink
☎ T 020 7588 0174   F 020 7638 8421
@ accountwebapps@primeuk.com
Market areas Accountancy

Website www.primeuk.com

UK Offices 1

REC Member No

Brief Description Prime Accountancy was formed in 1996 and has quickly established itself as a major contributor to the Prime Personnel Group. Their specialist team of consultants handle a broad range of recruitment covering all areas across Commerce and Industry and Banking. A well established team with exposure to many business sectors, which enables Prime to fully cover all areas of Accounts and give the service that is required to remain at the forefront of the recruitment market.

Preferred method of contact Apply on line or telephone for an appointment

Minimum requirements None

Type of business Contract and Permanent

Grade/Level of Appointments Graduate/Accounts Assistant to Senior level

Prime Banking

Head Office ✉ 11 Blomfield St, EC2M 7AY
⊖ Holborn
🚊 City Thameslink
☎ T 020 7588 0174   F 020 7638 8421
@ bankingwebapps@primeuk.com
Market areas Banking

Website www.primeuk.com

UK Offices 1

REC Member No

Brief Description Part of the Prime Personnel group, Prime Banking has established close and long standing relationships with many of the leading national and international Financial institutions. Their highly trained consultants, often recruited from within the financial community, undergo rigorous and continued training and development. Their relationships are based around world leading Financial Institutions, Investment, Merchant and Clearing Banks, Commodity Brokers, Fund Managers, etc. They have serviced many of these clients since their inception, while others have instructed them more recently as a result of their success with their major competitors.

Preferred method of contact Apply on line or telephone for an appointment

Minimum requirements None

Type of business Contract and Permanent

Grade/Level of Appointments All levels

Prime Executive

See Executive Search, page 103

Prime Temps

Head Office ✉ 11 Blomfield St, EC2M 7AY
            ⊖ Holborn
            🚇 City Thameslink
            ☎ T 020 7588 0174   F 020 7638 8421
            @ temps@primeuk.com
Market areas Accountancy and Banking, Secretarial

Website www.primeuk.com

UK Offices 1

REC Member No

Brief Description Part of Prime Personnel, the Prime Temporary division provides professional, experienced temps for blue chip organisations. In the City and West End, they specialise in Banking, Finance, Media, Accountancy, Secretarial, Property and IT. Their enduring success within the temporary market is in no small way attributed to the extremely close working relationship which exists between all the divisions and the temporary consultants. They possess a wealth of knowledge across their sectors and they utilise this knowledge to the best effects for their clients and candidates.

Preferred method of contact Apply on line or telephone for an appointment

Minimum requirements None

Type of business Temporary

Grade/Level of Appointments All levels

The Principle Partnership

See Secretarial, page 253

PSD Group Plc

Head Office ✉ 28 Essex St, WC2R 3AT
            ⊖ Temple
            🚇 Blackfriars
            ☎ T 020 7970 9700
            @ london@psdgroup.com
Market areas Finance, IT, Marketing, Engineering, Sales

Website www.psdgroup.com

UK Offices 4

REC Member No

Brief Description PSD opened its first office outside the UK in Singapore in early 1996. It has since added offices in Amsterdam, Paris, Frankfurt, Munich and Hong Kong. PSD currently operates out of 10 offices, each of which services specific sectors and disciplines. The four UK offices run down the spine of the country and are located in London, Manchester, Birmingham and Hayward's Heath. PSD's disciplines are Finance, IT, Marketing, HR, Property, Law, Customer Services, Purchasing, Sales, Front and Middle Office, Operations, Engineering. PSD Sectors are Banking, Business and Professional Services, Communications, Construction, Consumer, Electronics, Energy and Utilities, Financial Services, Pharmaceuticals, Software and Services, Public Sector.

Preferred method of contact Apply on line or telephone for an appointment

Minimum requirements None

Type of business Contract and Permanent

Grade/Level of Appointments All levels

Ranfurly Recruitment

Head Office ✉ 4th Floor, 61 Cheapside, EC2V 6AX
            ⊖ Bank
            🚇 Cannon St
            ☎ T 020 7489 8827   F 020 7329 3115
            @ recruit@ranfurly.co.uk
Market areas Investment Banking, Asset Management, Commerce and Communications

Website www.ranfurly.co.uk

UK Offices 1

REC Member No

Brief Description Ranfurly has been operating within the City of London for 15 years and has preferred supplier agreements with the premier Investment Banking and Asset Management firms. They pride themselves on providing the most professional and honest recruitment service within the City.

Preferred method of contact Apply on line or telephone for an appointment

Minimum requirements None

Type of business Temporary and Permanent

Grade/Level of Appointments General Administration to Fund Managers

Reed Accountancy Personnel

Head Office ✉ Reed Executive Plc, 145 Kensington High St, W8 7LP
            ☎ T 020 7313 7450   F 020 7313 7451

            ✉ 52 Welbeck St, W1M 1LA
            ⊖ Bond St
            🚇 Paddington
            ☎ T 020 7467 4690
Market areas Accountancy

23

✉ 181–183 Victoria St, SW1E 5NE
⊖ Victoria
🚆 Victoria
☎ T 020 7828 2691
Market areas   Accountancy

✉ 17 South Molton St, W1K 5QT
⊖ Bond St
🚆 Paddington
☎ T 020 7323 6958
Market areas   Accountancy

✉ 309 High Holborn, WC1V 7LU
⊖ Holborn
🚆 City Thameslink
☎ T 020 7400 1890
Market areas   Accountancy

✉ 76 Cannon St, EC4N 6AE
⊖ Cannon St
🚆 Cannon St
☎ T 020 7489 8005
Market areas   Accountancy

✉ 87 Moorgate, EC2M 6SA
⊖ Moorgate
🚆 Moorgate
☎ T 020 7638 1021
Market areas   Accountancy

Website www.reed.co.uk
UK Offices 250+
REC Member No

Brief Description A subsidiary of Reed Executive Plc established in 1960, Reed's growth has been dramatic and the company's stated ambition is to grow the business substantially. Reed has been organised into a number of separate operating companies to make this happen. Reed Accountancy Personnel recruits temporary and permanent personnel for the Accountancy sector.

Preferred method of contact Apply on line or telephone for an appointment
Minimum requirements None
Type of business Temporary and Permanent
Grade/Level of Appointments All levels

Reed Banking Personnel

Head Office ✉ Reed Executive Plc, 145 Kensington High St, W8 7LP
☎ T 020 7313 7450   F 020 7313 7451

✉ 87 Moorgate, EC2M 6SA
⊖ Moorgate
🚆 Moorgate
☎ T 020 7588 3544
Market areas   Banking

Website www.reed.co.uk
UK Offices 250+

REC Member No

Brief Description A subsidiary of Reed Executive Plc established in 1960, Reed's growth has been dramatic and the company's stated ambition is to grow the business substantially. Reed has been organised into a number of separate operating companies to make this happen. Reed Banking Personnel operates within the Banking sector.

Preferred method of contact Apply on line or telephone for an appointment
Minimum requirements None
Type of business Temporary and Permanent
Grade/Level of Appointments All levels

Resources Connection

Head Office ✉ 2nd Floor, 117 Houndsditch, EC3A 7BT
⊖ Aldgate
🚆 Fenchurch St
☎ T 020 7422 7780
@ london@resources-uk.com
Market areas   Accountancy, IT

Website www.resourcesconnection.co.uk
UK Offices 1
REC Member Yes

Brief Description Resources Connection was founded in 1996 as a wholly owned subsidiary of Deloitte & Touche in an effort to provide clients with that 'new way of getting things done'. Now an independent company, Resources has grown into an international force in the industry with 42 offices in major US cities and global offices in Hong Kong, London, Taipei, and Toronto. The company employs over 1500 employees.

Preferred method of contact Telephone for appointment
Minimum requirements Relevant industry exposure
Type of business Contract
Grade/Level of Appointments All levels

RHI Management Resources

Head Office ✉ 10–11 Austin Friars, EC2P 2JD
⊖ Bank
🚆 Cannon St
☎ T 020 7562 6500   F 020 7588 2959
@ city@rhimr.co.uk
Market areas   Accountancy

✉ Rex House, 10 Regent St, SW1Y 4PE
⊖ Piccadilly Circus
🚆 Charing Cross
☎ T 020 7389 6900   F 020 7389 6999
@ westend@rhimr.co.uk
Market areas   Accountancy

Website www.roberthalfmr.co.uk

UK Offices 9

REC Member Yes

Brief Description RHI Management Resources, A Robert Half International Company. Founded in 1948, pioneered specialised staffing services and today leads the world in the field. With more than 330 locations throughout UK, Europe, Australia, New Zealand and United States, the company is traded on the New York Stock Exchange and operates five separate divisions, each serving different markets. These are Robert Half, which specialises in placing permanent accounting and finance professionals; Accountemps – temporary Accounting, Banking and Finance Support personnel; RHI Management Resources – senior level Accounting and Finance Management on an individual or project-team basis; Office Team – temporary Administrative and Office Support personnel; RHI Consulting – permanent and contract IT specialists.

Preferred method of contact Apply on line or telephone for an appointment

Minimum requirements Senior level Accountancy exposure

Type of business Contract

Grade/Level of Appointments Senior level

Rice & Dore Associates

See **Executive Search, page 105**

Richmond & Co

Head Office ✉ 15 St Helens Place, EC3A 6DE
🚇 Liverpool St
🚃 Liverpool St
☎ T 020 7628 5550   F 020 7628 5551
@ main@richmondandco.co.uk
Market areas Investment Banking, Derivatives

Website www.richmondandco.co.uk

UK Offices 1

REC Member No

Brief Description Richmond & Co is a specialist Investment Banking Executive Search firm based in the City of London. They have significant depth of experience in the product sectors in which they operate. These include all aspects of Investment Banking, Fixed Income, Equities, Asset Management, Private Equity, Real Estate, Corporate Banking and Human Resources.

Preferred method of contact Apply on line or telephone for an appointment

Minimum requirements Relevant Banking exposure

Type of business Permanent

Grade/Level of Appointments All levels

Robert Half

Head Office ✉ Rex House, 10 Regent St, SW1Y 4PE
🚇 Piccadilly Circus
🚃 Charing Cross
☎ T 020 7389 6900   F 020 7389 6999
@ westend@roberthalf.co.uk
Market areas Accountancy and Banking

Website www.roberthalf.co.uk

UK Offices 19

REC Member Yes

Brief Description Robert Half International pioneered specialised staffing services and today leads the world in the field. There are more than 330 Robert Half International locations throughout Australia, New Zealand, Europe and the United States. Founded in 1948, the company is traded on the New York Stock Exchange and operates five separate divisions, each serving different markets. Robert Half specialises in recruiting services for Accounting and Finance professionals on a permanent basis. RHI Management Resources specialises in providing senior level Accounting and Finance Management talent on an individual and project-team basis. Office Team provides highly skilled temporary Administrative and Office Support personnel. RHI Consulting is for permanent and contract IT specialists. Accountemps specialise in temporary recruiting services for Accounting, Banking and Finance.

Preferred method of contact Apply on line or telephone for an appointment

Minimum requirements None

Type of business Permanent

Grade/Level of Appointments All levels

Robert Walters

Head Office ✉ 55 Strand, WC2N 5WR
🚇 Charing Cross
🚃 Charing Cross
☎ T 020 7379 3333   F 020 7509 8714
@ london@robertwalters.com
Market areas Accountancy and Banking, Legal, Technology, Sales and Marketing, Secretarial and Admin

Website www.robertwalters.com

UK Offices 3

REC Member Yes

Brief Description Operating across five continents, with 24 offices in 14 countries, Robert Walters is one of the leading global specialist recruitment and human resources outsourcing businesses. The Robert Walters brand stands for innovation, vision and leadership in the global recruitment market. They specialise in permanent, contract and interim recruitment across all industry sectors, including the world's leading Investment Banks and Multinational blue chip commercial clients. Operating at all levels of seniority, they manage the careers of the best people in the Accounting, Finance, Banking, Legal,

Technology, Sales and Marketing, HR, Call Centre, Support and Administration fields.

Preferred method of contact Apply on line or telephone for an appointment

Minimum requirements None

Type of business Temporary, Permanent and Contract

Grade/Level of Appointments All levels

ROC Recruitment

Head Office ✉ 27 Grosvenor St, London

    ☎ T 020 7318 1400 F 020 7499 9002

    ✉ Park House, 116 Park St, W1K 6NR

    ⊖ Marble Arch

    🚆 Paddington

    ☎ T 020 7318 1414 F 020 7409 1949

    @ roc@roc.co.uk

Market areas Accountancy and Banking, Retail, Hospitality, Education

Website www.roc.co.uk

UK Offices 3

REC Member Yes

Brief Description ROC Recruitment specialises in placing temporary and permanent staff within Accountancy and Banking, Retail, Education and Hospitality from offices in London and Manchester.

Preferred method of contact Apply on line or telephone for an appointment

Minimum requirements None

Type of business Temporary and Permanent

Grade/Level of Appointments All levels

Rochester Partnership

Head Office ✉ 7 St Helens Place, Bishopsgate, EC3 6AU

    ⊖ Liverpool St

    🚆 Liverpool St

    ☎ T 020 7256 9000 F 020 7256 9111

    @ rochester@rochpar.com

Market areas Accountancy and Banking, Insurance, Executive Search

Website www.rochpar.com

UK Offices 1

REC Member No

Brief Description Since its creation in 1982, The Rochester Partnership has focussed its activities on searches for individuals and teams in the financial markets. An independent company, Rochester continues to count a select group of leading global banks and financial institutions among its clients.

Preferred method of contact Apply on line or telephone for an appointment

Minimum requirements None

Type of business Permanent

Grade/Level of Appointments All levels

Russell Jones Associates

See **Executive Search, page 106**

Sheffield Haworth

See **Executive Search, page 107**

Shepherd Little and Associates

See **Financial Services and Insurance, page 126**

Spherion

Head Office ✉ 5 Queen St, EC4N 1SW

    ⊖ Blackfriars

    🚆 Blackfriars

    ☎ T 020 7390 7000 F 020 7390 2997

Market areas Accountancy and Banking, IT, Sales and Marketing, Financial Services, Secretarial

Website www.uk.spherion.com

UK Offices 6

REC Member No

Brief Description Spherion UK is part of the Spherion Corporation, a long-established market leader within the US recruitment industry. Established in 1946, the Spherion Corporation now provides Staffing, Technology and Outsourcing services to customers across the globe. Spherion UK links the best the US has to offer with leading UK brands whose experience and innovation spans generations. Within the UK market Spherion occupies a unique position, comprising of both newly formed divisions and the well-established UK brands FSS and Crone Corkill. This focus allows them to provide customers with a total recruitment solution across discipline, level, location and requirement that combines a fresh approach with traditionally founded, tried and tested business principles.

Preferred method of contact Apply on line or telephone for an appointment

Minimum requirements None

Type of business Temporary and Permanent

Grade/Level of Appointments All levels

Steve Mills Associates

Head Office ✉ 7 Copthall Avenue, EC2R 7NJ

    ⊖ Bank

    🚆 Cannon St

C T 020 7588 8800   F 020 7588 7458

@ admin@stevemills.co.uk

Market areas   Banking - Securities and Investments

Website www.stevemills.co.uk

UK Offices 1

REC Member No

Brief Description Steve Mills is based in the City of London and they offer 20 years specialist recruitment experience in Banking, Securities and Investment Management. Clients include an impressive selection of global banks and they aim to offer you unrivalled access to London's leading career opportunities.

Preferred method of contact Apply on line or telephone for an appointment

Minimum requirements Relevant Banking exposure

Type of business Temporary and Permanent

Grade/Level of Appointments All levels

Virtual Purple

See **IT and Telecoms, page 178**

Walker & Kutner

See **Secretarial, page 261**

Watson Jennings Day Partnership

Head Office   ✉   Bankside House, 107–112 Leadenhall St, EC3A 4AH
              ⊖   Bank
              ⊠   Liverpool St
              C   T 020 7891 2645   F 020 7891 2641
              @   wjdp@wjdp.com
Market areas   Banking

              ✉   29th Floor, 1 Canada Sq, E14 5DY
              ⊖   Canary Wharf
              ⊠   Canary Wharf
              C   T 020 7712 1542
              @   wjdp@wjdp.com
Market areas   Banking

Website www.wjdp.com

UK Offices 2

REC Member No

Brief Description WJD Partnership are a specialist financial recruitment consultancy based in the heart of the City of London. They offer a comprehensive search and selection process and undertake assignments throughout London and Europe. The WJD Partnership are retained by some of the world's leading financial institutions:

Investment Banks, Stockbrokers, Fund Managers and Global Custodians, specialising in recruiting individuals from Junior through to Senior Management within Operations, Middle Office, Front Office and IT for permanent, temporary and contract personnel. They place great emphasis on anticipating change in their market, to provide a proactive and professional service to their clients and candidates alike. If you are looking for staff or you are considering your next career move they work closely with you to ensure your requirements and aspirations are achieved.

Preferred method of contact Apply on line or telephone for an appointment

Minimum requirements None

Type of business Temporary and Permanent

Grade/Level of Appointments Junior to Senior Management level

Whitney Group

See **Executive Search, page 111**

Witan Jardine

Head Office   ✉   13 Southampton Place, WC1A 2AL
              ⊖   Holborn
              ⊠   City Thameslink
              C   T 020 7404 4004   F 020 7404 2865
              @   contactus@witanjardine.co.uk
Market areas   Banking, Finance, Media

Website www.witanjardine.co.uk

UK Offices 1

REC Member Yes

Brief Description Witan Jardine is a highly successful, independent and rapidly growing recruitment consultancy. Established for over 23 years their goal is to become the first point of contact for recruitment in London and the Home Counties, for a number of niche service sectors. These organisations' competitive edge rides on the skills and knowledge of their people. Witan Jardine see candidates and clients with an equal importance. Whatever your requirements you'll find that they can propose options that are not available anywhere else. They have developed a wealth of expertise within their markets and understand the importance of listening to your individual needs.

Preferred method of contact Apply on line or telephone for an appointment

Minimum requirements None

Type of business Temporary and Permanent

Grade/Level of Appointments All levels

Your Achilles' heel

Dealing with your weak spots, difficult questions, embarrassing pauses and horrible interviews

This chapter is taken from "Brilliant Answers to Tough Interview Questions" by Susan Hodgson, published by Prentice Hall, an imprint of Pearson Education, © Pearson Education Ltd 2002

Unless you are one of those rare people who has led a charmed life and found that every decision has turned out well and that fortune has always smiled on you, you are likely to have aspects of your past (be it poor examination results, a period of unemployment, a patchy work history, poor health record, etc.) that you don't want to be asked about at job interviews. Yet you know that, because these issues are part of your history, they are likely to emerge from your CV, application form or employment and character references, and are very likely to arouse a future employer's curiosity. Interviewers do want an explanation of results or circumstances that appear to contradict other evidence of your history and character, and leaves them wondering 'Why?'

Before preparing your answers on any tricky questions that may be applicable to you, you must remind yourself that interviewers ask these things because they genuinely want to know – they want to ascertain whether some weak spot was a temporary glitch or reflects a more pervasive problem. The good news is that they suspect it is the former – otherwise they would not have invited you to the interview in the first place. There can be a second reason why you may be questioned on these 'Achilles' heels' – interviewers know that you are likely to feel vulnerable on these and they want to see whether you become hostile or defensive, or whether you take the opportunity to use your skills of communication, persuasion, analysis and calm reason to offer plausible and convincing explanations.

A brief word about truth

This chapter does not promise to offer a rigorous analysis of the philosophical and moral place of truth in the competitive jungle of job hunting. It does, however, offer some common sense advice on this subject. If you are hiding something on your CV and/or during a job interview, you are unlikely to communicate so effectively or be as relaxed and natural as you would like to be. Things which you have chosen not to say, fictional exam results, jobs that you invent or references written by your mum to enhance your case may well trip you up. Employers almost always take up references before they employ you and if you have to hide the truth at an interview then you have to ask yourself how you are going to keep this up if you are the successful candidate. Remember also, that if an employer finds out later that you have not been

straight with them, they may use this as grounds for dismissal or other disciplinary procedures.

Here are some of the issues about which candidates feel anxious – and some suggested ways to deal with these.

Q   I see that you got very good GCSE results and yet your A level results are poor – what happened?

A   I was unsure of whether I wanted to stay on at school and do A levels, it was something my parents pushed for, but my heart was not really in it. I had become too interested in other things and I just didn't put in the effort I should.

A possible follow-up question to this that could easily provoke a defensive response might be as follows.

Q   Can I take it then, that if you don't like something, you stop working hard at it? What if we give you a job and you find there are parts of it you don't enjoy?

A   I have had a good work record for the past three years since I left school and I have had no difficulty in handling several fairly routine, repetitive tasks during that time. I have grown up a lot since I was 17; I seem to learn better in a work rather than a school environment. I am doing an evening course in website design though, and I am really enjoying that.

Q   There appears to be an eight-month gap on your CV. What were you doing during this time?

A   I had been temping for the previous two years and I really wanted something with more of a sense of direction. With hindsight, I might have done better to wait until I had something permanent before I gave up the temporary work, but I really wanted to concentrate on my job search and give it 100 per cent. I wasn't expecting the job market to plummet so badly during that time. I got my act together by doing a short, intensive course in secretarial skills and was very pleased to get back into the work environment.

Q   You only got a third class degree. We are really looking for someone with a good honours degree.

(Remember, whatever they say, they have still chosen to interview you.)

A   Of course, I was disappointed. I had hoped for an upper second and my first two years' results indicated that I would achieve this. I had a lot of personal problems during my final year, which are well behind me and sorted out now, but they did affect my result. My individual and group project results were good and I think these developed the communication, time management and information-gathering skills that I need for this particular post – so I know I am strong on useful, relevant work skills.

Q   From your CV, it looks as if you have taken six years out of the job market – how do you think you will fit in coping with the routine and the demands of work?

(Candidates should not have to see this as a negative area in their past, but sometimes it can feel that way.)

A   Yes, I took a break from paid work to have my children and see them settled into school, so I have not had salaried employment for the past few years, but I have actually been working very hard. Bringing up a family makes you deal with the unexpected as well as the routine and I often work a much longer day than I did when I was in paid employment. Besides, I certainly haven't forgotten all the skills I used in the drawing office. I keep up to date with the relevant trade press and more significantly by doing some drawing work for friends.

Tip

This one applies to answers on any topic, not just awkward ones. Avoid using apologetic sounding words or phrases such as 'only', a 'little', 'limited' or 'not much' when you describe any of your experience. Look for alternatives like 'useful', 'considerable', 'extensive' and 'relevant'.

Q   **I see that you were made redundant by your last employer nine months ago. How have you coped with this?**

A   It was not a complete surprise because the company had been in financial difficulties for a while and many of us were aware that our jobs might be under threat, nevertheless it was a shock and very hard at first. I've always been someone with an optimistic attitude, but this field is competitive at the moment. I enrolled on an IT course to give me some new design skills very soon after I lost my last job and I have also been doing some voluntary work for my local secondary school, helping with computer skills classes. My CAD skills have certainly developed significantly since leaving my last company and I am very eager to get back into full-time work.

Q   **You don't think you will have lost a bit of your edge and slipped out of the work routine during that time?**

(This is one possible, rather mean reply.)

A   Quite the opposite. I have filled my time constructively and increased my skills, but I really enjoyed work. I think my energy levels and enthusiasm are on top form and I intend them to stay that way.

Q   **It looks from your CV as if you haven't had much work experience at all – other candidates we are seeing today are likely to have had far more.**

A   I did think about working for a year before I went to university and I had intended to take on a part-time job while I was studying. In fact, my father was very ill for a major part of my course and I ended up helping out a lot at home and spending time with him and my family. My course was quite practical and, as you can see, I got a good result even with all the stress going on outside. I really believe I am capable of doing this job and doing it well and you do emphasise your high standard of training and induction.

A   It was really difficult to find the sort of work I wanted when I first left school. I was desperate to get into something with the media and it was hard for me to accept that that just may not have been possible at that time. I did do some voluntary work for my local hospital radio and some unpaid work experience with two local newspapers – I guess I should have mentioned those on my CV.

Tip

It is all too common for job applicants to dismiss part of their own useful experience as irrelevant. Voluntary work, work shadowing, work experience and helping out with a family business are frequent examples of this neglect.

Q   Why did you drop out of university before you had completed your course?

A   It was the wrong subject and the wrong time and place for me. I had been reluctant to carry on with my studies and I am afraid my first year results showed that. The evening job I was doing at the local sports centre was far more exciting to me and the manager was very happy with me. If I go back to studying I want it to be on a part-time basis and I want it to be a more practical course than the degree I started.

It is difficult when, as a candidate, you know that there are extremely private and personal reasons which have affected an area of your life at a particular time – it may have been a bereavement, serious illness of someone close to you, a broken relationship or marriage, or problems within your family at an important time during your schooling. You are reluctant to reveal information which feels personal and private, which might make you feel upset and your interviewer embarrassed and which quite frankly is beyond the scope of what a prospective employer has a reasonable right to know.

Balanced against this is your knowledge that the facts of your personal circumstances at the time offer a legitimate and understandable explanation for a drop in your work or academic performance. It is perfectly reasonable to say that you were affected by difficult personal circumstances that you would rather not discuss at an interview, but if it is something you feel comfortable about mentioning then do so. A family break-up during your school examinations or a marriage falling apart just as you applied for a promotion may be something you would rather reveal and get out of the way. Even the least well trained of interviewers should not then follow this up with a run of personal and intrusive questions. It is also helpful to add a comment suggesting that whatever a problem was, it is now behind you and is not affecting your performance any longer. That, after all, is what the person who is contemplating paying your salary and investing in your training and development really wants to know.

Q   You have changed jobs rather frequently in the last few years. Does this mean you get restless if you are in any job for a considerable length of time?

A   Some of my recent moves have been because I have needed to relocate to different places for personal reasons. I am now settled here and have recently bought a property in the area. Of all the jobs I have done in the past three years I really enjoyed my work at the finance company. I have very good references from them and the work I was doing looks very similar to the responsibilities you list in your advert and job spec.

A   Many of those jobs were temporary anyway and my employers in those situations were not expecting me to stay long, for example when I was providing Christmas or holiday cover. I did not want to commit myself to a career until

I was more sure of the direction in which I wanted to go. My temporary job in the local planning department gave me my first real involvement with work that touched on environmental issues and I have done a great deal of voluntary work with urban and rural environmental improvement projects, so I hope that demonstrates my enthusiasm and commitment to a career with your organisation – it feels like the opportunity I have been waiting for.

Q **You have requested us not to approach your current employer for a reference. Why aren't you happy for us to do this?**

A My current company may be looking at some cost-cutting measures and if they think I am looking elsewhere I may turn out to be one of them. I am quite happy with my work there, but I have been at that level for two and a half years now and I think the job you are offering is ideal. I feel sure I would enjoy it, but I can't guarantee that I shall be the successful candidate and I don't want to unsettle things with my current firm.

A My current manager has only been in the post for three months and if he were asked to write my reference I am not sure that he knows enough about my work, what it entails, what my strengths are to be able to do justice to my skills. I feel you would get far more relevant information from my previous boss, for whom I worked for four and a half years.

Q **Your reference shows that last year you had 15 days off work due to sickness. Is this a typical annual record for you?**

A No, far from it. Those 15 days were all in a block and it was because I had had an accident while on a skiing holiday. My attendance record up to then has been pretty good.

Q **Apart from your annual leave entitlement and public holidays, how many days were you absent from work last year?**

A Four – two were for dental surgery and the other two for an extremely heavy cold that meant I was useless on the telephone, but I am usually pretty hardy.

Health records are of concern to employers. Many organisations will use a pro forma reference request that they send to your current employer or your nominated referee. This form usually contains a section asking for details of how many days you have taken off work due to sickness, so your interviewer may already have access to accurate, factual information on this.

Q **What is your time keeping like?**

A Good, I am usually the first to arrive in the mornings and I dislike being late for any meeting, training session or anything. I think you owe it to your colleagues as well as your manager to be punctual.

Q **You left your last job without having another one lined up to go to. Wasn't that a bit risky?**

A Yes, I suppose it was, but I had never intended to stay in sales for that long and it felt like the right decision. There had been a lot of changes there recently and very few staff were happy. It takes a great deal for me to become discouraged, but I felt my wisest option was to leave and start looking for something else.

The sales work was useful, especially dealing with people and working under pressure – two things which I have become very good at. I'm sure they would be valuable in your customer support department.

Q   One of your references suggests that you sometimes lose your cool in the office. What is your reaction to this?

A   It has happened very occasionally, but I have always been quick to apologise if I have been unreasonable and it has certainly never happened in front of a client. I am aware of it, so I make an effort to keep calm and explain what is annoying or frustrating me. I think most of my colleagues would say that although I can be a little volatile, I am a helpful and supportive member of the department for the vast majority of the time.

Q   Have you ever been asked to resign?

A   No, but I have come close enough to it to resign of my own accord rather than waiting to be asked. We had undergone a restructuring with a new manager, with whom I admit I did not hit it off and yet I had worked successfully and productively there for ten years. I knew that cost cutting and streamlining measures were on the cards and I just had to accept that I was not flavour of the month. It was hard, but it was a useful lesson and I spent an interesting 18 months working as an independent consultant.

A   No, I am pleased to say that is not an experience I have had to go through.

A   Yes. It was the first job I had after I left school. I really wanted to get into anything to do with cars and somehow I ended up working for an insurance company – I don't think it was ever going to work out.

Tip

Don't shoot yourself in the foot. If you have had awful experiences – losing jobs through no fault of your own, or even as a result of your own actions – but these are in the past, and won't emerge through references, don't mention them.

What am I supposed to say?

Some interviewers will try to find out more about your strengths and weaknesses by confronting you with imaginary scenarios to see just how good you are at thinking on your feet. These questions are not designed with one 'right' answer, so don't waste time agonising over exactly what you think the correct solution is. What your interviewer is looking for is evidence of your common sense, your ability to take decisions under pressure and your capacity to know your own limits.

Q   You are the manager of a large supermarket and you receive an anonymous telephone call saying that a number of the baby food products you carry have been tampered with by a protest group. How do you react?

A   I would suspect it was probably a hoax, but of course, I would take every precaution in case it were not. If I had an assistant, I would ask them to arrange to cordon off the baby food aisle and see what could be done to stop any items getting through the checkouts. I would also make a calm announcement over the PA. I would telephone the police and also local press and radio to begin a recall of any suspect items. If I had no assistant, my priority would be to stop anyone buying any of the products in question and then to contact the police.

Q   You work for a company which has been involved in secret merger talks with another company – you are aware of this because it is your job to know, but you don't have any authority in these talks, or this deal. You are the last person in the office and you get a call from a member of the financial press saying that they have heard that this merger is taking place. What would you do?

A   I would say that they would have to speak to one of the directors of the company and that unfortunately none of them is available at the moment. I would check the diaries and give them the earliest possible time when they could call back again. If they pressed me, I would simply repeat my previous answer very calmly and very politely.

Q   You run the research and development section for your company and you have one designer in your section who is brilliant at his job, but very difficult to work with. He is unpredictable, bad tempered and unable to conform to the company rules on many occasions and yet there is no doubt he helps you make a lot of money because on a good day his ideas are brilliant. How do you deal with this?

A   I would have to look at whether we were losing other good staff because of him, how likely he would be to join one of our major competitors if we got rid of him, but most importantly whether there were things we could do to get him to work more effectively as a member of the whole team. I would start by talking to him and possibly involving the human resource department in this discussion and together we would all agree clear targets for improvements with a specific review period. I might also offer training and support if this seemed appropriate.

Tip

Get a friend to confront you with scenarios that they dream up (friends are capable of being far more sadistic than many real live interviewers). This will give you practice in marshalling your thoughts quickly.

Interviewers should not ask you questions about sex, religion or politics – indeed, many of these questions are illegal. They can, however, ask you questions about current affairs and general knowledge. Unless you are facing a particularly devious interviewer, these questions are not designed to reveal your political leanings, they are designed to test your ability to express your opinion, formulate an argument, defend a point of view. They won't usually pick really contentious issues. Expect questions such as the following.

Q   How would you improve the public transport system in this town/city?

Q   What steps would you take to integrate the student population more effectively into the local community?

Q   If you were suddenly given a million pounds to spend on improving this town, how would you spend it?

Q   How would you encourage more young people to continue with their education?

Q   Which story grabbed your attention in the news today?

Tip

> You will need to be well prepared for these questions if you are going for a job in current affairs media, policy development, etc. You may also find you face this type of question related specifically to your own profession, e.g. education, health, the environment, the legal system, etc., so consider carefully the major issues and talking points within your profession at this moment.

That was horrible

There are some interviews where it is not so much the questions that hit a raw nerve with you, but problems about the interview itself. Silences, questions you just can't answer or unusually aggressive interviewers.

Silence may be golden, it may be a beautiful thing on a deserted beach under a starry sky, but it loses its poetry and magic when it causes an embarrassing void in the flow of an interview conversation. To make matters worse, not all interview silence is the same kind of silence. There is the silence that means you have not got a clue what to say, the silence that means you know what the interviewer is getting at, but it is an awkward question and you need time to think about it or, the silence where you believe you have given a thorough, cogent and complete answer and yet your interviewer lets you down – he or she does not retort with the next question. In all three instances, resist the temptation to tell a joke, sing a song or rush out of the room in tears; there are more effective ways than these to deal with the situation.

If you really don't know the answer to a question, then you should say so. This problem is most likely to occur if you are being asked technical/professional questions that you do not know the answers to at this stage, or if you are being asked to provide factual information of some kind.

A   I am sorry, but that isn't an area I am familiar with at present, so I can't really give you any details on that.

A   I am not familiar with that particular data management system, though I would imagine it is quite similar to others that I have used and I am usually quick to get to grips with new systems.

A   I am sorry, but I haven't come across that particular term before, would you mind clarifying it for me?

A   I am afraid that is an area we did not cover on the course, but it is something I am very keen to learn more about.

A   I'm afraid that isn't a situation I have ever had to deal with, but I believe I would deal with it in the following way.

(Then go on to give specific details.)

A   That is a new area for me, so I am afraid I can't really answer, but I enjoy acquiring new knowledge and I do learn quickly.

A   That is not an area with which I am very familiar at the moment, but I see from your recruitment brochure that you offer a thorough induction programme and several training opportunities, so I would like to take advantage of one of these if I were to be offered a position with you.

A   I am not familiar with that legislation, but it is something I would make sure I brought myself up to speed on very quickly if you were to offer me this job.

A   I have never used that software before, but I would be happy to do any necessary training either through your training department or on an external course if that was more appropriate.

Tip

Replies like those above suggest a fair degree of personal confidence, showing that you don't get flustered if there is something you don't know. So, not only do you get yourself out of a tight spot, you demonstrate your good qualities in action – self-assurance, assertiveness, communication, honesty, eagerness to learn – but be careful, you may become so carried away with this list that you make it a positive art form to stop knowing the answers to questions.

It is entirely acceptable to ask for clarification if you don't understand a question, though do this in a way that does not make your interviewer look silly. 'I've no idea what you're on about' is not a response that will endear you to your interviewer.

A   I am sorry, I am not quite sure what you are asking. Could you ask me that question again please?

A   I am not sure where I should start with that, please could you give me a little bit more of an explanation?

Asking for a few moments to think about your answer can immediately remove the anxiety factor from a silence.

A   That's an interesting question, may I have a moment or two to collect my thoughts?

A   There is quite a lot I could say about that – can you bear with me while I think about it for a minute?

These responses are fine. Take it that you have overdone it if the interviewer goes away, makes a cup of coffee and deals with one or two vital telephone calls in the time you have taken to get your thoughts into some sort of order.

If you are faced with a situation where you think you have given a complete answer, but a silence ensues because you are not asked a further question, then you can always say

A   Is there anything you would like me to add?

A   Should I go on to tell you a little about how my previous job gave me some useful experience of dealing with these types of problems?

Encountering an aggressive interviewer is an unpleasant experience for a candidate to face. To some extent, this style of interview is currently out of fashion, but it could return at any moment, so it is wise to be prepared. Leaving aside the possibility that your interviewer simply has a personality problem, you have to ask yourself what is the rationale behind their decision to interview you in this way. It may be to determine how you react in a hostile situation and to discover aspects of your personality through other means than asking you to describe them. Keeping calm and avoiding hitting your adversary is a fundamental starting point. It is, however, important that you don't crumble under the pressure and that you do continue expressing your well-prepared answers clearly and assertively.

Remember the questions are not any more difficult, even if they are being asked in a rather unpleasant manner. It may be that the position you have applied for will mean that you are placed with some fairly aggressive colleagues or clients and if your interviewer is aware of this, they want to ascertain that you will be able to cope.

Once in a while, your interviewer is pleasant, but circumstances are difficult. Your interview is constantly interrupted by telephone calls or by people bursting into the room. Your interviewer probably feels even more flustered than you by this (unless it is some bizarre psychological test), but this is unlikely. Bad planning and time pressure or staff shortages are more likely explanations. Take a note of where the conversation broke off, so that you can get it back on track quickly if your interviewer is struggling with 'and where were we?' One candidate being interviewed for a job at a company based in a coastal town had their interview interrupted because their interviewer was a member of the local lifeboat crew and he was summoned to a rescue – so some interruptions have to be forgiven.

Tip

Aggressive-sounding questions often begin with the word 'Why'. 'Why did you take this decision?' 'Why did this problem arise?' Just keep smiling as you answer the questions being fired at you and try not to take the whole thing too personally.

Final tips for dealing with interview horrors

1. Prepare ahead for any areas where you know you may be vulnerable.

2. Ensure that those people whose names you are giving as referees know this beforehand and have given their permission for you to do so. This is not only courteous, but it means if there are any areas of concern, they may be prepared to discuss them with you in advance.

3. Accept that some interviews will go badly and you can't always redeem the situation.

4. Be candid and truthful, but don't give people information they don't ask for; you don't have to drag all the skeletons out of your cupboard.

5. Remember that you would never have been called for an interview if there was not a real chance that you could be the successful candidate, so be positive.

Bilingual

ACCESS Technology

See **Executive Search, page 75**

Active Recruitment

Head Office ✉ 3 Westminster Palace Gardens, Artillery Row, SW1P 1RL
⊖ St James's Park
🚊 Victoria
✆ T 020 7976 7551   F 020 7222 1743
@ active@awlt.com
Market areas Linguists, Interpreters and Translators

Website www.awlt.com
UK Offices 1
REC Member No
Brief Description Established in 1994, Active Recruitment initially specialised in finding employment for Japanese speaking candidates with international companies requiring Japanese speakers. Their candidate database now contains many candidates who are bilingual in languages other than Japanese who have expressed an interest in employment with international companies.
Preferred method of contact Apply on line or telephone for appointment
Minimum requirements Bilingual
Type of business Contract, Temporary and Permanent
Grade/Level of Appointments All levels

Appointments Bi-Language

Head Office ✉ Sussex House, 143 Long Acre, WC2E 9AD
⊖ Covent Garden
🚊 Charing Cross
✆ T 020 7836 7878   F 020 7836 7615
@ info@appointmentsbilanguage.co.uk
Market areas Language specialists, Secretarial

Website www.ablrecruit.co.uk
UK Offices 1
REC Member No
Brief Description Founded in 1991, Appointments Bi-Language specialises in high calibre Support staff, both with or without languages. It has a dedicated team of 15 employees, dealing with permanent, contract and temporary vacancies for major International organisations in London.
Preferred method of contact Apply on line or telephone for appointment

Minimum requirements Systems literate and minimum 50 wpm typing
Type of business Permanent, Temporary and Contract
Grade/Level of Appointments All levels

Ashford Associates

Head Office ✉ 36–38 Cornhill, EC3V 3NG
⊖ Bank
🚊 Cannon St
✆ T 020 7626 4592   F 020 7626 4590
@ admin@ashford-associates.co.uk
Market areas Language specialists

Website www.ashford-associates.co.uk
UK Offices 1
REC Member Yes
Brief Description Ashford Associates is a recruitment business and consultancy services provider located in the City of London. They pride themselves on providing an efficient service based on excellent relationships with a number of Japan-related companies. They have dealt with clients in the United Kingdom and Europe since 1993, introducing Japanese speakers and other Bilingual candidates to a variety of professions.
Preferred method of contact Apply on line or telephone for appointment
Minimum requirements Ideally language skills
Type of business Temporary and Permanent
Grade/Level of Appointments All levels

Bilinguagroup

Head Office ✉ 25 Maddox St, W1S 2QT
⊖ Oxford Circus
🚊 Charing Cross
✆ T 020 7493 6446   F 020 7493 0168
@ info@bilinguagroup.com
Market areas Language specialists

Website www.bilinguagroup.com
UK Offices 1
REC Member Yes
Brief Description Bilinguagroup is a full service provider of global Language solutions with offices in London, Paris and Frankfurt, supplying Interpreters, PAs, Support Staff, Managers and Directors with bi-lingual skills to the Legal, Sales, Marketing, IT, Call Centres, Financial and Insurance sectors.

Preferred method of contact Apply on line or telephone for appointment

Minimum requirements Fluent second language speaker

Type of business Permanent and Temporary

Grade/Level of Appointments PAs/Secretaries to Interpreters and Director level

Bilingual People Ltd

Head Office ✉ 38 Dover St, W1X 3RB
🚇 Green Park
🚋 Victoria
☎ T 020 7491 2400   F 020 7491 1900
@ admin@bilingualpeople.com
Market areas   Language specialists

Website www.bilingualpeople.com

UK Offices 1

REC Member No

Brief Description Established in 1992, Bilingual People is a dynamic international recruitment consultancy with offices in London and Frankfurt, specialising in the recruitment of multilingual professionals for temporary or permanent opportunities across all business sectors including International Trade, Banking, IT, Engineering, Legal, Media and Professional bodies.

Preferred method of contact Telephone for appointment

Minimum requirements Fluent second language speaker

Type of business Permanent and Temporary

Grade/Level of Appointments General Office/Support Roles

Boyce Recruitment

Head Office ✉ 5–7 John Princes St, W1M 9HD
🚇 Oxford Circus
🚋 Charing Cross
☎ T 020 7491 9800   F 020 7491 4893
@ enquiries@boycerecruitment.co.uk
Market areas   Language specialists

Website www.boycerecruitment.co.uk

UK Offices 1

REC Member No

Brief Description Boyce Recruitment was established in 1984 to meet the demands of multinational organisations in their search for multilingual personnel, providing the best temporary, contract and permanent staff with experience of working in an International environment to small and large institutions across the UK and Europe.

Preferred method of contact Telephone for appointment

Minimum requirements Fluent Written and Spoken English

Type of business Temporary, Permanent and Contract

Grade/Level of Appointments Graduate/Junior to Management level

Cannon Persona International Recruitment

Head Office ✉ 12 Nicholas Lane, EC4N 7BN
🚇 Cannon St
🚋 Cannon St
☎ T 020 7621 0055   F 020 7621 1001
@ info@cpir.com
Market areas   Language specialists

Website www.cpir.com

UK Offices 1

REC Member Yes

Brief Description Founded in 1986, Cannon Persona is a joint venture with Japan's largest recruitment company, The Pasona Group, providing an effective recruitment service to Japanese companies worldwide and to European based companies dealing with Japan, representing a large number of blue chip Japanese, European and American clients.

Preferred method of contact Apply on line or telephone for appointment

Minimum requirements Fluent Japanese speaker

Type of business Permanent and Temporary

Grade/Level of Appointments Secretarial to Senior Management

Centre People Appointments Ltd

Head Office ✉ 1 Lombard St, EC3V 9JT
🚇 Bank
🚋 Cannon St
☎ T 020 7929 5551   F 020 7929 5552
@ centrepeople@centrepeople.com
Market areas   Language specialists

Website www.centrepeople.com

UK Offices 1

REC Member Yes

Brief Description Established in 1986, Centre People specialises in providing bilingual candidates to Japanese clients based in the UK and Europe within the following sectors: IT/Telecoms, Sales and Marketing, Trading, with appointments ranging from Administration/Secretarial to Middle/Senior Management.

Preferred method of contact Apply on line or telephone for appointment

Minimum requirements British or European nationals with BA/MA in Japanese

Type of business Permanent

Grade/Level of Appointments Sales/Customer Service to Software Engineer/Project Management

Crone Corkill Group Plc – Language

Head Office ✉ 5 Queen St, EC4N 1SW
⊖ Mansion House
🚇 Blackfriars
☎ T 020 7390 7000   F 020 7390 2997
@ infolang@cronecorkill.co.uk

Market areas Language specialists

✉ 1 Stratton St, W1J 8LA
⊖ Green Park
🚇 Victoria
☎ T 020 7636 0800   F 020 7499 4300
@ infolang@cronecorhill.co.uk

Market areas Language specialists

Website www.cronecorkill.co.uk

REC Member Yes

Brief Description Part of the Spherion Corporation, Crone Corkill specialise in placing both temporary and permanent Secretaries, PAs, Legal Secretaries, Paralegals and Bi-linguists in many major national and international clients.

Preferred method of contact Apply on line or telephone for appointment

Minimum requirements None

Type of business Temporary and Permanent

Grade/Level of Appointments All levels

DISCO International Ltd

✉ 125 New Bond St, W1S 1DY
⊖ Bond St
🚇 Paddington
☎ T 020 7493 1533   F 020 7493 1019
@ info@discointer.co.uk

Market areas Language specialists

Website www.discointer.co.uk

UK Offices 1

REC Member No

Head Office Tokyo

Brief Description DISCO International Ltd was established in 1993 as a human resources firm specialising in Japanese–English bilingual recruitment. For almost a decade they have built their expertise by connecting thousands of candidates with cutting edge companies.

Preferred method of contact Apply on line or telephone for appointment

Minimum requirements Japanese/English bilingual skills

Type of business Permanent

Grade/Level of Appointments Graduates/1st Jobbers to Management level

DSA Bilingual Ltd

Head Office ✉ Suite 81–85, Kent House, 83–89 Regent St, W1R 7HF
⊖ Piccadilly Circus
🚇 Charing Cross
☎ T 020 7734 4469   F 020 7734 4005
@ jobs@dsabilingual.co.uk

Market areas Language specialists

Website www.dsabilingual.co.uk

UK Offices 1

REC Member No

Brief Description Established in 1990, DSA Bilingual is a privately owned company with a wide ranging client base, from banking and international legal firms to manufacturing companies. They are committed to providing a very personal service to their candidates as well as their clients and since their inception have built strong relationships with major organisations.

Preferred method of contact Telephone for appointment

Minimum requirements Bilingual

Type of business Temporary, Permanent and Contract

Grade/Level of Appointments Secretarial/PA to Translators/Office Managers

Euro London Appointments

Head Office ✉ Three Kings Ct, 150 Fleet St, EC4A 2DQ
⊖ Blackfriars
🚇 City Thameslink
☎ T 020 7583 0180   F 020 7583 7800
@ city@eurolondon.com

Market areas Language specialists

✉ 35 Dover St, W1X 3RA
⊖ Green Park
🚇 Victoria
☎ T 020 7518 4288   F 020 7518 4299
@ westend@eurolondon.com

Market areas Language specialists

Website www.eurolondon.com

UK Offices 2

REC Member No

Brief Description Euro London Appointments is the largest independent recruitment consultancy specialising in the provision of multilingual personnel throughout all industries. Established in 1990, Euro London has offices in London, Frankfurt, Paris and Windsor.

Preferred method of contact Telephone for appointment

Minimum requirements Language skills

Type of business Temporary, Permanent and Contract

Grade/Level of Appointments All levels

Euro London Appointments (Temporaries Division)

Head Office ✉ Three Kings Ct, 150 Fleet St, EC4A 2DQ
             ⊖ Blackfriars
             ☒ City Thameslink
             ☎ T 020 7583 0180   F 020 7353 0491
             @ temporaries@eurolondon.com
Market areas Language specialists

Website www.eurolondon.com

UK Offices 2

REC Member No

Brief Description Euro London Appointments is the largest independent recruitment consultancy specialising in the provision of multilingual personnel throughout all industries. Established in 1990, Euro London has offices in London, Frankfurt, Paris and Windsor.

Preferred method of contact Telephone for appointment

Minimum requirements Language Skills

Type of business Temporary

Grade/Level of Appointments All levels

Hays Call Centre Personnel – Multilingual

Head Office ✉ 141 Moorgate, EC2M 6TX
             ☎ T 020 7628 9999   F 020 7628 4698

             ✉ Charter House, 13–15 Carteret St, SW1H 9DJ
             ⊖ St James's Park
             ☒ Victoria
             ☎ T 020 7222 3832   F 01226 720813
             @ multilingual@hays-hpcc.com
Market areas Call Centre

Website www.haysworks.com

UK Offices 2

REC Member No

Brief Description Hays Personnel Services is a division of Hays plc, the business services group listed in the FTSE 100. Hays Personnel Services is Europe's leading specialist professional recruitment group. Hays Personnel Contact Centres provide on-site recruitment solutions for the rapidly expanding Call Centre industry. The business provides clients with fully trained and experienced staff to handle the demanding workloads of any Call Centre.

Preferred method of contact Apply on line or telephone for an appointment

Minimum requirements Language skills

Type of business Temporary and Permanent

Grade/Level of Appointments All levels

JAC

Head Office ✉ 12th Floor, Cannon Centre, 78 Cannon St, EC4M 6HH
             ⊖ Cannon St
             ☒ Cannon St
             ☎ T 020 7623 9900   F 020 7623 9911
             @ jobs@jac-recruitment.co.uk
Market areas Language specialists

Website www.jac-recruitment.co.uk

UK Offices 1

REC Member Yes

Brief Description Established in 1975 as part of the UK based Tazaki Group, JAC Recruitment is recognised as the premier recruitment consultancy for Japanese native speakers and Japanese speaking candidates in the UK and Europe. They pride themselves on the level of customer service that they provide to both clients and candidates. All of their consultants are highly trained and fluent in both Japanese and English, and have developed excellent working relationships with both the Japanese and major international companies located in the UK and mainland Europe.

Preferred method of contact Apply on line or telephone for an appointment

Minimum requirements Japanese language speaker

Type of business Temporary and Permanent

Grade/Level of Appointments All levels

The Language Business

Head Office ✉ 20 Bedford St, WC2E 9HP
             ⊖ Covent Garden
             ☒ Charing Cross
             ☎ T 020 7379 3189   F 020 7379 0624
             @ admin@languagebusiness.co.uk
Market areas Language specialists

Website www.languagebusiness.co.uk

UK Offices 1

REC Member Yes

Brief Description Established in 1989, The Language Business is a recruitment consultancy specialising in multilingual permanent and temporary placements. The majority of their vacancies are based in London and the Home Counties, with some overseas opportunities. They provide multilingual staff for leading companies in every sector of Commerce and Industry, from Graduate opportunities to more experienced personnel.

Preferred method of contact Telephone for appointment

Minimum requirements Language skills

Type of business   Temporary and Permanent
Grade/Level of Appointments   All levels

Language Matters

Head Office   ✉ 3rd Floor, 9 Irving St, WC2H 7AH
              ⊖ Leicester Sq
              🚃 Charing Cross
              ☏ T 020 7930 1811   F 020 7925 0056
              @ info@languagematters.co.uk
Market areas   Language specialists

Website   www.languagematters.co.uk
UK Offices   1
REC Member   No

Brief Description   Language Matters is a multilingual recruitment consultancy covering temporary, permanent and contract personnel in London, the Home Counties and Europe. They recruit from Junior to Executive level, including PA/Secretaries, Banking and Sales/Marketing professionals and Customer Services personnel. Their expertise covers sectors from Manufacturing to Professional and Financial Services.

Preferred method of contact   Apply on line or telephone for an appointment

Minimum requirements   Fluent second language speaker
Type of business   Permanent, Temporary and Contract
Grade/Level of Appointments   Junior/Graduate to Executive level

Language Recruitment Services Ltd

Head Office   ✉ 54–62 Regent St, W1R 5PJ
              ⊖ Piccadilly Circus
              🚃 Charing Cross
              ☏ T 020 7287 0424   F 020 7437 4141
Market areas   Language specialists

Website   www.lrsuk.com
UK Offices   1
REC Member   Yes

Brief Description   LRS is a specialist multilingual recruitment consultancy conveniently situated in the heart of Central London. They began back in 1987, as one of the few independent companies offering their candidates and clients a personal and professional service in the evolving Language sector.

Preferred method of contact   Apply on line or telephone for an appointment

Minimum requirements   Fluent second language speaker
Type of business   Permanent, Temporary and Contract
Grade/Level of Appointments   All levels

Merrow Language Recruitment

Head Office   ✉ 3rd Floor, 23 Bentinck St, W1U 2EZ
              ⊖ Bond St
              🚃 Paddington
              ☏ T 020 7935 5050   F 020 7935 5454
              @ recruit@merrow.co.uk
Market areas   Language specialists

Website   www.merrow.co.uk
UK Offices   1
REC Member   No

Brief Description   Merrow the language recruitment specialist has over 35 years of experience in the field of multilingual recruitment. Established in 1965 to fill an existing market niche, they are the most experienced and second to none in the area of language recruitment. They offer a highly focussed and comprehensive service across all industry sectors and at all levels of seniority within the multilingual market.

Preferred method of contact   Apply on line or telephone for an appointment

Minimum requirements   Language skills
Type of business   Temporary, Permanent and Contract
Grade/Level of Appointments   Administrative Assistant to Account Manager

People First Recruitment Ltd

Head Office   ✉ 46 Moorgate, EC2R 6EH
              ⊖ Moorgate
              🚃 Moorgate
              ☏ T 020 7256 9050   F 020 7256 9051
              @ mail@people-first.co.uk
Market areas   Language specialists, Secretarial

Website   www.people-first.demon.co.uk
UK Offices   1
REC Member   Yes

Brief Description   People First Recruitment is a small, specialised agency, which gives a personal, efficient, and friendly service to both clients and candidates. Their consultants work as a close-knit team in the fields of Japanese speaking and multi-lingual candidates in most disciplines, as well as Import/Export, and Support staff.

Preferred method of contact   Apply on line or telephone for an appointment

Minimum requirements   None
Type of business   Temporary and Permanent
Grade/Level of Appointments   All levels

Verity Appointments

See Secretarial, page 261

Construction and Property

Adrem Recruitment Ltd

Head Office ✉ 1st Floor, 41–42 Foley St, W1W 7TS
🚇 Goodge St
🚊 Euston
☎ T 020 7436 1616   F 020 7436 1335
@ info@adrem.uk.com
Market areas Architecture and Interior Design

Website www.adrem.uk.com
UK Offices 1
REC Member No

Brief Description Adrem is a specialist recruitment company operating at the heart of the Architectural and Design community with an enviable reputation for providing the right people for their clients.

Preferred method of contact Telephone for appointment

Minimum requirements None

Type of business Temporary and Permanent

Grade/Level of Appointments All levels

AMSA Ltd

Head Office ✉ 2 Great Malborough St, W1F 7HQ
🚇 Oxford Circus
🚊 Charing Cross
☎ T 020 7734 0532   F 020 7494 1509
@ recruit@amsa.co.uk
Market areas Architecture and Interior Design

Website www.amsa.co.uk
UK Offices 1
REC Member No

Brief Description Established for over 30 years, AMSA is a specialist recruitment consultancy providing services to Architects and Interior Designers covering all professional, technical and administrative staff appointments.

Preferred method of contact Telephone for appointment

Minimum requirements None

Type of business Permanent and Temporary

Grade/Level of Appointments Graduates/Juniors to Project Managers

Anders Elite

✉ Dashwood House, 69 Old Broad St, EC2M 1NQ
🚇 Liverpool St
🚇 Liverpool St
☎ T 020 7256 5555   F 020 7256 9898
@ london@anderselite.com
Market areas Building, Property, Engineering and Technical

Website www.anderselite.com
UK Offices 10
REC Member No

Head Office Capital House, 1 Houndwell Place, Southampton, SO14 1HU

Brief Description Established in 1983, Anders Elite (previously Anders Glaser Wills and Euro Elite) has a network of regional offices supplying permanent, contract and temporary staff to the Building, Property, Engineering and Technical industries.

Preferred method of contact Telephone for appointment

Minimum requirements None

Type of business Temporary, Permanent and Contract

Grade/Level of Appointments All levels

Anglo Technical

Head Office ✉ 25 Skylines Village, Limeharbour, E14 9TS
🚇 Crossharbour
🚊 Limehouse
☎ T 020 7531 5757   F 020 7538 4051
@ recruit@anglo.com
Market areas IT, Technical, Construction, Engineering

Website www.anglo.com
UK Offices 1
REC Member Yes

Brief Description Anglo Technical Recruitment was founded in 1984, with the expressed intention to provide the Construction industry with a high standard of professional service and give Construction professionals honest, high-calibre career management. Throughout the industry the name of Anglo has come to signify an expertise within the fields of Building, Building Services, Chemical, Civil, Environmental, Highways, Oil and Gas, Pharmaceutical, Power, Structures, Transportation and Water.

Preferred method of contact Apply on line or telephone for appointment

Minimum requirements Relevant industry exposure

Type of business Temporary and Permanent

Grade/Level of Appointments Site Supervisor to Project Manager/ Senior Engineer

Anthony Moss & Associates Ltd

Head Office ✉ AMA Energy Management, Suite 350, Prices House, 50–60 Eastcastle St, W1W 8EA
⊖ Oxford Circus
🚊 Charing Cross
☎ T 020 7323 2330   F 020 7323 3340
@ recruit@amoss.com
Market areas Engineering and Technical within the Oil and Gas Industry

Website www.amoss.com
UK Offices 1
REC Member No

Brief Description Anthony Moss & Associates (AMA) is the Energy and Management Division of the privately owned Malla Technical Recruitment Group which was founded in 1995. AMA undertakes assignments on behalf of both UK and International based operators and Integrated Service companies resourcing project management teams for joint venture activities.

Preferred method of contact Apply on line or telephone for appointment

Minimum requirements Relevant industry exposure

Type of business Contract and Permanent

Avery Associates Ltd

Head Office ✉ Glen House, Stag Place, SW1E 5AG
⊖ Victoria
🚊 Victoria
☎ T 020 7233 7712   F 020 7233 6364
@ info@aa2000.co.uk
Market areas Construction, Rail, Telecoms and Civil Engineering

Website www.aa2000.co.uk
UK Offices 1
REC Member No

Brief Description Avery Associates is the trading name of Avery 2000 Ltd and was established in 1980 to supply staff for the Construction, Civil Engineering, Rail and Telecoms industries for permanent, temporary and contract work.

Preferred method of contact Apply on line or telephone for appointment

Minimum requirements None

Type of business Permanent, Temporary and Contract

Grade/Level of Appointments All levels

Bluetec Recruitment

Head Office ✉ 61 Southwark St, SE1 0HL
⊖ London Bridge
🚊 London Bridge

☎ T 020 7861 8960   F 020 7861 8998
@ bluetecinfo@bluetec.co.uk
Market areas Construction, Public Sector, Engineering, Rail

Website www.bluetec.co.uk
UK Offices 1
REC Member Yes

Brief Description Bluetec Recruitment specialises in the temporary and permanent recruitment of Construction, Public Sector, Engineering and Rail workers.

Preferred method of contact Telephone for an appointment

Minimum requirements Previous professional experience

Type of business Temporary and Permanent

Grade/Level of Appointments All levels

Capita Technical Services Resourcing

Head Office ✉ New Loom House, 101 Back Church Lane, E1 1LU
⊖ Aldgate East
🚊 Fenchurch St
☎ T 020 7481 9779   F 020 7481 9889
@ london@capitatsr.co.uk
Market areas Construction and Property

Website www.capitatsr.co.uk
UK Offices 5
REC Member No

Brief Description Capita Technical Services Resourcing specialises in the Construction and Property industries, from Assistant Surveyors right through to Directors.

Preferred method of contact Apply on line or telephone for an appointment

Minimum requirements None

Type of business Permanent

Grade/Level of Appointments Assistant Surveyor to Director level

Catch 22 Facilities Support Services

Head Office ✉ 199 Victoria St, SW1E 5NE
⊖ Victoria
🚊 Victoria
☎ T 020 7630 5144   F 020 7834 7172
@ london@c22.co.uk
Market areas Facilities Management and Support Staff

Website www.c22.co.uk
UK Offices 2
REC Member Yes

Brief Description Established in 1982, Catch 22 is a privately owned employment agency which supplies all grades of Facilities Support staff and services to companies across the UK. All services are supported 24 hours a day through a dedicated helpdesk operation.

Preferred method of contact Telephone for appointment

Minimum requirements None

Type of business Temporary, Permanent and Contract

Grade/Level of Appointments Domestic/Helpdesk to Facilities Managers

Charles Birch Recruitment Ltd

⊠ Warnford Ct, 29 Throgmorton St, EC2N 2AT
⊖ Moorgate
🚆 Moorgate
☎ T 020 7588 6124   F 020 7588 6125
@ recruitment@charlesbirch.org
Market areas Secretarial, Facilities Management

Website www.charlesbirch.org

UK Offices 2

REC Member No

Head Office 1 Caxton Place, Roden St, Ilford, Essex, IG1 2AH

Brief Description With two offices in London and Essex, Charles Birch specialise in supplying both temporary and permanent personnel to a wide range of clients, with opportunities ranging from CAD Draughtsmen, Project Managers to Receptionist and Secretarial Support staff.

Preferred method of contact Telephone for appointment

Minimum requirements None

Type of business Temporary and Permanent

Grade/Level of Appointments All levels

Corps of Commissionaires

Head Office ⊠ 85 Cowcross St, EC1M 6PF
⊖ Farringdon
🚆 Farringdon
☎ T 020 7556 0601   F 020 7566 0502
@ kfaulkner@the-corps.co.uk
Market areas Security, Facilities Support

Website www.the-corps.co.uk

UK Offices 15

REC Member Yes

Brief Description The Corps is one of the UK's premier Security and Facilities Support organisations – as well as offering worldwide Security Consultancy and Undercover Operations. In the UK they provide high quality Uniformed Guarding and related facilities services, hi-tech equipment systems and advice to local and national companies, working through their network of 17 regional offices in England, Scotland, Wales and Northern Ireland.

Preferred method of contact Apply on line or telephone for appointment

Minimum requirements None

Type of business Temporary, Permanent and Contract

Grade/Level of Appointments Reception Security/Filing to Management Support/VIP Protection

CSL Right People

Head Office ⊠ Renown House, 33–34 Bury St, EC3A 5AR
⊖ Aldgate
🚆 Fenchurch St
☎ T 020 7626 2626   F 020 7626 0247
@ jobs@rightpeople.co.uk
Market areas Facilities Management, Building Services

Website www.rightpeople.co.uk

UK Offices 1

REC Member No

Brief Description CSL Right People are a specialist recruitment agency for the Building Services Maintenance and Facilities Management industries.

Preferred method of contact Telephone for appointment

Minimum requirements None

Type of business Permanent

Grade/Level of Appointments All levels

Daniel Owen Associates

⊠ 78–79 Long Lane, EC1A 9RP
⊖ Barbican
🚆 Barbican
☎ T 020 7600 7777   F 020 7600 2222
@ email@danielowen.co.uk
Market areas Construction

Website www.danielowen.co.uk

UK Offices 2

REC Member No

Head Office Hadwyn House, Field Rd, Reading, RG1 6AP

Brief Description Construction and allied industries are where Daniel Owen Associates have their roots. They are wholly focused on Construction industry staffing; they have supplied Building professionals, from Architects and Engineers to Surveyors and Site Managers, on a permanent and temporary basis since 1986.

Preferred method of contact Apply on line or telephone for an appointment

Minimum requirements None

Type of business Temporary and Permanent

Grade/Level of Appointments All levels

Daulton Construction Personnel Ltd

Head Office ✉ 2 Greycoat Place, SW1P 1SB
  ⊖ St James's Park
  🚃 Victoria
  ☎ T 020 7222 0817   F 020 7233 0734
  @ info@daultonpersonnel.co.uk
  Market areas Construction

Website www.daultonpersonnel.co.uk
UK Offices 1
REC Member No
Brief Description Daulton Construction Personnel Ltd was established in 1988 to provide a quality recruitment and selection consultancy to the Construction industry. From the beginning, Daulton Construction has employed specialists from within both the UK and International Construction industries.

Preferred method of contact Apply on line or telephone for appointment
Minimum requirements None
Type of business Permanent and Contract
Grade/Level of Appointments Graduate/Site level to Board level appointments

Eden Brown Recruitment Ltd

Head Office ✉ 17–29 Sun St, EC2M 2PT
  ⊖ Liverpool St
  🚃 Liverpool St
  ☎ T 020 7309 1300   F 020 7309 1313
  @ london@edenbrown.com
  Market areas Construction, Facilities Management, Architecture, Housing, Secretarial

Website www.edenbrown.com
UK Offices 5
REC Member Yes
Brief Description Over the past 12 years Eden Brown has led the UK recruitment industry. One of the very first to be Quality Assured (1993) and an Investor in People (1996) it has consistently innovated in terms of professionalism and customer service. Many initiatives such as Contractor Support services were first developed and supported by Eden Brown. Today Eden Brown is recognised as a leading staff supplier within a number of UK markets. With offices in London, Birmingham, Manchester, Bristol and Leeds it offers a networked nationwide service.

Preferred method of contact Apply on line or telephone for appointment
Minimum requirements None
Type of business Temporary, Permanent and Contract
Grade/Level of Appointments Office Juniors to Site Managers/ Directors

Estate Agency Recruitment

Head Office ✉ 3 Hornton Place, W8 4LZ
  ⊖ Kensington (Olympia)
  🚃 Kensington (Olympia)
  ☎ T 020 7938 3855   F 020 7938 3596
  @ jobs@estateagencyrecruit.co.uk
  Market areas Property

Website www.estateagencyrecruitment.co.uk
UK Offices 1
REC Member No
Brief Description Established in 1988, they are the first agency developed by Estate Agents to provide a quick and professional answer to the recruitment needs of the Property industry. Their experienced team offer a confidential and personal service, recruiting for a broad spectrum of the Property market, including the majority of corporate and independent Estate Agents.

Preferred method of contact Apply on line or telephone for appointment
Minimum requirements None
Type of business Permanent
Grade/Level of Appointments All levels

Extraman Ltd

See **Industrial, page 150**

Facilities Management Recruitment

Head Office ✉ 67 Chiltern St, W1J 6NJ
  ⊖ Baker St
  🚃 Marylebone
  ☎ T 020 7224 5204   F 020 7224 5206
  @ apply@fmr.co.uk
  Market areas Facilities Management

Website www.fmr.co.uk
UK Offices 1
REC Member No
Brief Description FMR are a highly professional recruitment and training company, providing solutions to personnel requirements in the Property and Facilities Management, Technical and Engineering professions. From offices in London, FMR recruits for clients all over the UK and overseas. The majority of their recruitment consultants are professionally qualified in the areas in which they recruit.

Preferred method of contact Telephone for appointment
Minimum requirements None
Type of business Temporary and Contract
Grade/Level of Appointments All levels

Facilities Recruitment Ltd

Head Office ✉ Blackfriars Foundry, 156 Blackfriars Rd, SE1 8EN
⊖ Blackfriars
🚊 Blackfriars
☎ T 020 7721 7333   F 020 7721 7335
@ info@facilitiesrecruit.co.uk
Market areas Facilities Management

Website www.facilitiesrecruit.co.uk

UK Offices 1

REC Member No

Brief Description Established in 1999, Facilities Recruitment provide sourcing and introduction services for professional Facilities personnel.

Preferred method of contact Apply on line or telephone for appointment

Minimum requirements None

Type of business Contract and Permanent

Grade/Level of Appointments All levels

Farlow & Warren Search and Selection – Construction

Head Office ✉ Unit 212–213 The Business Design Centre, 52 Upper St, N1 0QH
⊖ Highbury and Islington
🚊 Highbury and Islington
☎ T 020 7288 6211   F 020 7288 6208
@ constructionservices@farlowandwarren.co.uk
Market areas Interiors, Construction Services, Building Services

Website www.farlowandwarren.co.uk

UK Offices 1

REC Member No

Brief Description Farlow & Warren Search and Selection have been established for 10 years and have a wealth of experience of recruiting on a search and contingency basis to specialist niche market-places: Telecoms and IT, including Customer Service, Engineering, Sales, Networking and Transmission; Financial, including Life and Pensions and Financial Advisers; Construction, including Interior Fit-out, Facilities Managers, Construction Services and Building Services; Commercial, including Back Office, Secretarial, Administration, temporary and permanent.

Preferred method of contact Apply on line or telephone for an appointment

Minimum requirements None

Type of business Contract and Permanent

Grade/Level of Appointments All levels

Folio Personnel Ltd (Architecture Division)

Head Office ✉ Dorland House, 14–16 Regent St, SW1Y 4PH
⊖ Piccadilly Circus
🚊 Charing Cross
☎ T 020 7484 0602   F 020 7484 0601
@ cedgley@foliopersonnel.com
Market areas Architecture and Interior Design

Website www.foliopersonnel.com

UK Offices 1

REC Member No

Brief Description Established in 1994, Folio Personnel was founded to provide a professional service to the industry it serves. They offer a complete recruitment service for both temporary and permanent staff at all levels.

Preferred method of contact Apply on line or telephone for appointment

Minimum requirements None

Type of business Contract and Permanent

Grade/Level of Appointments All levels

Folio Personnel Ltd (Construction Division)

Head Office ✉ Dorland House, 14–16 Regent St, SW1Y 4PH
⊖ Piccadilly Circus
🚊 Charing Cross
☎ T 020 7484 0604   F 020 7484 0601
@ ipirrie@foliopersonnel.com
Market areas Construction

Website www.foliopersonnel.com

UK Offices 1

REC Member No

Brief Description Established in 1994, Folio Personnel was founded to provide a professional service to the industry it serves. They offer a complete recruitment service for both temporary and permanent staff at all levels.

Preferred method of contact Apply on line or telephone for appointment

Minimum requirements None

Type of business Contract and Permanent

Grade/Level of Appointments All levels

Folio Personnel Ltd (Graphic Design Division)

See Media, page 198

Folio Personnel Ltd (Sales and Marketing Division)

See **Sales and Marketing**, page 215

Folio Personnel Ltd (Shell and Core Division)

Head Office   ✉   Dorland House, 14–16 Regent St, SW1Y 4PH
     ⊖   Piccadilly Circus
     🚃   Charing Cross
     ☎   **T** 020 7484 0606   **F** 020 7484 0601
     @   ipirrie@foliopersonnel.com
Market areas   Shell and Core

Website www.foliopersonnel.com
UK Offices 1
REC Member No

Brief Description Established in 1994, Folio Personnel was founded to provide a professional service to the industry it serves. They offer a complete recruitment service for both temporary and permanent staff at all levels.

Preferred method of contact Apply on line or telephone for appointment

Minimum requirements None

Type of business Contract and Permanent

Grade/Level of Appointments All levels

Hays Executive Search – Property and Construction Practice

See **Executive Search**, page 92

Hays Montrose

Head Office   ✉   141 Moorgate, EC2M 6TX
     ☎   **T** 020 7628 9999   **F** 020 7628 4698

     ✉   3 Parker House, Admirals Way, E14 9UQ
     ⊖   South Quay
     🚃   Limehouse
     ☎   **T** 020 7987 8963   **F** 020 7987 0974
     @   docklands@hays-montrose.com
Market areas   Construction, Property, Architecture

     ✉   15 St Helens Place, EC3A 6DE
     ⊖   Liverpool St
     🚃   Liverpool St
     ☎   **T** 020 7588 6633   **F** 020 7588 6581
     @   city@hays-montrose.co.uk
Market areas   Construction, Property, Architecture

Website www.haysworks.com
UK Offices 40
REC Member No

Brief Description Hays Personnel Services is a division of Hays plc, the business services group listed in the FTSE 100. Hays Personnel Services is Europe's leading specialist professional recruitment group. Hays Montrose is the largest supplier of staff to the Construction, Property and Maintenance sector with over 40 offices in the UK, Ireland, Portugal and Australia. Exclusive recruitment agreements with the Chartered Institute of Building Services Engineers illustrates the reputation of Hays Montrose in this field.

Preferred method of contact Apply on line or telephone for an appointment

Minimum requirements None

Type of business Temporary and Permanent

Grade/Level of Appointments All levels

Hays Montrose Architecture Division

Head Office   ✉   141 Moorgate, EC2M 6TX
     ☎   **T** 020 7628 9999   **F** 020 7628 4698

     ✉   Abford House, 15 Wilton Rd, SW1V 1LT
     ⊖   Victoria
     🚃   Victoria
     ☎   **T** 020 7931 9310   **F** 01226 720718
     @   victoria.ar@hays-montrose.com
Market areas   Construction, Property, Architecture

Website www.haysworks.com
UK Offices 40
REC Member No

Brief Description Hays Personnel Services is a division of Hays plc, the business services group listed in the FTSE 100. Hays Personnel Services is Europe's leading specialist professional recruitment group. Hays Montrose is the largest supplier of staff to the Construction, Property and Maintenance sector with over 40 offices in the UK, Ireland, Portugal and Australia. Exclusive recruitment agreements with the Chartered Institute of Building Services Engineers illustrates the reputation of Hays Montrose in this field.

Preferred method of contact Apply on line or telephone for an appointment

Minimum requirements None

Type of business Temporary and Permanent

Grade/Level of Appointments All levels

Hays Montrose Building Services Division

Head Office   ✉   141 Moorgate, EC2M 6TX
     ☎   **T** 020 7628 9999   **F** 020 7628 4698

     ✉   Abford House, 15 Wilton Rd, SW1V 1LT
     ⊖   Victoria

🚇 Victoria
☎ T 020 7931 8941   F 01226 720721
@ victoria.bs@hays-montrose.com
Market areas Construction, Property, Architecture

Website www.haysworks.com

UK Offices 40

REC Member No

Brief Description Hays Personnel Services is a division of Hays plc, the business services group listed in the FTSE 100. Hays Personnel Services is Europe's leading specialist professional recruitment group. Hays Montrose is the largest supplier of staff to the Construction, Property and Maintenance sector with over 40 offices in the UK, Ireland, Portugal and Australia. Exclusive recruitment agreements with the Chartered Institute of Building Services Engineers illustrates the reputation of Hays Montrose in this field.

Preferred method of contact Apply on line or telephone for an appointment

Minimum requirements None

Type of business Temporary and Permanent

Grade/Level of Appointments All levels

Hays Montrose Civil and Structural Division

Head Office ✉ 141 Moorgate, EC2M 6TX
☎ T 020 7628 9999   F 020 7628 4698
✉ Abford House, 15 Wilton Rd, SW1V 1LT
🚇 Victoria
🚇 Victoria
☎ T 020 7931 7714   F 01226 720719
@ victoria.cs@hays-montrose.com
Market areas Construction, Property, Architecture

Website www.haysworks.com

UK Offices 40

REC Member No

Brief Description Hays Personnel Services is a division of Hays plc, the business services group listed in the FTSE 100. Hays Personnel Services is Europe's leading specialist professional recruitment group. Hays Montrose is the largest supplier of staff to the Construction, Property and Maintenance sector with over 40 offices in the UK, Ireland, Portugal and Australia. Exclusive recruitment agreements with the Chartered Institute of Building Services Engineers illustrates the reputation of Hays Montrose in this field.

Preferred method of contact Apply on line or telephone for an appointment

Minimum requirements None

Type of business Temporary and Permanent

Grade/Level of Appointments All levels

Hays Montrose Communications Division

Head Office ✉ 141 Moorgate, EC2M 6TX
☎ T 020 7628 9999   F 020 7628 4698
✉ Abford House, 15 Wilton Rd, SW1V 1LT
🚇 Victoria
🚇 Victoria
☎ T 020 7931 8823   F 01226 720724
@ victoria.cm@hays-montrose.com
Market areas Construction, Property, Architecture

Website www.haysworks.com

UK Offices 40

REC Member No

Brief Description Hays Personnel Services is a division of Hays plc, the business services group listed in the FTSE 100. Hays Personnel Services is Europe's leading specialist professional recruitment group. Hays Montrose is the largest supplier of staff to the Construction, Property and Maintenance sector with over 40 offices in the UK, Ireland, Portugal and Australia. Exclusive recruitment agreements with the Chartered Institute of Building Services Engineers illustrates the reputation of Hays Montrose in this field.

Preferred method of contact Apply on line or telephone for an appointment

Minimum requirements None

Type of business Temporary and Permanent

Grade/Level of Appointments All levels

Hays Montrose Construction Division

Head Office ✉ 141 Moorgate, EC2M 6TX
☎ T 020 7628 9999   F 020 7628 4698
✉ 1 Wilton Rd, Victoria, SW1V 1AB
🚇 Victoria
🚇 Victoria
☎ T 020 7828 7040   F 01226 720722
@ victoria.cn@hays-montrose.com
Market areas Construction, Property, Architecture

Website www.haysworks.com

UK Offices 40

REC Member No

Brief Description Hays Personnel Services is a division of Hays plc, the business services group listed in the FTSE 100. Hays Personnel Services is Europe's leading specialist professional recruitment group. Hays Montrose is the largest supplier of staff to the Construction, Property and Maintenance sector with over 40 offices in the UK, Ireland, Portugal and Australia. Exclusive recruitment agreements with the Chartered Institute of Building Services Engineers illustrates the reputation of Hays Montrose in this field.

Preferred method of contact Apply on line or telephone for an appointment

Minimum requirements None

Type of business Temporary and Permanent

Grade/Level of Appointments All levels

Hays Montrose Estate Agency Division

Head Office ✉ 141 Moorgate, EC2M 6TX
 ☎ T 020 7628 9999   F 020 7628 4698

 ✉ Abford House, 15 Wilton Rd, SW1V 1LT
 ⊖ Victoria
 🚆 Victoria
 ☎ T 020 7931 8647   F 01226 720724
 @ victoria.ea@hays-montrose.com

Market areas Construction, Property, Architecture

Website www.haysworks.com

UK Offices 40

REC Member No

Brief Description Hays Personnel Services is a division of Hays plc, the business services group listed in the FTSE 100. Hays Personnel Services is Europe's leading specialist professional recruitment group. Hays Montrose is the largest supplier of staff to the Construction, Property and Maintenance sector with over 40 offices in the UK, Ireland, Portugal and Australia. Exclusive recruitment agreements with the Chartered Institute of Building Services Engineers illustrates the reputation of Hays Montrose in this field.

Preferred method of contact Apply on line or telephone for an appointment

Minimum requirements None

Type of business Temporary and Permanent

Grade/Level of Appointments All levels

Hays Montrose Facilities Management Division

Head Office ✉ 141 Moorgate, EC2M 6TX
 ☎ T 020 7628 9999   F 020 7628 4698

 ✉ 1 Wilton Rd, Victoria, SW1V 1AB
 ⊖ Victoria
 🚆 Victoria
 ☎ T 020 7931 9933   F 01226 720705
 @ victoria.fm@hays-montrose.com

Market areas Construction, Property, Architecture

Website www.haysworks.com

UK Offices 40

REC Member No

Brief Description Hays Personnel Services is a division of Hays plc, the business services group listed in the FTSE 100. Hays Personnel Services is Europe's leading specialist professional recruitment group. Hays Montrose is the largest supplier of staff to the Construction, Property and Maintenance sector with over 40 offices in the UK,

Ireland, Portugal and Australia. Exclusive recruitment agreements with the Chartered Institute of Building Services Engineers illustrates the reputation of Hays Montrose in this field.

Preferred method of contact Apply on line or telephone for an appointment

Minimum requirements None

Type of business Temporary and Permanent

Grade/Level of Appointments All levels

Hays Montrose Labour Hire Division

Head Office ✉ 141 Moorgate, EC2M 6TX
 ☎ T 020 7628 9999   F 020 7628 4698

 ✉ 1 Wilton Rd, Victoria, SW1V 1AB
 ⊖ Victoria
 🚆 Victoria
 ☎ T 020 7931 8822   F 01226 720722
 @ victoria.lh@hays-montrose.com

Market areas Construction, Property, Architecture

Website www.haysworks.com

UK Offices 40

REC Member No

Brief Description Hays Personnel Services is a division of Hays plc, the business services group listed in the FTSE 100. Hays Personnel Services is Europe's leading specialist professional recruitment group. Hays Montrose is the largest supplier of staff to the Construction, Property and Maintenance sector with over 40 offices in the UK, Ireland, Portugal and Australia. Exclusive recruitment agreements with the Chartered Institute of Building Services Engineers illustrates the reputation of Hays Montrose in this field.

Preferred method of contact Apply on line or telephone for an appointment

Minimum requirements None

Type of business Temporary and Permanent

Grade/Level of Appointments All levels

Hays Montrose Liftstaff Division

Head Office ✉ 141 Moorgate, EC2M 6TX
 ☎ T 020 7628 9999   F 020 7628 4698

 ✉ Abford House, 15 Wilton Rd, SW1V 1LT
 ⊖ Victoria
 🚆 Victoria
 ☎ T 020 7931 8952   F 01226 720723
 @ victoria.ls@hays-montrose.com

Market areas Construction, Property, Architecture

Website www.haysworks.com

UK Offices 40

REC Member No

Brief Description Hays Personnel Services is a division of Hays plc, the business services group listed in the FTSE 100. Hays Personnel Services is Europe's leading specialist professional recruitment group. Hays Montrose is the largest supplier of staff to the Construction, Property and Maintenance sector with over 40 offices in the UK, Ireland, Portugal and Australia. Exclusive recruitment agreements with the Chartered Institute of Building Services Engineers illustrates the reputation of Hays Montrose in this field.

Preferred method of contact Apply on line or telephone for an appointment

Minimum requirements None

Type of business Temporary and Permanent

Grade/Level of Appointments All levels

Hays Montrose Maintenance Division

Head Office ✉ 141 Moorgate, EC2M 6TX
  ☎ T 020 7628 9999   F 020 7628 4698

✉ 1 Wilton Rd, Victoria, SW1V 1AB
  ⊖ Victoria
  ⊠ Victoria
  ☎ T 020 7931 7755   F 01226 720705
  @ victoria.ma@hays-montrose.com
Market areas   Construction, Property, Architecture

Website   www.haysworks.com
UK Offices 40
REC Member No

Brief Description Hays Personnel Services is a division of Hays plc, the business services group listed in the FTSE 100. Hays Personnel Services is Europe's leading specialist professional recruitment group. Hays Montrose is the largest supplier of staff to the Construction, Property and Maintenance sector with over 40 offices in the UK, Ireland, Portugal and Australia. Exclusive recruitment agreements with the Chartered Institute of Building Services Engineers illustrates the reputation of Hays Montrose in this field.

Preferred method of contact Apply on line or telephone for an appointment

Minimum requirements None

Type of business Temporary and Permanent

Grade/Level of Appointments All levels

Hays Montrose Process and Production Engineering Division

See Technical, page 267

Hays Montrose Property and Surveying Division

Head Office ✉ 141 Moorgate, EC2M 6TX
  ☎ T 020 7628 9999   F 020 7628 4698

✉ Kingsway House, 103 Kingsway, WC2B 6QX
  ⊖ Holborn
  ⊠ City Thameslink
  ☎ T 020 7405 6133   F 01226 720720
  @ holborn@hays-montrose.com
Market areas   Construction, Property, Architecture

Website   www.haysworks.com
UK Offices 40
REC Member No

Brief Description Hays Personnel Services is a division of Hays plc, the business services group listed in the FTSE 100. Hays Personnel Services is Europe's leading specialist professional recruitment group. Hays Montrose is the largest supplier of staff to the Construction, Property and Maintenance sector with over 40 offices in the UK, Ireland, Portugal and Australia. Exclusive recruitment agreements with the Chartered Institute of Building Services Engineers illustrates the reputation of Hays Montrose in this field.

Preferred method of contact Apply on line or telephone for an appointment

Minimum requirements None

Type of business Temporary and Permanent

Grade/Level of Appointments All levels

Hays Montrose Public Sector DLO Division

Head Office ✉ 141 Moorgate, EC2M 6TX
  ☎ T 020 7628 9999   F 020 7628 4698

✉ 1 Wilton Rd, Victoria, SW1V 1AB
  ⊖ Victoria
  ⊠ Victoria
  ☎ T 020 7931 8960   F 01226 720705
  @ victoria.ma@hays-montrose.com
Market areas   Construction, Property, Architecture

Website   www.haysworks.com
UK Offices 40
REC Member No

Brief Description Hays Personnel Services is a division of Hays plc, the business services group listed in the FTSE 100. Hays Personnel Services is Europe's leading specialist professional recruitment group. Hays Montrose is the largest supplier of staff to the Construction, Property and Maintenance sector with over 40 offices in the UK, Ireland, Portugal and Australia. Exclusive recruitment agreements with the Chartered Institute of Building Services Engineers illustrates the reputation of Hays Montrose in this field.

Preferred method of contact Apply on line or telephone for an appointment

Minimum requirements None

Type of business Temporary and Permanent

Grade/Level of Appointments All levels

Hays Montrose Public Sector DSO Division

Head Office ✉ 141 Moorgate, EC2M 6TX
              ☎ T 020 7628 9999   F 020 7628 4698

              ✉ 1 Wilton Rd, Victoria, SW1V 1AB
              ⊖ Victoria
              🚇 Victoria
              ☎ T 020 7931 8733   F 01226 720705
              @ victoria.ma@hays-montrose.com
Market areas Construction, Property, Architecture

Website www.haysworks.com

UK Offices 40

REC Member No

Brief Description Hays Personnel Services is a division of Hays plc, the business services group listed in the FTSE 100. Hays Personnel Services is Europe's leading specialist professional recruitment group. Hays Montrose is the largest supplier of staff to the Construction, Property and Maintenance sector with over 40 offices in the UK, Ireland, Portugal and Australia. Exclusive recruitment agreements with the Chartered Institute of Building Services Engineers illustrates the reputation of Hays Montrose in this field.

Preferred method of contact Apply on line or telephone for an appointment

Minimum requirements None

Type of business Temporary and Permanent

Grade/Level of Appointments All levels

Hays Montrose Rail Division

Head Office ✉ 141 Moorgate, EC2M 6TX
              ☎ T 020 7628 9999   F 020 7628 4698

              ✉ Abford House, 15 Wilton Rd, SW1V 1LT
              ⊖ Victoria
              🚇 Victoria
              ☎ T 020 7931 8953   F 01226 720701
              @ victoria.rs@hays-montrose.com
Market areas Construction, Property, Architecture

Website www.haysworks.com

UK Offices 40

REC Member No

Brief Description Hays Personnel Services is a division of Hays plc, the business services group listed in the FTSE 100. Hays Personnel Services is Europe's leading specialist professional recruitment group. Hays Montrose is the largest supplier of staff to the Construction, Property and Maintenance sector with over 40 offices in the UK, Ireland, Portugal and Australia. Exclusive recruitment agreements with

the Chartered Institute of Building Services Engineers illustrates the reputation of Hays Montrose in this field.

Preferred method of contact Apply on line or telephone for an appointment

Minimum requirements None

Type of business Temporary and Permanent

Grade/Level of Appointments All levels

Hays Montrose Social Housing Division

Head Office ✉ 141 Moorgate, EC2M 6TX
              ☎ T 020 7628 9999   F 020 7628 4698

              ✉ Abford House, 15 Wilton Rd, SW1V 1LT
              ⊖ Victoria
              🚇 Victoria
              ☎ T 020 7931 8989   F 01226 720724
              @ victoria.ta@hays-montrose.com
Market areas Construction, Property, Architecture

Website www.haysworks.com

UK Offices 40

REC Member No

Brief Description Hays Personnel Services is a division of Hays plc, the business services group listed in the FTSE 100. Hays Personnel Services is Europe's leading specialist professional recruitment group. Hays Montrose is the largest supplier of staff to the Construction, Property and Maintenance sector with over 40 offices in the UK, Ireland, Portugal and Australia. Exclusive recruitment agreements with the Chartered Institute of Building Services Engineers illustrates the reputation of Hays Montrose in this field.

Preferred method of contact Apply on line or telephone for an appointment

Minimum requirements None

Type of business Temporary and Permanent

Grade/Level of Appointments All levels

Hays Montrose Technical Admin Division

Head Office ✉ 141 Moorgate, EC2M 6TX
              ☎ T 020 7628 9999   F 020 7628 4698

              ✉ Abford House, 15 Wilton Rd, SW1V 1LT
              ⊖ Victoria
              🚇 Victoria
              ☎ T 020 7931 8989   F 01226 720724
              @ victoria.ta@hays-montrose.com
Market areas Construction, Property, Architecture

Website www.haysworks.com

UK Offices 40

REC Member No

Brief Description Hays Personnel Services is a division of Hays plc, the business services group listed in the FTSE 100. Hays Personnel Services is Europe's leading specialist professional recruitment group. Hays Montrose is the largest supplier of staff to the Construction, Property and Maintenance sector with over 40 offices in the UK, Ireland, Portugal and Australia. Exclusive recruitment agreements with the Chartered Institute of Building Services Engineers illustrates the reputation of Hays Montrose in this field.

Preferred method of contact Apply on line or telephone for an appointment

Minimum requirements None

Type of business Temporary and Permanent

Grade/Level of Appointments All levels

Hill McGlynn & Associates Ltd

    ✉ Strand Bridge House, 138–142 Strand, WC2R 1HH
    ⊖ Temple
    🚇 Charing Cross
    ✆ T 020 7240 4433   F 020 7240 2440
    @ london@hillmcglynn.com
Market areas Construction

Website www.hillmcglynn.com

UK Offices 7

REC Member No

Head Office 2nd Floor, 66–70 Oxford St, Southampton, SO14 3DL

Brief Description Hill McGlynn has over 25 years experience in recruiting Construction professionals. They work for a wide range of leading companies, from family run businesses to major multinationals. Whether you are looking for freelance work or a permanent position Hill McGlynn can help through their network of branches and specialist divisions.

Preferred method of contact Apply on line or telephone for an appointment

Minimum requirements None

Type of business Permanent and Contract

Grade/Level of Appointments Site Management to Board level

Judd Farris

Head Office ✉ 10 Golden Sq, W1F 9JA
    ⊖ Piccadilly Circus
    🚇 Charing Cross
    ✆ T 020 7494 2555   F 020 7494 3033
    @ enquiries@juddfarris.co.uk
Market areas Property and Construction

Website www.juddfarris.co.uk

UK Offices 3

REC Member No

Brief Description From their offices in London, Manchester and Bristol, Judd Farris are able to offer a complete recruitment service throughout the UK and Ireland. In addition they have an extensive worldwide exposure in the Asia Pacific, Australasian and European Markets. Their clients include businesses throughout the Property and Construction industries, from Consultancies to Property companies, Retailers, Leisure Operators, Developers, Funds and Institutional Investors to Contractors, Accountancy firms and Private Investors.

Preferred method of contact Apply on line or telephone for an appointment

Minimum requirements None

Type of business Permanent

Grade/Level of Appointments All levels

LJB & CO

Head Office ✉ The Maples, 144 Liverpool Rd, N1 1LA
    ⊖ Angel
    🚇 Kings Cross
    ✆ T 020 7609 7769   F 020 7607 7378
    @ search@ljbrecruit.com
Market areas Building Services, Construction, Facilities Management, Civil, Structural

Website www.ljbrecruit.com

UK Offices 1

REC Member No

Brief Description LJB & Co is an established independent technical and management recruitment consultancy based in London. During the past 10 years they have assembled and developed a team of experienced and capable consultants who are dedicated to providing a value-added service in their individual areas of expertise within Building Services, Construction, Facilities Management, Civil and Structural, Project Management.

Preferred method of contact Telephone for appointment

Minimum requirements Relevant industry exposure

Type of business Contract and Permanent

Grade/Level of Appointments CAD Operators/Design Engineers to Quantity Surveyors/Contracts Directors

MacDonald & Company

Head Office ✉ 40a Dover St, W1S 4NW
    ⊖ Green Park
    🚇 Victoria
    ✆ T 020 7629 7220   F 020 7629 3990
    @ property@macdonald.co.uk
Market areas Property, Construction, Legal

Website www.macdonald.co.uk

UK Offices 5

REC Member No

Brief Description Established in 1994 and independently owned, MacDonald & Company specialises exclusively in the recruitment of Property, Legal and Construction professionals. Since their formation, they have handled countless assignments for practices, consultancies and businesses. Their services are provided by a team that consists predominately of qualified Property professionals, specialising in fields such as General Practice, Investment, Property Management, Project Management, Building or Quantity Surveying and Facilities Management.

Preferred method of contact Apply on line or telephone for an appointment

Minimum requirements None

Type of business Permanent

Grade/Level of Appointments Graduates/1st Jobbers to Management level

Malla

Head Office ✉ 77 Cornhill, EC3V 3QQ
⊖ Bank
🚂 Cannon St
☎ T 020 7556 1122   F 0870 242 9488
@ recruit@malla.com
Market areas Construction, Building Services, Transport and Utilities

Website www.malla.com

UK Offices 2

REC Member No

Brief Description Malla specialises in providing staff to the Construction, Facilities Management and Utilities sectors, Railway and Trades industries from offices in London and Cardiff.

Preferred method of contact Apply on line or telephone for an appointment

Minimum requirements None

Type of business Temporary, Permanent and Contract

Grade/Level of Appointments All levels

Morson Group

✉ Lillie Bridge Depot, Lillie Rd, SW6 1TP
⊖ Barons Ct
🚂 Kensington (Olympia)
☎ T 020 7918 7765   F 020 7918 7764
@ grahamm@morson.com
Market areas Engineering, Utilities, Aerospace, Construction

✉ 63–81 Pelham St, SW7 2NJ
⊖ South Kensington
🚂 Victoria
☎ T 020 7918 5461   F 020 7918 5042
@ richarde@morson.com
Market areas Engineering, Utilities, Aerospace, Construction

✉ 4th Floor, Tavistock Sq, WC1X 9HX
⊖ Russell Sq
🚂 Euston
☎ T 020 7383 0409   F 020 7383 0411
@ garthp@morson.com
Market areas Engineering, Utilities, Aerospace, Construction

Website www.morson.com

UK Offices 11

REC Member No

Head Office Manchester

Brief Description Formed in 1969, the Morson Group has grown steadily, broadening its range of services aimed at supporting and providing solutions to Manpower Resourcing and Project Management/Engineering Design for a variety of organisations.

Preferred method of contact Apply on line or telephone for an appointment

Minimum requirements None

Type of business Permanent and Contract

Grade/Level of Appointments All levels

Network Design

Head Office ✉ 34 Mortimer St, W1W 7JS
⊖ Oxford Circus
🚂 Charing Cross
☎ T 020 7580 5151   F 020 7580 6350
@ get.work@networkdesign.cc
Market areas Architecture and Interior Design, Graphic Design, Design Management

Website www.networkdesign.cc

UK Offices 1

REC Member No

Brief Description For over a decade, Network Design has been recognised as being at the forefront of the Design industry. During this time, they have successfully provided quality applicants at various levels within the Design industry, specifically in the areas of Architecture and Interior Design, Graphic Design and Design Management, and the ever-emerging New Media sector. They are a highly professional team, all with experience in the industry. This allows them to maintain a greater level of understanding and an accurate perception of their clients' requirements. Their success lies in recognising that a company is likely to be as individual as the applicant who will eventually become part of it.

Preferred method of contact Apply on line or telephone for an appointment

Minimum requirements Previous professional experience

Type of business Permanent

Grade/Level of Appointments All levels

Phoenix Resourcing Services Ltd

Head Office   ✉   Phoenix House, 56 Borough High St, SE1 1XF
    ⊖   London Bridge
    🚇   London Bridge
    ☎ T 020 7089 7777   F 020 7089 7778
    @   info@prsjobs.com
Market areas   Building Services, Engineering, FM Industry

Website www.prsjobs.com
UK Offices 1
REC Member No

Brief Description Phoenix Resourcing Services specialise in the sectors of Building Services and Facilities Management.

Preferred method of contact Apply on line or telephone for an appointment

Minimum requirements None

Type of business Contract and Permanent

Grade/Level of Appointments All levels

RGB Consultants Ltd

Head Office   ✉   6–10 Lexington St, W1F 9AF
    ⊖   Piccadilly Circus
    🚇   Charing Cross
    ☎ T 020 7287 3333   F 020 7287 0007
    @   london@rgbgroup.uk.com
Market areas   Construction, New Media

Website www.rgbconsultants.co.uk
UK Offices 3
REC Member Yes

Brief Description RGB Group is a dynamic recruitment company that provides staff to the Construction and New Media industries. They have ambitious plans for future growth and recognise that this can only be realised though the ongoing delivery of a quality recruitment service that will add value to a client's business.

Preferred method of contact Apply on line or telephone for an appointment

Minimum requirements None

Type of business Permanent

Grade/Level of Appointments All levels

RIBA Appointments Bureau

Head Office   ✉   1–3 Duffin St, EC1Y 8NA
    ✉   66 Portland Place, W1B 1AD
    ⊖   Regent's Park
    🚇   Marylebone
    ☎ T 020 7580 9588   F 020 7636 4108
    @   appointments@inst.riba.org
Market areas   Architecture

Website www.riba-jobs.com
UK Offices 1
REC Member No

Brief Description RIBA Employment for Architects and all Architectural Employment from the Recruitment Consultancy of the Royal Institute of British Architects. They deal with vacancies throughout the fields of Architecture and Interior Design, for all UK-resident members of the profession (not just RIBA Members), including experienced Technicians, Assistants, Architectural Computer Aided Design personnel, Interior Designers, Clerks of Works etc.

Preferred method of contact Apply on line or telephone for an appointment

Minimum requirements Previous professional experience

Type of business Permanent

Grade/Level of Appointments All levels

Robert Giles

See **Technical, page 269**

The Synergy Group

See **Secretarial, page 259**

TeamSales

Head Office   ✉   25 Princess Rd, NW1 8JR
    ⊖   Camden Town
    🚇   Kentish Town
    ☎ T 020 7209 2499
    @   temps@team-sales.co.uk
Market areas   New Homes

Website www.team-sales.co.uk
UK Offices 1
REC Member Yes

Brief Description TeamSales specialise in the placement of both temporary and permanent staff in the New Homes industry. They can provide Sales Negotiators, Part Exchange Co-ordinators, Housing Association Specialists, Market Researchers and Telesales, Field Sales Managers and Directors. Established in 1988, TeamSales is a dynamic organisation both proactive and reactive to customers' needs. First hand knowledge of the New Homes industry from Site to Director level.

Preferred method of contact Apply on line or telephone for an appointment

Minimum requirements None

Type of business Temporary and Permanent

Grade/Level of Appointments Site to Director level

TED Recruitment Ltd

Head Office ✉ 2nd Floor, Neville House, 277–279 Bethnal Green Rd, E2 6AH
⊖ Shoreditch
🚊 Liverpool St
✆ T 020 7613 5555   F 020 7613 1191
@ info@tedrecruitment.com
Market areas Building, Construction, Petrochemical, Oil and Gas

Website www.tedrecruitment.co.uk
UK Offices 1
REC Member No
Brief Description Established in 1981, TED is a technical recruitment consultancy specialising in the supply of professional people to the Building Construction and Petrochemical/Oil & Gas industries, both in the UK and overseas.
Preferred method of contact Apply on line or telephone for an appointment
Minimum requirements None
Type of business Temporary and Permanent
Grade/Level of Appointments All levels

Tempest Search & Selection Ltd

See Executive Search, page 109

Walbrook Architectural Appointments

Head Office ✉ 66 Red Lion St, WC1R 4NA
⊖ Holborn
🚊 City Thameslink
✆ T 020 7405 8787   F 020 7404 5300
@ office@walbrook.net
Market areas Architecture and Interior Design

Website www.walbrook.net
UK Offices 1
REC Member Yes
Brief Description Walbrook Appointments is a specialist Architectural and Interior Design recruitment consultancy. Established

in 1970 and located in the centre of London, near the offices of many major Architectural practices, Walbrook has been playing a pivotal role in the provision of Architectural staff and Interior Designers for over 30 years.
Preferred method of contact Apply on line or telephone for an appointment
Minimum requirements Previous professional experience
Type of business Temporary and Permanent
Grade/Level of Appointments All levels

Workstream Ltd

✉ Docklands Business Centre, Tiller Ct, 16 Tiller Rd, E14 8PX
⊖ Canary Wharf
🚊 Limehouse
✆ T 020 7515 6567
@ london@workstream.co.uk
Market areas Construction

Website www.workstream.co.uk
UK Offices 3
REC Member No
Head Office The Old Stables, Newton Morrell, Nr Bicester, Oxon, OX27 8AG

Brief Description Workstream was founded in 1988 with the aim of providing a totally professional service for clients and candidates within the Construction industry. Because of this focus, Workstream has continued to grow rapidly with more and more clients and candidates benefiting from their services. They now have three branches (London, Central and Bristol) with more expected soon: London – handling East London, the South East and Anglia; Central – Southern England, West London and the Midlands; Bristol – Wales and the South West.
Preferred method of contact Apply on line or telephone for an appointment
Minimum requirements None
Type of business Temporary and Permanent
Grade/Level of Appointments All levels

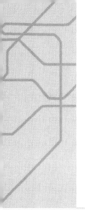

The killer CV

What it is and how to produce it

This chapter is taken from "Killer CVs and Hidden Approaches" by Graham Perkins, published by Prentice Hall, an imprint of Pearson Education, © Pearson Education Ltd 2001

The killer CV and the professional assassin have a lot in common. Just as real life contract killers have none of the glitz, glamour and gadgetry of The Jackal, so the killer CV has no truck with being flashy or gimmicky. There are no short cuts, no magic wands. The qualities that make a killer are:

→   a clear goal;
→   complete single mindedness in pursuing it;
→   total efficiency – no waste of either time or energy;
→   awareness of risks, and a thorough understanding of how to avoid them;
→   outright determination to eliminate the opposition;
→   complete mastery of all the tools of the trade;
→   total professionalism.

When applying these qualities to the preparation of a CV there are two aspects to consider – content and presentation. Good presentation will never make up for weak content, but it is all too easy to ruin strong content by poor presentation. That is why the first two stages in preparing your CV are all about what you are going to include – and what you are going to leave out.

Getting started

The preparation of your CV involves several stages:

→   gathering together the information;
→   selecting those facts which will enable you to achieve your purpose;
→   choosing a layout which is easy to assimilate and conveys a professional impression of you;
→   finding words which get your message across in a vivid and individual manner;
→   reviewing your draft;
→   editing it;
→   checking it.

The reviewing and editing stages must be repeated – over and over if necessary – until you are completely satisfied that your CV is going to do you justice.

The first stage, the assembling of the necessary facts, should involve comparatively little effort.

Stage two, on the other hand, is not nearly as straightforward. It is here that so many people start to go astray and, instead of producing a killer CV, end up by shooting themselves in the foot.

The first, and most common, error is to concentrate on the wrong person. Your CV may be about you but it is – or, rather, should be – written for the recipient. Busy recruiters and decision makers do not want to have to wade through your entire life history. Still less do they want to be told irrelevant details about your family and leisure interests. What they do want to know is how you are going to add value to their organisation.

So, put yourself into the shoes of the kind of person to whom you are going to be sending your CV. Take a sheet of paper and write down at the top of it what that person will want to see in order to be persuaded to take the action you are after – calling you in for a meeting, for example. Then, keeping that sheet of paper in front of you all the time, start selecting the relevant facts.

You should find that your problem lies in being spoilt for choice. Be ruthless. Include only those skills, strengths, achievements and so on that really do make you stand out. This will not only ensure that you produce the best possible CV, but will also be valuable preparation for an ultimate meeting, helping you to concentrate your mind on your key assets and the ways in which they will benefit your prospective employer.

If, by any chance, you find that your problem is too little choice, rather than too much, there are two possible explanations. Either you are targeting the wrong kind of opportunity or you did not do your initial self-appraisal thoroughly enough.

CV suicide

If you are to be ruthless in selecting only those assets which are going to ensure that your CV achieves its objective, then you must be even more ruthless in dealing with other matters which probably do not need to be mentioned at all, and in avoiding some of the more common risks and pitfalls. Here are some examples.

➔ Leisure interests should appear on your CV only if they positively strengthen your application – for example, active involvement in professional and trade associations, or pursuits which demonstrate qualities like fitness and tenacity. Any that are not directly relevant add nothing, except clutter. Oddball interests are a distinct liability – do not risk being labelled a weirdo.

➔ Political and religious affiliations are even more risky. Keep them to yourself, at least until you find out what your prospective employer's views are.

➔ Voluntary/community work falls into the same category as leisure interests, i.e. to be omitted unless directly relevant. While some potential employers may admire your public spiritedness, others may fear that you will always be running off to do good works instead of staying late in the office when you are needed.

→ It is not necessary to provide references at this stage, except in the case of public sector applications.

→ Addresses and telephone numbers of employers are also superfluous.

→ Beware of jargon, and of abbreviations which – though universally recognised in your current environment – may be meaningless to the person reading your CV.

→ If possible, avoid the risk of either over- or under-pricing yourself by omitting details of your remuneration. Should it be specifically asked for, deal with it in your covering letter.

→ Reasons for leaving jobs are a potential minefield. Let them wait for the interview.

→ Career goals and ambitions are another dicey area. Unless you are sure they match both the specific job and the future prospects in the organisation in question, leave them out.

→ Once you have made a statement in your CV, you have invited the reader to ask you to justify it at interview, so do not include anything you cannot prove, if challenged to do so.

→ Explain gaps between jobs, otherwise people may jump to an unfavourable conclusion.

→ In particular, avoid lies. Be sparing with the truth, if you must, by omitting things completely, but do not risk getting caught in the act of trying to deceive – it will be the end of your chances of the job in question. Professional recruiters check, as a matter of routine, whether candidates actually have the qualifications they claim, while all sorts of other matters – such as dates of employment and details of salary and benefits – are verified in the course of taking up references.

How to present yourself

You should present your CV the same way you would present yourself for an interview: smart, positive, professional – conveying an image of efficiency but not going over the top by being flashy or too smooth. The following specific points need to be kept in mind.

→ **Length**

A couple of pages should be enough, three at the outside. If you need to list out technical information (this may apply, for example, to IT people, academics or scientists), do so in an appendix attached to the back of your CV. Do not enclose photocopies of reference letters, detailed job descriptions or certificates relating to professional qualifications.

→ **Spacing**

Do not, however, sacrifice legibility on the altar of brevity. Three well-spaced pages, using bullets, indents, clear margins and so on, will produce a more favourable impression on a tired-eyed recruiter than two cramped ones. This is why a one-page CV, for all its apparent advantages, is not generally to be recommended.

→ **Priority**

Assuming, then, that you are going to have to rely on gaining sufficient interest from your reader to ensure that they do turn the page, remember to put 'first things first'. After providing only the absolutely necessary personal details (name, address, telephone number, e-mail address, professional qualifications, relevant educational details and any foreign languages spoken), go straight into your most relevant experience and achievements.

→ **Typography**

Stick to a single typeface. Mixing them creates a messy effect. Choose a clean, businesslike typeface like Times New Roman and use a size that will not cause eye strain – 12 point is ideal. Achieve variety by the use of capitalisation and emboldening.

Be verbally lean

Presentation is not just about layout. It is also about the words you use – or, rather, not just the words you do use, but also the ones you do not. The first rule is that every single word you employ in your CV must earn its keep, otherwise it has no business being there.

Start at the beginning. What are you going to put at the top? 'Curriculum vitae'? Does anyone really need telling that? So why put it there? Why not just head the sheet with your name?

Economise on space, as well as words. You want your reader to get to the important stuff as quickly as possible. Your address need take up only one line. Do not forget the post code – its omission is likely to be considered either careless or unbusinesslike. Another single line will be enough for your telephone numbers. Since recipients of CVs may want to contact you during working hours, include not just your home number but also an office number or your mobile. These days contact information should also include your e-mail address.

Avoid, by the way, taking economy with words to the extreme of omitting contact information completely on the grounds that it is on your covering letter. The two documents can, and often do, become separated.

'Age'? No, use 'Date of Birth' instead. There is no more certain way of making a CV look tired than by forgetting to update it when you have a birthday.

Marital status and numbers of children are optional. Include them only if they help. Many employers prefer the impression of stability which is given by someone who is married with two-point-four children. On the other hand, if a job involves a lot of travel away from home, it could be an advantage to state that you are single.

Then, after dealing with qualifications, education and languages, you come to your most recent job – or, if you are really convinced it is going to do you more good than harm, your personal profile. Either way, you need to be aware of a couple more words which should be avoided at all costs: 'I' and 'me'. Once you start using them, you have to go on doing so, and there is no easier way of making yourself sound nauseatingly egocentric. Remember who the CV is for? It is supposed to be a reader-centred document, not a you-centred one.

The way to avoid those two pronouns, by the way, is not to put the whole thing in the third person. Recruiters loathe the kind of CV which has apparently been written by someone other than the subject, e.g. 'Smith spent 10 years with XYZ Co.' The correct method is to eliminate not only 'I' and 'me', but also a lot of other unnecessary little words like 'a', 'an' and 'the' by scrapping full grammatical English and using note form.

Creating an impact

Compare the following examples for snappiness and impact:

→   I installed a fully computerised accounting system which resulted in a reduction in the amount of time it took to produce the monthly reporting package from thirteen days to seven days.

→   **Installed fully computerised accounting system, reducing time taken to produce monthly reporting package from 13 days to 7.**

Writing in note form also ensures that you avoid two more pet hates of people who read a lot of CVs – long sentences and heavy wedges of solid text.

The clearest way to set out your career history is to put dates to the left (months are not necessary, just years are sufficient), and indent the text. State your job title and, unless the company is a household name, indicate its size and what it does. Rather than detailing duties, which are often largely self-evident from the job title, list achievements. Give some thought to why the company was better off for your contribution and get this across in a succinct but striking manner.

Unless an earlier job is particularly relevant to your current application, go into more detail on your current or most recent position and progressively less as you work backwards. If you had several short periods of employment right at the beginning of what is now a lengthy career, you can summarise them rather than listing them individually.

Finding fresh words

If eliminating words that do not earn their keep is one half of the job, then making those words you do use earn not only their keep, but also a handsome bonus, is the other half. The English language is an exceptionally rich one, with many alternative terms for any one noun or verb, adjective or adverb. Do not be lazy. Avoid serving up the same tired old words that everyone else is using. Take the trouble to find the words that precisely describe what you want to convey, words which express the individualism that makes you unique, rather than just another faceless candidate, desperate for a job.

Study the suggestions in the word lists which follow, but do not stop there. Make use of the thesaurus on your word-processing package too. Each time you want to describe something, consider all the alternatives. Select the one that sits comfortably on your shoulders, like a well-fitting jacket. Avoid using outlandish terms just to be different – you can achieve a striking impact simply by careful thought and accurate choice.

To take one or two examples of how to make your personal qualities shine through, here are a couple which have impressed recruiters.

→ A recruitment consultant who was trying to fill a vacancy for an auditor to work for a large European financial institution – not exactly the sort of job that has the majority of people jumping up and down with excitement – was struck by a CV which said, 'Particularly enjoyed audits of international organisations in finance sector'. The applicant had not only drawn attention to relevant experience, but had also personalised that statement.

→ Another candidate, working in a business where security was vital, said, 'Regarded by my boss as the safest pair of hands in the whole company'. This applicant had correctly identified the fact that reliability was what the reader of the CV would place at the top of the person specification for the job in question, not executive Rambo qualities like being dynamic and results oriented.

Get the idea? All right, now have a go yourself. The word lists are on the next page (they are all action words, not adjectives), and a sample CV layout follows on the two pages after that.

At first glance the sample CV may not look dramatically different from many others you have seen, and this is quite intentional. Gimmicks and unfamiliar formats do more harm than good. What is different from so many CVs that recruiters receive, and reject, is that this CV makes it so easy for its readers to pick out the kinds of things they want to see – Hilary Brown's international exposure, computer systems experience and so on – as well as making the excellent career progression stand out. Careful selection and the elimination of all irrelevancies, combined with clear layout, means that this CV sells itself – or, rather, its writer. Does yours do the same?

Reviews and wraps

In any professional organisation, a draft report always gets reviewed carefully before dispatch, whether it is being presented to a committee or board, or being sent off to clients. This review process usually involves someone other than the writer taking a look at the draft. A fresh pair of eyes often spots things the writer, who has been too closely immersed in it for too long, may no longer have the objectivity to notice.

Achievement	Initiative	Leadership	Problem solving
accelerated	created	controlled	analysed
accomplished	designed	developed	corrected
achieved	devised	directed	cut
attained	established	drove	eliminated
carried out	extended	guided	ended
completed	formulated	headed	evaluated
conducted	generated	inspired	examined
delivered	improvised	led	identified
demonstrated	initiated	managed	investigated
doubled	instituted	organised	refined
effected	introduced	revitalised	reduced
enhanced	launched	undertook	reorganised
enlarged	originated		repositioned
exceeded	pioneered		reshaped
expanded	redesigned		resolved
expedited	set up		restructured
finished	started		revamped
implemented			reviewed
improved			revised
increased			simplified
negotiated			solved
obtained			streamlined
perfected			strengthened
performed			tackled
produced			traced
secured			trimmed
succeeded			turned round
surpassed			uncovered
tripled			unified
won			utilised

HILARY BROWN, BA, FCA

Address: 23 Laburnum Gardens, Suburbia on Thames, Middlesex
                 MX9 9XM

Telephone: Home: 01999 000999   Office: 01999 989898

                 Mobile: 09090 900990   E-mail: HilaryB@servprov.co.uk

Date of birth: 17/9/64

Career History

1999 to date   **Global Computer Corporation**
                 (Turnover £4billion worldwide, £600million Europe)

2001 to date   **Financial Controller, Europe**

                 Report to VP, Europe, plus functionally to VP, Finance in
                 Chicago.
                 Control 6 staff in London plus further 12 on continent.

                 Achievements

                 • Introduced centralised treasury system covering all
                   seven European subsidiaries, reducing interest paid
                   on overdrafts by 24%.
                 • Reduced average debtor days throughout Europe
                   by 18%.
                 • Implemented completely new computerised
                   accounting systems, cutting time taken to produce
                   monthly reporting package from 11 days to 7.

1999-2001   **Finance Manager, Global France**

                 • Set up accounting systems in newly established
                   French subsidiary, joining as only the fourth person
                   recruited at greenfield site.
                 • As member of small management team, helped
                   develop the company to sales of £35million and
                   second highest profitability in Europe.

1993-1999	**International Fragrances Corporation**
	(Cosmetics distributor, Turnover £900million)

1997-1999   **Management Accountant**

Based at worldwide headquarters in London. Responsible for budget preparation and management reporting: setting timetables, ensuring figures received on time from 23 subsidiaries, checking accuracy, consolidating and producing commentary for parent company board.

1995-1997   **Systems Accountant**

Co-ordination between group MIS department and users on all new accounting systems, from initial specification through to successful implementation.

1993-1995   **Operational Auditor**

Genuine operational auditing, rather than internal checking function. Visited 14 different subsidiaries in Europe, the Far East and Australasia.

1986-1993   **Coopers & Andersen**

Articled to this major international firm of Chartered Accountants. Rose to Audit Manager, achieving all promotions at earliest possible opportunities. Audit clients were mainly international groups, both US and UK owned, in the manufacturing and service sectors.

Qualifications: FCA

Education: Bristol University: BA
(1st class), History

Languages: Fluent French

Other Interests   Member of Institute's Anglo-French liaison group

Run half marathons

65

So, when you have had a first go at reviewing and editing, and have tried to antici-pate – and answer – the questions you think the reader might want answered, ask someone else to have a look at your draft. Find someone qualified to pass a reason-ably expert judgement. While colleagues or friends may be able to help, you could kill two birds with one stone and actually use your CV to do a bit of networking, especially if you are sounding out a new area you wish to move into.

Get more than one view if possible. Each person will have his or her own quirks, and you will never please everyone 100 per cent, but listen for the consensus. Try asking the question, 'If you were ploughing through two or three hundred CVs, would mine stand out?'

And when, finally, you really do have the best effort you can possibly produce – and have run your word-processor's spellcheck over it – take care, if you are using hard copy rather than e-mail, not to let yourself down with your printing and stationery. The aim here should be for a crisp, professional appearance without going over the top. An excessively glossy presentation will turn recruiters off just as quickly as a tatty, amateurish one, probably because it smacks of a factory produced bulk mailshot.

You do not, therefore, have to spend a fortune on a laser printer. A decent bubble jet will produce a perfectly acceptable result.

Having taken the trouble to achieve high-quality printing, avoid – if at all possible – faxing your CV. The print always lacks crispness, and the paper creates a distinctly tacky impression.

The same need for a balanced approach applies to stationery as it does to print qual-ity. Fancy folders are not appreciated, at least not in the UK, but do print out on a decent quality white paper, even when you are running your CV through a photo-copier. White? Yes. Although cream, buff or pale blue are generally acceptable, a main board director of a highly regarded merchant bank was recently seen to cast a CV abruptly aside with the comment, 'Blue paper! No way am I going to employ someone who sends in a CV on blue paper!'

You may not be able to predict all the whims of the people you are targeting, but there is no point in taking avoidable risks. Keep the presentation professional and then let the carefully chosen content do the rest.

International aspects

The first point that needs to be made is that you need to translate your CV into the language in question or, in some cases, languages – plural. In Belgium it is custom-ary to have a CV available in French, Flemish and, if you are dealing with subsidiar-ies of UK or US corporations, English too.

Custom and practice varies enormously from one country to another. In America you never mention age or date of birth (age discrimination is illegal), and you omit details of marital status, children, religion and nationality. You also print your resumé on an American paper size, not on A4. In Germany you give greater promi-

nence to qualifications. In France it used to be the norm to attach a photograph, but is now becoming less so.

What it all adds up to is the fact that you just have to have local knowledge, gained either through previous personal experience of working in the country in question or through obtaining advice and guidance from people who do have that knowledge.

Customer Services

Call Centre Placements

Head Office ✉ 2nd Floor, 42–43 Lower Marsh, SE1 7RG
⊖ Lambeth North
🚃 Waterloo
☎ T 020 7928 5111   F 020 7928 5070
@ recruitment@ccpps.com
Market areas Call Centre, Telesales, Customer Service

Website www.ccpps.com
UK Offices 1
REC Member Yes

Brief Description Call Centre Placements are a specialist recruitment agency for the Telebusiness sector covering temporary, permanent and contract solutions across the board for a range of clients including Telecommunications, Travel, Logistics, Food and Beverages, Automotive and Utilities.

Preferred method of contact Apply on line or telephone for appointment

Minimum requirements None

Type of business Temporary, Permanent and Contract

Grade/Level of Appointments Telemarketing to Business Development/Sales Manager

Hays Call Centre Personnel

Head Office ✉ 141 Moorgate, EC2M 6TX
☎ T 020 7628 9999   F 020 7628 4698

✉ Charter House, 13–15 Carteret St, SW1H 9DJ
⊖ St James's Park
🚃 Victoria
☎ T 020 7222 5200   F 01226 720778
Market areas Call Centre

Website www.haysworks.com
UK Offices 2
REC Member No

Brief Description Hays Personnel Services is a division of Hays plc, the Business Services group listed in the FTSE 100. Hays Personnel Services is Europe's leading specialist professional recruitment group. Hays Personnel Contact Centres provide on-site recruitment solutions for the rapidly expanding Call Centre industry. The business provides clients with fully trained and experienced staff to handle the demanding workloads of any Call Centre.

Preferred method of contact Apply on line or telephone for an appointment

Minimum requirements None

Type of business Temporary and Permanent

Grade/Level of Appointments All levels

Hays Call Centre Personnel – Multilingual

See **Bilingual, page 41**

Select Appointments

See **Secretarial, page 256**

Teleresources

See **Sales and Marketing, page 219**

Domestic

Aunt Jessica Cares

Head Office ✉ Abford House, 15 Wilton Rd, SW1V 1LT
⊖ Victoria
🚃 Victoria
☎ T 020 7630 0044   F 020 7630 8585
@ enquiry@auntjessicacares.co.uk
Market areas Childcare, Housekeeping, Domestic

Website www.auntjessicacares.co.uk
UK Offices 1
REC Member No
Brief Description Aunt Jessica Cares specialises in supplying staff within the Care sector for the modern household, ranging from part-time Housekeeper, Nanny to Housekeeper with a nursing background.
Preferred method of contact Telephone for appointment
Minimum requirements Childcare background
Type of business Permanent
Grade/Level of Appointments All levels

Beauchamp Bureau

Head Office ✉ 186 Sloane St, SW1X 9QR
⊖ Sloane Sq
🚃 Victoria
☎ T 020 7259 6999   F 020 7245 6213
@ enquiries@beauchampbureau.co.uk
Market areas Secretarial, Domestic

Website www.beauchampbureau.co.uk
UK Offices 1
REC Member No
Brief Description Beauchamp Bureau is an independent consultancy, founded over 10 years ago offering the complete and unusual combination of Domestic and Commercial recruitment, ranging from Graduates/Juniors, Secretaries, Chauffeurs, Nannies to Estate Managers, Office Managers and Financial Controllers.
Preferred method of contact Apply on line or telephone for appointment
Minimum requirements None
Type of business Permanent and Temporary
Grade/Level of Appointments All levels

Childminders

Head Office ✉ 6 Nottingham St, W1U 5EJ
⊖ Baker St
🚃 Marylebone
☎ T 020 7935 3000   F 020 7224 0305
@ perrec@aol.com
Market areas Childcare

Website www.babysitter.co.uk
UK Offices 1
REC Member Yes
Brief Description Childminders was formed over 34 years ago to provide responsible, caring, professional Babysitters. Now acknowledged as London's leading Babysitting service, they provide low-cost local Babysitters at short notice for families throughout London, the suburbs and the Thames Valley.
Preferred method of contact Apply on line or telephone for appointment
Minimum requirements None
Type of business Temporary
Grade/Level of Appointments All levels

Greycoat Placements Ltd

Head Office ✉ Grosvenor Gardens House, 35–37 Grosvenor Gardens, SW1W 0BS
⊖ Victoria
🚃 Victoria
☎ T 020 7233 9950   F 020 7592 0096
@ info@greycoatplacements.co.uk
Market areas Domestic

Website www.greycoatplacements.co.uk
UK Offices 1
REC Member Yes
Brief Description Part of the Empressaria Group, Greycoat Placements specialises in matching top quality staff to their clients' specific needs. They offer a wide range of Domestic and Commercial staff, both temporary and permanent: Housekeepers, Cooks and Chefs, Couples, Daily Cleaners, Porters, Caretakers, Chauffeurs, Butlers and Household Managers, Valets, Companions and Carers.
Preferred method of contact Telephone for appointment
Minimum requirements None
Type of business Temporary and Permanent
Grade/Level of Appointments All levels

Kensington Nannies

Head Office ✉ 3 Hornton Place, W8 4LZ
⊖ High St Kensington
🚃 Kensington (Olympia)

C T 020 7937 2333   F 020 7937 1027

@ nannies@easynet.co.uk

Market areas Nannies

Website www.kensington-nannies.co.uk

UK Offices 1

REC Member Yes

Brief Description Kensington Nannies are London's longest established Nanny agency. Run by the same consultants for over 30 years, it is able to offer its clients and Nannies continuity which results in both returning time and time again.

Preferred method of contact Telephone for appointment

Minimum requirements Previous professional experience

Type of business Temporary and Permanent

Grade/Level of Appointments All levels

London Care Plc

Head Office ✉ 291–299 Borough High St, SE1 1JG
- ⊖ London Bridge
- ⊠ London Bridge
- **C** T 020 7939 9300   F 020 7939 9301
- **@** ho@londoncare.co.uk

Market areas Domestic, Care

✉ Suite 3, Dormers Ct, 18–36 Thomas Rd, E1 7BJ
- ⊖ Limehouse
- ⊠ Limehouse
- **C** T 020 7537 7979   F 020 7537 7878
- **@** limehouse@londoncare.co.uk

Market areas Domestic, Care

✉ 6 Archway Business Centre, 19–23 Wedmore St, N19 4RU
- ⊖ Tufnell Park
- ⊠ Kentish Town
- **C** T 020 7272 9290   F 020 7561 1872
- **@** holloway@londoncare.co.uk

Market areas Domestic, Care

✉ 2nd Floor, 2–6 Atlantic Rd, SW9 8HY
- ⊖ Brixton
- ⊠ Brixton
- **C** T 020 7326 7844   F 020 7326 7845
- **@** brixton@londoncare.co.uk

Market areas Domestic, Care

Website www.londoncare.co.uk

UK Offices 9

REC Member Yes

Brief Description Since its creation in 1995, London Care has experienced considerable growth to the extent that the company now numbers nine offices across London, the South-East and the East of England. With over 60 full-time Management staff and over 2,000 Care Support staff, they are already one of the largest Domiciliary Care providers operating in the UK.

Preferred method of contact Apply on line or telephone for an appointment

Minimum requirements None

Type of business Temporary, Permanent and Contract

Grade/Level of Appointments All

The London Nanny Company

Head Office ✉ Collier House, 163–169 Brompton Rd, SW3 1PY
- ⊖ Knightsbridge
- ⊠ Victoria
- **C** T 020 7591 4444   F 020 7581 9199
- **@** all@londonnannycompany.co.uk

Market areas Childcare, Nannies

Website www.londonnannycompany.co.uk

UK Offices 1

REC Member No

Brief Description The London Nanny Company was established in 1996, specialising in trained/experienced British Nannies and Maternity Nurses. Nanny Connection was established in 1987 and has developed an excellent reputation in placing Australian and New Zealand Nannies who are well know for their 'roll up your sleeves and get stuck in' attitude. The two companies merged in February 1998.

Preferred method of contact Apply on line or telephone for an appointment

Minimum requirements Relevant experience

Type of business Temporary and Permanent

Grade/Level of Appointments All levels

Marylebone Nursery Nursing Service

See **Education**, page 73

Occasional & Permanent Nannies

Head Office ✉ 2 Cromwell Place, SW7 2JE
- ⊖ South Kensington
- ⊠ Victoria
- **C** T 020 7225 1555   F 020 7589 4966
- **@** all@nannyworld.co.uk

Market areas Childcare, Nannies, Butlers, Cooks

Website www.nannyworld.co.uk

UK Offices 1

REC Member Yes

Brief Description Occasional & Permanent Nannies provide the traditional Nanny with modern day efficiency. With 45 years experience, they believe they offer the best professional service and personal attention to ensure that Nannies introduced through them will be successful.

Preferred method of contact Apply on line or telephone for an appointment

Minimum requirements Relevant experience

Type of business Temporary and Permanent

Grade/Level of Appointments All levels

Platinum Recruitment International Ltd

See **Hospitality and Leisure, page 143**

SLM Recruitment

Head Office   ✉   10 Lower Belgrave St, SW1W 0LJ
         ⊖   Victoria
         🚆   Victoria
         ☎   T 020 7730 9991   F 020 7730 9777
         @   info@slmrecruitment.co.uk
   Market areas   Nanny and Domestic

Website www.slmrecruitment.co.uk

UK Offices 1

REC Member Yes

Brief Description SLM Recruitment are a well established introductory agency specialising in the placement of all categories of Domestic staff and Nannies within private residences throughout the UK and overseas. They were founded in Belgravia, London in 1995.

Preferred method of contact Apply on line or telephone for an appointment

Minimum requirements None

Type of business Temporary and Permanent

Grade/Level of Appointments All levels

Top Notch Nannies and Brilliant Babysitters

Head Office   ✉   49 Harrington Gardens, SW7 4JU
         ⊖   Gloucester Rd
         🚆   Victoria
         ☎   T 020 7259 2626
         @   theteam@topnotchnannies.com
   Market areas   Childcare, Nannies

Website www.topnotchnannies.com

UK Offices 1

REC Member Yes

Brief Description Top Notch Nannies is one of the top Nanny agencies in the world. They specialise in matching top notch clients with top notch Nannies, Mother's Helps, Maternity Nurses and Babysitters. Their sister company, British Doulas, is Britain's specialist in training and placing Doulas in Britain. They also own Regal Housekeepers which places top Domestic staff in Britain and abroad.

Preferred method of contact Telephone for appointment

Minimum requirements Relevant experience

Type of business Temporary and Permanent

Grade/Level of Appointments All levels

Education

ASA Education

Head Office ⊠ 52–54 Carter Lane, EC4V 5EA
⊖ Blackfriars
🚃 Blackfriars
☎ T 020 7246 4777   F 020 7246 4739
@ educate@asagroup.co.uk
Market areas   Education

Website www.asagroup.co.uk
UK Offices 1
REC Member Yes

Brief Description ASA was founded in 1973 to deal specifically with Legal Secretarial positions, expanding into professional Legal recruitment, contract Locums, Education, Banking, IT and Medical sectors.

Preferred method of contact Telephone for appointment

Minimum requirements Previous industry exposure

Type of business Permanent, Temporary and Contract

Grade/Level of Appointments All levels

Celsian Group – Education

⊠ 5th Floor, New Zealand House, 80 Haymarket, SW1Y 4TE
⊖ Piccadilly Circus
🚃 Charing Cross
☎ T 020 7930 4932   F 020 7930 4934
@ enquiries@celsiangroup.co.uk
Market areas   Education

Website www.celsiangroup.co.uk
UK Offices 24
REC Member Yes

Head Office Albany Place, Hyde Way, Welwyn Garden City, Herts, AL7 3BG

Brief Description Part of Carlisle Group UK, Celsian is the new collective brand name unveiled in 2002 for the following divisions: Recruit Education Services, Recruit Employment Care, Agency Cover and First Call.

Preferred method of contact Apply on line or telephone for appointment

Minimum requirements None

Type of business Permanent, Temporary and Contract

Grade/Level of Appointments All levels

Classroom Ltd

Head Office ⊠ Walmar House, 296 Regent St, W1B 3AW
⊖ Oxford Circus
🚃 Charing Cross
☎ T 020 7636 0600   F 020 7299 7444
@ enquiries@classroomteachers.co.uk
Market areas   Teaching

Website www.classroomteachers.co.uk
UK Offices 1
REC Member Yes

Brief Description Based in the West End, Classroom Ltd specialise in the long and short term supply of experienced Teachers to a variety of schools across London and the Home Counties.

Preferred method of contact Telephone for appointment

Minimum requirements Qualified Teachers

Type of business Temporary and Permanent

Grade/Level of Appointments All levels

Hays Education

Head Office ⊠ 141 Moorgate, EC2M 6TX
☎ T 020 7628 9999   F 020 7628 4698
⊠ 1 Wilton Rd, Victoria, SW1V 1AB
⊖ Victoria
🚃 Victoria
☎ T 020 7931 9040   F 020 7630 7146
@ london@hays-education.co.uk
Market areas   Teaching, Education

Website www.haysworks.com
UK Offices 14
REC Member No

Brief Description Hays Personnel Services is a division of Hays plc, the Business Services group listed in the FTSE 100. Hays Personnel Services is Europe's leading specialist professional recruitment group. Hays Education is a market leader in supply Teaching and Nursery Nurse recruitment with a client base of over 10,000 schools and an expanding national office network.

Preferred method of contact Apply on line or telephone for an appointment

Minimum requirements Previous professional experience

Type of business Temporary, Permanent and Contract

Grade/Level of Appointments All levels

Long Term Teachers

Head Office ✉ 26 Mortimer St, W1W 7RB
- Oxford Circus
- Charing Cross
- ☎ T 020 7436 4949   F 020 7436 4979
- @ info@longtermteachers.com

Market areas Education, Teachers

Website www.longtermteachers.com

UK Offices 2

REC Member Yes

Brief Description Long Term concentrate solely on the placement of Teachers in long term posts in Primary, Secondary and Special Needs Schools and are the only London agency to do so. As former teachers, their founders are committed to education, and to the provision of a positive experience for those working in London's schools. Long term Teachers offer personalised support and advice for Teachers, both before and after they start their positions, an excellent rate of pay, and a service dedicated to finding them the right long term position.

Preferred method of contact Apply on line or telephone for an appointment

Minimum requirements Previous professional experience

Type of business Contract

Grade/Level of Appointments All levels

Marylebone Nursery Nursing Service

Head Office ✉ 110 Princedale Rd, W11 4NH
- Holland Park
- Paddington
- ☎ T 020 7727 2743   F 020 7243 2559
- @ info@maryleboneservices.co.uk

Market areas Nursery Nursing Staff

Website www.maryleboneservices.co.uk

UK Offices 1

REC Member Yes

Brief Description Marylebone Nursery Nursing Service was established in 1974 to provide temporary Nursery Nursing Staff to Day Nurseries, Creches, Family Centres and Nursery Schools throughout Greater London.

Preferred method of contact Apply on line or telephone for an appointment

Minimum requirements Relevant industry exposure

Type of business Temporary and Permanent

Grade/Level of Appointments All levels

Masterlock

See Secretarial, page 248

Protocol Teachers

Head Office ✉ 40–43 Chancery Lane, WC2A 1JA
- Chancery Lane
- City Thameslink
- ☎ T 020 7440 8440   F 020 7404 5133

Market areas Teaching, Education

Website www.protocol-teachers.com

UK Offices 1

REC Member No

Brief Description Protocol Teachers is part of the Protocol Group of companies, which provides three types of service within the education and training sectors: Staffing Solutions to Colleges of Further Education, Training on a nationwide basis, Software and Facilities Management services. They supply both temporary and permanent Teaching staff for Mainstream and Special Needs Schools, from Nursery right up to A-Level standards, as well as Nursery Nurses and Classroom Assistants.

Preferred method of contact Apply on line or telephone for an appointment

Minimum requirements Previous professional experience

Type of business Temporary, Permanent and Contract

Grade/Level of Appointments All levels

Reed Education

Head Office ✉ Reed Executive Plc, 145 Kensington High St, W8 7LP
- ☎ T 020 7313 7450   F 020 7313 7451

✉ 376 Holloway Rd, N7 6PN
- Holloway Rd
- Finsbury Park
- ☎ T 020 7697 1609

Market areas Education

Website www.reed.co.uk

UK Offices 250+

REC Member No

Brief Description A subsidiary of Reed Executive Plc established in 1960, Reed's growth has been dramatic and the company's stated ambition is to grow the business substantially. Reed has been organised into a number of separate operating companies to make this happen. Reed Education is the specialist division dealing with the Education marketplace.

Preferred method of contact Apply on line or telephone for an appointment

Minimum requirements Previous professional experience

Type of business Contract and Permanent

Grade/Level of Appointments All levels

ROC Recruitment

See **Hospitality and Leisure, page 144**

Select Education

✉ Salisbury House, London Wall, EC2M 5QQ
⊖ Moorgate
🚊 Moorgate
☎ **T** 020 7588 4216   **F** 020 7588 4243
@ finsburycircus-ed@select.co.uk
Market areas Education

Website www.selecteducation.co.uk

UK Offices 35

REC Member Yes

Head Office Luton

Brief Description Select Education plc is a specialist division of Vedior, the world's third-largest staffing services group. Select Education plc is established as a leading UK and global Educational staffing specialist. They regularly provide Teaching staff for more than 13,000 days each week to Nursery, Primary, Secondary and Special Schools throughout England, Wales and Northern Ireland. With a unique network of 35 offices across the UK, Select Education provides a quality, individual service to the 10,000+ Teachers and Support staff registered with them, and to their 15,000 customer schools.

Preferred method of contact Apply on line or telephone for an appointment

Minimum requirements None

Type of business Temporary and Permanent

Grade/Level of Appointments All levels

Stafflink

Head Office ✉ 138 Lower Rd, SE16 2UG
⊖ Rotherhithe
🚊 Bermondsey
☎ **T** 020 7252 2212   **F** 020 7252 2901
@ info@staff-link.co.uk
Market areas Education, Housing, Care, Catering

Website www.staff-link.co.uk

UK Offices 1

REC Member No

Brief Description Established in 2000, Stafflink is one of the UK's prominent recruitment advertising networks, selection agencies, and a leading search firm in Europe. Each of their specialist divisions is headed by a consultant with relevant experience in their industry.

Preferred method of contact Telephone for appointment

Minimum requirements None

Type of business Temporary and Permanent

Grade/Level of Appointments All levels

Verity Education Ltd

Head Office ✉ 10 South Molton St, W1K 5QJ
☎ **T** 020 7493 0437   **F** 020 7493 0647
✉ 47 South Molton St, W1K 5RY
⊖ Bond St
🚊 Paddington
☎ **T** 020 7629 8786   **F** 020 7629 8828
@ info@verityeducation.com
Market areas Education

Website www.verityeducation.com

UK Offices 2

REC Member Yes

Brief Description Verity Education was established in 1995 and has become a major name in the field of Education recruitment. They are approved by the DfES and a member of the REC. They offer a free service to Teachers who have qualified in the UK or overseas and also place Nursery Nurses and Classroom Assistants with schools. They have built their reputation on providing a thoroughly professional and personal service to both Teachers and client schools. Their measure of success is the large number of Teachers who come to them through recommendations.

Preferred method of contact Apply on line or telephone for an appointment

Minimum requirements Previous professional experience

Type of business Temporary and Permanent

Grade/Level of Appointments All levels

Executive Search

ACCESS Technology

- ✉ 75 Cannon St, EC4N 5BN
- ⊖ Cannon St
- ⊠ Cannon St
- ℂ T 020 7556 7033   F 020 7556 7001
- @ info.uk@accesstech.com
- **Market areas** Executive Search

Website www.accesstech.com
UK Offices 1
REC Member No
Head Office Tokyo

Brief Description Established in 1992, Access Technology's dedicated consultancy team works face to face with both IT professionals and clients to provide them with an Executive Search service. Clients range from start ups to Fortune 500 companies. Access Technology is Japan's leading licensed High-Tech Executive Search firm with locations in Chicago, Sydney, San Francisco, Tokyo, London and Wellington.

Preferred method of contact Interviews are by appointment only – please make initial contact by telephone or email

Minimum requirements None

Type of business Permanent

Grade/Level of Appointments All levels up to Senior Management

Adderley Featherstone Plc

- ✉ 56 Queen Anne St, W1M 9LA
- ⊖ Oxford Circus
- ⊠ Charing Cross
- ℂ T 020 7317 3116   F 020 7317 3115
- @ snicholson@adderley-featherstone.plc.uk
- **Market areas** Executive Search

Website www.adderley-featherstone.plc.uk
UK Offices 7
REC Member No
Head Office Bowcliffe Ct, Bowcliffe Hall, Braham, Leeds LS23 6LW

Brief Description Established in 1991, Adderley Featherstone is an independent Consulting firm with traditional values, integrity, a modern outlook and an outstanding record of success in filling Board and Senior Management positions. Core activity is in the £50k–£150k pa range, specialising in Interim and Permanent opportunities.

Preferred method of contact Interviews are by appointment only - please make initial contact by telephone or email

Minimum requirements Industry and Commerce experience at Management/Board level

Type of business Permanent, Interim
Grade/Level of Appointments Board and Senior Management

Albemarle Interim Management Plc

- **Head Office** ✉ 26–28 Great Portland St, W1W 8QT
- ⊖ Oxford Circus
- ⊠ Charing Cross
- ℂ T 020 7079 3737   F 020 7631 1881
- @ managers@albemarle.co.uk
- **Market areas** Interim Management

Website www.albemarle.co.uk
UK Offices 1
REC Member No

Brief Description Albemarle is one of the world's leading providers of Interim Management services and a part of the Select Group, one of the world's top three international staffing organisations. With over 16 years experience in an industry they helped to create, it is no surprise that their portfolio contains some of the UK's brightest companies and a host of International clients. Interim Managers come from a wide range of industry sectors. Many have a business degree in addition to their technical qualifications and typically have held senior management positions, usually at Board or Head of Function level.

Preferred method of contact Interviews are by appointment only – please make initial contact by telephone or email

Minimum requirements Demonstrable history of achievements, effective communication and inter-personal skills; applicants must also pass a stringent interview process and have qualifications verified with first class, detailed references

Type of business Contract
Grade/Level of Appointments Senior Management

Alderwick Consulting Ltd

- **Head Office** ✉ 95 Fetter Lane, EC4A 1EP
- ⊖ Chancery Lane
- ⊠ City Thameslink
- ℂ T 020 7400 2100   F 020 7242 3560
- @ acl@alderwick.com
- **Market areas** Executive Search

Website www.alderwick-consulting.co.uk
UK Offices 1
REC Member No

Brief Description Alderwick Consulting provides tailored solutions to Human Resources issues, focusing on sourcing Business and Finance professionals for Commercial, Industrial and Financial Services companies. Principal areas of expertise are Search and Selection, Recruitment Advertising, Psychometric Testing, Job Analysis and Skills Testing.

Preferred method of contact Telephone for appointment

Minimum requirements Professional Accountancy qualification

Type of business Permanent

Grade/Level of Appointments Junior Management and above

Alexander Hughes Ltd

Head Office ✉ 14–16 Lower Regent St, SW1Y 4PH
⊖ Piccadilly Circus
🚊 Charing Cross
☎ **T** 020 7331 1800 **F** 020 7331 1888
@ company@alexander-hughes.co.uk
Market areas Executive Search

Website www.alexander-hughes.co.uk

UK Offices 1

REC Member No

Brief Description Alexander Hughes is one of the original British Executive Search firms with a successful track record of over 30 years. Part of Alexander Hughes International with a Paris HQ, the group along with Alexander Hughes Selection and Interim Management specialises at the highest levels of management across all areas of business.

Preferred method of contact Telephone for appointment

Minimum requirements None

Type of business Permanent

Grade/Level of Appointments Senior Management and Board level

Alistair Ames

Head Office ✉ 211 Piccadilly, W1J 9HF
⊖ Piccadilly Circus
🚊 Charing Cross
☎ **T** 020 7917 1855 **F** 020 7917 1856
@ mail@alistairaimes.co.uk
Market areas Executive Search

Website www.alastairames.co.uk

UK Offices 1

REC Member No

Brief Description Established in 1986.

Preferred method of contact Telephone for appointment

Minimum requirements None

Type of business Permanent

Grade/Level of Appointments All levels

Allemby Hunt

Head Office ✉ 28 Austin Friars, EC2N 2QQ
⊖ Bank
🚊 Cannon St
☎ **T** 020 7638 0900 **F** 020 7638 2300
@ info@allembyhunt.co.uk
Market areas Executive Search

Website www.allembyhunt.co.uk

UK Offices 1

REC Member No

Brief Description Allemby Hunt is a specialist Financial Services Search and Selection consultancy, providing a highly professional, targeted service to clients by utilising their considerable market knowledge and contacts to produce reliable, efficient and cost effective recruitment solutions.

Preferred method of contact Telephone for appointment

Minimum requirements Financial Services exposure

Type of business Permanent

Grade/Level of Appointments Middle to Senior Management

Anderson Recruitment Ltd

See **IT and Telecoms, page 153**

Anthony Taylor

Head Office ✉ Suite 8, 10 College Terrace, E3 5AN
⊖ Mile End
🚊 Stratford
☎ **T** 020 7729 6638 **F** 0709 233 2058
@ london@anthonytaylor.com
Market areas Executive Search

Website www.anthonytaylor.dial.pipex.com

UK Offices 1

REC Member No

Brief Description Anthony Taylor Search and Selection specialises in Senior Executive recruitment ranging from Qualified Accountants/Solicitors to Board level appointments across a broad range of Industry and Commerce.

Preferred method of contact Telephone for appointment

Minimum requirements None

Type of business Permanent
Grade/Level of Appointments Junior Management to Board level/ Non Executive appointments

Armstrong International Ltd

Head Office ✉ 1 Angel Ct, EC2R 7HJ
⊖ Bank
🚇 Cannon St
☎ T 020 7606 0002   F 020 7606 2800
Market areas Executive Search

Website www.armstrongint.com
UK Offices 1
REC Member No

Brief Description Armstrong International is Europe's leading Financial Services Executive Search firm. They are a high-growth company and intent on expanding aggressively over the next 4 years to become the number one global Senior-level Financial Services Executive Search firm. They understand the objectives and needs of today's decision makers and provide a fast, professional, tailored and long-term solution to their recruitment requirements.

Preferred method of contact Apply on line or telephone for an appointment
Minimum requirements Senior Financial Services exposure
Type of business Permanent
Grade/Level of Appointments All levels

Ashton Penney Partnership Ltd

Head Office ✉ Marcol House, 289–293 Regent St, W1R 7PD
⊖ Piccadilly Circus
🚇 Charing Cross
☎ T 020 7659 0600   F 020 7659 0601
@ info@ashtonpenney.com
Market areas Executive Search

Website www.ashtonpenney.com
UK Offices 6
REC Member No

Brief Description Ashton Penney provides high quality Interim Managers or Turnaround Management professionals with proven Interim Management experience, for a wide range of temporary assignments ranging from Project Management to Chief Executives and Managing Directors.

Preferred method of contact Apply on line or telephone for appointment
Minimum requirements None
Type of business Contract
Grade/Level of Appointments Middle to Senior Management

Astbury Marsden & Partners Ltd

Head Office ✉ Augustine House, 64 Austin Friars, EC2N 2HA
⊖ Bank
🚇 Cannon St
☎ T 020 7930 1222   F 020 7930 1234
@ mail@astburymarsden.com
Market areas Executive Search

Website www.astburymarsden.com
UK Offices 1
REC Member No

Brief Description Established in 1995, Astbury Marsden is one of Europe's fastest growing and leading recruitment firms specialising in the provision of Middle/Senior Management and Board level solutions. The company source experienced Finance, IT, Strategy and Investment Banking executives.

Preferred method of contact Telephone for appointment
Minimum requirements Graduate level with professional qualification
Type of business Permanent
Grade/Level of Appointments Middle to Senior Management

Austin Benn Ltd

Head Office ✉ 3rd Floor, 3 Lombard St, EC3V 9AA
⊖ Bank
🚇 Cannon St
☎ T 020 7623 7330   F 020 7623 7261
@ london@austinbenn.co.uk
Market areas Executive Search

Website www.austinbenn.co.uk
UK Offices 7
REC Member No

Brief Description Founded over 20 years ago, Austin Benn is one of the UK's leading executive recruitment firms finding Support, Management and HR professionals for such diverse sectors as Financial Services, IT, Telecoms, Consumer Goods and Manufacturing.

Preferred method of contact Apply on line or telephone for appointment
Minimum requirements None
Type of business Permanent
Grade/Level of Appointments Graduate to Finance/Marketing/ Managing Director

Barkers Norman Broadbent

Head Office ✉ Dorland House, 20 Regent St, SW1Y 4PH
☎ T 020 7484 0000   F 020 7484 0001

✉ 30 Farrindon St, EC4 4EA
⊖ Farringdon

🚊 Farringdon
C T 020 7634 1200   F 020 7489 9330
@ webmaster@bnb-global.com
Market areas Executive Search

Website www.bnb-global.com
UK Offices 15
REC Member No
Brief Description BNB Resources Plc is a leading Human Resources Solutions provider offering a complete service in Executive Search, Management Selection, On-line Recruitment Advertising, Outsourcing, Interim Management, Training, Public Relations and Marketing in the UK and internationally.
Preferred method of contact Telephone for appointment
Minimum requirements None
Type of business Permanent
Grade/Level of Appointments All levels

Barry Latchford Associates

Head Office ✉ 6 New Bridge St, EC4V 6AB
🚇 Blackfriars
🚊 Blackfriars
C T 020 7583 3923   F 020 7842 0851
@ mail@barrylatchford.com
Market areas Executive Search

Website www.barrylatchford.com
UK Offices 1
REC Member No
Brief Description Established in 1980, Barry Latchford Associates work with companies who require the best talent within the IT and Management Consultancy sectors, supplying senior staff and teams to the Big 5 consultancies, e-Business, corporate and blue chip companies.
Preferred method of contact Telephone for appointment
Minimum requirements Background in IT and Management Consultancy
Type of business Permanent
Grade/Level of Appointments Senior Management to Board level

Bartlett Scott Edgar

Head Office ✉ 65–67 Wilson St, EC2A 2LT
🚇 Liverpool St
🚊 Liverpool St
C T 020 7562 5700   F 020 7562 5702
@ b.cernuschi@barlett.co.uk
Market areas Executive Search

Website www.bartlett.co.uk
UK Offices 2

REC Member No
Brief Description Formed in June 2000 through the merger of two long established and successful agencies, Barlett Merton and Scott Edgar, delivers innovative and cost effective recruitment solutions.
Preferred method of contact Telephone for appointment
Minimum requirements Previous professional experience
Type of business Permanent
Grade/Level of Appointments All levels

Beeley & Co

Head Office ✉ 33 Cornhill, EC3V 3ND
🚇 Bank
🚊 Cannon St
C T 020 7398 1800   F 020 7929 0202
@ enquiries@beeley.co.uk
Market areas Executive Search

Website www.beeley.co.uk
UK Offices 1
REC Member No
Brief Description Established in 1995 to provide retainer based search services focused exclusively on the Asset Management industry.
Preferred method of contact Telephone for appointment
Minimum requirements Asset Management experience
Type of business Permanent
Grade/Level of Appointments Senior level

BIE Interim Executive

Head Office ✉ 22 Queen Annes Gate, SW1H 9AA
🚇 St James's Park
🚊 Victoria
C T 020 7222 1010   F 020 7222 2215
@ info@bieinterim.com
Market areas Executive Search

Website www.bieinterim.com
UK Offices 1
REC Member Yes
Brief Description BIE is the UK's leading specialist provider of senior level Interim Executives. It comprises a team of consultants with over 28 years experience in this field. Established in 1996, BIE has been awarded preferred supplier status to 3i plc, has been the recommended supplier of the IOD and has now produced – in association with the CBI – the CBI/BIE Guide to Interim Executive Management.
Preferred method of contact Apply on line or telephone for an appointment
Minimum requirements Senior level Management exposure

Type of business Contract

Grade/Level of Appointments Senior level

Blackwood Group Ltd

Head Office ✉ 77 Cornhill, EC3V 3QQ
       ⊖ Bank
       🚇 Cannon St
       ☎ T 020 7220 0270   F 020 7220 0271
       @ enquiries@blackwoodgroup.com
Market areas Executive Search

Website www.blackwoodgroup.com

UK Offices 1

REC Member No

Brief Description Established in 1999, Blackwood Group are a specialist recruitment consultancy focusing on Investment Banking, Private Equity, Private Banking and the Technology sectors.

Preferred method of contact Telephone for appointment

Minimum requirements Previous professional experience

Type of business Permanent

Grade/Level of Appointments All levels

The Bloomsbury Group

Head Office ✉ 1 Southampton St, WC2R 0LR
       ⊖ Charing Cross
       🚇 Charing Cross
       ☎ T 020 7379 1100   F 020 7240 6362
       @ info@thebloomsburygroup.com
Market areas Executive Search

Website www.thebloomsburygroup.com

UK Offices 1

REC Member Yes

Brief Description The Bloomsbury Group was established as a Partnership in 1989 to provide an Executive Search service to the Financial sector. The firm's clients include Investment Banks, Fund Managers, Private Equity Houses, Consulting Firms and Professional Practices. The Bloomsbury Group is London based but conducts international assignments in all the major financial centres, as well as more remote locations such as Moscow, Istanbul and Vietnam.

Preferred method of contact Apply on line or telephone for an appointment

Minimum requirements Relevant industry exposure

Type of business Permanent

Grade/Level of Appointments Mid to Senior Management level

Blue 10 Ltd

Head Office ✉ 13–14 Golden Sq, W1F 9JF
       ⊖ Piccadilly Circus
       🚇 Charing Cross
       ☎ T 020 7494 3292   F 020 7434 9833
       @ info@blue10.net
Market areas Executive Search

Website www.blue10.net

UK Offices 1

REC Member No

Brief Description Blue 10 specialises in the sourcing, selection and placement of New Media, Marketing and Sales personnel.

Preferred method of contact Telephone for appointment

Minimum requirements Previous professional experience

Type of business Permanent

Grade/Level of Appointments All levels

Bluestone Ltd

Head Office ✉ Cornhill House, 59–60 Cornhill, EC3V 3PD
       ⊖ Bank
       🚇 Cannon St
       ☎ T 020 7929 5885   F 020 7929 5638
       @ bsl@bluestone.ltd.uk
Market areas Executive Search

Website www.bluestone.ltd.uk

UK Offices 1

REC Member No

Brief Description Bluestone is a Search and Selection recruitment company focused exclusively on the Financial Services and associated professional providers marketplace.

Preferred method of contact Telephone for appointment

Minimum requirements Previous professional experience

Type of business Permanent

Grade/Level of Appointments All levels

Bower & Company

Head Office ✉ 23–29 Walbrook, EC4N 8LD
       ⊖ Cannon St
       🚇 Cannon St
       ☎ T 020 7929 5040   F 020 7929 5030
       @ info@bowerco.com
Market areas Executive Search

Website www.bowerco.com

UK Offices 1

REC Member No

Brief Description Bower & Company is synonymous with top of the range, assignment based recruitment solutions particularly in the TMT sectors. Principal areas of expertise include both the use of IT and the business issues within Banking and Financial Services, the Mobile and Fixed Wire Telecommunications industries, and the emerging e-Business and Knowledge Management technologies.

Preferred method of contact Apply on line or telephone for appointment

Minimum requirements Previous professional experience

Type of business Permanent

Grade/Level of Appointments Mid to Senior level

Boyden International

✉ 52 Cornhill, EC3 3PD
🚇 Bank
🚉 Cannon St
☎ T 020 7980 3000   F 020 7980 3030
@ financial@boyden-int.co.uk
Market areas Executive Search

✉ 24 Queen Ann's Gate, SW1H 9AA
🚇 St James's Park
🚉 Victoria
☎ T 020 7222 9033   F 020 7222 8838
@ london@boyden.com
Market areas Executive Search

Website www.boyden-int.co.uk

UK Offices 2

REC Member No

Head Office 364 Elwood Avenue, Hawthorne, NY 10532

Brief Description Part of Boyden Global, Boyden London has been established in London since 1996 with its core business being Executive Search, and also Advertised Recruitment, Interim Executive Management. It operates Director appointments on behalf of the Institute of Directors across five sectors: Financial Services, Healthcare/Pharmaceuticals, Consumer Products, Information and Communication Technology and e-Business.

Preferred method of contact Telephone for appointment

Minimum requirements Previous professional experience

Type of business Contract and Permanent

Grade/Level of Appointments Senior to Board level

BPA Search and Selection Ltd

Head Office ✉ County Mark House, 50 Regent St, W1B 5RD
🚇 Piccadilly Circus
🚉 Charing Cross
☎ T 020 7432 4533   F 020 7432 4534
@ barrie@bpasearch.co.uk
Market areas Executive Search

Website www.bpasearch.co.uk

UK Offices 1

REC Member No

Brief Description Established in 1993, BPA is a retained search consultancy focusing solely on Tax professionals for major Accountancy firms, large multinationals and Banking institutions seeking qualified Tax professionals at Partner level.

Preferred method of contact Telephone for appointment

Minimum requirements Tax professional

Type of business Permanent

Grade/Level of Appointments Partner/Partner Designate to Director level

Bucher/Rugman & Partners

Head Office ✉ Audley House, 13 Palace St, SW1E 5HX
🚇 Victoria
🚉 Victoria
☎ T 020 7630 9090   F 020 7630 9808
@ mail@bucher-rugman.co.uk
Market areas Executive Search

Website www.bucher-rugman.co.uk

UK Offices 1

REC Member No

Brief Description Founded in 1994, Bucher/Rugman & Partners are part of Allied Partnership International.

Preferred method of contact Telephone for appointment

Minimum requirements Previous professional experience

Type of business Permanent

Grade/Level of Appointments All levels

Bull Thompson International

Head Office ✉ 8 Upper St Martins Lane, WC2H 9DF
🚇 Leicester Sq
🚉 Charing Cross
☎ T 020 7240 3561   F 020 7836 9812
@ london@bullthompson.com
Market areas Executive Search

Website www.bullthompson.com

UK Offices 2

REC Member No

Brief Description Founded in 1968, Bull Thompson International is a consultancy specialising in the recruitment of Board Directors, Senior Management and Executives from offices in London and the Thames Valley and associate offices in the USA, Europe and Far East operating across various sectors including Healthcare, Travel, Communications, FMCG, IT, Financial Services, Utilities and Retail.

Preferred method of contact Telephone for appointment

Minimum requirements Previous managerial exposure
Type of business Permanent and Contract
Grade/Level of Appointments Senior Manager to Board level

Minimum requirements None
Type of business Permanent, Contract
Grade/Level of Appointments Graduate/Junior to Board level

Calibre One

Head Office ✉ 38 Welbeck St, W1G 8DD
 ⊖ Bond St
 🚇 Paddington
 ☎ T 020 7070 3000 F 020 7070 3001
 @ info@calibreone.com
Market areas Executive Search

Website www.calibreone.com
UK Offices 1
REC Member Yes

Brief Description Calibre One is a leading international Executive Search organisation that provides tailored solutions for the talent resourcing issues that face the businesses of today. With offices in London and San Francisco, the company comprises two separate, but closely related practice areas, which focus on Permanent and Interim Management appointments. Their Interim Management practice provides Senior Management support to businesses in all sectors. Their Executive Search practice specialises in building senior management teams for High Technology and Media businesses and the businesses that invest in them both. Both practices employ recruitment consultants of unparalleled quality supported by advanced technology, processes and systems.

Preferred method of contact Apply on line or telephone for appointment
Minimum requirements Previous managerial exposure
Type of business Permanent and Contract
Grade/Level of Appointments Senior Management to Board level

Camron James

Head Office ✉ Fleetway House, 25 Farringdon St, EC4A 4SR
 ⊖ St Pauls
 🚇 City Thameslink
 ☎ T 020 7415 2860 F 020 7332 2496
 @ iainmcadam@camronjames.com
Market areas Executive Search

Website www.camron-james.co.uk
UK Offices 2
REC Member No

Brief Description Part of the SR Group, Camron James is a niche Executive Search and Selection firm focusing exclusively on the Consultancy market within Management Consultancy firms, Industry and Banking across the UK and internationally from offices in London, Leeds, Hong Kong and Sydney.

Preferred method of contact Telephone for appointment

Capital Markets Consulting Ltd

Head Office ✉ 1 Berkeley St, Mayfair, W1J 8DJ
 ⊖ Green Park
 🚇 Victoria
 ☎ T 020 7016 9798 F 020 7016 9100
 @ questions@cmcx.com
Market areas Executive Search

Website www.cmcx.com
UK Offices 1
REC Member No

Brief Description Capital Markets Consulting Ltd (CMC) is an Executive Search and Consulting company specialising in Recruitment and Management Consultancy assignments within Global Capital and Financial Markets with expertise in the sectors of Fixed Income Derivatives and Research, with opportunities for Juniors and seasoned professionals.

Preferred method of contact Apply on line or telephone for appointment
Minimum requirements Graduate level and above
Type of business Permanent
Grade/Level of Appointments Graduates to Senior Management

Carter James Ltd

Head Office ✉ 1st Floor, Berkeley Sq House, Berkeley Sq, W1J 6BS
 ⊖ Green Park
 🚇 Victoria
 ☎ T 020 7629 2666 F 020 7491 8053
 @ response@carterjames.co.uk
Market areas Executive Search

Website www.carterjames.co.uk
UK Offices 1
REC Member No

Brief Description Carter James are a search and adsearch recruitment consultancy specialising in senior level management within four key areas: Human Resources, Finance and Accountancy, Private Equity/Private Banking, Credit/Risk for leading international organisations.

Preferred method of contact Telephone for appointment
Minimum requirements Senior Management experience
Type of business Permanent and Contract
Grade/Level of Appointments Senior level

Carter Murray

Head Office   ✉   Fleetway House, 25 Farringdon St, EC4A 4SR
       ⊖   St Pauls
       🚆   City Thameslink
       ☏   T 020 7415 2840   F 020 7332 9053
       @   davidkeddie@cartermurray.co.uk
Market areas   Executive Search

Website www.thesrgroup.com

UK Offices 2

REC Member No

Brief Description Part of the SR Group, Carter Murray is a niche Search and Selection firm focusing on the recruitment of Senior Support Management into the Professional Services sector. They specialise in the areas of Finance, Strategy/Change Management, Marketing/Business Development and General Management and IT. Assignments handled typically include recruiting Financial Controllers/ Directors, Marketing Managers/Directors, Business/Strategy Managers, IT Managers/Directors and Practice Directors/Chief Executives. Indicative of their professionalism and success in handling these assignments is the amount of new business they receive from recommendations by leading external advisers to the Professional Services market.

Preferred method of contact Telephone for appointment

Minimum requirements Previous professional experience

Type of business Permanent

Grade/Level of Appointments Senior level

Cavendish Knight

Head Office   ✉   8 Hanover St, W1S 1YE
       ⊖   Oxford Circus
       🚆   Charing Cross
       ☏   T 020 7290 2694   F 020 7290 2643
       @   info@cavendishknight.co.uk
Market areas   Executive Search

Website www.cavendishknight.co.uk

UK Offices 1

REC Member No

Brief Description Cavendish Knight is an Executive Search and Selection consultancy specialising in FMCG Sales and Marketing vacancies.

Preferred method of contact Apply on line or telephone for appointment

Minimum requirements Previous professional experience

Type of business Permanent

Grade/Level of Appointments All levels

CF Appointments Ltd

Head Office   ✉   Lloyds Ct, 1 Goodman's Yard, E1 8AT
       ⊖   Tower Hill
       🚆   Fenchurch St
       ☏   T 020 7953 1190   F 020 7952 1191
       @   enquiries@cfappointments.com
Market areas   Executive Search

Website www.cfappointments.com

UK Offices 1

REC Member Yes

Brief Description Established in 1984 as a charity, more recently CF Appointments redefined itself as an Executive Search and Selection business specialising in Senior Executive and Trustee appointments in the Charity and Not for Profit sectors.

Preferred method of contact Telephone for appointment

Minimum requirements Previous professional experience

Type of business Permanent

Grade/Level of Appointments Finance Director to Chief Executive

Chamberlains Personnel Services Ltd

Head Office   ✉   211 Piccadilly, W1J 9LD
       ⊖   Piccadilly Circus
       🚆   Charing Cross
       ☏   T 0870 607 1340   F 0870 607 1341
       @   contact@chamberlains-international.co.uk
Market areas   Executive Search

Website www.chamberlains-international.com

UK Offices 1

REC Member No

Brief Description Established in 1981, Chamberlains Personnel Services enjoys international exposure and specialises in HR, Training, Financial Services and Legal placements.

Preferred method of contact Telephone for appointment

Minimum requirements Previous professional experience

Type of business Permanent

Grade/Level of Appointments All levels

Chapple Ltd

Head Office   ✉   60 Lombard St, EC3V 9EA
       ⊖   Bank
       🚆   Cannon St
       ☏   T 020 7384 3092   F 020 7201 6543
       @   theteam@chapple.ltd.uk
Market areas   Executive Search

Website www.chapple.ltd.uk

UK Offices 2

REC Member No

Brief Description Based in the City, Chapple Recruitment specialise in Executive Search and Selection for the following industry sectors: Law, Investment Banking, Corporate Communications and Human Resources.

Preferred method of contact Telephone for appointment

Minimum requirements Previous professional experience

Type of business Permanent and Contract

Grade/Level of Appointments All levels

Chartwell Search & Selection

Head Office ✉ St Georges House, 14–17 Wells St, W1T 3PD
🔴 Oxford Circus
🚆 Charing Cross
☎ **T** 020 7636 5444   **F** 020 7636 5445
@ info@chartwellsearch.co.uk
Market areas Executive Search

Website www.chartwellsearch.co.uk

UK Offices 1

REC Member No

Brief Description Chartwell Search and Selection was established 10 years ago by experienced Search and Selection staff to cover a range of sectors including Telecoms, Retail, Manufacturing, Services, Public Sector and Management Consultancy for both permanent and contract appointments.

Preferred method of contact Apply on line or telephone for appointment

Minimum requirements Previous professional experience

Type of business Permanent and Contract

Grade/Level of Appointments Middle to Senior Management

Chatworth Rowe & Partners

Head Office ✉ 45 Cornhill, EC3V 3PD
🔴 Bank
🚆 Cannon St
☎ **T** 020 7623 2263   **F** 020 7626 2766
@ post@chatworthrowe.co.uk
Market areas Executive Search

Website www.chatworthrowe.co.uk

UK Offices 1

REC Member No

Brief Description Chatworth Rowe & Partners is an independent consultancy established by experienced practitioners specialising in the placement of key individuals in Law, Compensation and Benefits, HR, Insurance, Banking, Actuarial and Fund Management.

Preferred method of contact Telephone for appointment

Minimum requirements Previous professional experience

Type of business Permanent

Grade/Level of Appointments Middle to Senior Management

Commodity Appointments Ltd

Head Office ✉ 1 Gracechurch St, EC3V 0DD
🔴 Monument
🚆 Cannon St
☎ **T** 020 7626 3666   **F** 020 7621 0804
@ mail@commodityappointments.com
Market areas Executive Search

Website www.commodityappointments.com

UK Offices 1

REC Member No

Brief Description Commodity Appointments is a Search and Selection consultancy focused on the Commodity Markets within the following areas: Energy, Power, Global Metals, Soft Commodities and Emerging Commodities.

Preferred method of contact Telephone for appointment

Minimum requirements Graduate level/Previous professional experience

Type of business Permanent

Grade/Level of Appointments Graduate/Trader to Director level

Cossar Lindsay Recruitment Ltd

Head Office ✉ 2 London Wall Buildings, London Wall, EC2M 5UU
🔴 Moorgate
🚆 Moorgate
☎ **T** 020 7242 0558
@ cv@cossarlindsay.co.uk
Market areas Executive Search

Website www.cossarlindsay.co.uk

UK Offices 1

REC Member No

Brief Description Established in 1995, Cossar Lindsay focuses on Recruitment and Executive Search in the international Commodity Markets. They cover positions at all levels in Metals, Energy, Chemicals and Foodstuffs, both Physicals and Futures, placing permanent staff in major traders in the UK and across Europe.

Preferred method of contact Apply on line or telephone for appointment

Minimum requirements Ideally languages/1 year's relevant exposure/Graduate level

Type of business Permanent

Grade/Level of Appointments Graduate/Trainee Broker to Broker/Risk Manager

Cripps Sears & Partners

Head Office ✉ 52 Lincoln Inn Fields, WC2A 3LZ
⊖ Holborn
🚉 City Thameslink
☎ T 020 7440 8999   F 020 7242 0515
@ info@crippssears.com
Market areas Executive Search

Website www.crippssears.com
UK Offices 2
REC Member No

Brief Description Established in 1973, Cripps Sears provides senior level Executive Search services through specialist practice groups in the following sectors: Energy, Financial Services, Legal, Property/Construction, IT/e-Commerce.

Preferred method of contact Apply on line or telephone for appointment

Minimum requirements Previous professional experience

Type of business Permanent

Grade/Level of Appointments Senior level

Criterion Search

Head Office ✉ (The Curzon Partnership) 50 Regent St, London
☎ T 020 7470 7160

✉ 35 Piccadilly, W1J 0DW
⊖ Piccadilly Circus
🚉 Charing Cross
☎ T 020 7479 7280   F 020 7479 7281
@ mail@criterionsearch.co.uk
Market areas Executive Search

Website www.criterionsearch.co.uk
UK Offices 1
REC Member No

Brief Description Part of The Curzon Partnership, Criterion Search has an exceptional track record of successfully completing assignments and gaining repeat business. In the 3 years since they were established, over half of their clients have returned with further requirements. Recruiting for positions with basic salaries between £45k and £100k is their area of expertise.

Preferred method of contact Telephone for appointment

Minimum requirements Previous professional experience

Type of business Permanent

Grade/Level of Appointments Middle Management and upwards

D'Arcy & Co

Head Office ✉ 37 Lombard St, EC3V 9BQ
⊖ Bank
🚉 Cannon St
☎ T 020 7929 8666   F 020 7929 8665
Market areas Executive Search

Website www.darcy-co.com
UK Offices 1
REC Member No

Brief Description D'Arcy & Co is an independently owned and managed Executive Search firm specialising in Investment Banking, Private Equity and Technology. They undertake searches for Managing Director and Chief Executive Officer positions through to Associates, placing permanent, highly experienced professionals in key decision maker roles.

Preferred method of contact Apply on line or telephone for an appointment

Minimum requirements Previous professional experience

Type of business Permanent

Grade/Level of Appointments Associates to Managing Director/Chief Executive Officer

David Ledger Associates

Head Office ✉ 35 Finlay St, SW6 6HE
⊖ Putney Bridge
🚉 Wimbledon
☎ T 020 7736 0770   F 020 7371 0608
@ dla@davidledger.co.uk
Market areas Executive Search

Website www.davidledger.co.uk
UK Offices 1
REC Member No

Brief Description David Ledger Associates was established in 1997 to provide a highly personalised and confidential Executive Search and Selection service specialising in appointments in the UK Finance and Leasing industry.

Preferred method of contact Telephone for appointment

Minimum requirements Finance/Leasing exposure

Type of business Permanent

Grade/Level of Appointments Middle and Senior Executive appointments

The Davis Co Ltd

Head Office ✉ 1st Floor, 45–49 Mortimer St, W1N 8JL
⊖ Oxford Circus
🚉 Marylebone
☎ T 020 7323 6696   F 020 7323 6697
Market areas Executive Search

Website www.daviscompany.co.uk
UK Offices 1
REC Member No

Brief Description Since 1982 The Davis Company has established a proven understanding and knowledge of the Media and Marketing recruitment marketplaces, placing permanent and contract personnel into a variety of clients ranging from IT and Telecoms to Financial Services.

Preferred method of contact Apply on line or telephone for an appointment

Minimum requirements None

Type of business Permanent

Grade/Level of Appointments Graduate to Senior level

Deacon Search

Head Office	✉	88 Kingsway, WC2B 6AA
	⊖	Holborn
	🚆	City Thameslink
	✆	T 020 7681 6514 F 020 7681 6594
	@	solutions@deaconsearch.com
Market areas		Executive Search

Website www.deaconsearch.com

UK Offices 1

REC Member No

Brief Description Deacon Search specialises exclusively in Retained Legal Search in relation to Partner and Senior Lawyer strategic requirements. They have met with considerable success and established a strong track record in the Legal Search market acting for top 10, US, medium-sized West End and niche firms.

Preferred method of contact Telephone for an appointment

Minimum requirements Previous professional experience

Type of business Permanent

Grade/Level of Appointments Senior level

Digby Morgan Consulting

Head Office	✉	Roxburghe House, 273–287 Regent St, W1B 2HA
	⊖	Oxford Circus
	🚆	Charing Cross
	✆	T 020 7907 2828 F 020 7495 4474
	@	mail@digby-morgan.com
Market areas		Executive Search

Website www.digby-morgan.com

UK Offices 1

REC Member No

Brief Description Digby Morgan is a specialist Executive Search, Selection and Human Resources consultancy. Established in 1988, their success is built on proven expertise within niche markets. They focus on HR recruitment and provide innovative resourcing solutions to leading organisations within the Financial, Professional Services and Technology sectors as well as several FTSE 100 companies.

Preferred method of contact Telephone for appointment

Minimum requirements Ideally 6 months exposure within HR

Type of business Contract and Permanent

Grade/Level of Appointments Graduate/Personnel Administrator to Head of HR/Board level

Drayton Finch Ltd

Head Office	✉	Durrant House, 8–13 Chiswell St, EC1Y 4XY
	⊖	Moorgate
	🚆	Moorgate
	✆	T 020 7496 0000 F 020 7496 9988
	@	enquiries@draytonfinch.com
Market areas		Executive Search

Website www.draytonfinch.com

UK Offices 1

REC Member No

Brief Description Drayton Finch concentrate in the highly specialised Search and Selection Asset Management sector.

Preferred method of contact Apply on line or telephone for appointment

Minimum requirements Previous professional experience

Type of business Permanent

Grade/Level of Appointments All levels

Eban Ltd

Head Office	✉	The Garden House, 6 Eccleston Place, SW1W 9NF
	⊖	Victoria
	🚆	Victoria
	✆	T 020 7730 5800 F 020 7730 5831
	@	ann.semple@eban.co.uk
Market areas		Executive Search

Website www.eban.co.uk

UK Offices 1

REC Member No

Brief Description Eban was established in Hong Kong in 1995. The London Office opened in 1997 and the Tokyo office in 1999. Eban concentrates on research-driven retained assignments for a select number of global Investment Banking groups, with a focus in Asia, Japan and Europe on all aspects of the Global Markets, particularly: Equity Markets, Debt Capital Markets, Fund Management and Senior Financial Management positions.

Preferred method of contact Telephone for appointment

Minimum requirements Previous professional experience

Type of business Permanent

Grade/Level of Appointments Analysts/Researchers to Head of Trading/Chief Executive Officer

Elements

Head Office ✉ Henrietta House, 17–18 Henrietta St, WC2E 8QH
⊖ Covent Garden
🚊 Charing Cross
☎ T 020 7484 5005   F 020 7484 5105
Market areas Executive Search

Website www.elementsgroup.co.uk
UK Offices 6
REC Member Yes
Brief Description Established in 1998, Elements have experienced consistent growth year on year and are now recognised as one of the leading specialist recruitment consultancies within the UK, supplying the very best talent to multi-national blue chip organisations. Capitalising on over 40 years experience within the Financial Services market, they are committed to developing their reputation as the consultancy of choice in terms of advice, service and delivery for both their clients and candidates. They employ a team of highly skilled Business Managers who are able to consult across the broad spectrum of roles that exist within their market. Whether in the field of Pensions, Investments or Protection, or within the disciplines of Broker Sales, IFA or Employee Benefits, they understand and appreciate the key issues.

Preferred method of contact Apply on line or telephone for an appointment
Minimum requirements None
Type of business Contract and Permanent
Grade/Level of Appointments All levels

Elliott Ross Associates

Head Office ✉ 150 Minories, EC3N 1LS
⊖ Aldgate
🚊 Fenchurch St
☎ T 020 7264 2224   F 020 7264 2269
@ reply@elliott-ross.co.uk
Market areas Executive Search

Website www.elliott-ross.co.uk
UK Offices 1
REC Member No
Brief Description Elliott Ross is a specialist Risk Management Search and Selection consultancy in the Global Financial Markets. The core of their activities are concentrated around the Risk Management, Actuarial Consulting, Quantitative Analytics and Third Party Risk/Trading systems of their clients where they work to provide recruitment solutions in specific business areas. These are the disciplines of Investment Consulting, Risk Consulting, Employee Consulting and Third Party Risk/Trading, Systems Development, Integration and Implementation.

Preferred method of contact Apply on line or telephone for appointment
Minimum requirements Previous professional experience

Type of business Contract and Permanent
Grade/Level of Appointments All levels

Ellis Fairbank Plc

✉ 32 Dover St, W1S 4NE
⊖ Green Park
🚊 Victoria
☎ T 020 7529 2600   F 020 7529 2601
@ contactus@ellisfairbank.co.uk
Market areas Executive Search

Website www.ellisfairbank.co.uk
UK Offices 3
REC Member No
Head Office Ellis Fairbank House, Manor Rd, Leeds, LS18 4DX
Brief Description Ellis Fairbank Plc is a market leader in recruitment. Established in 1991, they are one of the top 10 independent recruitment companies in the UK. Offering bespoke recruitment solutions across a wide range of sectors and industries, they attract, assess and select candidates at all levels, from recent graduates to senior level candidates, including non-executive and interim appointments.

Preferred method of contact Apply on line or telephone for appointment
Minimum requirements None
Type of business Permanent
Grade/Level of Appointments Graduate to Senior level

Executive Match Recruitment Consultancy

Head Office ✉ 1 Adam St, WC2N 6AE
⊖ Charing Cross
🚊 Charing Cross
☎ T 020 7930 7000   F 020 7930 8888
@ vacancies@e-m.co.uk
Market areas Executive Search

Website www.e-m.co.uk
UK Offices 1
REC Member No
Brief Description Established in 1993, Executive Match's experience and expertise has led to unrivalled relationships with the world's most prestigious employers. They focus upon delivering the best opportunities to the best candidates. To achieve this their consultants and researchers utilise a unique combination of the latest Search and Selection methodologies focusing on Consulting, Finance, Media and Sales recruitment.

Preferred method of contact Apply on line or telephone for appointment
Minimum requirements Previous professional experience

Type of business Contract and Permanent
Grade/Level of Appointments All levels

Executive Selection Associates

Head Office ✉ Craven House, 121 Kingsway, WC2B 6PA
      ⊖ Holborn
      🚆 City Thameslink
      ✆ T 020 7721 8022   F 020 7721 8025
      @ info@e-s-a.co.uk
Market areas Executive Search

Website www.e-s-a.co.uk
UK Offices 1
REC Member Yes

Brief Description Formed in 1985, with an MBO in 2001, Executive Selection Associates is a specialist retained led Search and Selection consultancy supplying Middle to Senior and Executive Management throughout specific sectors of industry. By cultivating excellent customer relationships, they have developed the reputation of being one of the UK's leading consultancies within their market sector. They work in both the Public and Private sectors, from major blue chip well established organisations to the new and fast emerging companies.

Preferred method of contact Apply on line or telephone for an appointment
Minimum requirements Relevant management exposure
Type of business Permanent
Grade/Level of Appointments Mid to Senior Management level

Farlow & Warren Search and Selection – Construction

See Construction and Property, page 47

Farlow & Warren Search and Selection – Financial

See Financial Services and Insurance, page 121

Farlow & Warren Search and Selection – Telecoms & IT

See IT and Telecoms, page 161

Farn Williams

Head Office ✉ 13–15 Vine Hill, EC1R 5FW
      ⊖ Farringdon
      🚆 Farringdon
      ✆ T 020 7309 0300   F 020 7837 0001
      @ information@farnwilliams.com
Market areas Executive Search

Website www.farnwilliams.co.uk
UK Offices 1
REC Member No

Brief Description Farn Williams is a high quality international search firm. They specialise in recruiting local and expatriate professionals for international companies and financial institutions in the EMEA region. Their practices specialise by function, geography and industry sector enabling them to rapidly focus on relevant searches: Finance and Accounting (including Leasing and Vendor Finance), Technology, and Central and Eastern Europe (including Oil and Gas).

Preferred method of contact Telephone for appointment
Minimum requirements Previous professional experience
Type of business Permanent
Grade/Level of Appointments All levels

Firth Ross Martin

Head Office ✉ Bell Ct House, 11 Blomfield St, EC2M 7AY
      ⊖ Moorgate
      🚆 Moorgate
      ✆ T 020 7786 6950   F 020 7382 9417
      @ search@firthrossmartin.com
Market areas Executive Search

Website www.firthrossmartin.com
UK Offices 2
REC Member No

Brief Description Part of the Blomfield Group, Firth Ross Martin was founded in 1983 and is acknowledged as one of the UK's leading Executive Search firms. Their prime areas of focus continue to be Investment Banking, Securities Trading and Asset Management, where they continue to demonstrate the full range of consultancy skills required to provide effective solutions to clients' senior level resourcing needs.

Preferred method of contact Apply on line or telephone for an appointment
Minimum requirements Relevant industry exposure
Type of business Permanent
Grade/Level of Appointments Senior level

Fleet Search and Selection

Head Office ✉ 30 -32 Ludgate Hill, EC4M 7DR
      ⊖ Blackfriars
      🚆 City Thameslink
      ✆ T 020 7246 6500   F 020 7246 6501

@ careers@fleetsearch.co.uk
Market areas Executive Search

Website www.fleetsearch.co.uk

UK Offices 1

REC Member No

Brief Description Fleet Search and Selection is a professional consultancy specialising in appointments from Director to Recently Qualified personnel, in the City, Europe and Middle East Financial Services sectors. They are dedicated to the highest level of service to both candidate and client alike and pride themselves on their attention to detail and time effective solutions to the recruitment process. Specifically, whilst conducting searches for Investment Banks and other Financial Services institutions they provide: Traders, Sales, Business Auditors, Technology Auditors, Audit Executives, Risk Managers, Quantitative Finance and Research Analysts and Compliance Executives.

Preferred method of contact Apply on line or telephone for appointment

Minimum requirements Previous professional experience

Type of business Permanent

Grade/Level of Appointments Recently Qualified to Director level

---

Fletcher Jones Ltd

Head Office ✉ 150 Minories, EC3N 1LS
🚇 Aldgate
🚆 Fenchurch St
C T 020 7264 2272   F 020 7264 2270
@ responses@fletcher-jones.co.uk
Market areas Executive Search

Website www.fletcherjones.co.uk

UK Offices 2

REC Member No

Brief Description Fletcher Jones Executive Search and Selection is an independent consultancy with offices in Edinburgh and London providing creative recruitment solutions to a broad range of clients throughout the UK. Fletcher Jones was incorporated in 1986 to provide a bespoke Executive Search service for senior positions. They are one of the UK's best resourced regional Search and Selection consultancies with a national client base, covering a range of industries including: Consumer, Energy, Financial Services, Industrial, Media, Professional Practice, Public Sector, Technology and Telecoms.

Preferred method of contact Telephone for appointment

Minimum requirements Previous professional experience

Type of business Permanent

Grade/Level of Appointments Senior level

The Foundry

Head Office ✉ 41 Shelton St, WC2H 9HG
🚇 Covent Garden
🚆 Charing Cross
C T 020 7240 5115   F 020 7240 5501
@ best@the-foundry.co.uk
Market areas Executive Search

Website www.the-foundry.co.uk

UK Offices 1

REC Member No

Brief Description The consultant team at The Foundry has over 16 years experience developed within the Communications sector. Many of their clients have remained loyal over the years and they are consistently attracting and retaining new clients. They may be PR consultancies, Organisational Change Communication consultancies and Public Affairs businesses or the In-house Communications departments of a broad range of organisations from the Public and Not for Profit sectors to Commercial companies of considerable international standing.

Preferred method of contact Apply on line or telephone for appointment

Minimum requirements Relevant Management Exposure

Type of business Permanent

Grade/Level of Appointments Senior level appointments

Fox Rodney Search

Head Office ✉ 78 Cannon St, EC4N 6NQ
🚇 Cannon St
🚆 Cannon St
C T 020 7618 6433   F 020 7618 8593
@ afox@foxrodneysearch.com
Market areas Executive Search

Website www.foxrodneysearch.com

UK Offices 1

REC Member No

Brief Description Established in 2000, Fox Rodney Search specialises in Legal Executive Search. Their experience has involved them in some of the most significant recruitment assignments in the Legal market, ranging from individual Partners, Teams and Senior In-house Legal Advisors to US Law firms, start-ups and mergers.

Preferred method of contact Telephone for appointment

Minimum requirements Previous professional experience

Type of business Permanent

Grade/Level of Appointments Partner and Senior level

FR Europe

Head Office ✉ The Ziggurat, 60–66 Saffron Hill, EC1N 8QX
　　　　　⊖ Farringdon
　　　　　🚆 Farringdon
　　　　　☎ T 020 7729 0929
　　　　　@ infolondon@freurope.com
Market areas Executive Search

Website www.freurope.com

UK Offices 4

REC Member Yes

Brief Description FR Europe is an Executive Search organisation operating across a range of industry sectors.

Preferred method of contact Apply on line or telephone for appointment

Minimum requirements Relevant industry exposure

Type of business Permanent

Grade/Level of Appointments Graduate calibre to Director level

The Freshman Consultancy

Head Office ✉ 1 Royal Exchange Avenue, EC3V 3LT
　　　　　⊖ Bank
　　　　　🚆 Cannon St
　　　　　☎ T 020 7623 4220
　　　　　@ research@freshman.co.uk
Market areas Executive Search

Website www.freshman.co.uk

UK Offices 1

REC Member No

Brief Description The Freshman Consultancy is a specialist Executive Search and Selection firm for the Internet and Digital business. They have a broad client base and a strong record of achievement within e-Commerce, New Media services and the Global Investment community.

Preferred method of contact Telephone for appointment

Minimum requirements Previous professional experience

Type of business Permanent and Contract

Grade/Level of Appointments All levels

Garner International Ltd

Head Office ✉ 6 Derby St, W1J 7AD
　　　　　⊖ Green Park
　　　　　🚆 Victoria
　　　　　☎ T 020 7629 8822　F 020 7629 8833
　　　　　@ info@garnerinternational.co.uk
Market areas Executive Search

Website www.garnerinternational.com

UK Offices 1

REC Member No

Brief Description Garner International is part of the Constellation Corporation Plc, with offices in Malaysia and Singapore. The practice has an in-depth and specialised knowledge in Technology, Media, Retail, Telecoms, Consumer Goods, Life Sciences, and Personal and Corporate Finance.

Preferred method of contact Telephone for appointment

Minimum requirements Previous professional experience

Type of business Permanent

Grade/Level of Appointments All levels

Gecko Search Ltd

Head Office ✉ 36–42 New Inn Yard, EC2A 3EY
　　　　　⊖ Old St
　　　　　🚆 Old St
　　　　　☎ T 020 7739 9970
　　　　　@ nero@gecko-search.co.uk
Market areas Executive Search

Website www.gecko-search.co.uk

UK Offices 1

REC Member No

Brief Description Gecko Search specialise in the Search and Selection of Senior Commercial, Creative and Technical appointments in New Media.

Preferred method of contact Telephone for appointment

Minimum requirements Previous professional experience

Type of business Permanent

Grade/Level of Appointments Senior level

Global Markets Recruitment Ltd

Head Office ✉ 12 Mason Avenue, EC2V 5BB
　　　　　⊖ Bank
　　　　　🚆 Cannon St
　　　　　☎ T 020 7600 4744　F 020 7600 4717
　　　　　@ info@globalmarkets.co.uk
Market areas Executive Search

Website www.globalmarkets.co.uk

UK Offices 1

REC Member No

Brief Description Global Markets Search was incorporated in 1992 to address the specialist recruiting requirements of the Financial Services community. Their market specialisations are: Debt, Equity, Corporate Finance, Financial Operations, New Media, Risk Management, Economics and Strategy, Asset Management, Private Banking, Emerging Markets and Financial Marketing.

Preferred method of contact Apply on line or telephone for appointment

Minimum requirements Previous professional experience

Type of business Permanent

Grade/Level of Appointments All levels

Hanover Fox International Ltd

Head Office ✉ 10–12 Cork St, W1S 3NP
🚇 Piccadilly Circus
🚂 Charing Cross
📞 T 020 7851 2800   F 020 7851 2801
@ aft@hanoverfox.co.uk
Market areas Executive Search

Website www.hanoverfox.co.uk

UK Offices 2

REC Member No

Brief Description With offices in London and Bristol, Hanover Fox specialise in senior appointments using Search and Selection methods to identify key individuals across a broad range of industry sectors for clients across the UK and worldwide.

Preferred method of contact Telephone for appointment

Minimum requirements Previous professional experience

Type of business Permanent

Grade/Level of Appointments Senior level

Hanover Matrix

Head Office ✉ 12 St James Sq, SW1Y 4RB
🚇 Piccadilly Circus
🚂 Charing Cross
📞 T 020 7849 6032   F 020 7849 6152
@ info@hanovermatrix.com
Market areas Executive Search

Website www.hanovermatrix.co.uk

UK Offices 1

REC Member No

Brief Description Hanover Matrix is one of Europe's leading providers of Executive Search solutions. Founded in London in 1990 and employee owned, Hanover Matrix has grown to more than 25 professional personnel working in several offices throughout Europe, placing senior level appointments from Middle Management to Chief Executive Officer/Board Level within various clients across the UK and Europe.

Preferred method of contact Telephone for appointment

Minimum requirements Previous professional experience

Type of business Permanent

Grade/Level of Appointments Middle Management to Chief Executive Officer level

Hardy Financial

Head Office ✉ Horatio House, 22 Candahar Rd, SW11 2QB
🚇 Clapham Common
🚂 Clapham Junction
📞 T 020 7652 7366   F 020 7738 0934
@ search@hardyfinancial.co.uk
Market areas Executive Search

Website www.hardyfinancial.co.uk

UK Offices 1

REC Member No

Brief Description Hardy Financial was established in 1996 as a specialist Executive Search consultancy in Financial recruitment, focusing on Fund Management and Equity Sales, Research and Trading. They are particularly strong in the Japanese and Asian markets, but have also been building a European franchise.

Preferred method of contact Telephone for appointment

Minimum requirements Relevant industry exposure

Type of business Permanent

Grade/Level of Appointments Middle to Senior Management level

HARP Wallen

Head Office ✉ The Media Centre, 131–151 Great Titchfield St, W1W 5BB
🚇 Great Portland St
🚂 Euston
📞 T 020 7072 2360   F 020 7072 2366
@ harpwallen@harpwallen.co.uk
Market areas Executive Search

Website www.harpwallen.co.uk

UK Offices 1

REC Member No

Brief Description HARP Wallen Ltd Executive Recruitment combines a wealth of experience with a unique understanding of the Travel, Leisure, Conference and Incentive industries. An independent consultancy, they recruit at Middle to Senior Management level across a broad spectrum of skill sectors including Sales, Product, Marketing, Commercial, Account Management, Operations, Call Centre Management, Customer Service and Finance.

Preferred method of contact Apply on line or telephone for an appointment

Minimum requirements Previous managerial exposure

Type of business Permanent

Grade/Level of Appointments Middle to Senior Management level

Harper Halsey Laroche

Head Office ✉ Grafton House, 2–3 Golden Sq, W1R 3AD
 ⊖ Piccadilly Circus
 🚊 Charing Cross
 ℂ T 020 7287 1115   F 020 7494 3549
 @ krista@hhlrecruitment.co.uk
Market areas Executive Search

Website www.hhlrecruitment.co.uk

UK Offices 1

REC Member Yes

Brief Description Established in 1989, Harper Halsey Laroche is an established Search and Selection consultancy specialising in the Retail sector.

Preferred method of contact Apply on line or telephone for an appointment

Minimum requirements None

Type of business Permanent

Grade/Level of Appointments Graduate/Sales Consultant to Regional Business Manager

Harvey Nash International Search & Selection

Head Office ✉ 13 Bruton St, W1J 6QA
 ⊖ Green Park
 🚊 Victoria
 ℂ T 020 7333 0033   F 020 7333 0032
 @ harveynash@harveynash.com
Market areas Executive Search

Website www.harveynash.com

UK Offices 3

REC Member No

Brief Description Harvey Nash International Search & Selection are one of Europe's leading Executive Search and Selection firms. In the UK they have continued to dominate their market and the division has four IT industry focused practices: IT Services, Telecommunications, End-user IT and e-Business – and a Generalist practice consisting of Financial Services, Healthcare, Retail and FMCG. Their clients range from blue chip global organisations and high growth Telecom companies to New Technology start ups.

Preferred method of contact Apply on line or telephone for an appointment

Minimum requirements Previous professional experience

Type of business Permanent

Grade/Level of Appointments All levels

Hays City

Head Office ✉ 141 Moorgate, EC2M 6TX
 ⊖ Moorgate
 🚊 Moorgate
 ℂ T 020 7786 9585   F 01279 642088
 @ hays.city@hays-hps.com
Market areas Executive Search

Website www.haysworks.com

UK Offices 1

REC Member No

Brief Description Hays Personnel Services is a division of Hays plc, the Business Services group listed in the FTSE 100. Hays Personnel Services is Europe's leading specialist professional recruitment group. Hays City is a Contingency Search and Selection division operating across the Banking and Finance sectors, recruiting Senior Finance, Operations and Middle Office staff within the salary bracket of £40k–£120k.

Preferred method of contact Telephone for appointment

Minimum requirements Previous professional experience

Type of business Permanent

Grade/Level of Appointments Mid to Senior Management level

Hays Executive Search – Main Board Services Practice

Head Office ✉ 141 Moorgate, EC2M 6TX
 ℂ T 020 7628 9999   F 020 7628 4698
 ✉ Mansfield House, 1st Floor, 1 Southampton St, WC2R 0LR
 ⊖ Covent Garden
 🚊 Charing Cross
 ℂ T 020 7520 5999   F 020 7379 0357
 @ uk@hays-executive.com
Market areas Executive Search

Website www.haysworks.com

UK Offices 3

REC Member No

Brief Description Hays Personnel Services is a division of Hays plc, the Business Services group listed in the FTSE 100. Hays Personnel Services is Europe's leading specialist professional recruitment group. Hays Executive Search and Selection provides a Senior Management Search and Selection service in the UK and across Europe. With offices in London, Hamburg, Paris and Prague, their experienced consultants recruit across a range of disciplines and sectors at Executive level.

Preferred method of contact Apply on line or telephone for an appointment

Minimum requirements Previous professional experience

Type of business Permanent

Grade/Level of Appointments Senior Management level

Hays Executive Search – Property and Construction Practice

Head Office ✉ 141 Moorgate, EC2M 6TX
　　　　　　 ☎ T 020 7628 9999   F 020 7628 4698

　　　　　　 ✉ Charter House, 13–15 Carteret St, SW1H 9DJ
　　　　　　 ⊖ St James's Park
　　　　　　 ⊟ Victoria
　　　　　　 ☎ T 020 7931 0444   F 020 7931 7231
　　　　　　 @ london@hays-executive.com

Market areas Executive Search

Website www.haysworks.com

UK Offices 3

REC Member No

Brief Description Hays Personnel Services is a division of Hays plc, the Business Services group listed in the FTSE 100. Hays Personnel Services is Europe's leading specialist professional recruitment group. Hays Executive Search and Selection provides a Senior Management Search and Selection service in the UK and across Europe. With offices in London, Hamburg, Paris and Prague, their experienced consultants recruit across a range of disciplines and sectors at Executive level.

Preferred method of contact Apply on line or telephone for an appointment

Minimum requirements Previous professional experience

Type of business Permanent

Grade/Level of Appointments Senior Management level

Hays Executive Search – Public Sector Practice

Head Office ✉ 141 Moorgate, EC2M 6TX
　　　　　　 ☎ T 020 7628 9999   F 020 7628 4698

　　　　　　 ✉ Mansfield House, 1st Floor, 1 Southampton St, WC2R 0LR
　　　　　　 ⊖ Covent Garden
　　　　　　 ⊟ Charing Cross
　　　　　　 ☎ T 020 7520 5960   F 020 7520 5961
　　　　　　 @ covent-garden.ps@hays-ap.com

Market areas Executive Search

Website www.haysworks.com

UK Offices 3

REC Member No

Brief Description Hays Personnel Services is a division of Hays plc, the Business Services group listed in the FTSE 100. Hays Personnel Services is Europe's leading specialist professional recruitment group.

Hays Executive Search and Selection provides a Senior Management Search and Selection service in the UK and across Europe. With offices in London, Hamburg, Paris and Prague, their experienced consultants recruit across a range of disciplines and sectors at Executive level.

Preferred method of contact Apply on line or telephone for an appointment

Minimum requirements Previous professional experience

Type of business Permanent

Grade/Level of Appointments Senior Management level

Heidrick & Struggles Associates

Head Office ✉ 3 Burlington Gardens, W1S 3EP
　　　　　　 ⊖ Green Park
　　　　　　 ⊟ Victoria
　　　　　　 ☎ T 020 7075 4000   F 020 7075 4001
　　　　　　 @ london@heidrick.com

Market areas Executive Search

Website www.heidrick.com

UK Offices 2

REC Member No

Brief Description The opening of the London office in 1968 was Heidrick & Struggles first step into Europe. The office is the largest in the European network and its evolution has been characterised by a continuous quest for excellence and the pioneering of new concepts in response to – and in advance of – their clients' needs. Their sector specialists have long operated on a pan-European basis and the firm is independently acknowledged as the pioneer of the speciality practice group concept. This sector focus and associated expertise now extends throughout their worldwide network.

Preferred method of contact Apply on line or telephone for an appointment

Minimum requirements Senior Management exposure

Type of business Contract and Permanent

Grade/Level of Appointments Senior level to Board appointments

Heyman Woodworth Search and Selection Ltd

Head Office ✉ 5th Floor, Goldsmith House, 137–141 Regent St, W1B 4HZ
　　　　　　 ⊖ Piccadilly Circus
　　　　　　 ⊟ Charing Cross
　　　　　　 ☎ T 020 7287 6116   F 020 7287 7121
　　　　　　 @ billy@heymanwoodworth.co.uk

Market areas Executive Search

Website www.heymanwoodworth.co.uk

UK Offices 1

REC Member No

Brief Description Heyman Woodworth was established in early 1999 and remains the only recruitment consultancy in the UK that provides Forces Officers to Commercial and Banking organisations both with and without technical commercial experience. Specialists in the placement of ex-Forces Officers and Defence professionals.

Preferred method of contact Apply on line or telephone for an appointment

Minimum requirements Ex-Armed Forces Officers and Defence experience

Type of business Permanent

Grade/Level of Appointments All levels

HLR Associates Ltd

Head Office ✉ 33 Davies St, W1K 4LR
🔵 Bond St
🚆 Paddington
☎ T 020 7316 3000   F 020 7316 3030
@ info@hlrassociates.co.uk
Market areas Executive Search

Website www.hlrassociates.co.uk
UK Offices 1
REC Member No

Brief Description HLR Associates Ltd is a highly respected Senior Executive Search firm which has been dedicated to the Hospitality, Leisure, Travel and Tourism industries since 1994. These industry sectors are now broadening into Sport, Gaming, Property and Communications, with particular emphasis on filling Senior Management and Board level positions.

Preferred method of contact Apply on line or telephone for an appointment

Minimum requirements Previous professional experience

Type of business Permanent

Grade/Level of Appointments Senior level

Hogarth Davies Lloyd

Head Office ✉ Halton House, 20–23 Holborn, EC1N 2JD
🔵 Chancery Lane
🚆 City Thameslink
☎ T 020 7404 7440   F 020 7404 7663
@ info@hogarthdavieslloyd.com
Market areas Executive Search

Website www.hogarthdavieslloyd.com
UK Offices 1
REC Member No

Brief Description Established in 1995, Hogarth Davies Lloyd provides a unique Executive Search service based upon relevant market experience and specialises in Investment Banking and the Law.

Preferred method of contact Telephone for appointment

Minimum requirements Previous professional experience

Type of business Permanent

Grade/Level of Appointments Senior level

Hoggett Bowers

Head Office ✉ 7–9 Breams Buildings, EC4A 1DT
🔵 Chancery Lane
🚆 City Thameslink
☎ T 020 7964 9100   F 020 7964 9101
Market areas Executive Search

Website www.hoggett-bowers.com
UK Offices 4
REC Member No

Brief Description Hoggett Bowers believes that telling anything less than the complete truth wastes everyone's time. The trust they have built up with their clients means that they never have to pull punches. This approach ensures everyone, even unsuccessful candidates, take away something positive from the process. Although they work to specific client briefs, they are always happy to talk to Senior Executives looking for new opportunities or who would like to develop a relationship with them.

Preferred method of contact Apply on line or telephone for an appointment

Minimum requirements Previous professional experience

Type of business Permanent and Interim

Grade/Level of Appointments Mid to Senior Management level

Horton International (UK) Ltd

Head Office ✉ 24 Buckingham Gate, SW1E 6LB
🔵 Victoria
🚆 Victoria
☎ T 020 7630 0200   F 020 7630 0322
@ london@horton-intl.com
Market areas Executive Search

Website www.horton-intl.co.uk
UK Offices 1
REC Member No

Brief Description The UK Firm of Horton International was founded in 1970. Today the group has 30 offices in 26 countries located in the economic and industrial centres of Europe, the Americas and the Asia-Pacific region. Horton International provides resourcing and organisational solutions globally, nationally and regionally to its clients across a wide range of industries and sectors.

Preferred method of contact Telephone for appointment

Minimum requirements Previous professional experience

Type of business Permanent

Grade/Level of Appointments Mid to Senior Management level

Howgate Sable

Head Office ✉ Dover House, 34 Dover St, W1S 4NG
             ⊖ Green Park
             🚆 Victoria
             ☎ T 020 7495 1234   F 020 7317 0920
             @ london@howgate-sable.com
Market areas Executive Search

Website www.howgate-sable.com

UK Offices 5

REC Member No

Brief Description Howgate Sable is a leading independent Search and Selection consultancy working with a broad range of clients and candidates. With an enviable track record of success, they develop partnerships with their clients across a complete range of business sectors in the UK, Europe and throughout the world.

Preferred method of contact Apply on line or telephone for an appointment

Minimum requirements Previous professional experience

Type of business Permanent

Grade/Level of Appointments All levels

HW Search & Selection

Head Office ✉ Linen Hall, 162–168 Regent St, W1R 5TB
             ⊖ Piccadilly Circus
             🚆 Charing Cross
             ☎ T 020 7734 7444   F 020 7734 2060
             @ info@hwselect.com
Market areas Executive Search

Website www.hwselect.com

UK Offices 1

REC Member No

Brief Description HW Search & Selection specialises in the Retained Search of experienced Legal Professionals at Managing and Senior Partner level, as well as IT Professionals in the global community. Their successes to date combine the best elements of the larger Executive Search firms with the speed of the Contingency practitioners. They are particularly knowledgeable in the areas of Computer and Information Technology, Intellectual Property, Biotechnology and Pharmaceuticals.

Preferred method of contact Telephone for appointment

Minimum requirements Systems Development/Management exposure

Type of business Permanent and Contract

Grade/Level of Appointments Senior Management level to Director

Ian Jones & Partners Ltd

Head Office ✉ 5 Aldford St, W1K 2AF
             ⊖ Marble Arch
             🚆 Paddington
             ☎ T 020 7493 1120   F 020 7493 1151
             @ info@ianjonesandpartners.com
Market areas Executive Search

Website www.ianjonesandpartners.com

UK Offices 1

REC Member No

Brief Description Ian Jones & Partners was founded in 1996, and handles search assignments for Executive appointments, at salary levels from £100k to in excess of £300k, and for the appointment of Chairmen and Non-Executive Directors.

Preferred method of contact Apply on line or telephone for an appointment

Minimum requirements Previous professional experience

Type of business Permanent

Grade/Level of Appointments Senior level

Impact Executives

Head Office ✉ 13 Bruton St, W1J 6QA
             ⊖ Green Park
             🚆 Victoria
             ☎ T 020 7314 2011   F 020 7314 2020
             @ info@impactexecutives.com
Market areas Technology, Accountancy and Banking, Government, Retail, Healthcare

Website www.impactexecutives.com

UK Offices 1

REC Member Yes

Brief Description Harvey Nash plc, the global resource solutions group, acquired Impact Executives from Management Consultants, PA Consulting. Impact Executives was merged with Harvey Nash's Interim business IMIT (Interim Management for IT) to create a leading global Interim Management provider. Impact Executives can offer its clients an unrivalled level of service and support, providing them with high quality Interim Executives at all levels who deliver competitive solutions at speed. With access to a global network, Impact Executives provides support for clients on a national or international basis.

Preferred method of contact Telephone for appointment

Minimum requirements Relevant industry exposure at Board or Senior Director level

Type of business Contract

Grade/Level of Appointments Senior level

JCL Search

Head Office ✉ 78 Austin Friars, EC2N 2QQ
⊖ Bank
🚆 Cannon St
☎ T 020 7726 0000   F 020 7638 2300
@ info@jclsearch.co.uk
Market areas Executive Search

Website www.jclsearch.co.uk

UK Offices 1

REC Member No

Brief Description JCL Search is a Search consultancy specialising in the strategic recruitment of Lawyers and Senior Management for the Legal profession worldwide.

Preferred method of contact Telephone for appointment

Minimum requirements Previous professional experience

Type of business Permanent

Grade/Level of Appointments Senior level

JCR Executive Search

Head Office ✉ 1 Cromwell Place, SW7 2JE
⊖ South Kensington
🚆 Victoria
☎ T 020 7581 2977   F 020 7581 1766
@ jcr@jcr.co.uk
Market areas Executive Search

Website www.jcr.co.uk

UK Offices 1

REC Member No

Brief Description The JCR Group has a 20 year track record within the Search industry and prides itself on its integrity and professionalism, as well as its friendly approach to candidates and clients alike.

Preferred method of contact Telephone for appointment

Minimum requirements Previous professional experience

Type of business Permanent

Grade/Level of Appointments All levels

Kenexa

✉ 8 Duncannon St, WC2N 4JF
⊖ Charing Cross
🚆 Charing Cross

☎ T 020 7484 5056   F 020 7484 5115
Market areas Executive Search

Website www.kenexa.com

UK Offices 1

REC Member No

Head Office USA

Brief Description Kenexa was founded as an Executive Search firm. They have rapidly become a premier and international provider of Executive Search services in the Financial Services and Healthcare markets.

Preferred method of contact Apply on line or telephone for an appointment

Minimum requirements Senior managerial exposure

Type of business Permanent

Grade/Level of Appointments Senior to Board level

Kettlefish

Head Office ✉ 10 Regents Wharf, All Saints St, N1 9RL
⊖ Kings Cross
🚆 Kings Cross
☎ T 020 7551 4794   F 020 7551 4793
@ contacts@kettlefish.com
Market areas Executive Search

Website www.kettlefish.co.uk

UK Offices 1

REC Member No

Brief Description Part of the Bernard Hodes Group, Kettlefish specialise in the Executive Search market.

Preferred method of contact Telephone for appointment

Minimum requirements Previous professional experience

Type of business Permanent

Grade/Level of Appointments Senior level

Kingston Smith Executive Selection

Head Office ✉ Quadrant House, 80–82 Regent St, W1B 5RP
⊖ Piccadilly Circus
🚆 Charing Cross
☎ T 020 7304 4646   F 020 7304 4647
Market areas Executive Search

Website www.kingstonsmith.co.uk

UK Offices 1

REC Member No

Brief Description Kingston Smith Executive Selection recruits for people in the Marketing Services and Entertainment sectors.

Preferred method of contact Apply on line or telephone for an appointment

Minimum requirements Previous professional experience

Type of business Permanent

Grade/Level of Appointments All levels

Korn Ferry International

✉ 123 Buckingham Palace Rd, SW1W 9DZ
🚇 St James's Park
🚌 Victoria
☎ **T** 020 7312 3100   **F** 020 7312 3130
Market areas Executive Search

Website www.kornferry.co.uk

UK Offices 2

REC Member No

Head Office USA

Brief Description Korn Ferry opened its first offices in Europe in 1972. Three decades later, the firm is an established leader in European human capital solutions, with more than 20 offices throughout the region. For more than 30 years, Korn Ferry International has been a leader in executive recruitment, conducting over 80,000 senior-level searches for clients worldwide. Today they are one of the world's premier providers of executive human capital solutions, with services ranging from Corporate Governance and Chief Executive Officer recruitment to Executive Search, Middle Management recruitment, Strategic Management Assessment and Executive Coaching and Development. They cover the broadest range of global industries, everything from Investment Banking and Pharmaceuticals to Retail, Technology, Energy and Entertainment.

Preferred method of contact Apply on line or telephone for an appointment

Minimum requirements Relevant Management exposure

Type of business Permanent

Grade/Level of Appointments Middle Management to Chief Executive Officer level

Latimer International

Head Office ✉ Countymark House, 50 Regent St, W1R 6LP
🚇 Piccadilly Circus
🚌 Charing Cross
☎ **T** 020 7470 7178   **F** 020 7470 7183
@ latimer@latimerinternational.com
Market areas Executive Search

Website www.latimerinternational.com

UK Offices 1

REC Member No

Brief Description Latimer International was formed in 1991 and has focused on providing recruitment services, principally in the form of Search (head-hunting), to businesses in emerging and fast moving sectors for positions within the £50,000 to £200,000 salary range.

Since its inception it has operated in the growth markets of Cable and Satellite, Mobile Communications, Telecommunications, Multi-media, Entertainment, Retail, Consulting, e-Commerce and the Internet.

Preferred method of contact Apply on line or telephone for an appointment

Minimum requirements Relevant management exposure

Type of business Permanent

Grade/Level of Appointments HR Executives/General Management to Executive Board level

LKRC

Head Office ✉ 1st Floor, 66 Great Russell St, WC1B 3BN
🚇 Tottenham Court Rd
🚌 Euston
☎ **T** 020 7831 4140   **F** 020 7831 1171
@ info@lkrc.co.uk
Market areas Executive Search

Website www.lkrc.co.uk

UK Offices 1

REC Member Yes

Brief Description LKRC is an independent London based consultancy, specialising in recruiting Consulting Profile professionals into Management Consultants' Internal Consulting departments, within blue chip corporate and project based positions in industry.

Preferred method of contact Apply on line or telephone for an appointment

Minimum requirements Relevant industry exposure

Type of business Contract and Permanent

Grade/Level of Appointments Communications Consultant to Change Programme Specialist

Lomond Consulting Ltd

Head Office ✉ Berkeley Sq House, Berkeley Sq, W1X 6EA
🚇 Green Park
🚌 Victoria
☎ **T** 020 7887 6023   **F** 020 7887 6100
@ info@lomond.uk.com
Market areas Executive Search

Website www.lomond.uk.com

UK Offices 3

REC Member No

Brief Description With three offices across the UK, Lomond Consulting specialises in placing experienced professionals in management positions for a wide range of clients from Mobile Telecoms to Technology.

Preferred method of contact Telephone for appointment

Minimum requirements Previous managerial exposure

Type of business Permanent

Grade/Level of Appointments Middle to Senior Management level

Longbridge International Plc

Head Office ✉ 6th Floor, 85 Gracechurch St, EC3V 0AA
⊖ Monument
🚊 Cannon St
☎ T 020 7208 5858   F 020 7208 5859
@ info@longbridge.com
Market areas Executive Search

Website www.longbridge.com

UK Offices 3

REC Member No

Brief Description Longbridge is a Human Capital consultancy offering a range of solutions to support the implementation of corporate strategic objectives. These solutions include Executive Search and Selection, Practice Mergers and Acquisitions, Personnel Development and Business Strategy.

Preferred method of contact Telephone for appointment

Minimum requirements Relevant management exposure

Type of business Permanent

Grade/Level of Appointments Senior level

Madison Maclean Group

Head Office ✉ Hamilton House, 1 Temple Avenue, EC4Y 0HA
⊖ Blackfriars
🚊 Blackfriars
☎ T 020 7489 2040   F 020 7489 2001
@ mail@madisonmaclean.com
Market areas Executive Search

Website www.madisonmaclean.com

UK Offices 1

REC Member No

Brief Description Madison Maclean Ltd is a specialist Search and Selection consultancy, founded in 1998 focusing on sourcing the highest calibre professionals for the Telecoms, Media, Investment Banking and Technology sectors.

Preferred method of contact Apply on line or telephone for an appointment

Minimum requirements Relevant Management Exposure

Type of business Permanent

Grade/Level of Appointments Middle to Senior Management level

Management Search Executive Ltd

Head Office ✉ 12 Harley St, W1G 9PG
⊖ Regent's Park
🚊 Marylebone
☎ T 020 7323 3506   F 020 7323 3505
@ search@mseltd.co.uk
Market areas Executive Search

Website www.mseltd.co.uk

UK Offices 1

REC Member Yes

Brief Description Specialists in the Hospitality industry who fully understand its diversities and complexities, Management Search Executive handle Senior Management positions on an exclusive basis.

Preferred method of contact Telephone for appointment

Minimum requirements Relevant Management Exposure

Type of business Permanent

Grade/Level of Appointments Senior Management level

Mansion House Executives Ltd

Head Office ✉ 78 Old Broad St, EC2M 1QP
⊖ Bank
🚊 Cannon St
☎ T 020 7496 3399   F 020 7496 3388
@ info@mansionhouse.co.uk
Market areas Executive Search

Website www.mansionhouse.co.uk

UK Offices 1

REC Member Yes

Brief Description Mansion House is a specialist Executive Search and Selection firm focusing on the General Insurance, Life, Pensions and Investment Markets, Insurers, Brokers, Consultancy Practices, Third Party Administrators, Bancassurers, Life Companies, IFAs and Corporations. Their clients are predominately UK based, however they also handle assignments for clients in Europe and worldwide. They have handled successful projects at executive level in the following areas: Chief Executive Officers, Underwriting and Broking, Sales, Marketing, Operations, HR, Compliance, Actuarial and Finance and Risk Management.

Preferred method of contact Apply on line or telephone for an appointment

Minimum requirements Relevant industry exposure

Type of business Permanent

Grade/Level of Appointments Middle to Senior Management level

Marshall Warburton

Head Office ✉ 5 St Johns Lane, EC1M 4BH
⊖ Farringdon

🚋 Farringdon
☎ T 020 7250 4710   F 020 7251 4648
@ info@marsh-warb.co.uk
Market areas Executive Search

Website www.marshallwarburton.co.uk

UK Offices 1

REC Member No

Brief Description Marshall Warburton is a successful and innovative recruitment organisation. Their principal areas of expertise are: Investment Banking, IT and Consumer Practice. The company was established with the aim of bridging the gap between the top traditional search firms and the 'City' agency recruiters. Marshall Warburton has established itself at the forefront of innovative recruiting solutions by establishing an on-line presence with www.doublecuff.com – a niche Financial Services Career Management website which has gained a reputation as a strong brand, synonymous with sector specific financial market positions.

Preferred method of contact Telephone for appointment

Minimum requirements Relevant Management Exposure

Type of business Permanent

Grade/Level of Appointments Senior level appointments

MBS Group

Head Office ✉ 3 Primrose Mews, Sharpleshall St, NW1 8YW
🚇 Chalk Farm
🚋 Kentish Town
☎ T 020 7722 1221
@ info@thembsgroup.co.uk
Market areas Executive Search

Website www.thembsgroup.co.uk

UK Offices 1

REC Member No

Brief Description Founded in 1987, MBS has evolved into a specialist Retail and Consumer Brands Executive Search practice bringing solutions through strategic people-power planning. A thorough knowledge of Retail and Brands, and an incisive approach to companies and individuals, has enabled this team to achieve a high level of client satisfaction. MBS Media was formed in 1999 to enable their clients to acquire key management and strategic skills for the new economy disciplines and propositions. Leveraging the expertise within their team, MBS Media has evolved into a multi-disciplinary area, successfully working with clients spanning the Media arena, including Telecommunications and Entertainment.

Preferred method of contact Telephone for appointment

Minimum requirements Relevant industry management exposure

Type of business Permanent

Grade/Level of Appointments Senior Management level

McCabe & Barton

Head Office ✉ 27 Austin Friars, EC2N 2AA
🚇 Bank
🚋 Cannon St
☎ T 020 7628 0704
@ info@mccabebarton.com
Market areas Executive Search

Website www.mccabebarton.com

UK Offices 1

REC Member No

Brief Description Based in the City, McCabe & Barton specialise in senior level IT recruitment for Financial Markets, Technology, Software Houses, placing key individuals in clients across the London market.

Preferred method of contact Telephone for appointment

Minimum requirements Senior level IT experience

Type of business Permanent

Grade/Level of Appointments Senior Analyst Programmer/ Technical Project Manager to Head of Finance and IT

Mellor Watts International

Head Office ✉ High Holborn House, 52–54 High Holborn, WC1V 6RL
🚇 Chancery Lane
🚋 City Thameslink
☎ T 020 7692 0500   F 020 7692 0501
@ info@mwi-uk.com
Market areas Executive Search

Website www.mwi-uk.com

UK Offices 1

REC Member No

Brief Description Mellor Watts International is an Executive Search firm with an enviable and formidable reputation within the Media, Entertainment and Marketing sectors. Their founding partners have 50 years combined Board-level experience in Media and Communications and are unique in the respect that they specialise solely within these markets.

Preferred method of contact Telephone for appointment

Minimum requirements Relevant Management Exposure

Type of business Permanent

Grade/Level of Appointments Middle/Senior Management to Board level

Menswear and Womenswear Executives

Head Office ✉ 207 Regent St, W1B 4ND
🚇 Oxford Circus
🚋 Charing Cross
☎ T 020 7434 2644   F 020 7434 1451

@ mwe@rossgroup.co.uk
Market areas Executive Search

Website www.rossgroup.co.uk
UK Offices 2
REC Member Yes
Brief Description Part of The Ross Group and established over 30 years, Menswear and Womanswear Executives are one of the world's leaders in Fashion Executive Search.
Preferred method of contact Telephone for appointment
Minimum requirements Previous professional experience
Type of business Permanent
Grade/Level of Appointments Senior level

Mercer Gray

Head Office ✉ 4th Floor, Venture House, 27–29 Glasshouse St, W1R 5RG
🚇 Piccadilly Circus
🚆 Charing Cross
☎ T 020 7494 6622   F 020 7494 6633
@ executive@mercergray.co.uk
Market areas Executive Search

Website www.mercergray.co.uk
UK Offices 1
REC Member No
Brief Description Mercer Gray is a leading IT recruitment services company operating across a range of business sectors. Employing a variety of Search and Selection techniques they provide high-quality, proactive and client-focused solutions to Public and Private Sector organisations, both in the UK and abroad.
Preferred method of contact Telephone for appointment
Minimum requirements Relevant systems exposure
Type of business Permanent
Grade/Level of Appointments Sales Consultant/Business Analyst to IT Manager/Head of IT

MGM International

✉ New Premier House, 150 Southampton Row, WC1B 5AL
🚇 Holborn
🚆 City Thameslink
☎ T 020 7278 7500   F 020 7278 7600
@ info@mgmint.com
Market areas Executive Search

Website www.mgmint.com
UK Offices 3
REC Member No
Head Office West Yorkshire

Brief Description MGM International specialise in using Executive Search methods to attract the highest calibre personnel for a range of clients ranging from IT and Telecoms to FMCG and Finance Markets for blue chip and international organisations.
Preferred method of contact Telephone for an appointment
Minimum requirements Senior Management exposure
Type of business Permanent
Grade/Level of Appointments Senior level appointments

Michael Lamb Associates

Head Office ✉ 25 Carnaby St, W1F 7DE
🚇 Oxford Circus
🚆 Charing Cross
☎ T 020 7734 8111   F 020 7287 8568
@ recruit@mlamichaellamb.com
Market areas Executive Search

Website www.mlamichaellamb.com
UK Offices 1
REC Member No
Brief Description Michael Lamb Associates was founded in 1989. They provide a professional recruitment service to the Property sector throughout the UK and Europe, taking time and effort to fully understand the organisations and individuals they assist, with the aim of bringing the mutual objectives of both parties together. There are two divisions within the company: Michael Lamb Associates and MLA Recruitment. Michael Lamb Associates has a reputation as a market leader in the fields of Executive Search and Advertised Selection for individual retained assignments. Retained clients include Property Consultancies, Development and Investment Companies, Banks, Institutions, Funds and Management Consultancies. Assignments cover the spectrum of Property disciplines, typically in the Commercial sector.
Preferred method of contact Apply on line or telephone for an appointment
Minimum requirements Relevant industry exposure
Type of business Permanent
Grade/Level of Appointments Surveyors and Property professionals at all levels

Michael William Associates td

Head Office ✉ 6 Cochrane House, Admirals Way, E1 9UD
🚇 South Quay
🚆 Limehouse
☎ T 020 7538 0097   F 020 7538 4569
@ mwa@mwa-ltd.co.uk
Market areas Executive Search

Website www.mwa-ltd.com
UK Offices 1

REC Member No

Brief Description Michael Williams Associates are a leading niche Financial Executive Search firm. Initiated in 1992, the firm has built its foundations on providing a highly professional, innovative and efficient recruitment service to become an industry leader. They have dedicated themselves to the Foreign Exchange Market sector.

Preferred method of contact Apply on line or telephone for an appointment

Minimum requirements Relevant industry exposure

Type of business Permanent

Grade/Level of Appointments Senior level appointments

Michelangelo Associates

Head Office ⊠ Austin Friars House, 2—6 Austin Friars, EC2N 2HD
⊖ Bank
🚇 Cannon St
☎ T 020 7456 6999   F 020 7456 6925
@ search@michelangelo.co.uk
Market areas Executive Search

Website www.michelangelo.co.uk

UK Offices 1

REC Member No

Brief Description Michelangelo Associates, international Search, Selection and Recruitment specialists, have a proven track record in the placement of key personnel which extends throughout Europe and the major financial centres worldwide.

Preferred method of contact Apply on line or telephone for an appointment

Minimum requirements Relevant industry exposure

Type of business Permanent

Grade/Level of Appointments Across all levels

The Miles Partnership

Head Office ⊠ Rotherwick House, 19—21 Old Bond St, W1S 4PX
⊖ Green Park
🚇 Victoria
☎ T 020 7495 7772   F 020 7495 7773
@ postbox@miles-partnership.com
Market areas Executive Search

Website www.miles-partnership.com

UK Offices 1

REC Member No

Brief Description The Miles Partnership provides Executive Search services to UK and international clients across a range of sectors. The firm comprises four partners and is supported by an outstanding research team. The Miles Partnership works at the highest levels of industry, recruiting Chairmen, Chief Executive Officers, Directors as well as Non-Executive Directors, and their clients include many of the world's most successful companies.

Preferred method of contact Telephone for appointment

Minimum requirements Senior managerial exposure

Type of business Permanent

Grade/Level of Appointments Senior level appointments

Mineral Ltd

Head Office ⊠ Zetland House, 5—25 Scrutton St, EC2A 4HG
⊖ Liverpool St
🚇 Liverpool St
☎ T 020 7729 8771   F 020 7729 0771
Market areas Executive Search

Website www.mineral-resourcing.co.uk

UK Offices 1

REC Member No

Brief Description Mineral Ltd was established to provide quality Search and Selection solutions to the Business Consulting and Leading Edge Technology communities. Employing only experienced consultants with proven track records of delivery has, in combination with a proactive and rigorous approach to candidate sourcing, allowed Mineral to establish an enviable list of clients in a short period of time.

Preferred method of contact Apply on line or telephone for an appointment

Minimum requirements None

Type of business Contract and Permanent

Grade/Level of Appointments All levels

Morgan Hunt

Head Office ⊠ 172 Drury Lane, WC2B 5QR
⊖ Covent Garden
🚇 Charing Cross
☎ T 020 7419 8900   F 020 7419 8999
@ morgan.hunt@morganhunt.com
Market areas Executive Search

Website www.morganhunt.com

UK Offices 1

REC Member Yes

Brief Description Morgan Hunt was established in 1994 and provides an Executive Recruitment service specifically aimed at the Financial sector.

Preferred method of contact Telephone for appointment

Minimum requirements Relevant industry exposure

Type of business Permanent

Grade/Level of Appointments Middle to Senior Management level

Networking People

Head Office ✉ Cambridge House, 373–375 Euston Rd, NW1 3AR
⊖ Euston Sq
🚇 Euston
☎ T 020 7953 0000   F 020 7953 0001
@ enquiries@npuk.com
Market areas Executive Search

Website www.npuk.com

UK Offices 1

REC Member Yes

Brief Description Networking People was established in 1998. They understand that in the new economy, an ambitious company's life is focused on winning the race for market leadership and capitalisation. They understand that with the right teams of IT people, expanding firms gain critical competitive edge, allowing them to scale rapidly to market-defining levels, realising their corporate vision. They partner hyper-growth technology firms at venture capital stage(s) and multinational conglomerates, innovating and delivering creative resource solutions for the supply of high demand and emerging technology specialists.

Preferred method of contact Apply on line or telephone for an appointment

Minimum requirements Previous professional experience

Type of business Permanent

Grade/Level of Appointments All levels

Next Generation IT Recruitment

Head Office ✉ 22a Theobalds Rd, WC1X 8PF
⊖ Chancery Lane
🚇 City Thameslink
☎ T 020 7253 0101   F 020 7553 3979
@ info@nextgen-it.com
Market areas Executive Search

Website www.nextgen-it.com

UK Offices 2

REC Member No

Brief Description Next Generation IT Recruitment are a venture capital backed recruitment organisation providing global resource solutions for its clients. Through the ongoing diversification within the industry, Next Generation has realised the need to be a total resource provider. Their services include High-level Search and Selection, Managed Resource, Retained Services, and Flexible Resource. All of which are delivered through specialist consultants using their leading edge ASP database solution.

Preferred method of contact Telephone for appointment

Minimum requirements Previous professional experience

Type of business Contract and Permanent

Grade/Level of Appointments All levels

NMC-Ennismore Partnership Ltd

✉ 48–50 Mortimer St, W1N 7DG
⊖ Oxford Circus
🚇 Charing Cross
☎ T 020 7436 7667   F 020 7436 7677
@ london@nijsse-international.com
Market areas Executive Search

Website www.nijsse-international.com

UK Offices 1

REC Member No

Head Office Netherlands

Brief Description Founded in The Netherlands in 1983, NMC-Nijsse International Executive Search has grown to become one of the leading Executive Search companies in Europe. It has offices in Amsterdam, Brussels, Frankfurt, Lisbon, London, Madrid, Milan, Paris and Zurich and works through affiliated offices in Scandinavia and Eastern Europe.

Preferred method of contact Apply on line or telephone for appointment

Minimum requirements Previous professional experience

Type of business Permanent

Grade/Level of Appointments Senior level

Norman Broadbent

Head Office ✉ 20 Regent St, SW1Y 4PH
⊖ Piccadilly Circus
🚇 Charing Cross
☎ T 020 7484 0000   F 020 7484 0001
@ enquiries@normanbroadbent.com
Market areas Executive Search

Website www.normanbroadbent.com

UK Offices 6

REC Member Yes

Brief Description Norman Broadbent are one of the world's leading recruitment consultancies, experts in Executive Recruitment. They work in partnership with leading and emerging companies in many different fields, helping them attract, recruit and retain the key individuals who will drive their future growth.

Preferred method of contact Apply on line or telephone for an appointment

Minimum requirements Previous professional experience

Type of business Permanent

Grade/Level of Appointments All levels

Odgers Ray & Berndtson

Head Office ✉ 11–12 Hanover Sq, W1S 1JJ
⊖ Oxford Circus
🚇 Charing Cross
☎ T 020 7529 1111   F 020 7529 1000
@ info@ray-berndtson.co.uk
Market areas Executive Search

✉ 16 St Martin's le Grand, EC1A 4N
⊖ St Pauls
🚇 City Thameslink
☎ T 020 7397 8600   F 020 7397 8601
@ info@ray-berndtson.co.uk
Market areas Executive Search

Website www.odgers.com
UK Offices 5
REC Member Yes
Brief Description Recruitment has significant impact on a company's success. Odgers Ray & Berndtson recruits people who help their clients to excel. As the only privately owned major Search business in the UK, they offer successful recruitment solutions across a wide range of sectors. They are determined to be the best Executive Recruitment firm in their chosen markets. Their work is creative, rigorous and comprehensive and their clients benefit from the market intelligence which good Search creates.

Preferred method of contact Telephone for appointment
Minimum requirements Previous professional experience
Type of business Permanent
Grade/Level of Appointments Senior level

Options Group

✉ 27 Hanson St, W1W 6TR
⊖ Goodge St
🚇 Euston
☎ T 020 7909 1900   F 020 7909 1901
@ ccusack@optionsgroup.com
Market areas Executive Search

Website www.optionsgroup.com
UK Offices 1
REC Member No
Head Office USA
Brief Description The Options Group is a global Executive Search firm with offices strategically positioned in many of the world's leading business and financial centres. Founded in 1992, the Options Group has rapidly grown to become one of the leading 100 Executive Recruitment firms worldwide. Their cross border focus, dedicated team of industry and research specialists and cutting-edge technological platform provide them a distinct advantage over competition. The Options Group has built a global network of partnerships across the world's financial markets and with Fortune 500 companies in many of the major growth industries.

Preferred method of contact Apply on line or telephone for an appointment
Minimum requirements Previous professional experience
Type of business Permanent
Grade/Level of Appointments Mid to Senior Management level

Options Search & Selection

Head Office ✉ 20 King St, EC2V 8EG
⊖ Mansion House
🚇 Cannon St
☎ T 020 7600 8008   F 020 7600 8699
@ london@optionssearch.com
Market areas Executive Search

Website www.optionssearch.com
UK Offices 2
REC Member No
Brief Description Established since 1990, Options Search & Selection have over a decade of expertise in providing bespoke recruitment solutions nationwide for a wide range of Financial Service companies. Their specialist divisions concentrate on Compliance, Training, Broker Consultants, Marketing, IFA and Administration positions and their aim is to provide unparalleled standards of the highest level.

Preferred method of contact Telephone for appointment
Minimum requirements Previous professional experience
Type of business Permanent
Grade/Level of Appointments All levels

Oxygen Executive Search

Head Office ✉ Marble Arch Tower, 55 Bryanston St, W1H 7AA
⊖ Marble Arch
🚇 Paddington
☎ T 020 7905 7123   F 020 7905 7111
@ info@oxygenpeople.com
Market areas Executive Search

Website www.oxygenpeople.com
UK Offices 1
REC Member No
Brief Description Oxygen was founded by Ian Lloyd, Emily Heller (both ex-Odgers), joined later by Valerie Fairbank (from CCG). All three have extensive Search experience, working with clients across a wide range of industry sectors, both in the UK and internationally. The Oxygen team now includes experienced Consultants with a variety of sector specialisations, supported by an excellent Research team. In an overcrowded recruitment marketplace, Oxygen is focused on Senior Management roles in the 'marzipan layer', i.e. Executives in the £100,000–£250,000 salary range, and Non-Executive Directors for small and medium-sized businesses. Oxygen's philosophy is based on

quality, professionalism, personal service and direct involvement of a Partner or Senior Consultant in each assignment.

Preferred method of contact Telephone for appointment

Minimum requirements Previous professional experience

Type of business Permanent

Grade/Level of Appointments Senior level

Personnel Resources Recruitment Ltd

Head Office ✉ 75 Grays Inn Rd, WC1X 8US
🚇 Chancery Lane
🚊 City Thameslink
☎ T 020 7242 6321   F 020 7831 7121
@ mail@personnelresources.co.uk
Market areas Executive Search

Website www.personnelresources.co.uk

UK Offices 1

REC Member No

Brief Description Since 1988, Personnel Resources has provided a market-leading Executive Recruitment service for Market Research professionals of all levels and disciplines. This position is achieved from a specialist consultant team with first-hand market sector knowledge plus painstaking attention to providing a high-quality and discreet service backed by unparalleled access to the widest range of applicants and unadvertised opportunities.

Preferred method of contact Apply on line or telephone for an appointment

Minimum requirements None

Type of business Permanent

Grade/Level of Appointments Graduate to Director level

Praxis

✉ 1 Hay Hill, Berkeley Sq, W1X 7LF
🚇 Green Park
🚊 Victoria
☎ T 020 7495 2442   F 020 7409 2557
@ info@praxisinterim.com
Market areas Executive Search

Website www.praxisinterim.com

UK Offices 5

REC Member No

Head Office Birmingham

Brief Description Praxis is a subsidiary of Professional Staff plc, a NASDAQ quoted group providing temporary and permanent Executive staffing to the Science, Technology and Management sectors. Established in 1989, Praxis was a pioneer of Interim Management in the UK. The growth of Praxis has mirrored the expansion of the market as a whole. Today they are one of the leading specialist providers of professional Interim Managers to Industry, Commerce and the

Professions. They are proud to count many top national and multinational organisations among their clients.

Preferred method of contact Apply on line or telephone for an appointment

Minimum requirements Relevant management exposure

Type of business Interim and Permanent

Grade/Level of Appointments All levels

Premmit Associates Ltd

Head Office ✉ 33 Eccleston Sq, SW1V 1PB
🚇 Victoria
🚊 Victoria
☎ T 020 7834 7253   F 020 7834 3544
@ info@premmit.com
Market areas Executive Search

Website www.premmit.co.uk

UK Offices 1

REC Member No

Brief Description Premmit Associates Ltd is a London-based Executive Search and Selection consultancy firm targeting Top and Middle Management in all the major management functions: ie General Management, Sales and Marketing, Finance, Production, Personnel and specifically Engineering. Premmit Associates pride themselves on quality and the efficient provision of experienced professionals to meet even the most specialised requirements, anywhere in the world.

Preferred method of contact Apply on line or telephone for an appointment

Minimum requirements Previous professional experience

Type of business Permanent

Grade/Level of Appointments Mid to Senior Management level

Prime Executive

Head Office ✉ 11 Blomfield St, EC2M 7AY
🚇 Holborn
🚊 City Thameslink
☎ T 020 7588 0174   F 020 7638 8421
@ executive@primeuk.com
Market areas Executive Search

Website www.primeuk.com

UK Offices 1

REC Member No

Brief Description Part of the Prime Personnel Group, Prime Executive was established in 1995 in order to provide a more complete recruitment service with the addition of a Search and Selection capability. Since its inception Prime Executive has established a reputation for providing one of the leading services in its specialist markets. Operating in complementary areas such as Project and Structured Finance together with senior Banking and Accountancy positions, Prime Executive is ideally placed to not only create its own niche position but also build upon the excellent reputation and relationships gained by Prime Personnel over its 30 year history.

Preferred method of contact Apply on line or telephone for an appointment

Minimum requirements Previous professional experience

Type of business Permanent

Grade/Level of Appointments All levels

Project Partners Ltd

Head Office 6 Laurence Pountney Hill, EC4R OBL
⊖ Cannon St
🚇 Cannon St
☎ T 020 7929 1800   F 020 7929 1200
@ enquiries@projpartners.com
Market areas Executive Search

Website www.projpartners.com

UK Offices 1

REC Member No

Brief Description Project Partners is an Executive Search consultancy specialising in IT recruitment exclusively to Investment Banking and Asset Management sectors.

Preferred method of contact Telephone for appointment

Minimum requirements Previous professional experience

Type of business Permanent

Grade/Level of Appointments Mid to Senior Management level

Prospect

Head Office 3rd Floor, Charles House, 7 Leicester Place, WC2H 7BY
⊖ Leicester Sq
🚇 Charing Cross
☎ T 020 7439 1919   F 020 7437 1791
@ info@prospectmsl.com
Market areas Executive Search

Website www.prospectmsl.com

UK Offices 1

REC Member No

Brief Description Prospect are specialists in Digital Technology and New Media.

Preferred method of contact Telephone for appointment

Minimum requirements Previous professional experience

Type of business Permanent

Grade/Level of Appointments All levels

Questor International Ltd

Head Office ✉ Liberty House, 222 Regent St, W1B 5TR
⊖ Oxford Circus
🚇 Charing Cross
☎ T 020 7297 2001   F 020 7297 2101
@ info@questorint.com
Market areas Executive Search

Website www.questorint.com

UK Offices 1

REC Member No

Brief Description Founded in 1996, Questor International are a Generalist practice working across all industry sectors and functional remits. Organisational success depends on the skills and teamwork of the workforce. Questor works in partnership with its clients to identify the core skills essential to any given role and ensure that these criteria are rigorously applied throughout the recruitment exercise. They care about success, so they build honest, informal and productive relationships at every level of their business.

Preferred method of contact Apply on line or telephone for an appointment

Minimum requirements Previous professional experience

Type of business Permanent

Grade/Level of Appointments All levels

Quorum International Search Ltd

Head Office ✉ 19–21 Grosvenor Gardens, SW1W OEB
⊖ Victoria
🚇 Victoria
☎ T 020 7630 6400
@ uk@qisearch.com
Market areas Executive Search

Website www.qisearch.com

UK Offices 1

REC Member No

Brief Description Established in 1997, Quorum International is a specialist Executive Search company delivering accelerated solutions for acquiring human capital through the acquisition of teams and executives. Their team is a select group of the best researchers, consultants, and account managers in the industry. With offices in London, Paris, Munich, Amsterdam, Stockholm, Milan and Madrid, they provide extensive reach and unparalleled market research within Europe's Technology, Telecommunications and Consulting marketplace. Quorum's seven geographic locations allow them to manage and accelerate the delivery of major local, national, or Pan-European projects.

Preferred method of contact Telephone for appointment

Minimum requirements Previous professional experience

Type of business Permanent

Grade/Level of Appointments Mid to Senior Management level

Reed Technology Group

Head Office ✉ Reed Executive Plc, 145 Kensington High St, W8 7LP
         C T 020 7313 7450 F 020 7313 7451

         ✉ 6th Floor, Fairgate House, 78 New Oxford St,
           WC1A 1HB
         ⊖ Holborn
         🚊 City Thameslink
         C T 020 7255 2882

Market areas Executive Search, IT

Website www.reed.co.uk

UK Offices 250+

REC Member No

Brief Description A subsidiary of Reed Executive Plc established in 1960, Reed's growth has been dramatic and the company's stated ambition is to grow the business substantially. Reed has been organised into a number of separate operating companies to make this happen. Reed Technology Group is the IT specialist division of Reed. It comprises three operating divisions containing dedicated teams specialising in Computing, Telecoms, Datacoms and New Media.

Preferred method of contact Apply on line or telephone for an appointment

Minimum requirements Previous professional experience

Type of business Permanent

Grade/Level of Appointments All levels

Renoir Partners

Head Office ✉ 93–95 Wigmore St, W1U 1QW
         ⊖ Bond St
         🚊 Paddington
         C T 020 7224 1900 F 020 7317 2872
         @ info@renoirpartners.com

Market areas Executive Search

Website www.renoirpartners.com

UK Offices 1

REC Member No

Brief Description Renoir Partners specialise in placing Chief Executive Officers, Board Directors and Senior Level Executives into Early Stage Technology companies in Europe, North America and Asia. Their approach is based on understanding and responding quickly and effectively to their clients' strategic needs. It's a true partnership approach. Their people have decades of experience working with business leaders from a broad spectrum of Technology companies around the world, both large and small and bring a wealth of strategic insight to the table.

Preferred method of contact Telephone for appointment

Minimum requirements Previous professional experience

Type of business Permanent

Grade/Level of Appointments Senior level

Retail Executives

Head Office ✉ 207 Regent St, W1B 4ND
         ⊖ Oxford Circus
         🚊 Charing Cross
         C T 020 7434 4448 F 020 7434 1451
         @ retailexecs@rossgroup.co.uk

Market areas Executive Search

Website www.rossgroup.co.uk

UK Offices 2

REC Member Yes

Brief Description Part of The Ross Group, Retail Executives have been established for over 30 years and during this time have placed some of the most prominent and illustrious names in the industry.

Preferred method of contact Telephone for appointment

Minimum requirements Previous professional experience

Type of business Permanent

Grade/Level of Appointments Senior level

Rice & Dore Associates

Head Office ✉ 33 Great St Helen's, EC3A 6AP
         ⊖ Bank
         🚊 Cannon St
         C T 020 7070 9000 F 020 70170 9001
         @ enquiries@riceanddore.com

Market areas Executive Search

Website www.riceanddore.com

UK Offices 1

REC Member No

Brief Description Rice & Dore Associates works on a retainer basis with a select number of the world's leading Investment Banks and Asset Management companies.

Preferred method of contact Apply on line or telephone for an appointment

Minimum requirements Previous professional experience

Type of business Permanent

Grade/Level of Appointments Mid to Senior Management level

Richmond & Co

See **Accountancy and Banking, page 25**

Roger Steare Consulting Ltd

Head Office   ✉   46 Aldgate High St, EC3N 1AL
  ⊖   Aldgate
  🚊   Fenchurch St
  ☎   T 020 7744 7788   F 020 7744 7789
  @   roger.steare@rogersteare.com

Market areas   Executive Search

Website   www.rogersteare.com

UK Offices   1

REC Member   Yes

Brief Description   Roger Steare Consulting has developed an approach to Executive Search and Selection which gives clients the benefits of positive employer branding; quality research; effective advertising; rigorous assessment and selection; induction coaching and an innovative, equitable fee structure.

Preferred method of contact   Telephone for appointment

Minimum requirements   Previous professional experience

Type of business   Permanent

Grade/Level of Appointments   All levels

Russell Jones Associates

Head Office   ✉   Broadgate Ct, 199 Bishopsgate, EC2M 3TY
  ⊖   Liverpool St
  🚊   Liverpool St
  ☎   T 020 7814 7955   F 020 7814 6609
  @   info@russell-jones.co.uk

Market areas   Executive Search

Website   www.russell-jones.co.uk

UK Offices   1

REC Member   No

Brief Description   Russell Jones Associates are a Search and Selection consultancy providing recruitment solutions to the Global Financial Markets. Areas of specialty include: Investment Banking, Corporate Finance, Mergers and Acquisitions, High Yield/Leverage Finance, Securitisation Law, Banking, International Capital Markets, IT, Trading, Risk Management, e-Commerce, Management Consultancy. Their client base includes a select number of market leaders within the Investment Banking, Legal and Management Consultancy arenas.

Preferred method of contact   Apply on line or telephone for an appointment

Minimum requirements   Relevant management exposure

Type of business   Permanent

Grade/Level of Appointments   Senior level appointments

Russell Reynolds Associates

Head Office   ✉   24 St James's Sq, SW1Y 4HZ
  ⊖   St James's Park
  🚊   Victoria
  ☎   T 020 7839 7788   F 020 7839 9395
  @   info@russellreynolds.com

Market areas   Executive Search

Website   www.russellreynolds.com

UK Offices   1

REC Member   Yes

Brief Description   Founded in 1969, Russell Reynolds Associates is a global Executive Recruitment and Management Assessment firm that delivers solutions to organisational challenges through the recruitment of exceptional leaders. Based in 32 wholly owned offices, their associates work in more than 40 practice areas to provide specialised industry and functional expertise to clients in major markets around the world.

Preferred method of contact   Apply on line or telephone for an appointment

Minimum requirements   Senior managerial exposure

Type of business   Permanent

Grade/Level of Appointments   Senior level appointments

Ruston Poole International

Head Office   ✉   Cording House, 34 St James's St, SW1A 1HD
  ⊖   Green Park
  🚊   Victoria
  ☎   T 020 7930 3001   F 020 7930 3002
  @   search@rustonpoole.com

Market areas   Executive Search

Website   www.rustonpoole.com

UK Offices   1

REC Member   No

Brief Description   Ruston Poole International plc is one of Europe's leading Executive Search groups, specialising in recruiting Senior Management for the international Healthcare, Pharmaceutical and Bioscience industries. They work across borders throughout Europe and through associates and affiliates in North America and the Pacific Rim.

Preferred method of contact   Apply on line or telephone for an appointment

Minimum requirements   Senior managerial exposure

Type of business   Permanent

Grade/Level of Appointments   Senior level appointments

Sabre International Search

Head Office ✉ 19 Mansion Mews, SW7 5AF
⊖ South Kensington
🚊 Victoria
📞 T 020 7835 0600 F 020 7835 0548
@ xel@sabresearch.com
Market areas Executive Search

Website www.sabresearch.com
UK Offices 1
REC Member No
Brief Description Established in 1969, Sabre International Search specialises in placing Middle and Senior level Executives into a range of clients from FMCG, Marketing, Oil and Gas, IT, Retail, Engineering and Financial Services.
Preferred method of contact Telephone for appointment
Minimum requirements Relevant Management Exposure
Type of business Contract and Permanent
Grade/Level of Appointments Mid to Senior Management level

Sammons Associates

✉ 7–8 Philpot Lane, EC3M 8AA
⊖ Monument
🚊 Cannon St
📞 T 020 7398 2400
Market areas Executive Search

Website www.sammons.co.uk
UK Offices 1
REC Member Yes
Head Office Hastings
Brief Description Part of the Sammon Group, Sammons Associates is an Executive Search consultancy which helps leading Banks, Security Houses and Financial Institutions to find and recruit the best qualified senior staff in key areas, including Equity Analysis and Sales, Fixed Income, Foreign Exchange, Treasury and Derivatives Sales, Fund Management, Compliance and Risk Management. Their executive team operates in the UK and overseas.
Preferred method of contact Apply on line or telephone for an appointment
Minimum requirements Previous professional experience
Type of business Permanent
Grade/Level of Appointments Senior level

Sequoia Consulting Ltd

Head Office ✉ Bradstock House, 52–53 Russell Sq, WC1B
⊖ Russell Sq
🚊 Kings Cross

📞 T 020 7580 2553 F 020 7580 2771
Market areas Executive Search

Website www.sequoiaconsulting.co.uk
UK Offices 1
REC Member No
Brief Description Sequoia Consulting Ltd is a specialist Financial Markets Search and Recruitment firm based in London.
Preferred method of contact Apply on line or telephone for an appointment
Minimum requirements Relevant industry exposure
Type of business Permanent
Grade/Level of Appointments All levels

Sheffield Haworth

Head Office ✉ 36 Queen St, EC4R 1BN
⊖ Mansion House
🚊 Cannon St
📞 T 020 7236 2400 F 020 7236 0316
@ postmaster@sheffield-haworth.com
Market areas Executive Search

Website www.sheffield-haworth.com
UK Offices 1
REC Member Yes
Brief Description Established in 1993, Sheffield Haworth is now one of the leading Financial Executive Search consultancies in the UK and overseas, employing over 50 professionals in three regional offices, and with a client list that includes a significant number of leading global Financial Services companies. The sectors in which they specialise include Equities/Equity Capital Markets, Fixed Income/Debt Capital Markets, Treasury, Foreign Exchange, Derivatives, Corporate Finance, Private Equity, Wealth and Asset Management, IT, Infrastructure, Legal, Structured and Asset Finance, Project Finance and Private Banking.
Preferred method of contact Apply on line or telephone for an appointment
Minimum requirements Relevant industry exposure
Type of business Permanent
Grade/Level of Appointments Mid to Senior Management level

Skillcapital

Head Office ✉ 1 Angel Ct, EC2R 7HJ
⊖ Bank
🚊 Cannon St
📞 T 020 7762 0000 F 020 7762 0011
@ enquiries@skillcapital.com
Market areas Executive Search

Website www.skillcapital.com

UK Offices 1

REC Member No

Brief Description Skillcapital is a boutique Executive Search firm focusing on the recruitment of Chief Executive Officer and Executive Board level management for Private Equity and Venture Capital backed companies. They also recruit senior level Investment professionals into these funds.

Preferred method of contact Apply on line or telephone for an appointment

Minimum requirements Relevant senior level exposure

Type of business Permanent

Grade/Level of Appointments Senior Chief Executive Officer and Executive Board level Management

Southwestern Business Resources

✉ 1st Floor, Cloister Ct, 22–26 Farringdon Lane, EC1R 3AJ

⊖ Farringdon

🚇 Farringdon

☎ T 020 7253 1441   F 020 7253 1551

Market areas Executive Search

Website www.sbreurope.com

UK Offices 1

REC Member Yes

Head Office USA

Brief Description Established in 1982, Southwestern Business Resources is a privately held full-service Executive Search firm that works internationally through offices and recruiters located throughout the United States, the United Kingdom, and Latin America.

Preferred method of contact Apply on line or telephone for an appointment

Minimum requirements Previous professional experience

Type of business Permanent

Grade/Level of Appointments All levels

Spencer Stuart Ltd

✉ 16 Connaught Place, W2 2ED

⊖ Marble Arch

🚇 Paddington

☎ T 020 7298 3333   F 020 7298 3388

@ sfenton@spencerstuart.com

Market areas Executive Search

Website www.spencerstuart.com

UK Offices 3

REC Member No

Head Office Chicago, USA

Brief Description Spencer Stuart is a leading Management Consulting firm specialising in senior-level Executive Search and Board Director appointments. For 45 years, they have been at the forefront of their industry, creating a blend of Management Consulting and Executive Search that is best described as executive talent management and is focused on the long term success of their clients. It is a global company whose core practice has reached 52 offices in 25 countries since its founding.

Preferred method of contact Apply on line or telephone for an appointment

Minimum requirements Relevant senior managerial exposure

Type of business Permanent

Grade/Level of Appointments Senior level

Springman Tipper Campbell Partnership

Head Office ✉ Bond St House, 14 Clifford St, W1X 1RE

⊖ Piccadilly Circus

🚇 Charing Cross

☎ T 020 7499 9892   F 020 7499 7546

@ stcp@stcp.co.uk

Market areas Executive Search

Website www.stcp.co.uk

UK Offices 1

REC Member Yes

Brief Description S+T+C+P Partnership is the UK member firm of USP (United Search Partners), a partnership of independent firms in 16 international locations, dedicated to clients whose operations span countries and markets across the world. USP is a worldwide resource of experienced Search professionals, united by shared values and the same rigorous approach to handling high-level Executive Search assignments.

Preferred method of contact Telephone for appointment

Minimum requirements Senior level Management exposure

Type of business Permanent

Grade/Level of Appointments Senior level

Stanford Resourcing Ltd

Head Office ✉ 33 Throgmorton St, EC2N 2BR

⊖ Bank

🚇 Cannon St

☎ T 020 7397 3388   F 020 7397 3389

@ joepacelli@stanfordresourcing.com

Market areas Executive Search

Website www.stanfordresourcing.com

UK Offices 1

REC Member No

Brief Description Stanford Resourcing is an international Search consultancy specialising in the recruitment of Lawyers. Their clients include some of the leading names within Private Practice (both UK and US Law firms) and Investment Banking. During the last 12 month period, their consultants have conducted searches in London, Paris, Hong Kong, Singapore, Tokyo, New York and Sydney.

Preferred method of contact Telephone for appointment

Minimum requirements Qualified Lawyers only

Type of business Permanent

Grade/Level of Appointments All levels

Star Executives

Head Office ✉ 7 Fitzroy Mews, W1T 6DQ
⊖ Warren St
🚇 Euston
☎ T 020 7387 6969   F 020 7387 6999
@ info@starexecutives.com
Market areas   Executive Search

Website www.starexecutives.com

UK Offices 1

REC Member Yes

Brief Description Based in the West End, Star Executive Search and Selection specialise in placing middle to senior level Executives across a broad range of industries.

Preferred method of contact Apply on line or telephone for an appointment

Minimum requirements None

Type of business Permanent

Grade/Level of Appointments Mid to Senior Management level

Technology Project Services

See **Technical, page 270**

Tempest Search & Selection Ltd

Head Office ✉ 60 Neal St, WC2H 9PA
⊖ Covent Garden
🚇 Charing Cross
☎ T 020 7379 6011   F 020 7379 6013
@ info@tempest-uk.com
Market areas   Executive Search

Website www.tempest-uk.com

UK Offices 2

REC Member No

Brief Description Tempest Search & Selection Ltd was established in 1994, primarily to meet the requirements of clients for an integrated consultancy service. They concentrate on Project Management, Construction Management, Management

Consultancies and Senior Professionals within the Construction and Property industry.

Preferred method of contact Apply on line or telephone for an appointment

Minimum requirements Relevant industry exposure

Type of business Permanent

Grade/Level of Appointments Mid to Senior Management level

TFPL Ltd

See **Media, page 205**

Thomas Telford Recruitment Consultants

Head Office ✉ Thomas Telford House, 1 Heron Quay, E14 4JA
⊖ Canary Wharf
🚇 Limehouse
☎ T 020 7665 2464
Market areas   Executive Search

Website www.thomastelford.com

UK Offices 1

REC Member Yes

Brief Description Thomas Telford Recruitment is the leading recruitment consultancy specialising in the Construction, Process and Energy sectors, to which it supplies principally Civil and Chemical Engineers, including Technician grades. They provide a full range of recruitment services including Database Search, Executive Search, Executive Selection and Placement of contract staff. Thomas Telford Recruitment is the official recruitment consultancy of the Institution of Civil Engineers.

Preferred method of contact Apply on line or telephone for an appointment

Minimum requirements None

Type of business Permanent

Grade/Level of Appointments All levels

Thorburn Geiger Group

Head Office ✉ 6 Broad St Place, EC2M 7JH
⊖ Moorgate
🚇 Moorgate
☎ T 020 7628 2299   F 020 7628 1199
@ london@thorburngeiger.com
Market areas   Executive Search

Website www.thorburngeiger.com

UK Offices 2

REC Member No

Brief Description Thorburn Geiger are international Management Consultants operating from a control base in Switzerland with consultants strategically located throughout Europe, the USA and worldwide. The company's activities are soundly based on over 25 years experience spanning a wide range of market sectors and multinational businesses. Thorburn Geiger can provide objective, fresh ideas, Strategic Plans, Training, Implementation, Executive Search and Recruitment, temporary Executive Assistance and Board Members in any discipline on a contract basis.

Preferred method of contact Apply on line or telephone for an appointment

Minimum requirements Relevant Management Exposure

Type of business Temporary and Permanent

Grade/Level of Appointments Senior level appointments

TMP Worldwide Executive Search

Head Office ✉ Chancery House, 53–64 Chancery Lane, WC2A 1QU
C T 020 7406 5000

✉ The Adelphi, 12th Floor, 1–11 John Adam St, WC2N 6HT
⊖ Charing Cross
🚇 Charing Cross
C T 020 7451 9400   F 020 7451 9401
Market areas Executive Search

Website www.tmp.com

UK Offices 30+

REC Member No

Brief Description Human capital has become the most critical component of any organisation. Meeting these challenges off- and online is TMP Worldwide, an interactive company with a unique suite of Global Career Solutions and a client base that includes more than 90 of the Fortune 100 and more than 490 of the Fortune 500. Expertise in this area is one reason why TMP is the largest recruitment advertising agency in the world. They sell, market, and brand employers to talent on a global scale. This is accomplished through product offerings such as: Media Research/Planning/Buying, Strategic Hiring Plans, Creative Services, On-campus Recruiting, the Web-based Intern Center, and Interactive.

Preferred method of contact Apply on line or telephone for an appointment

Minimum requirements Previous professional experience

Type of business Temporary and Permanent

Grade/Level of Appointments All levels

Torus Partnership

Head Office ✉ 150 Minories, EC3N 1LS
⊖ Aldgate
🚇 Fenchurch St
C T 020 7264 2112   F 020 7265 0736
Market areas Executive Search

Website www.toruspartnership.com

UK Offices 1

REC Member No

Brief Description Torus Partnership specialise in using Search methods to attract the highest calibre professionals within the Financial Services sector for clients across London.

Preferred method of contact Apply on line or telephone for an appointment

Minimum requirements Senior managerial exposure

Type of business Permanent

Grade/Level of Appointments Senior level appointments

Veredus Executive Resourcing

Head Office ✉ Plumtree Ct, EC4A 4HT
⊖ Chancery Lane
🚇 City Thameslink
C T 020 7213 2965   F 020 7213 5545
@ peter.john@veredus.co.uk
Market areas Executive Search

Website www.veredus.co.uk

UK Offices 4

REC Member Yes

Brief Description Veredus Executive Resourcing (formerly know as Pricewaterhouse Coopers Executive Search & Selection and Interim Management) is renowned for providing intelligent, pioneering and highly professional Recruitment and Interim Management solutions for both Public and Private Sector clients.

Preferred method of contact Apply on line or telephone for an appointment

Minimum requirements Relevant Management Exposure

Type of business Permanent and Interim

Grade/Level of Appointments Senior level

Voices of Experience Ltd

Head Office ✉ 100 Pall Mall, SW1Y 5HP
⊖ Green Park
🚇 Victoria
C T 020 7664 8925   F 020 7664 8927
@ stephen.cooke@voices-of-experience.com
Market areas Executive Search

Website www.voices-of-experience.com

UK Offices 1

REC Member No

Brief Description Voices of Experience Ltd is a professional Search and Selection firm specialising in Non-Executive Directors and Non-Executive Chairmen. Their clients include publicly quoted companies, leveraged buyouts, privately owned family firms, venture capital-funded start-ups and the Public Sector. They believe that Non-Executives play a vital role, not only in corporate governance but, increasingly, in sharing their experience with Executive Management teams.

Preferred method of contact Apply on line or telephone for an appointment

Minimum requirements Previous professional experience

Type of business Permanent

Grade/Level of Appointments All levels

Walker Hamill ltd

Head Office ✉ 103–105 Jermyn St, SW1Y 6EE
     ⊖ Piccadilly Circus
     🚆 Charing Cross
     📞 T 020 7839 4444 F 020 7839 5857
     @ contactus@walker-hamill.co.uk
Market areas Executive Search

Website www.walkerhamill.com

UK Offices 1

REC Member No

Brief Description Walker Hamill identifies and attracts the very best quality individuals on behalf of the leading employers within their respective fields. They work with a vast range of companies such as Private Equity firms, Investment Banks and Strategy Consulting firms to source the world's best qualified and most successful Executives.

Preferred method of contact Apply on line or telephone for an appointment

Minimum requirements Previous professional experience

Type of business Temporary and Permanent

Grade/Level of Appointments Mid to Senior Management level

Wheat

Head Office ✉ 33 Throgmorton St, EC2N 2BR
     ⊖ Bank
     🚆 Cannon St
     📞 T 020 7397 3340 F 020 7397 3341
Market areas Executive Search

Website www.wheatsearch.com

UK Offices 1

REC Member No

Brief Description Wheat is a newly established, specialist Search firm providing a range of recruitment services to clients within the Wholesale and Retail Financial sectors and the associated Management Consultancy community. The company was founded by

individuals who have worked closely together for the past 10 years and have built up a powerful franchise and collegiate work ethic.

Preferred method of contact Apply on line or telephone for an appointment

Minimum requirements Previous professional experience

Type of business Permanent

Grade/Level of Appointments All levels

Whitehead Mann GKR

Head Office ✉ 11 Hill St, W1J 5LG
     ⊖ Hyde Park Corner
     🚆 Victoria
     📞 T 020 7290 2000 F 020 7290 2050
     @ uklondon@wmann.com
Market areas Executive Search

Website www.wmann.com

UK Offices 3

REC Member No

Brief Description Whitehead Mann GKR was established in 1976 and operates within a variety of sectors.

Preferred method of contact Apply on line or telephone for an appointment

Minimum requirements Previous professional experience

Type of business Permanent

Grade/Level of Appointments All levels

Whitney Group

Head Office ✉ 10 Hallam St, W1N 6DJ
     ⊖ Great Portland St
     🚆 Euston
     📞 T 020 7307 5757 F 020 7631 5317
Market areas Executive Search

Website www.whitneygroup.com

UK Offices 2

REC Member No

Brief Description Whitney Group cover a range of sectors including Banking, Financial Services, Property, Media and IT/Telecoms.

Preferred method of contact Apply on line or telephone for an appointment

Minimum requirements Previous professional experience

Type of business Permanent

Grade/Level of Appointments All levels

Fashion and Retail

Berkeley Search & Selection

Head Office ✉ 118 Piccadilly, W1J 7NW
⊖ Green Park
🚊 Victoria
☎ T 020 7355 5045   F 020 7355 5022
@ info@berkeley-search.com
Market areas Fashion, Retail

Website www.berkeley-search.com

UK Offices 1

REC Member No

Brief Description Founded in 1994, Berkeley Search & Selection's portfolio of clients are both nationally and internationally based across the following sectors: Footwear and Accessories, Fashion, Retail, Mail Order industries and Corporate Clothing.

Preferred method of contact Telephone for appointment

Minimum requirements Fashion, Retail related experience

Type of business Temporary and Permanent

Grade/Level of Appointments Buyers to Director level

Denza International Ltd

Head Office ✉ 11 St George St, W1S 2FD
⊖ Oxford Circus
🚊 Charing Cross
☎ T 020 7499 5047   F 020 7629 8376
@ vanessa@denza.co.uk
Market areas Fashion

Website www.denza.co.uk

UK Offices 1

REC Member No

Brief Description Denza have a great deal of experience within Fashion recruitment and have as a consequence accumulated a vast database of Designers and Fashion companies both in the UK and overseas.

Preferred method of contact Apply on line or telephone for appointment

Minimum requirements Ideally Fashion exposure

Type of business Permanent

Grade/Level of Appointments Junior Designer to Senior Designer/ Management

The Fashion Personnel Group

Head Office ✉ 21 Great Titchfield St, W1W 8BA
⊖ Goodge St
🚊 Euston
☎ T 020 7436 0220   F 020 7436 0088
@ info@fashionpersonnel.co.uk
Market areas Fashion, Retail

Website www.fashionpersonnel.co.uk

UK Offices 2

REC Member Yes

Brief Description Fashion Personnel supply all levels of permanent and temporary staff operating across all disciplines of the Fashion and Retail industries. Their staff are trained consultants from industry backgrounds and actively place professionals throughout the UK, Europe and internationally.

Preferred method of contact Apply on line or telephone for appointment

Minimum requirements None

Type of business Permanent and Temporary

Grade/Level of Appointments Graduates to Senior level

Freedom Recruitment

Head Office ✉ 50 Great Malborough St, W1F 7JS
⊖ Oxford Circus
🚊 Charing Cross
☎ T 020 7734 9779   F 020 7734 1101
@ info@freedomrecruit.com
Market areas Retail and Fashion, Accountancy and Finance, Secretarial, Banking

Website www.freedomrecruit.com

UK Offices 1

REC Member Yes

Brief Description Established in 1997, Freedom Recruitment aims to provide high quality, low profile recruitment for clients in six sectors where their expertise allows them to take an innovative approach to finding the best candidates available – in the shortest possible time: Retail, Fashion Production, Accounting and Finance, Office Support and Banking. Freedom Recruitment is in an enviable position of having excellent word of mouth referrals from both candidates and clients alike. This attracts a very good level of high profile clients and blue chip organisations who use their services. Attracting clients of this calibre provides Freedom with a high quantity of fantastic opportunities for candidates.

Preferred method of contact Telephone for appointment

Minimum requirements None

Type of business Temporary and Permanent

Grade/Level of Appointments All levels

Harper Halsey Laroche

See Executive Search, page 91

Indesign

Head Office ✉ 1 Ashland Place, W1U 4AQ
- ⊖ Baker St
- 🚆 Marylebone
- ☎ **T** 020 7935 7485   **F** 020 7486 1349
- @ l@indesignrecruitment.co.uk

Market areas Design

Website www.indesignrecruitment.co.uk

UK Offices 1

REC Member No

Brief Description Established in 1968, Indesign has long enjoyed an international reputation for finding the right Design talent for its world class clients from the most junior Design appointment to the most senior.

Preferred method of contact Telephone for appointment

Minimum requirements Design experience

Type of business Permanent

Grade/Level of Appointments Graduate to Senior level

Menswear and Womenswear Appointments

Head Office ✉ 207 Regent St, W1B 4ND
- ⊖ Oxford Circus
- 🚆 Charing Cross
- ☎ **T** 020 7439 6031   **F** 020 7434 1451
- @ mwa@rossgroup.co.uk

Market areas Fashion

Website www.rossgroup.co.uk

UK Offices 2

REC Member Yes

Brief Description Part of The Ross Group, established over 30 years and specialists in Fashion recruitment, Menswear and Womenswear Appointments have grown with some of the High Street's most prominent names. Their specialist sectors include: Retail Operations, Retail Head Office, Human Resources, Design and Technical/Production.

Preferred method of contact Telephone for appointment

Minimum requirements None

Type of business Permanent

Grade/Level of Appointments Junior to Senior Management level

Menswear and Womenswear Executives

See Executive Search, page 98

Meridian Retail

Head Office ✉ 22 Bristol Gardens, W9 2JQ
- ⊖ Maida Vale
- 🚆 Queens Park
- ☎ **T** 020 7436 9555   **F** 020 7266 5819
- @ search@meridianretail.co.uk

Market areas Retail

Website www.meridianretail.co.uk

UK Offices 1

REC Member No

Brief Description Meridian Retail are a highly personalised Retail recruitment consultancy, working across all sectors of the industry. As consultants they work hard to build a close relationship with their clients and candidates, handling national and international assignments from their London based office.

Preferred method of contact Telephone for appointment

Minimum requirements Ideally Retail exposure

Type of business Permanent

Grade/Level of Appointments Merchandise Supervisor/Team Leader to Area Manager/Operations Manager

Reinforcements

Head Office ✉ 207 Regent St, W1B 4ND
- ⊖ Oxford Circus
- 🚆 Charing Cross
- ☎ **T** 020 7494 0050   **F** 020 7434 1451
- @ reinforcements@rossgroup.co.uk

Market areas Retail, Fashion, Travel

Website www.rossgroup.co.uk

UK Offices 2

REC Member Yes

Brief Description Part of The Ross Group, Reinforcements were established in 1988 to provide temporary and short term contracts for the Retail, Fashion and Travel industries.

Preferred method of contact Telephone for appointment

Minimum requirements None

Type of business Temporary and Contract

Grade/Level of Appointments Junior to Management level

Retail Executives

See Executive Search, page 105

Retail Human Resources Plc

Head Office ✉ 14 Bristol Gardens, W9 2JG
🚇 Warwick Ave
🚃 Paddington
☎ T 020 7432 8888 F 020 7289 1968
@ enquiries@rhr.co.uk
Market areas Retail

Website www.retailhumanresources.com
UK Offices 6
REC Member No

Brief Description Established in 1988, Retail Human Resources has many long-standing relationships with leading retailers. Operating out of six cities and employing over 100 employees, RHR has grown from humble beginnings to become the largest Retail recruitment company in the UK and Eire.

Preferred method of contact Apply on line or telephone for an appointment

Minimum requirements None

Type of business Permanent

Grade/Level of Appointments All levels

Retail People

Head Office ✉ 207 Regent St, W1B 4ND
🚇 Oxford Circus
🚃 Charing Cross
☎ T 020 7434 4123 F 020 7434 1451
@ retailpeople@rossgroup.co.uk
Market areas Retail

Website www.rossgroup.co.uk
UK Offices 2
REC Member Yes

Brief Description Part of The Ross Group, Retail People are undoubtedly one of the market leaders in General Retail recruitment. Their specialist sectors include: Retail Operations, Retail Head Office, Human Resources, Call Centres and Customer Service.

Preferred method of contact Telephone for appointment

Minimum requirements None

Type of business Permanent

Grade/Level of Appointments Junior to Management level

ROC Recruitment

See Accountancy and Banking, page 26

Smith and Pye Limited

Head Office ✉ 17 Willow St, EC2A 4BH
🚇 Old St
🚃 Old St
☎ T 020 7739 1010 F 020 7739 2744
@ cake@smithandpye.com
Market areas Fashion

Website www.smithandpye.com
UK Offices 1
REC Member No

Brief Description Established in 1994, Smith and Pye is a leading Fashion consultancy introducing companies worldwide to Fashion Designers and Trend Forecasters across all levels, with clients comprising of Couture houses, International Brands/Retailers and Manufacturers.

Preferred method of contact Apply on line or telephone for an appointment

Minimum requirements Relevant industry exposure

Type of business Permanent

Grade/Level of Appointments Junior Designer to Senior Designer/ Management

Success Appointments

Head Office ✉ 7 Air St, W1R 5RJ
🚇 Piccadilly Circus
🚃 Charing Cross
☎ T 020 7287 7722 F 020 7734 1692
@ info@successrecruit.co.uk
Market areas Retail, Secretarial, Design, Technical, Sales, Buying, Merchandising

Website www.successrecruit.co.uk
UK Offices 2
REC Member Yes

Brief Description Success Appointments is the UK's leading specialist Retail recruitment consultancy. Since their launch in 1988, they have established a first class reputation throughout the industry. Based in the heart of London and Manchester, they have become an integral part of the UK Retail culture.

Preferred method of contact Apply on line or telephone for an appointment

Minimum requirements None

Type of business Temporary and Permanent

Grade/Level of Appointments All levels

Tiro Resource Solutions Ltd

See Media, page 205

Improve your chances... of getting the right job

By Sarah de Carteret, National Graduate Recruitment Manager, Deloitte & Touche.
© Deloitte & Touche 2003

So, now it's time to start thinking about starting your career – but just how do you get that perfect job?

Choosing the career for you...

Let's start at the very beginning – research. It may sound boring, but you need to make sure you are applying for a job that you *really* want to do. In this day and age, a wealth of information is at your fingertips, not only in books, directories and career magazines, but also on the internet. Your early research will be useful when you turn up for the interview too, as any employer is going to want to know *why* you want *that job* in that *particular company*.

Find out what the job is really like. For example, if you are thinking about working in investment banking, try to strip away the glamour and understand what you will really be doing day-to-day. In addition to this, try to build a picture of the lifestyle you will need to get used to.

It is worth attending employer presentations and careers fairs so that you can talk to people who are doing the job. Also, look out for 'drop-in' sessions which many employers run. At Deloitte & Touche we often organise these sessions with university careers services, and find we are kept very busy giving advice about the careers we have on offer and how to go about applying for a graduate position.

Applying...

Once you have decided on the career, you then need to start completing applications. This is a time-consuming task but it's worth noting that at Deloitte & Touche we reject around 60 per cent of applicants – why? Often we believe this is because candidates have tried to 'cut and paste' answers into different employer application forms. Although this saves time, it often means candidates have not read and therefore not answered questions properly.

On other occasions applicants do not meet the basic entry criteria (such as gaining a certain number of UCAS points) or leave out key information, assuming that the recipient of the form will be able to guess what is missing. Another common mistake is to imagine that the application form is on a par with an e-mail to a friend – typos, no capital letters, abbreviations and slang are seen all too often, and do not impress employers!

In an application form, employers are usually trying to assess *competencies* – in other words, the skills, attitudes and behaviours that are important in the job you are applying for. Questions will often be focused around team working, taking responsibility, commitment and motivation as well as your academic achievements. Spend time thinking about *your personal* achievements, both academically and in your outside interests – employers generally want well-rounded individuals rather than pure academics – and pick your best examples to demonstrate your skills.

If you are really at a loss, look out for employer or careers service-led talks on completing application forms.

Tip

Spend your time completing a handful of good quality application forms, rather than filling in dozens badly.

The dreaded first interview...

So, you've impressed someone enough on paper to get invited in, but how do you keep up the good work? Usually, selection processes are made up of two stages. The first stage will usually consist of an interview and some sort of psychometric test, either based on ability or personality. The second interview stage can become more complex, with some organisations running assessment centres, which may involve you participating in a variety of activities designed to test your abilities.

For any interview, *preparation* is key, so all the research you have done into your career choice and the careful completion of your application form will be useful at this stage.

An interviewer will often cover the key points on your application form so it is worth reviewing it just before the interview. It is also worth preparing a range of other examples to demonstrate your skills. Think about giving examples that demonstrate your potential as an employee, and if you have relevant experience tell the interviewer.

Although it is tempting, don't reel off strings of buzz-words if you have no good examples to back up your statements. As an example, if you claim you are a good leader, make sure you have thought of at least three examples where you were able to demonstrate your leadership skills, as a good interviewer will probe this assertion. Finally, prepare some questions to ask your interviewer. These should be pertinent to you and may involve 'personal' questions such as 'Why did you join this firm?' or something related to the industry such as 'What do you think are the major challenges facing your business at the present time?'

In terms of nerves, most people are somewhat apprehensive about an interview, however it is important that nerves do not affect your performance adversely. Remember the following points.

→ An interview is an adult-to-adult discussion – you should not feel intimidated, after all you are talking about someone you know very well for most of the interview!

→ Many interviewers are trained in interviewing skills, and should not need to put you under undue pressure or make you feel nervous.

→ If you do feel terribly uncomfortable with your interviewer, ask yourself why. Do you really want to work for an organisation that uses someone like that to recruit for their firm?

→ If you suffer from 'clammy palms', try this technique before shaking hands with your interviewer. As you stand up to meet them, subtly brush your hands on your trouser legs/skirt!

→ Keep up appropriate eye contact with your interviewer, sit up straight and try not to fidget as this will give away the fact you are nervous.

As you leave the first interview, it is worthwhile to reflect on what went well and what perhaps you found more difficult. Jot down a few notes for future reference, and make sure you polish up the areas that you struggled with before any further interviews.

Many careers services and large employers run practice interview sessions. The advantage of having a mock interview is that you will be given useful feedback on your performance, which you can then build upon for the real thing. (If you go to an employer session, check that these are confidential and therefore will not impact on future applications you might want to make there.)

Getting to the final stage...

The second interview usually takes a similar format to the first, but is likely to cover some different competency areas. In addition, it is normal for a second interviewer to pick up on any concerns from the first interview, to question you further about your career choice, sell the job to you and answer any of your questions.

In addition to an interview, many employers utilise other selection 'tools', which are often referred to as an assessment centre. These typically involve you participating in more than one exercise used to assess your ability, and again many are based around testing your competencies. Some employers take potential recruits away to hotels and put them through a gruelling process, involving exercises such as group discussions, presentations, case studies and interviews. Many, however, use a shortened version; for example, at Deloitte & Touche we use a two-stage process, which includes a case study exercise and two interviews.

In terms of preparation for assessment centre exercises, make sure you are up to speed with current business news, and that you have some understanding of the main working practices used by that employer. Many of these exercises revolve around real-life business issues.

It is hard to prepare for group exercises but reviewing your own performance in other team situations is worthwhile. Employers are usually looking for candidates who can recognise the balance between being too quiet and not participating, and being overly enthusiastic and taking over at the expense of other candidates' participation. If you think you have been 'taking over', remember to modify your behaviour appropriately. Listening to others, defining a team objective, allocating roles at the start and keeping an eye on the time are all qualities that your observers will be watching for.

Once the day is over, the final piece of advice is to review how it all went. Consider how you performed in the interview and note down any areas where you felt you struggled to give a strong answer. Think about how others might have perceived your performance in other exercises and again make a note. Most importantly, reflect on the sorts of people you met during the day, and the overall 'feeling' you got about the company. Is it the sort of job you would like to do, or the sort of firm you would like to work for?

Inevitably, you will not be successful at all interviews, but make sure you take something positive away from your experience. The right job will come along and by the time it does, you will be fully prepared to get it!

Financial Services and Insurance

Accredited Personnel Insurance Agency

Head Office ✉ 71a Wentworth St, E1 7TD
⊖ Aldgate East
🚇 Fenchurch St
☎ T 020 7375 1357   F 020 7375 3730
@ sonja_accreditpersonnel@compuserve.com
Market areas   Insurance, Re-insurance

Website www.accredit.co.uk
UK Offices 2
REC Member No
Brief Description Accredited Personnel Insurance Agency is a City based privately owned recruitment consultancy specialising in the Insurance and Re-insurance markets for clients across London and Essex.
Preferred method of contact Apply on line or telephone for appointment
Minimum requirements Ideally Insurance/Reinsurance background
Type of business Permanent
Grade/Level of Appointments All levels

Aldrich & Co

Head Office ✉ 106 Salisbury House, London Wall, EC2M 5QQ
⊖ Moorgate
🚇 Moorgate
☎ T 020 7588 8999   F 020 7588 8998
@ info@aldrich.co.uk
Market areas   Financial Services

Website www.aldrich.co.uk
UK Offices 1
REC Member No
Brief Description Aldrich & Company specialise in Support recruitment for the Financial Services industry. Based in the heart of the City, clients include the world's leading Investment Banks and Investment Management houses.
Preferred method of contact Telephone for appointment
Minimum requirements None
Type of business Permanent, Temporary and Contract
Grade/Level of Appointments All levels

Allegis Group Ltd

See Secretarial, page 229

Amery Cooper Financial Recruitment Consultants

See Accountancy and Banking, page 5

Andersons (UK) Ltd

See Accountancy and Banking, page 6

Armstrong International Ltd

See Executive Search, page 77

Badenoch & Clark

See Accountancy and Banking, page 6

Banking Additions

See Accountancy and Banking, page 7

Beaumont Leslie Thomas (BLT)

Head Office ✉ Quality House, 5–9 Quality Ct, WC2A 1HP
⊖ Chancery Lane
🚇 City Thameslink
☎ T 020 7405 3404   F 020 7405 3310
@ css@blt.co.uk
Market areas   Management Consultancy, Voluntary Sector, Human Resources, Taxation

Website www.blt.co.uk
UK Offices 1
REC Member No
Brief Description Launched in 1987, BLT's aim was to become the leading recruitment consultancy in the following specialist areas: Taxation, Management Consultancy, Human Resources, Company Secretarial and Voluntary Sector.
Preferred method of contact Apply on line or telephone for appointment
Minimum requirements Previous professional experience
Type of business Permanent
Grade/Level of Appointments Senior level

Bowmaker Sharpe Ltd

Head Office ✉ 22a Theobalds Rd, WC1X 8PF
⊖ Chancery Lane
🚇 City Thameslink
☎ T 020 7242 4444 F 020 7242 5757
@ recruit@bowmaker-sharpe.co.uk
Market areas Financial Services

Website www.bowmaker-sharpe.co.uk

UK Offices 1

REC Member No

Brief Description Established in 1999, Bowmaker Sharpe have grown to be one of the UK's leading specialists for the supply of staff to the Financial Services sector for Retail and Corporate Banking, Mortgages, Pensions, Investments, Life Assurance and Insurance.

Preferred method of contact Apply on line or telephone for appointment

Minimum requirements Financial Services background

Type of business Permanent

Grade/Level of Appointments All levels

Brewer Morris

Head Office ✉ Fleetway House, 25 Farringdon St, EC4A 4SR
⊖ St Pauls
🚇 Cannon St
☎ T 020 7415 2800 F 020 7332 9053
@ matthewphelps@brewermorris.co.uk
Market areas Taxation

Website www.brewermorris.com

UK Offices 2

REC Member No

Brief Description Brewer Morris was established in 1987 as the UK's first recruitment consultancy to focus exclusively on the recruitment of Taxation professionals. Part of the SR Group, Brewer Morris' clients include leading Accountancy firms, Legal profession, National and Local Practices, Plcs, Financial institutions and corporations.

Preferred method of contact Telephone for appointment

Minimum requirements Previous professional experience

Type of business Permanent

Grade/Level of Appointments Tax Assistants/Accountants to Tax Partner/Head of Tax

Cameron Kennedy

Head Office ✉ 125 High Holborn, WC1V 6ZX
⊖ Holborn

🚇 City Thameslink
☎ T 020 7430 0011 F 020 7404 4333
@ andrew@cameronkennedy.com
Market areas IT, Financial Services, Banking, Hotel and Leisure, Insurance

Website www.cameronkennedy.com

UK Offices 1

REC Member Yes

Brief Description Cameron Kennedy is a specialist recruitment consultancy specialising in four key niche areas: Financial Selection; IT; Life, Pensions and Insurance; and Hotel and Leisure, ranging from Support staff to Board level appointments.

Preferred method of contact Apply on line or telephone for appointment

Minimum requirements None

Type of business Temporary, Permanent and Contract

Grade/Level of Appointments Graduate/1st Jobber to Board level

City Executive Consultants Ltd

See Accountancy and Banking, page 10

Darwin Rhodes – General Insurance Division

Head Office ✉ 5 Dryden St, WC2E 9NB
☎ T 020 7829 8378 F 020 7829 8381

✉ 10 Fenchurch Avenue, EC3M 5BN
⊖ Monument
🚇 Cannon St
☎ T 020 7663 5660 F 020 7663 5800
@ gi@dr-city.com
Market areas Insurance, Actuarial, Financial Planning

Website www.darwinrhodes.com

UK Offices 3

REC Member No

Brief Description Darwin Rhodes Ltd was established in 1996 and is now one of the World's leading recruitment consultancies specialising in the placement of Actuarial, Employee Benefits, Insurance and Financial Planning professionals.

Preferred method of contact Apply on line or telephone for appointment

Minimum requirements None

Type of business Permanent

Grade/Level of Appointments Graduates/Trainee Consultants to Qualified Actuaries/Risk Analysts

Darwin Rhodes - Life and Pensions Division

Head Office ✉ 5 Dryden St, WC2E 9NB
　　　　　　🚇 Covent Garden
　　　　　　🚆 Charing Cross
　　　　　　📞 T 020 7829 8378　F 020 7829 8381
　　　　　　@ recruit@darwinrhodes.com
Market areas　Insurance, Actuarial, Financial Planning

Website　www.darwinrhodes.com
UK Offices　3
REC Member　No

Brief Description　Darwin Rhodes Ltd was established in 1996 and is now one of the worlds leading recruitment consultancies specialising in the placement of actuarial, employee benefits, insurance and financial planning professionals.

Preferred method of contact　Apply on line or telephone for appointment

Minimum requirements　None
Type of business　Permanent
Grade/Level of Appointments　Graduates/Trainee Consultants to Qualified Actuaries/Risk Analysts

Davies Kidd

Head Office ✉ Hamilton House, 1 Temple Avenue, EC4Y 0HA
　　　　　　🚇 Blackfriars
　　　　　　🚆 Blackfriars
　　　　　　📞 T 020 7489 2053　F 020 7353 0612
　　　　　　@ careers@davies-kidd.co.uk
Market areas　Taxation, Audit, Public Practice

Website　www.davies-kidd.co.uk
UK Offices　1
REC Member　No

Brief Description　Davies Kidd aim to provide advice and assistance of the highest quality for all candidates, at all levels of the profession, through to Partners and Directors. To achieve this they rely on a detailed knowledge of the Practice market combined with a responsive, down-to-earth, friendly, professional approach.

Preferred method of contact　Apply on line or telephone for appointment

Minimum requirements　None
Type of business　Permanent
Grade/Level of Appointments　Graduates/Juniors to Directors/ Partners

Diamond Resourcing Plc

See **Sales and Marketing, page 214**

Edge Recruitment

See **Accountancy and Banking, page 11**

Elements

See **Executive Search, page 86**

Elliott Bauer Ltd

Head Office ✉ 2nd Floor, 103 Cannon St, EC4N 5AD
　　　　　　🚇 Cannon St
　　　　　　🚆 Cannon St
　　　　　　📞 T 020 7283 4004　F 020 7283 4050
　　　　　　@ recruitment@elliottbauer.com
Market areas　Actuarial, Life and Pensions

Website　www.elliottbauer.com
UK Offices　1
REC Member　No

Brief Description　Elliott Bauer is a Human Resource Management consultancy providing long term solutions to Human Resource problems. They have a proven track record within the field of Actuarial recruitment, covering all aspects of the profession. Their extensive client base covers all the major employers within this sector, and offers candidates the chance to explore the opportunities available to them, from entry level Graduate roles through to those at Director level.

Preferred method of contact　Apply on line or telephone for appointment

Minimum requirements　None
Type of business　Contract and Permanent
Grade/Level of Appointments　Graduate to Senior Manager

Farlow & Warren Search and Selection – Financial

Head Office ✉ Unit 212–213 The Business Design Centre, 52 Upper St, N1 0QH
　　　　　　🚇 Highbury and Islington
　　　　　　🚆 Highbury and Islington
　　　　　　📞 T 020 7288 6211　F 020 7288 6208
　　　　　　@ financialservices@farlowandwarren.co.uk
Market areas　Financial Services, Pensions

Website　www.farlowandwarren.co.uk
UK Offices　1
REC Member　No

Brief Description　Farlow & Warren Search and Selection have been established for 10 years and have a wealth of experience of recruiting on a Search and Contingency basis to specialist niche marketplaces: Telecoms and IT including Customer Service, Engineering, Sales, Networking and Transmission; Financial including Life and Pensions and Financial Advisers; Construction including Interior Fit-out, Facilities Managers, Construction Services and Building Services; Commercial including Back Office, Secretarial, Administration, temporary and permanent.

Preferred method of contact Apply on line or telephone for an appointment

Minimum requirements None

Type of business Contract and Permanent

Grade/Level of Appointments All levels

The Gaap Group

Head Office ✉ Grafton House, 2–3 Golden Sq, W1F 9HR
🚇 Piccadilly Circus
🚆 Charing Cross
☎ T 020 7437 8899   F 020 7437 8677
@ info@gaaps.com
Market areas Financial Services, Actuarial

Website www.gaaps.com
UK Offices 1
REC Member No

Brief Description Over the last decade Gaaps has proved to be consistently successful in the area of Actuarial recruitment. So much so that clients have asked them to take on tasks far beyond their original brief, from Advertising to Benchmarking, Assessment Centres to Graduate Recruitment Programmes. The Gaaps of today is an international Human Resource consultancy that firmly puts the Human back into Human Resources.

Preferred method of contact Apply on line or telephone for appointment

Minimum requirements None

Type of business Contract and Permanent

Grade/Level of Appointments Graduate to Senior level

Goodman Mason Ltd
See **Accountancy and Banking, page 13**

Grove Recruitment Solutions

Head Office ✉ The Linen Hall, 162–168 Regent St, W1B 5TB
🚇 Piccadilly Circus
🚆 Charing Cross
☎ T 020 7851 6800   F 020 7851 6801
@ grs@grove-group.com
Market areas Financial Services, Actuarial, HR

Website www.grove-group.com
UK Offices 1
REC Member Yes

Brief Description Grove Recruitment provides business solutions for recruitment needs across a range of specialist and rare skills within the areas of Financial Services, Finance and HR. Their business grows by word of mouth, and by approaching top quartile individuals and companies. The company has already built a reputation as an ethical and professional solution provider respected by many leading firms.

Preferred method of contact Apply on line or telephone for an appointment

Minimum requirements Ideally relevant industry exposure

Type of business Permanent

Grade/Level of Appointments All levels

Hanover Search & Selection
See **Accountancy and Banking, page 14**

Hays Inter-Selection

Head Office ✉ 141 Moorgate, EC2M 6TX
☎ T 020 7628 9999   F 020 7628 4698

✉ Roman Wall House, 1–2 Crutched Friars, EC3N 2HT
🚇 Tower Hill
🚆 Fenchurch St
☎ T 020 7480 7220   F 020 7481 9888
@ fs.london@hays-interselection.co.uk
Market areas Insurance, Actuarial, Financial Services

Website www.haysworks.com
UK Offices 15
REC Member No

Brief Description Hays Personnel Services is a division of Hays plc, the Business Services group listed in the FTSE 100. Hays Personnel Services is Europe's leading specialist professional recruitment group. Hays Inter-Selection is the UK's largest specialist Insurance and Financial Services recruitment consultancy, placing General Insurance, Sales, Business Development, Technical, Compliance and Administrative staff at all levels.

Preferred method of contact Apply on line or telephone for an appointment

Minimum requirements None

Type of business Temporary and Permanent

Grade/Level of Appointments All levels

Hays Investment Personnel

Head Office ✉ 141 Moorgate, EC2M 6TX
☎ T 020 7628 9999   F 020 7628 4698

✉ 105–107 Bishopsgate, EC2M 3UE
🚇 Liverpool St
🚆 Liverpool St
☎ T 020 7588 0182   F 020 7588 4436

@ bishopsgate@hays-investment.co.uk
Market areas Financial Services, Securities

Website www.haysworks.com
UK Offices 1
REC Member No

Brief Description Hays Personnel Services is a division of Hays plc, the Business Services group listed in the FTSE 100. Hays Personnel Services is Europe's leading specialist professional recruitment group. Hays Investment Personnel is a specialist division dedicated to the recruitment of permanent, temporary and contract staff for Integrated Securities houses, Stockbrokers, Global Custodians and Asset Management houses.

Preferred method of contact Apply on line or telephone for an appointment

Minimum requirements None

Type of business Temporary, Permanent and Contract

Grade/Level of Appointments All levels

Hays Taxation Personnel

Head Office ✉ 141 Moorgate, EC2M 6TX
☎ T 020 7628 9999 F 020 7628 4698

✉ Mansfield House, 1st Floor, 1 Southampton St, WC2R 0LR
⊖ Covent Garden
🚊 Charing Cross
☎ T 020 7520 5959 F 020 7520 5969
@ holborn.tax@hays-ap.co.uk

Market areas Taxation

Website www.haysworks.com
UK Offices 9
REC Member No

Brief Description Hays Personnel Services is a division of Hays plc, the Business Services group listed in the FTSE 100. Hays Personnel Services is Europe's leading specialist professional recruitment group. Hays Taxation Personnel is the UK's premier provider of Tax professionals to firms in Practice, Commerce, Industry and Finance. Hays Taxation Personnel draws on the resources of the country's largest specialists in Financial recruitment with a network of 125 offices.

Preferred method of contact Apply on line or telephone for an appointment

Minimum requirements None

Type of business Temporary and Permanent

Grade/Level of Appointments All levels

HD+L Selection

Head Office ✉ Halton House, 20–23 Holborn, EC1N 2JD
⊖ Chancery Lane

🚊 City Thameslink
☎ T 020 7405 0000 F 020 7405 2222
@ hdl@hdl.co.uk
Market areas Financial Services, Legal, Banking

Website www.hdl.co.uk
UK Offices 1
REC Member No

Brief Description HD+L Selection is an associated business of Hogarth Davies Lloyd Executive Search. Hogarth Davies Lloyd was established at the beginning of 1995 and it has since met with considerable success and now enjoys a number of well established retained relationships, specialising in Financial Services, Legal and Banking for Graduates through to Finance Directors/Lawyers.

Preferred method of contact Apply on line or telephone for an appointment

Minimum requirements Previous professional experience

Type of business Permanent

Grade/Level of Appointments Graduates to Finance Directors/Lawyers

Hillman Saunders

Head Office ✉ 78 Leadenhall St, EC3A 3DH
⊖ Bank
🚊 Cannon St
☎ T 020 7929 0707 F 020 7929 1666
@ mail@hillmansaunders.com
Market areas Financial Services, Insurance, Secretarial

Website www.hillmansaunders.com
UK Offices 3
REC Member No

Brief Description Hillman Saunders was established in the late 1980s and has four specialist divisions – Insurance, Financial Services (Life and Pensions), e-Business and Secretarial – staffed by consultants who have a proven track record and who are fully conversant with the mechanics of their specialist field. Their client base is extensive and consists of many renowned and respected FT top 500 companies.

Preferred method of contact Apply on line or telephone for an appointment

Minimum requirements None

Type of business Temporary and Permanent

Grade/Level of Appointments All levels

IMR Recruitment

See **Accountancy and Banking, page 17**

123

Indigo Selection – Commerce and Accounting Division

See **Accountancy and Banking, page 17**

IPS Group Ltd

Head Office ✉ Lloyds Avenue House, 6 Lloyds Avenue, EC3N 3ES
⊖ Tower Hill
🚊 Fenchurch St
☎ **T** 020 7481 8111   **F** 020 7481 0994
@ enquiries@ipsgroup.co.uk
Market areas   Financial Services

Website www.ipsgroup.co.uk

UK Offices 4

REC Member No

Brief Description Established in 1970, IPS Group has evolved to service the dynamic changes in the Insurance and Financial Services industry whilst retaining its strong reputation for providing a high quality professional and friendly recruitment service. IPS prides itself on offering a high quality recruitment solution based on strong business relationships with key players in the market and a thorough understanding of individuals' requirements within specialist sectors.

Preferred method of contact Apply on line or telephone for an appointment

Minimum requirements None

Type of business Temporary, Permanent and Contract

Grade/Level of Appointments All levels

James Associates

Head Office ✉ Samian House, 85 Borough High St, SE1 1NH
⊖ London Bridge
🚊 London Bridge
☎ **T** 020 7357 7400   **F** 020 7357 7407
@ mail@jamesjobs.com
Market areas   Financial Services

Website www.jamesjobs.com

UK Offices 1

REC Member No

Brief Description James Associates was formed over 5 years ago and deals exclusively with recruitment in the Financial Services industry. They operate from an office in London Bridge near the City of London and predominately cover London and the Home Counties. Their clients are varied and include national and smaller IFAs, Wealth Management, Employee Benefits and Actuarial consultancies, Accountancy and Solicitor practices, Investment houses, Fund Managers, IT consultancies, and branches and head offices of Life and Pension providers.

Preferred method of contact Apply on line or telephone for an appointment

Minimum requirements None

Type of business Temporary and Permanent

Grade/Level of Appointments All levels

JH Consulting Ltd

See **Accountancy and Banking, page 17**

Jonathan Wren

See **Accountancy and Banking, page 18**

Joslin Rowe

See **Accountancy and Banking, page 18**

L&G Recruitment Ltd

Head Office ✉ 2nd Floor, 6 Minories, EC3N 1BJ
⊖ Aldgate
🚊 Fenchurch St
☎ **T** 020 7481 1475   **F** 020 7481 4951
@ consultants@lgrecruitment.co.uk
Market areas   Insurance, Catering, Teaching, Secretarial, Driving

Website www.lgrecruitment.co.uk

UK Offices 1

REC Member Yes

Brief Description L&G Recruitment Consultants was established in 1989 and since then has provided high quality, client focused recruitment services to numerous firms in Central London. Their Insurance Division deals predominantly with the Lloyds and London Insurance Markets in the City and the Home Counties. The L&G Catering Division deals exclusively with the provision of temporary Waiting and Bar staff to some of London's premier venues. The newest division, Teaching and Education, was set up in response to an increasing need for qualified Teachers for Primary and Secondary Schools in and around Central London.

Preferred method of contact Apply on line or telephone for an appointment

Minimum requirements None

Type of business Temporary, Permanent and Contract

Grade/Level of Appointments Trainees to Qualified Teachers/Chefs

Law & Finance International

Head Office	85 Gracechurch St, EC3V 0AA
	Bank
	Cannon St
	T 020 7208 5800 **F** 020 7208 5888
@	ssinger@lfionline.com
Market areas	Legal, Financial Services, Insurance, Banking, Technology

Website www.lfionline.com

UK Offices 1

REC Member No

Brief Description Founded in 1989 as a specialist legal recruitment consultancy, LFI has expanded to meet the growing staffing needs of the Professional Services, Financial Services and Technology sectors. As their clients and markets have developed, they have expanded organically and through acquisitions to ensure that they could meet the needs of their clients and candidates.

Preferred method of contact Apply on line or telephone for an appointment

Minimum requirements None

Type of business Permanent

Grade/Level of Appointments Administration/Secretarial to Solicitors/Senior Management

Lime Street Recruitment

Head Office	Lloyds Avenue House, 6 Lloyds Avenue, EC3N 3AX
	Aldgate
	Fenchurch St
	T 020 7977 7730 **F** 020 7977 7731
@	jobs@limestreet.co.uk
Market areas	Financial Services

Website www.limestreet.co.uk

UK Offices 1

REC Member Yes

Brief Description Lime Street Recruitment are an experienced and creative team specialising in resourcing for the General Insurance and Financial Services market. Recruiting extensively for companies in London and nationwide, they can provide temporary, permanent and contract staff from Junior to Director level.

Preferred method of contact Apply on line or telephone for an appointment

Minimum requirements None

Type of business Temporary, Permanent and Contract

Grade/Level of Appointments Junior/Graduate to Director level

Mansion House Executives Ltd

See **Executive Search, page 97**

Mortgage Recruitment

Head Office	8 Ely Place, EC1N 6RY
	Farringdon
	Farringdon
	T 020 7831 3329 **F** 020 7242 0528
@	mail@mrec.co.uk
Market areas	Mortgage Staff, Secretarial

Website www.mrec.co.uk

UK Offices 1

REC Member No

Brief Description Established for over 12 years, Mortgage Recruitment specialises solely in the recruitment of experienced Mortgage staff. They provide a very wide range of permanent, temporary and contract staff at all levels from Senior Management to temporary Clerical. Their clients include Building Societies, Centralised Lenders, Banks, Insurance Companies, Third Party Administrators, Application Packagers, Indemnity Insurers and major Brokers.

Preferred method of contact Apply on line or telephone for an appointment

Minimum requirements None

Type of business Temporary, Permanent and Contract

Grade/Level of Appointments Administration to Senior Management

Norman Broadbent

See **Executive Search, page 101**

Reed Insurance Selection

Head Office	Reed Executive Plc, 145 Kensington High St, W8 7LP
	T 020 7313 7450 **F** 020 7313 7451
	37–39 Lime St, EC3M 7AY
	Bank
	Cannon St
	T 020 7621 0733
Market areas	Insurance

Website www.reed.co.uk

UK Offices 250+

REC Member No

Brief Description A subsidiary of Reed Executive Plc established in 1960, Reed's growth has been dramatic and the company's stated ambition is to grow the business substantially. Reed has been organised into a number of separate operating companies to make this happen. Reed Insurance Selection is the UK's leading Insurance recruitment organisation with over 40 years industry experience. In today's marketplace talented Insurance and Financial Services professionals are at a premium.

Preferred method of contact Apply on line or telephone for an appointment

Minimum requirements None

Type of business Temporary and Permanent

Grade/Level of Appointments All levels

Rochester Partnership

See **Accountancy and Banking, page 26**

Royce Appointments

Head Office   ✉   150 The Minories, EC3N 1LS
   ⊖   Aldgate
  🚃   Fenchurch St
  📞   T 020 7264 2125   F 020 7553 0194
  @   recruit@royceappointments.com
Market areas   Insurance, Re-insurance, IT for Insurance Industry

Website www.royceappointments.com

UK Offices 1

REC Member Yes

Brief Description Royce Appointments Ltd began trading in February 1996 and specialise in Insurance and Re-insurance recruitment. There are many different career paths, and they recruit at every level of expertise.

Preferred method of contact Apply on line or telephone for an appointment

Minimum requirements None

Type of business Temporary and Permanent

Grade/Level of Appointments Insurance Trainee to Senior Underwriter

Shearer Darnell Recruitment Ltd

See **Secretarial, page 257**

Shepherd Little and Associates

Head Office   ✉   Cleary Ct, 21–23 St Swithins Lane, EC4N 8AD
  ⊖   Bank
  🚃   Cannon St
  📞   T 020 7645 8888   F 020 7626 9400
  @   recruit@slauk.com
Market areas   Financial Services, Banking

Website www.shepherdlittle.com

UK Offices 1

REC Member Yes

Brief Description Shepherd Little is a long established specialist Financial Services recruitment consultancy, based in the heart of the City of London. They have sound business relationships with most of the major Banks and Asset Management firms. As a preference their consultants are recruited from within the industry for which they themselves recruit. This gives them a high level of understanding and technical expertise when dealing with clients, line managers, HR and applicants alike. Their consultants are skilled interviewers who are well trained in giving excellent open and honest career advice.

Preferred method of contact Apply on line or telephone for an appointment

Minimum requirements None

Type of business Temporary and Permanent

Grade/Level of Appointments Junior Staff to Senior Director

Torus Partnership

See **Executive Search, page 110**

Graduates

Abraxas Plc

See **IT and Telecoms**, page 152

CareerFever Ltd

Head Office ✉	New Penderel House, 283–288 High Holborn, WC1V 7HG
⊖	Chancery Lane
🚃	City Thameslink
☎	T 020 7420 1950 F 020 7420 1955
@	info@careerfever.co.uk
Market areas	Graduates

Website www.careerfever.co.uk

UK Offices 1

REC Member No

Brief Description CareerFever was founded in 1999 to realise an entirely new concept in the field of Employment Market Communications with over 200 major clients across Europe, offering Graduates a unique virtual reality, 3D interactive platform through which they can apply for positions with the UK's leading recruiters They have offices in Netherlands, Spain, Belgium, Sweden and France.

Preferred method of contact Telephone for appointment

Minimum requirements Graduate level

Type of business Permanent

Grade/Level of Appointments Graduate level upwards

Graduate Appointments Ltd

Head Office ✉	Covden House, 7a Langley St, WC2H 9JA
⊖	Covent Garden
🚃	Charing Cross
☎	T 020 7447 5500 F 020 7379 0113
@	info@gradapps.co.uk
Market areas	Graduates

Website www.graduateappointments.com

UK Offices 1

REC Member No

Brief Description Graduate Appointments was founded in 1963, and is the among the longest established Graduate recruitment consultancies in London. Their team consists of specialist Graduate recruitment consultants whose aim is to provide a professional service in terms of matching job opportunities with Graduates into their chosen career path. They assist graduates who are focused on their chosen career path and who are proactively seeking employment. All

degree disciplines are accepted and any relevant work experience is advantageous.

Preferred method of contact Apply on line or telephone for appointment

Minimum requirements Ideally 6 months postgraduate experience

Type of business Permanent

Grade/Level of Appointments All levels

Graduate Recruitment Company

Head Office ✉	3rd Floor, 40–44 Clipstone St, W1W 5DW
⊖	Goodge St
🚃	Euston
☎	T 020 7854 8800 F 020 7854 8885
@	enquiries@pfj.co.uk
Market areas	Graduates

Website www.graduate-recruitment.co.uk

UK Offices 2

REC Member Yes

Brief Description Part of Phee Farrier Jones Recruitment Company, the Graduate Recruitment Company was established in 1992 as a Media Sales recruitment consultancy. From an initial team of three they now have over 50 staff in two offices placing candidates across a range of sectors from Media to Recruitment to Information and Research to Technology. Their reputation speaks for itself with over a third of their candidates coming via personal recommendation.

Preferred method of contact Apply on line or telephone for appointment

Minimum requirements None

Type of business Permanent and Temporary

Grade/Level of Appointments All levels

JPA Graduates

Head Office ✉	14–15 Lower Grosvenor Place, SW1W 0EX
⊖	Victoria
🚃	Victoria
☎	T 020 7821 0300 F 020 7821 0299
@	graduate@j-p-a.co.uk
Market areas	Sales

Website www.j-p-a.co.uk

UK Offices 1

REC Member Yes

Brief Description JPA was established in 1998 with the aim of providing companies with the highest calibre of employee covering a wide range of Sales sector jobs.

127

Preferred method of contact Apply on line or telephone for an appointment

Minimum requirements None

Type of business Temporary and Permanent

Grade/Level of Appointments Graduate to Senior level

Milkround

Head Office ✉ 26 Charlotte St, W1T 2NE
⊖ Goodge St
🚃 Euston
☎ T 020 7419 5190   F 020 7419 5191
@ info@milkround.com
Market areas Graduates

Website www.milkround.com

UK Offices 1

REC Member No

Brief Description Milkround was founded in 1997 with the sole aim of matching top quality graduates with leading employers. Since then it has created a dominant brand within its target market place.

Preferred method of contact Apply on line or telephone for an appointment

Minimum requirements Graduates Only

Type of business Permanent

Grade/Level of Appointments Graduates

next4GRADS

Head Office ✉ 4 Great James St, WC1N 7AD
☎ T 020 7404 6664   F 020 7404 6662

✉ Hill Flower Strong, 4 Great James St, WC1N 3DB
⊖ Chancery Lane
🚃 City Thameslink
☎ T 020 7404 6664   F 020 7404 6662
@ next4grads@globalnet.co.uk
Market areas Graduates

Website www.next4grads.co.uk

UK Offices 1

REC Member No

Brief Description next4GRADS is the Graduate recruitment division of Hills Flower Strong — a recruitment consultancy which specialises in finding suitable positions for candidates of all levels of experience from Graduate to Senior Management in a range of business sectors.

Preferred method of contact Apply on line or telephone for an appointment

Minimum requirements None

Type of business Temporary and Permanent

Grade/Level of Appointments All levels

Healthcare

Abbey Exec/AES Contract Services

Head Office ✉ 26–31 Shoreditch High St, E1 6PG
⊖ Liverpool St
🚆 Liverpool St
☎ T 020 7377 0256   F 020 7377 8472
@ info@abbetexec.co.uk
Market areas Catering, Healthcare, Maintenance, Secretarial, Transport and Distribution

Website www.abbeyexec.co.uk

UK Offices 1

REC Member No

Brief Description Abbey Exec are a Support Services recruitment company supplying temporary and contract staff to a variety of clients including Private and NHS Hospitals, Facilities Management companies, London Borough councils, Hotels and major blue chip companies.

Preferred method of contact Apply on line or telephone for appointment

Minimum requirements None

Type of business Temporary and Contract

Grade/Level of Appointments All levels

Access Medical

Head Office ✉ 3rd Floor, 402 Holloway Rd, N7 6PN
⊖ Holloway Rd
🚆 Finsbury Park
☎ T 020 7700 2234   F 020 7700 3704
@ info@accesslocums.com
Market areas Healthcare

Website www.accesslocums.com

UK Offices 1

REC Member Yes

Brief Description Access Medical are a recruitment agency dedicated to the specific task of finding work for Physiotherapists and Occupational Therapists. As specialists in this area, they understand the needs of both the candidate and the employer. They work throughout the whole of England, Scotland and Wales, with Private and NHS Hospitals, Social Services and Local Authorities, helping them to find the staff they require.

Preferred method of contact Apply on line or telephone for appointment

Minimum requirements Previous professional experience

Type of business Permanent and Contract
Grade/Level of Appointments All levels

Arabian Careers Ltd

Head Office ✉ 7th Floor, Berkeley Sq House, Berkeley Sq, W1X 5LB
⊖ Green Park
🚆 Victoria
☎ T 020 7495 3285
@ recruiter@arabiancareers.com
Market areas Healthcare

Website www.arabiancareers.com

UK Offices 1

REC Member No

Brief Description Arabian Careers Ltd specialises in the worldwide recruitment of Healthcare professionals for hospitals and other healthcare settings in Saudi Arabia, ranging from Support Staff to Doctors and Dentists in General Practice.

Preferred method of contact Apply on line or telephone for appointment

Minimum requirements Previous professional experience

Type of business Permanent

Grade/Level of Appointments All levels

ASA Medical

Head Office ✉ 52–54 Carter Lane, EC4V 5EA
⊖ Blackfriars
🚆 Blackfriars
☎ T 020 7246 4755   F 020 7489 0840
@ medical@asagroup.co.uk
Market areas Medical

Website www.asagroup.co.uk

UK Offices 1

REC Member Yes

Brief Description ASA was founded in 1973 to deal specifically with Legal Secretarial positions, expanding into Professional Legal recruitment, contract Locums, Education, Banking, IT and Medical sectors.

Preferred method of contact Telephone for appointment

Minimum requirements None

Type of business Permanent, Temporary and Contract

Grade/Level of Appointments All levels

Barnett Personnel Ltd

See **Secretarial, page 231**

Beresford Blake Thomas Ltd

Head Office	✉	14 Buckingham Palace Rd, SW1W 0QP
	⊖	Victoria
	🚊	Victoria
	☎	**T** 020 7233 8999 **F** 020 7233 8004
	@	care@bbt.co.uk
Market areas		Social Care, Nursing, Veterinary to Doctors, Health Professionals

Website www.bbt.co.uk

UK Offices 15

REC Member Yes

Brief Description Part of the Select Group, BBT was founded in 1990. BBT is established as a truly international specialist recruitment company, providing temporary and permanent staff to the Technical, Health and Social Care sectors with offices across the UK and worldwide.

Preferred method of contact Apply on line or telephone for appointment

Minimum requirements None

Type of business Temporary and Permanent

Grade/Level of Appointments All levels

Blue Arrow Care

	✉	5 Great Queen St, WC2B 5DG
	⊖	Holborn
	🚊	Holborn
	☎	**T** 020 7440 8300 **F** 020 7831 4306
	@	staff@bluearrow.co.uk
Market areas		Healthcare
	✉	41 Goodge St, W1T 2PY
	⊖	Goodge St
	🚊	Euston
	☎	**T** 020 7637 3800 **F** 020 7637 3600
	@	staff@bluearrow.co.uk
Market areas		Healthcare

Website www.bluearrow.co.uk

UK Offices 250

REC Member Yes

Head Office 800 The Boulevard, Capability Green, Luton, LU1 3BA

Brief Description Part of the Corporate Services Group (CSG), Blue Arrow was founded over 40 years ago to become one of the UK's largest recruitment businesses with a network of over 250 locations in the UK, providing temporary, permanent and contract staff across Office, Catering, Construction, Healthcare, Technical and Industrial sectors.

Preferred method of contact Telephone for appointment

Minimum requirements None

Type of business Temporary, Permanent and Contract

Grade/Level of Appointments All levels

BNA (British Nursing Association)

	✉	5a Heath St, NW3 6TT
	⊖	Hampstead
	🚊	West Hampstead
	☎	**T** 020 7435 3881 **F** 020 7431 8846
	@	info@bna.co.uk
Market areas		Nursing and Healthcare
	✉	2nd Floor, 7–13 Camberwell Rd, SE5 0EZ
	⊖	Kennington
	🚊	Brixton
	☎	**T** 020 7703 5288 **F** 020 7274 6556
	@	info@bna.co.uk
Market areas		Nursing and Healthcare
	✉	1st Floor, A Block, St Pancras Hospital, 4 St Pancras Way, NW1 0PE
	⊖	Camden Town
	🚊	Kentish Town
	☎	**T** 020 7530 3997 **F** 020 7530 5411
	@	info@bna.co.uk
Market areas		Nursing and Healthcare
	✉	'Nurses Bank', The Colonnades, Guys Hospital, St Thomas St, SE1 9RT
	⊖	London Bridge
	🚊	London Bridge
	☎	**T** 020 7955 2919 **F** 020 7955 8824
	@	info@bna.co.uk
Market areas		Nursing and Healthcare
	✉	3rd Floor, 443 Oxford St, W1C 2NA
	⊖	Bond St
	🚊	Paddington
	☎	**T** 020 7629 9030 **F** 020 7495 4847
	@	info@bna.co.uk
Market areas		Nursing and Healthcare

Website www.bna.co.uk

UK Offices 160+

REC Member No

Head Office The Colonnades, Beaconsfield Close, Hatfield, Herts, AL10 8YD

Brief Description Part of the Nestor Healthcare Group Plc, BNA was founded in 1949 and is the nation's leading Nursing and Care agency, providing staff in all areas of Healthcare from Care Assistants to Nurses for Private Hospitals and Trusts, Nursing Homes, Industry, Homecare, Prisons and Schools across the UK.

Preferred method of contact Telephone for appointment

Minimum requirements None

Type of business Temporary
Grade/Level of Appointments Care Assistants to Nurses

BSR Locums

Head Office ✉ Suite 60, Wickham House, 10 Cleveland Way, E1 4TR
⊖ Bethnal Green
🚃 Liverpool St
📞 T 020 7791 1444   F 020 7791 1222
@ locums@bsrgroup.co.uk
Market areas Locum Doctors

Website www.bsrlocums.com
UK Offices 1
REC Member Yes

Brief Description BSR are dedicated to providing the highest quality Medical recruitment services to both the NHS and Private sector. BSR specialise in assisting Doctors at all grades by finding Locum and Substantive posts throughout the UK and abroad.

Preferred method of contact Apply on line or telephone for appointment

Minimum requirements BMA registered

Type of business Contract and Permanent

Grade/Level of Appointments All levels

Capital Staffing Services

See Hospitality and Leisure, page 139

Celsian Group – Health

✉ 5th Floor, New Zealand House, 80 Haymarket, SW1Y 4TE
⊖ Piccadilly Circus
🚃 Charing Cross
📞 T 020 7930 2094   F 020 7930 4934
@ enquiries@celsiangroup.co.uk
Market areas Healthcare

Website www.celsiangroup.co.uk
UK Offices 24
REC Member Yes

Head Office Albany Place, Hyde Way, Welwyn Garden City, Herts, AL7 3BG

Brief Description Part of Carlisle Group UK, Celsian is the new collective brand name unveiled in 2002 for the following divisions: Recruit Education Services, Recruit Employment Care, Agency Cover and First Call.

Preferred method of contact Apply on line or telephone for appointment

Minimum requirements None
Type of business Permanent, Temporary and Contract
Grade/Level of Appointments All levels

Colvin Nursing Agency

Head Office ✉ 95 Heath St, NW3 6SS
⊖ Hampstead
🚃 West Hampstead
📞 T 020 7794 9323   F 020 7433 3706
@ eve@colvin-nursing.co.uk
Market areas Nursing and Healthcare

Website www.colvin-nursing.co.uk
UK Offices 1
REC Member Yes

Brief Description Colvin Nursing specialises in the placement of qualified and auxiliary Nurses in the home on a permanent or temporary, live-in residential or non-residential basis. For 22 years the name of Colvin has been synonymous with excellence, meeting the personal needs of those requiring care at home.

Preferred method of contact Telephone for appointment
Minimum requirements Nursing background
Type of business Temporary, Permanent and Contract
Grade/Level of Appointments Nursing Auxiliaries to Registered General Nurses

Corinth Healthcare Ltd

✉ 4 Cornwall Gardens , SW7 4AJ
⊖ Gloucester Rd
🚃 Victoria
📞 T 020 7589 3250   F 020 7589 3256
@ enquiries@corinthhealthcare.com
Market areas Healthcare

Website www.corinth.co.uk
REC Member No
Head Office 5 Theobald Ct, Theobald St, Borehamwood, Herts, WD6 4RN

Brief Description Established in 1968, Corinth Healthcare is the leading specialist agency for Healthcare professionals looking for work in the UK. They have over 4,000 people working for them at any one time and their network of contacts spans the UK as well as those developed through offices in Australia, New Zealand and South Africa.

Preferred method of contact Telephone for appointment
Minimum requirements Healthcare experience
Type of business Temporary, Permanent and Contract
Grade/Level of Appointments All levels

Drake International Ltd

See Secretarial, page 237

Elite Medical Services Ltd

Head Office ✉ 20 Grosvenor Place, SW1X 7HN
        Hyde Park Corner
        Victoria
        T 020 7235 1900   **F** 020 7235 1700
        @ recruit@elitemedical.co.uk
Market areas   Healthcare, Social Work

Website   www.elitemedical.co.uk
UK Offices   1
REC Member   No

Brief Description   Established in 1995, Elite Recruitment specialises in the placement of locum and permanent staff in NHS Trusts, Social Services, the Pharmaceutical industry and numerous Private Clinics throughout the UK.

Preferred method of contact   Apply on line or telephone for appointment

Minimum requirements   Previous professional experience

Type of business   Contract and Permanent

Grade/Level of Appointments   All levels

Elizabeth Norman International

See Sales and Marketing, page 214

Fairstaff Agency Ltd

Head Office ✉ 29–31 Oxford St, W1D 2DR
        Tottenham Court Rd
        Euston
        T 020 7439 2051   **F** 020 7287 0850
        @ enquiries@fairstaff.com
Market areas   Secretarial

Website   www.fairstaff.com
UK Offices   1
REC Member   Yes

Brief Description   Fairstaff has been established for nearly 19 years as a specialist agency for the Health Service and Public Sector. They are based in the heart of London and are proud of their reputation for providing high quality Office Staff to their Health and Public Sector clients. They manage prestigious Trust contracts in Central London and are therefore able to offer regular work to experienced, conscientious staff.

Preferred method of contact   Apply on line or telephone for appointment

Minimum requirements   None

Type of business   Temporary
Grade/Level of Appointments   All levels

Firstpoint Healthcare

         ✉ Copenhagen House, 5–10 Bury St, EC3A 5AT
          Aldgate
          Fenchurch St
          T 0845 130 5150   **F** 020 7375 9395
          @ info@firstpointhealthcare.com
Market areas   Healthcare

Website   www.firstpointhealthcare.com
UK Offices   7
REC Member   Yes
Head Office   Birmingham

Brief Description   Over the last 8 years, Firstpoint Healthcare has grown rapidly to become one on the largest independent providers of Healthcare personnel in the UK, and the fourth largest in Europe. They have expanded from their original base in Birmingham to open offices in key locations across the UK, and overseas in Australia and Canada.

Preferred method of contact   Apply on line or telephone for an appointment

Minimum requirements   None

Type of business   Temporary, Permanent and Contract

Grade/Level of Appointments   Administration/Clerical to Management

Geneva Health International Ltd

Head Office ✉ 2nd Floor, 128–129 Cheapside, EC2V 6BT
        Bank
        Cannon St
        T 020 7600 0859   **F** 020 7600 0944
        @ info@genevahealth.com
Market areas   Healthcare

Website   www.genevahealth.com
UK Offices   1
REC Member   Yes

Brief Description   Geneva is an international group of companies recruiting Nurses, Doctors and other Health professionals from around the world to work for Hospitals and Health employers in Australia, Canada, the Middle East, New Zealand, Saudi Arabia, the US and the UK. They cover the world from their hub locations in London and Auckland and support offices in Sydney, Melbourne and Wellington. They have many leading Private and Public Hospitals and Health Services as clients and are constantly building their database of Health professionals and Health jobs into one of the most comprehensive in the world.

Preferred method of contact   Apply on line or telephone for appointment

Minimum requirements Previous professional experience

Type of business Permanent and Contract

Grade/Level of Appointments Junior Clinical to Senior Executive

Grosvenor Nursing Agency

✉ 77 Denmark Hill, SE5 8RS
⊖ Brixton
🚇 Denmark Hill
☎ T 020 7703 9820   F 020 7701 8231
@ info@grosvenor-nursing.com
Market areas Healthcare

✉ House 10, The Residence, Newham General Hospital, Glen Rd, Plaistow, E13 6SL
⊖ Plaistow
☎ T 020 7363 8295   F 020 7363 8333
@ info@grosvenor-nursing.com
Market areas Healthcare

✉ 151 Hornsey Rd, N7 6DU
⊖ Holloway Rd
☎ T 020 7609 6222   F 020 7700 0589
@ info@grosvenor-nursing.com
Market areas Healthcare

Website www.grosvenor-nursing.com

UK Offices 3

REC Member No

Head Office Hatfield

Brief Description Part of Nestor Healthcare Group, Grosvenor was established in 1986 and has a strong reputation for delivering high quality Mental Health Care staff and Health Care services. Services include: supply of Health Care workers (Nurses and Auxiliaries) for short, medium and long term assignments; Nurse Bank Management; recruitment of specialist Mental Health Nurses and General Nurses for permanent posts; and Emergency Support service.

Preferred method of contact Apply on line or telephone for an appointment

Minimum requirements None

Type of business Contract, Temporary and Permanent

Grade/Level of Appointments All levels

Health Professionals Recruitment

Head Office ✉ 46 Queen Anne St, W1G 8HQ
⊖ Bond St
🚇 Paddington
☎ T 020 7935 8885   F 020 7935 8883
@ maria@healthprofessionals.com
Market areas Nursing

Website www.healthprofessionals.com

UK Offices 1

REC Member Yes

Brief Description Health Professionals is a Nursing recruitment company that concentrates solely on securing employment for specialist Registered Nurses, both full time and day to day. They are located in the centre of London's medical district. If you are interested in nursing in London, or any other part of the UK, the team at Health Professionals can help you through every step of your preparation.

Preferred method of contact Apply on line or telephone for an appointment

Minimum requirements Previous professional experience

Type of business Temporary and Permanent

Grade/Level of Appointments All levels

Hudson Shribman – Scientific Division

Head Office ✉ Vernon House, Sicilian Avenue, WC1A 2QH
⊖ Holborn
🚇 City Thameslink
☎ T 020 7269 0900   F 020 7404 5773
@ info@hs-scientific.co.uk
Market areas Scientific

Website www.hudson-shribman.co.uk

UK Offices 2

REC Member No

Brief Description Established in 1977, Hudson Shribman has firmly held the belief since its inception that the human resource is the most critical factor in determining the health and success of any organisation.

Preferred method of contact Apply on line or telephone for an appointment

Minimum requirements None

Type of business Temporary, Permanent and Contract

Grade/Level of Appointments Student to Board level appointments

Lifeline Personnel

See **Secretarial, page 247**

London Care Plc

See **Domestic, page 70**

Medacs

✉ 6 Paddington St, W1U 5BE
⊖ Baker St
🚇 Marylebone
☎ T 0800 783 0322   F 020 7224 4924

@ pharmacists@medacs.com

Market areas Healthcare

Website www.medacs.com

UK Offices 2

REC Member Yes

Head Office Skipton

Brief Description Medacs are part of Blue Arrow, one of the largest UK recruitment agencies. Since their first Doctor was placed in June 1992, Medacs has gone through a period of sustained growth to become the largest provider of temporary Healthcare professionals to the NHS. Discover the benefits of work with the UK's leading supplier of Healthcare professionals. Medacs supply locum and permanent Doctors to the National Health Service, Private Hospitals, the Prison Service, Cruise Ships and the Retail and Commercial sectors.

Preferred method of contact Apply on line or telephone for an appointment

Minimum requirements Ideally relevant medical exposure

Type of business Contract and Permanent

Grade/Level of Appointments Medical Administrators to Pharmacists/Consultants/Doctors

---

Montagu Nurses

Head Office ⊠ 18 Nottingham Place, W1U 5NQ
      ⊖ Baker St
      🚇 Marylebone
      ☎ T 020 7486 0818   F 020 7486 1531
      @ nurses@montagugroup.co.uk

Market areas Nurses, Carers

Website www.montagugroup.co.uk

UK Offices 1

REC Member Yes

Brief Description Montagu Nurses specialise in providing top Nurses and Carers to Hospitals, Nursing Homes and private patients own homes. Established in 1928, they are licensed to practice by Westminster City Council and the Department of Employment. Their office is staffed by an efficient caring team of Nurses who possess an in-depth knowledge of Nursing in London and client requirements.

Preferred method of contact Telephone for an appointment

Minimum requirements None

Type of business Temporary and Permanent

Grade/Level of Appointments All levels

MySwift

Head Office ⊠ 33 St James's Sq, SW1Y 4JS
      ⊖ St James's Park
      🚇 Victoria
      ☎ T 020 7661 9333   F 020 7661 9444

@ info@myswift.co.uk

Market areas Locum Doctors

Website www.myswift.co.uk

UK Offices 1

REC Member Yes

Brief Description MySwift was formed by Healthcare professionals in partnership with The Royal Bank of Scotland to provide a specialist Medical recruitment service focused on supplying locum Doctors for General Practice and Hospitals throughout the UK.

Preferred method of contact Apply on line or telephone for an appointment

Minimum requirements Previous professional experience

Type of business Contract

Grade/Level of Appointments All levels

Piers Meadows Recruitment

Head Office ⊠ 34 South Molton St, W1K 5RG
      ⊖ Bond St
      🚇 Paddington
      ☎ T 020 7629 6799   F 020 7629 6727
      @ info@piersmeadows.co.uk

Market areas Occupational Therapists and Physiotherapists

Website www.piersmeadows.co.uk

UK Offices 1

REC Member No

Brief Description Piers Meadows Recruitment is a specialist recruitment consultancy involved in the recruitment of Occupational Therapists and Physiotherapists throughout the United Kingdom. They aim to provide a personalised, friendly, and efficient service, finding their candidates the right permanent, locum or short-term contract position. They focus specifically on their candidates' needs, placing them where they want, when they want, specialising in what they want. So whether you are looking for a job now or in the future PMR can help.

Preferred method of contact Apply on line or telephone for an appointment

Minimum requirements Previous professional experience

Type of business Contract and Permanent

Grade/Level of Appointments All levels

Platinum Nursing

Head Office ⊠ 77 Oxford St, W1R 1RB
      ⊖ Tottenham Court Rd
      🚇 Euston
      ☎ T 020 7659 2424   F 020 7659 2134
      @ info@pr-international.co.uk

Market areas Nursing, Healthcare

Website www.pr-international.co.uk

UK Offices 1

REC Member No

Brief Description Platinum Nursing Ltd is managed by a team of qualified Nurses and Health professionals with a wealth of experience in caring for others. As part of the Platinum Recruitment International Group of Companies, they are dedicated to supporting the UK Healthcare market with a complete range of Health and Social Care support, providing training and specialist Healthcare services.

Preferred method of contact Apply on line or telephone for an appointment

Minimum requirements Previous professional experience

Type of business Contract and Permanent

Grade/Level of Appointments All levels

Praxis

See Executive Search, page 103

Pulse Healthcare Appointments

Head Office   ✉   1st Floor, 80 High Holborn, WC1V 6LS
  ⊖   Holborn
  ☃   City Thameslink
  ☎ T 020 7959 1000   F 020 7959 1001
Market areas   Healthcare

Website www.pulse-agency.com

UK Offices 1

REC Member Yes

Brief Description A member of the Match Group of companies, Pulse Healthcare Appointments operates across the length and breadth of the Healthcare market.

Preferred method of contact Apply on line or telephone for an appointment

Minimum requirements None

Type of business Temporary and Permanent

Grade/Level of Appointments All levels

Reed Healthcare International

Head Office   ✉   Reed Executive Plc, 145 Kensington High St, W8 7LP
  ☎ T 020 7313 7450   F 020 7313 7451

  ✉   44 Denmark Hill, SE5 8RZ
  ⊖   Denmark Hill
  ☃   Brixton
  ☎ T 020 7326 7501
Market areas   Healthcare

  ✉   Fairgate House, 78 New Oxford St, WC1A 1HB
  ⊖   Holborn

  ☃   City Thameslink
  ☎ T 020 7636 9329
Market areas   Healthcare

Website www.reed.co.uk

UK Offices 250+

REC Member No

Brief Description A subsidiary of Reed Executive Plc established in 1960, Reed's growth has been dramatic and the company's stated ambition is to grow the business substantially. Reed has been organised into a number of separate operating companies to make this happen. Reed Healthcare has been providing Nurses, Social Carers and Health professionals to clients in both the NHS and Private Sector nationwide for over 40 years.

Preferred method of contact Apply on line or telephone for an appointment

Minimum requirements None

Type of business Contract and Permanent

Grade/Level of Appointments All levels

Ruston Poole International

See Executive Search, page 106

Smile Healthcare

Head Office   ✉   20 Borough High St, SE1 9QG
  ⊖   London Bridge
  ☃   London Bridge
  ☎ T 020 7403 4191   F 020 7407 2989
  @   london@smilehealthcare.co.uk
Market areas   Healthcare, Social Work

Website www.smilehealthcare.co.uk

UK Offices 1

REC Member Yes

Brief Description Smile Healthcare is part of Corinth Healthcare, the leading specialist agency for Healthcare professionals looking for work in the UK. For over 30 years they've been helping Healthcare professionals, such as Therapists and Social Workers, find the right job, in the right place with the best pay.

Preferred method of contact Apply on line or telephone for an appointment

Minimum requirements Previous professional experience

Type of business Temporary and Permanent

Grade/Level of Appointments All levels

Southern Cross Employment Agency Ltd

Head Office   ✉   4 Pelham St, SW7 2NG
  ⊖   South Kensington

🚇 Victoria
☎ T 020 7589 9005
@ info@southerncrossdental.com
Market areas Dental Staff

Website www.southerncrossdental.com

UK Offices 1

REC Member No

Brief Description Southern Cross have nearly 40 years experience in the profession recruiting throughout Greater London and the rest of the UK. Based in Central London Southern Cross Dental will work with you to secure the Dental position or Dental personnel you are seeking.

Preferred method of contact Apply on line or telephone for an appointment

Minimum requirements None

Type of business Temporary and Permanent

Grade/Level of Appointments Receptionists to Dentists

SSC Staff Consultants

See **Sales and Marketing, page 218**

Strand Nurses Bureau

Head Office ✉ Brettenham House, 1 Lancaster Place, WC2E 7RN
🚇 Covent Garden
🚇 Charing Cross
☎ T 020 7836 6397   F 020 7240 6324
@ info@strandnursing.co.uk
Market areas Nursing, Care Assistants

Website www.strandnursing.co.uk

UK Offices 1

REC Member Yes

Brief Description Strand Nurses Bureau has been established since 1974. During this time they have gained a reputation for efficiency, reliability and professionalism. They provide a 24 hour service and are able to supply qualified Nurses, experienced Nursing Assistants and Carers in long and short term positions.

Preferred method of contact Apply on line or telephone for an appointment

Minimum requirements Previous professional experience

Type of business Temporary and Permanent

Grade/Level of Appointments All levels

Sugarman Group

See **Secretarial, page 258**

Talentmark Ltd

Head Office ✉ 11 Westbourne Grove, W2 4UA
🚇 Paddington
🚇 Paddington
☎ T 020 7229 2266   F 020 7229 3549
@ enquiries@talentmark.com
Market areas Consumer Healthcare, Pharmaceuticals

Website www.talentmark.com

UK Offices 1

REC Member No

Brief Description Talentmark is a specialist recruiter for the Pharmaceutical, Biotech and other Healthcare industries. They were the first company to specialise in recruitment for this sector – over 30 years ago – and remain at the forefront of Healthcare recruitment today.

Preferred method of contact Apply on line or telephone for an appointment

Minimum requirements Relevant industry exposure

Type of business Contract and Permanent

Grade/Level of Appointments Mid to Senior Management level

Vera Employment Agency

Head Office ✉ 240 Upper St, N1 1RU
🚇 Highbury and Islington
🚇 Highbury and Islington
☎ T 020 7359 5454   F 020 7704 2970
Market areas Nursing

Website www.veranursing.co.uk

UK Offices 1

REC Member Yes

Brief Description Vera Nursing Agency prides itself as the agency for everyone. Their objective is to provide professional, dedicated and quality Nurses of all specialities and Critical Nurses and Midwives. Vera Nursing has always been known as the agency that supplies Midwives no matter what time of the day or night. This is achieved by their 24 hour telephone service. At the same time they provide support care and respect to all their Nurses whose needs they hold very high.

Preferred method of contact Apply on line or telephone for an appointment

Minimum requirements Previous professional experience

Type of business Temporary

Grade/Level of Appointments All levels

Hospitality and Leisure

AA Appointments

See Secretarial, page 227

Abbey Exec/AES Contract Services

See Healthcare, page 129

Abbey Recruitment (London Co)

Head Office   ✉   18 James St, W1U 1EQ
  ⊖   Bond St
  🚇   Victoria
  ☎   T 020 7495 4342   F 020 7495 4345
  @   paul@abbeyrecruitment.co.uk
Market areas   Catering and Hospitality

Website   www.abbeyrecruitment.co.uk

UK Offices   1

REC Member   No

Brief Description   At Abbey Recruitment you'll find a dedicated team providing an honest, efficient employment service in all areas of Catering including Chefs, Managers and Hospitality staff. Their enthusiasm and commitment ensures that candidates and clients alike are given the best service. Applicants are selected for their dedication to the industry, and offered extremely competitive wages and benefits. Clients include International Hotels, Guide Listed Restaurants and Modern Themed Restaurants.

Preferred method of contact   Apply on line or telephone for appointment

Minimum requirements   None

Type of business   Temporary and Permanent

Grade/Level of Appointments   All levels

Adecco Hotel and Catering

  ✉   18 Devonshire Row, EC2M 4RH
  ⊖   Moorgate
  🚇   Moorgate
  ☎   T 020 7247 2992   F 020 7247 3375
  @   122.hotel.&catering@adecco.co.uk
Market areas   Hospitality, Chefs, Catering

Website   www.adecco.co.uk

UK Offices   358

REC Member   No

Head Office   Adecco House, Elstree Way, Borehamwood, Herts, WD6 1HY

Brief Description   Adecco is the only personnel services company in the world to offer such a comprehensive range of services with such a geographic reach, from general to highly specialised staffing, temporary and permanent placement, Human Resource consulting and Career Management. Formed from the merger of Adia Alfred Marks and Ecco Employment in 1997, its group companies include Office Angels, Computer People, Ajilon, Accountants on Call (AOC) and Jonathan Wren.

Preferred method of contact   Walk in, telephone or e-mail – candidates will normally be required to make an appointment for interview

Minimum requirements   None

Type of business   Contract, Temporary and Permanent

Grade/Level of Appointments   All levels up to Senior Management

Admiral Catering

Head Office   ✉   72 Wells St, W1P 3RD
  ⊖   Oxford Circus
  🚇   Euston
  ☎   T 020 7580 8446   F 020 7580 8447
  @   careers@admiralgroup.com
Market areas   Hospitality and Catering

  ✉   67 Farringdon Rd, EC1M 3JB
  ⊖   Farringdon
  🚇   Farringdon
  ☎   T 020 7831 5200   F 020 7831 4993
  @   careers@admiralgroup.com
Market areas   Hospitality and Catering

Website   www.admiralgroup.com

UK Offices   2

REC Member   Yes

Brief Description   Established in 1995, the Admiral Group is a market leader in providing permanent and temporary personnel at all levels within the Catering and Hospitality sector.

Preferred method of contact   Apply on line or telephone for appointment

Minimum requirements   None

Type of business   Temporary and Permanent

Grade/Level of Appointments   Junior to Senior Management

Angel Human Resources Plc

See Secretarial, page 229

Appleton Management

Head Office   ✉   125 High Holborn, WC1V 6QA
     ⊖   Holborn
     🚊   Holborn
     ☎   T 020 7831 1122   F 020 7831 2244
     @   contact@theeventpeople.co.uk
  Market areas   Catering, Hospitality and Leisure

Website   www.theeventpeople.co.uk

UK Offices   1

REC Member   Yes

Brief Description   Appleton is an established recruitment and event resources consultancy supplying the Catering, Leisure and Hospitality industry both within the UK and internationally. Their service incorporates permanent recruitment, temporary recruitment and event resources. They currently enjoy established relationships with some of the finest companies within the industry who have given them a reputation for providing effective high quality recruitment solutions. They created event people in response to client demand to extend the staff recruitment services at events to providing a wide range of resources. These include: Event Management, Mobile Staff Accommodation, Logistics, Ticketing, Set Up and Breakdown Crews and Event Catering. This area of their business continues to expand with their services being utilised at most of the premiere sporting events in the UK.

Preferred method of contact   Apply on line or telephone for appointment

Minimum requirements   None

Type of business   Temporary, Permanent and Contract

Grade/Level of Appointments   Graduate/1st Jobber to Executive/ Management level

Aptus Personnel

See Industrial, page 150

Berkeley Scott Group Plc

     ✉   64 Charlotte St, W1T 4QD
     ⊖   Goodge St
     🚊   Euston
     ☎   T 020 7299 6720   F 020 7299 6721
     @   central.temp/perm@bsgplc.co.uk
  Market areas   Hospitality and Leisure

     ✉   154 Bishopsgate, EC2M 4LN
     ⊖   Liverpool St
     🚊   Liverpool St
     ☎   T 020 7377 1817   F 020 7377 1199
     @   central.city@bsgplc.co.uk
  Market areas   Hospitality and Leisure

     ✉   Sutherland House, 5–6 Argyll St, W1V 1AD
     ⊖   Oxford Circus
     🚊   Charing Cross
     ☎   T 020 7025 1444   F 020 7025 1444
     @   chefs.london@bsgplc.com
  Market areas   Hospitality and Leisure

     ✉   3rd Floor, Sutherland House, 5–6 Argyll St, W1F 7TE
     ⊖   Oxford Circus
     🚊   Charing Cross
     ☎   T 020 7025 1400   F 020 7025 1402
     @   express.london@bsgplc.com
  Market areas   Hospitality and Leisure

Website   www.berkeley-scott.com

UK Offices   14

REC Member   No

Head Office   Berkeley House, 11–13 Ockford Rd, Godalming, Surrey, GU7 1QU

Brief Description   Berkeley Scott Group is the leading specialist in the Hospitality and Leisure sector supplying temporary and permanent staff from 14 offices across the UK to Hotels, Restaurants, High Street Retail, Health and Fitness, Facilities Management, Sports Venues and Arenas.

Preferred method of contact   Apply on line or telephone for appointment

Minimum requirements   None

Type of business   Temporary and Permanent

Grade/Level of Appointments   All levels

Blue Arrow Catering

     ✉   4 Moorfields, EC2Y 9AA
     ⊖   Moorgate
     🚊   Moorgate
     ☎   T 020 7588 4134   F 020 7588 4149
     @   staff@bluearrow.co.uk
  Market areas   Hospitality and Catering

     ✉   69 Buckingham Palace Rd, SW1W 0QU
     ⊖   Victoria
     🚊   Victoria
     ☎   T 020 7931 0913
     @   staff@bluearrow.co.uk
  Market areas   Hospitality and Catering

Website   www.bluearrow.co.uk

UK Offices   250

REC Member   Yes

Head Office   800 The Boulevard, Capability Green, Luton, LU1 3BA

Brief Description   Part of the Corporate Services Group (CSG), Blue Arrow was founded over 40 years ago to become one of the UK's largest recruitment businesses with a network of over 250 locations in the UK, providing temporary, permanent and contract staff across Office, Catering, Construction, Healthcare, Technical and Industrial sectors.

Preferred method of contact   Telephone for appointment

Minimum requirements None

Type of business Temporary, Permanent and Contract

Grade/Level of Appointments All levels

Blues Agency Ltd

Head Office ✉ 19 Oxberry Ave, SW6 5SP
🔄 Putney Bridge
🚃 Wimbledon
☎ T 020 7381 4747   F 020 7736 8132
Market areas Hospitality and Catering

Website www.bluesagency.co.uk

UK Offices 1

REC Member No

Brief Description Founded in 1979, Blues has been providing temporary and permanent Cooks, Waiters/Waitresses, Butlers and Kitchen Staff to corporate and private clients throughout the UK and overseas markets.

Preferred method of contact Apply on line or telephone for an appointment

Minimum requirements None

Type of business Temporary and Permanent

Grade/Level of Appointments All levels

C&M Travel Recruitment Ltd

Head Office ✉ 1 Carthusian St, EC1M 6DZ
🔄 Barbican
🚃 Barbican
☎ T 020 7490 8700   F 020 7490 8701
@ enq@candm.co.uk
Market areas Travel

Website www.candm.co.uk

UK Offices 3

REC Member Yes

Brief Description C&M Recruitment specialise in all levels of staffing for the Travel industry including Airlines, Car Hire, Hotels, Business Travel and Foreign Exchange across the UK with online training services available on all CRS systems.

Preferred method of contact Telephone for appointment

Minimum requirements None

Type of business Temporary and Permanent

Grade/Level of Appointments Graduate/Junior to Company Director

Capital Staffing Services

Head Office ✉ 82 Borough High St, SE1 1LL
🔄 London Bridge
🚃 London Bridge
☎ T 020 7407 8686   F 020 7407 8687
@ enquiries@capitalstaffing.co.uk
Market areas Catering, Nursing

Website www.css-nursing.com, www.css-catering.co.uk

UK Offices 1

REC Member Yes

Brief Description Capital Staffing is an established Catering and Nursing recruitment agency based in London.

Preferred method of contact Apply on line or telephone for appointment

Minimum requirements Ideally previous professional experience

Type of business Temporary, Permanent and Contract

Grade/Level of Appointments Across all levels

Chelsea Staff Bureau

Head Office ✉ 262a Fulham Rd, SW10 9EL
🔄 Gloucester Rd
🚃 Victoria
☎ T 020 7849 3920   F 020 7849 3929
@ chelsea.staff@talk21.com
Market areas Hospitality and Catering

Website www.chelseastaffbureau.co.uk

UK Offices 1

REC Member No

Brief Description Chelsea Staff Bureau specialise in the recruitment of Hospitality and Catering staff.

Preferred method of contact Telephone for appointment

Minimum requirements None

Type of business Temporary and Permanent

Grade/Level of Appointments All levels

Chess Partnership

Head Office ✉ 14a Ganton St, W1F 7QT
🔄 Oxford Circus
🚃 Charing Cross
☎ T 020 7025 1888   F 020 7025 1889
@ recruitment@chess-partnership.com
Market areas Hospitality and Catering

Website www.chess-partnership.com

UK Offices 2

REC Member No

Brief Description Part of the Chess Group of Companies, Chess Partnership specialises in recruitment for the Hospitality and Facilities Management sectors both in the UK and overseas. With offices in London and Nottingham, Chess Partnership provide staff to all areas including Hotels, Restaurants, Conference and Banqueting Events.

Preferred method of contact Apply on line or telephone for appointment

Minimum requirements None

Type of business Temporary and Contract

Grade/Level of Appointments All levels

Christophers Personnel Ltd

Head Office ✉ 68–70 Kings Rd, SW3 4UD
⊖ Sloane Sq
🚇 Victoria
📞 T 020 7581 3990   F 020 7581 5777
@ christopherspers@btconnect.com
Market areas   Catering and Hospitality

Website www.christopherspersonnel.co.uk

UK Offices 1

REC Member No

Brief Description Christophers Personnel specialise in providing Hospitality staff.

Preferred method of contact Telephone for appointment

Minimum requirements None

Type of business Temporary and Permanent

Grade/Level of Appointments All levels

City Centre Group

See Secretarial, page 235

Collins King and Associates

Head Office ✉ 30 Maiden Lane, WC2E 7JS
⊖ Covent Garden
🚇 Charing Cross
📞 T 020 7240 0066   F 020 7240 8888
@ info@collinsking.co.uk
Market areas   Hospitality

Website www.collinsking.co.uk

UK Offices 1

REC Member Yes

Brief Description Collins King and Associates are an established firm of Hospitality recruitment specialists based in the heart of London's West End. Their primary focus is the sourcing of high quality Kitchen and Management personnel to the Hospitality industry. Their client

base includes many of the UK's leading Hotel, Restaurant and Contract Catering companies.

Preferred method of contact Apply on line or telephone for appointment

Minimum requirements Ideally relevant industry exposure

Type of business Temporary and Permanent

Grade/Level of Appointments Junior Chef to General Manager/ Events Manager

CTI Group

✉ 207–209 Regent St, W1R 7DD
⊖ Piccadilly Circus
🚇 Charing Cross
📞 T 020 7734 9412   F 020 7734 9414
@ cti-uk@cti-usa.com
Market areas   Cruise Ship, Hotel, Resorts

Website www.cti-usa.com

UK Offices 1

REC Member No

Head Office Fort Lauderdale, Florida, USA

Brief Description Established in 1986, CTI Group has built a reputation of dependability and integrity on a strong dedication to the needs and expectations of both clients and candidates. CTI Group supplies to the following distinguished clients: Carnival Cruise Lines, Celebrity Cruises, Crystal Cruises, Disney Cruise Line amongst others.

Preferred method of contact Apply on line or telephone for appointment

Minimum requirements None

Type of business Permanent

Grade/Level of Appointments All levels

Exclusive Recruitment

Head Office ✉ Glyn House, 16 City Rd, EC1Y 2AA
⊖ Old St
🚇 Old St
📞 T 020 7588 4100   F 020 7588 4502
@ enquiries@exclusiverecruitment.com
Market areas   Hospitality, Secretarial

Website www.exclusiverecruitment.com

UK Offices 1

REC Member No

Brief Description Exclusive Recruitment (Reception Exclusive) has been established for over 15 years. It was set up to fill a gap in the market specialising purely in Front Office vacancies for Hotels. They are now highly regarded in the Hotel industry, and is often the first 'port of call' for a Hotel seeking to fill a Front Office vacancy. In 1997 they expanded into Office/Company Reception due to an increasing demand from clients. This has allowed Exclusive Recruitment to grow in reputation and continue to develop new relationships with clients though word of mouth and recommendations. They have forged links with international agencies to provide both international candidates for their clients, and opportunities for candidates wishing to further their careers overseas.

Preferred method of contact Apply on line or telephone for an appointment

Minimum requirements None

Type of business Temporary and Permanent

Grade/Level of Appointments All levels

Grapevine International

Head Office ✉ 63–66 Hatton Garden, EC1N 8LE
⊖ Chancery Lane
🚊 City Thameslink
☎ T 020 7430 2266   F 0845 1300 744
@ office@grapevine-int.co.uk
Market areas   Hospitality

Website www.grapevine-int.co.uk

UK Offices 1

REC Member No

Brief Description Grapevine International is an international executive recruitment firm specialising in the Hotel and Catering industry founded in 1989, with offices in Hong Kong and Spain and associate offices in Germany, South Africa. Sister company Grapevine International Services Ltd supplies Training, Consultancy and ancillary services such as Stocktaking, Payroll Computations.

Preferred method of contact Apply on line or telephone for appointment

Minimum requirements Previous professional experience

Type of business Permanent

Grade/Level of Appointments Mid to Senior Management level

Greycoat Placements Ltd

See **Domestic, page 69**

HARP Wallen

See **Executive Search, page 90**

HLR Associates Ltd

See **Executive Search, page 93**

Jubilee Persona

Head Office ✉ 47 Dean St, W1D 5BE
⊖ Tottenham Court Rd
🚊 Euston
☎ T 020 7437 5074   F 020 7287 3298
@ jubileepersona@btinternet.com
Market areas   Hospitality, Chefs, Catering

Website www.jubileepersona.com

UK Offices 1

REC Member No

Brief Description Established for over 23 years, Jubilee Persona supplies the Catering industry with quality staff for kitchens large and small in individual Restaurants and major Catering organisations. Jubilee's extensive contacts built, developed and maintained in complete confidence ensure that they have access to a wealth of clients and quality candidates.

Preferred method of contact Telephone for appointment

Minimum requirements None

Type of business Temporary and Permanent

Grade/Level of Appointments All levels

Kerry Robert Associates

Head Office ✉ 100 Pall Mall, SW1Y 5HP
⊖ St James's Park
🚊 Victoria
☎ T 020 7321 3891   F 020 7321 3892
@ recruitment@kerryrobert.com
Market areas   Hospitality and Catering

Website www.kerryrobert.com

UK Offices 1

REC Member No

Brief Description Kerry Robert Associates recruit exclusively for the Hotel, Restaurant and Catering industries. They specialise in the recruitment of Operational Management and Financial appointments at both unit and corporate levels throughout the UK.

Preferred method of contact Apply on line or telephone for an appointment

Minimum requirements Ideally relevant industry exposure

Type of business Permanent

Grade/Level of Appointments All levels

Keystone Employment Group – Catering & Hospitality

Head Office ✉ 272–276 Pentonville Rd, N1 9JY
☎ T 020 7837 6444   F 020 7833 7783

✉ 219 Oxford St, W1D 2LM
⊖ Oxford Circus
🚆 Charing Cross
☎ T 020 7434 1313   F 020 7434 3762
Market areas Catering and Hospitality

Website www.keystone-recruitment.co.uk

UK Offices 4

REC Member Yes

Brief Description Keystone was originally formed in London in 1948. It was one of the first and largest privately owned employment agencies placing Secretarial and General Office staff. Their greatest assets are the people who work for them, they are the reason why clients and candidates are recommended to use the Keystone Group services — their ability to listen and understand people's needs, to work in partnership with them to achieve success, and more importantly client and candidate satisfaction.

Preferred method of contact Apply on line or telephone for an appointment

Minimum requirements None

Type of business Temporary and Permanent

Grade/Level of Appointments All levels

L&G Recruitment Ltd

See **Financial Services and Insurance, page 124**

Lister Charles Partnership

Head Office ✉ 36 Tavistock St, WC2E 7PB
⊖ Covent Garden
🚆 Charing Cross
☎ T 020 7240 2224   F 020 7836 0036
@ lcp@lister-charles.co.uk
Market areas Leisure and Hospitality

Website www.lister-charles.co.uk

UK Offices 1

REC Member No

Brief Description No matter which area of the Leisure and Hospitality industry you work in, Lister Charles are perfectly placed to find you the right job — one which will enhance and develop your career and get you off the treadmill of your current role. They cover the broadest spectrum of industry disciplines across the broadest spectrum of industry sectors, so no matter if you are looking for a job as a Chef or as a Restaurant Manager, a Health and Fitness Club General Manager or a Senior Manager in the Brewing and Pub Retailing sector, they can help.

Preferred method of contact Apply on line or telephone for an appointment

Minimum requirements Ideally relevant industry exposure

Type of business Contract and Permanent

Grade/Level of Appointments Fitness Instructor/Chef to Operations Manager/Area Manager

Lumley Employment Co Ltd

Head Office ✉ 85 Charlwood St, SW1V 4PB
⊖ Pimlico
🚆 Victoria
☎ T 020 7630 0545   F 020 7976 6000
@ admin@lumleyscooks.co.uk
Market areas Corporate Hospitality, Catering

Website www.lumleyscooks.co.uk

UK Offices 2

REC Member No

Brief Description Lumleys have been providing Catering staff of the highest calibre since 1972, specialising in Corporate Hospitality and Private Entertaining. They supply all types of staff from Cooks, Assistants to Butlers whether it is a formal business lunch or a villa in the South of France.

Preferred method of contact Telephone for appointment

Minimum requirements None

Type of business Temporary, Permanent and Contract

Grade/Level of Appointments Waiters/Catering Assistants to Butlers/Chefs

Management Search Executive Ltd

See **Executive Search, page 97**

Mayday Group

Head Office ✉ 21 Great Chapel St, W1F 8FP
⊖ Tottenham Court Rd
🚆 Euston
☎ T 020 7434 2627
@ mayday@maydaygroup.co.uk
Market areas Catering

✉ 2 Shoreditch High St, E1 6PG
⊖ Liverpool St
🚆 Liverpool St
☎ T 020 7377 1352
@ mayday@maydaygroup.co.uk
Market areas Catering

Website www.maydaygroup.co.uk

UK Offices 3

REC Member Yes

Brief Description With three offices across London, Mayday specialises in temporary and permanent staffing solutions for clients across the UK.

Preferred method of contact Apply on line or telephone for an appointment

Minimum requirements None

Type of business Temporary and Permanent

Grade/Level of Appointments Administration to Head Chef

Mise en Place

Head Office	✉	Suite 18, Grafton House, 2–3 Golden Sq, W1F 9HR
	⊖	Piccadilly Circus
	⊜	Charing Cross
	☎	T 020 7439 3440 F 020 7439 3441
	@	info@miseenplaceuk.com
Market areas		Catering

Website www.miseenplaceuk.com

UK Offices 1

REC Member No

Brief Description Since the company was first formed in 1997 they have put into place hundreds of skilled workers who have contributed to their companies' profitability. Mise en Place specialises in the permanent placement of Catering staff throughout London and the UK, with clients ranging from Private Clubs to guide listed Restaurants and major UK and international Hotels.

Preferred method of contact Apply on line or telephone for an appointment

Minimum requirements None

Type of business Permanent

Grade/Level of Appointments Bar Staff/Sous Chef to Head Chef/Management level

Mosimann's Creative Chefs

Head Office	✉	11b West Halkin, SW1X 8JL
	✉	4 William Blake House, Bridge Lane, SW11 3AD
	⊖	Clapham Common
	⊜	Clapham Junction
	☎	T 020 7326 8355 F 020 7326 8350
	@	chefs@mosimann.com
Market areas		Hospitality, Chefs

Website www.mosimann.com

UK Offices 4

REC Member No

Brief Description Mosimann's Creative Chefs was founded in 1996 in combination with culinary experts to offer a service as a consultancy specialising in recruiting highly qualified members of staff within the Food and Beverage sector. Following the principle of Anton Mosimann to work with only the best, Creative Chefs can and will provide the exclusive service of Executive Search consultancy for their clients and applicants worldwide.

Preferred method of contact Apply on line or telephone for an appointment

Minimum requirements Previous professional experience

Type of business Permanent

Grade/Level of Appointments All levels

New Frontiers Ltd

Head Office	✉	23 Islington High St, N1 9LQ
	⊖	Angel
	⊜	Old St
	☎	T 020 7833 9977
	@	jobs@newfrontiers.co.uk
Market areas		Travel

Website www.newfrontiers.co.uk

UK Offices 5

REC Member Yes

Brief Description New Frontiers specialise in recruiting people into all sectors of the Travel industry. Since 1993, they have helped hundreds of people find fantastic careers in major Travel companies and prestigious independent organisations across the UK. New Frontiers have offices in strategic locations across the UK as well as recruitment partners in Auckland, Johannesburg and Sydney.

Preferred method of contact Apply on line or telephone for an appointment

Minimum requirements None

Type of business Temporary, Permanent and Contract

Grade/Level of Appointments All levels

Occasional & Permanent Nannies

See **Domestic, page 70**

Platinum Recruitment International Ltd

Head Office	✉	77 Oxford St, W1R 1RB
	⊖	Tottenham Court Rd
	⊜	Euston
	☎	T 020 7659 2034 F 020 7659 2134
	@	info@pr-international.co.uk
Market areas		Hospitality, Domestic

Website www.pr-international.co.uk

UK Offices 1

REC Member No

Brief Description Platinum Recruitment International Ltd is run by a team of consultants who specialise in recruiting staff for Housekeeping, Food and Beverage and Cleaning departments. They have specialised experience in different parts of Hotel Management and Personnel Management. They supply many London Hotels,

Schools, Hospitals and Restaurants and they offer a service of excellence, quality and value.

Preferred method of contact Apply on line or telephone for an appointment

Minimum requirements None

Type of business Temporary and Permanent

Grade/Level of Appointments All levels

Profile Management

Head Office ✉ 38–39 Maiden Lane, WC2E 7JS
            ⊖ Covent Garden
            ☒ Charing Cross
            ☎ T 020 7557 6060   F 020 7557 6061
Market areas Hospitality and Leisure, Sales and Marketing

Website www.pmsr.com

UK Offices 1

REC Member Yes

Brief Description Profile's mission is to become the first choice when selecting a specialist consultant for Management appointments in the Luxury Hospitality industry. Operating worldwide from offices in London, Paris and New York, and with associates in Germany and Australia, clients are able to draw on the experience they have gained in over 20 years in their specialist field; also from the knowledge of their team of over 20 consultants. The majority of the team has benefited from having had careers in Hotels and Restaurants working for companies, which in several cases, have become important clients. They are committed to providing all Profile's employees with comprehensive training in order to ensure a consistent level of service based on high quality candidates and a quick response time.

Preferred method of contact Apply on line or telephone for an appointment

Minimum requirements None

Type of business Temporary and Permanent

Grade/Level of Appointments All levels

Regent Recruitment

Head Office ✉ 2nd Floor, 37 Albemarle St, W1X 3FB
            ⊖ Green Park
            ☒ Victoria
            ☎ T 020 7629 9401   F 020 7629 9402
            @ info@regentrecruitment.com
Market areas Hospitality

Website www.regentrecruitment.com

UK Offices 2

REC Member No

Brief Description Established in 1996 to cater to the country's highest profile Restaurants and Hotels, Regent Recruitment is now recognised by, and represented in, many of the world's most elite

eating establishments. With a dedicated core of recruitment professionals and a company ethos that puts communication and care over clumsy convenience they have successfully paved the way for over a thousand quality candidates into quality jobs. Based in the heart of Mayfair, they run their head office to suit the needs of their customers. Their site acts as a tool for clients scouting for applicants to fill specific vacancies – from Front of House to Premier Chefs. And for candidates, applicants themselves, who are actively seeking employment through Regent Recruitment.

Preferred method of contact Apply on line or telephone for an appointment

Minimum requirements None

Type of business Temporary and Permanent

Grade/Level of Appointments All levels

ROC Recruitment

Head Office ✉ 27 Grosvenor St, London
            ☎ T 020 7318 1400   F 020 7499 9002

            ✉ 65 London Wall, EC2M 5TP
            ⊖ Moorgate
            ☒ Moorgate
            ☎ T 020 7256 9040   F 020 7256 9044
            @ roc@roc.co.uk
Market areas Accountancy and Banking, Retail, Hospitality, Education

Website www.roc.co.uk

UK Offices 3

REC Member Yes

Brief Description ROC Recruitment specialises in placing temporary and permanent staff within Accountancy and Banking, Retail, Education and Hospitality from offices in London and Manchester.

Preferred method of contact Apply on line or telephone for an appointment

Minimum requirements None

Type of business Temporary and Permanent

Grade/Level of Appointments All levels

The Sportsweb Agency

Head Office ✉ Cloisters House, 8 Battersea Park Rd, SW8 4BG
            ⊖ Clapham Common
            ☒ Clapham Junction
            ☎ T 020 7622 8500   F 020 7622 2225
Market areas Leisure

Website www.thesportsweb.co.uk

UK Offices 1

REC Member No

Brief Description The Sportsweb is the largest agency in the UK specialising in the Health and Leisure Industry. They have a particularly strong focus in London and the Home Counties and have expanded their existing client base to service companies across the UK and Europe. With the introduction of their Executive Search division in late 2000 they are also now operating in the Middle East and Far East.

Preferred method of contact Apply on line or telephone for an appointment

Minimum requirements None

Type of business Permanent

Grade/Level of Appointments All levels

Susan Hamilton Personnel Services

See Secretarial, page 258

T&T Recruitment & Resourcing Ltd

Head Office ✉ 5–7 Folgate St, E1 6BX
          ⊖ Liverpool St
          🚋 Liverpool St
          ☎ T 020 7426 9370   F 020 7051 4979
          @ info@t-trecruitment.co.uk
Market areas Hotel and Leisure, Travel, Tour Operations, Executive Secretarial

Website www.t-trecruitment.co.uk

UK Offices 2

REC Member Yes

Brief Description T&T Recruitment & Resourcing Limited has been established since 1983 as a specialist recruitment agency. They pride themselves on providing comprehensive recruitment solutions to applicants and clients alike. Unlike general High Street agencies T&T only recruit within specialist areas. They also ensure that their recruitment consultants have the relevant industry background enabling them to understand your every need. Their specialist divisions are: Travel, Tour Operations, Hotel and Leisure, Payroll and HR, Communications and Executive Secretarial.

Preferred method of contact Apply on line or telephone for an appointment

Minimum requirements None

Type of business Temporary and Permanent

Grade/Level of Appointments All levels

Travel Jobshop Ltd

Head Office ✉ 31 High Holborn, WC1V 6AX
          ⊖ Chancery Lane
          🚋 City Thameslink
          ☎ T 020 7242 7150   F 020 7405 5468
          @ careers@traveljobshop.co.uk
Market areas Travel

Website www.traveljobshop.co.uk

UK Offices 1

REC Member No

Brief Description Part of the Select Appointments Group, Travel Jobshop can help whether you are looking for permanent or temporary work in the Travel industry.

Preferred method of contact Apply on line or telephone for an appointment

Minimum requirements Relevant industry exposure

Type of business Temporary and Permanent

Grade/Level of Appointments All levels

Travel People

Head Office ✉ 207 Regent St, W1B 4ND
          ⊖ Oxford Circus
          🚋 Charing Cross
          ☎ T 020 7439 6111   F 020 7434 1451
          @ travelpeople@rossgroup.co.uk
Market areas Travel

Website www.rossgroup.co.uk

UK Offices 2

REC Member Yes

Brief Description Part of The Ross Group, Travel People pride themselves on having the most advanced technology in their sector. Their areas of expertise include Tour Operations, Business Travel and Retail Travel.

Preferred method of contact Telephone for appointment

Minimum requirements None

Type of business Permanent

Grade/Level of Appointments All levels

Travel Trade Recruitment

Head Office ✉ Lloyds Ct, 1 Goodmans Yard, E1 8AT
          ⊖ Tower Hill
          🚋 Fenchurch St
          ☎ T 020 7953 1179   F 020 7953 1327
          @ enquiries@traveltraderecruitment.co.uk
Market areas Travel

Website www.traveltraderecruitment.co.uk

UK Offices 5

REC Member No

Brief Description Travel Trade Recruitment are a traditional style recruitment agency specialising in placing both permanent and temporary staff within the Travel industry. Their success is based upon their high standards of service combined with total commitment from their consultants who are all ex-Travel professionals who have had extensive training within the recruitment industry. Their portfolio of clients specialise in Business Travel, Tour Operations, Retail Travel Reservations, Sales and Marketing, Hotels, Accounts, Ticketing and Administration.

Preferred method of contact Apply on line or telephone for an appointment

Minimum requirements None

Type of business Temporary and Permanent

Grade/Level of Appointments All levels

Veritas

Head Office ✉ 4th Floor, 4 Cromwell Place, SW7 2JE
⊖ South Kensington
🚋 Victoria
☎ T 020 7589 5969   F 020 7225 2299
@ office@veritas.uk.com
Market areas Hospitality

Website www.veritas.uk.com

UK Offices 1

REC Member Yes

Brief Description Veritas was established in 2001. They believe in consistency and in being straightforward with their candidates and clients. The decision to start Veritas was prompted by an urge to build a consultancy that offered an efficient but dynamic approach to recruitment. They value the 'personal approach' and pride themselves on working with total integrity and confidentiality.

Preferred method of contact Apply on line or telephone for an appointment

Minimum requirements None

Type of business Temporary and Permanent

Grade/Level of Appointments All levels

VIP International

Head Office ✉ VIP House, 17 Charing Cross Rd, WC2H 0EP
⊖ Charing Cross
🚋 Charing Cross
☎ T 020 7930 0541   F 020 7930 2860
@ vip@vipinternational.co.uk
Market areas Hospitality and Catering

Website www.vipinternational.co.uk

UK Offices 1

REC Member No

Brief Description VIP International was established over 30 years ago to service the growing international requirement for trained, and experienced Hotel professionals. VIP is widely accepted as the world's first specialist international Hotel recruitment company. Since VIP's formation, they have been privileged to assist almost all leading Hospitality companies with their requirements, in just about every area where there are operations of an internationally recognised standard; whether it be a luxury Hotel in Tokyo, a Cruise Liner in Alaska or a Mining Camp in Kazakhstan.

Preferred method of contact Apply on line or telephone for an appointment

Minimum requirements None

Type of business Temporary and Permanent

Grade/Level of Appointments All levels

West One Hotel & Catering Consultancy

Head Office ✉ 24 Haymarket, SW1Y 4DG
⊖ Piccadilly Circus
🚋 Charing Cross
☎ T 020 7287 4800
Market areas Hotel and Catering

Website www.w-one.co.uk

UK Offices 1

REC Member No

Brief Description West One Hotel & Catering Consultancy was formed in early 1996 to satisfy the demands of clients and candidates alike, requiring a quality and more focused approach to recruitment tailored to suit their specific needs. It is a young company with a fresh new approach to recruitment and employment within the Hotel and Catering industry, the UK's largest employer of skilled staff.

Preferred method of contact Apply on line or telephone for an appointment

Minimum requirements None

Type of business Temporary and Permanent

Grade/Level of Appointments All levels

Wise Owls Ltd

See **Secretarial**, page 262

146

Human Resources

Barbara Wren & Associates

Head Office ✉ Southbank House, Black Prince Rd, SE1 7SJ
⊖ Lambeth North
🚉 Waterloo
☎ T 020 7582 5341   F 020 7587 1604
@ enquiries@bwren.co.uk
Market areas   HR

Website www.bwren.co.uk

UK Offices 1

REC Member No

Brief Description Founded in 1990, Barbara Wren has achieved impressive growth using Search and Selection techniques closely geared to the needs of HR organisations resourcing their HR Management functions. These cover Personnel, Employee Industrial Relations, Training and Development, Compensation and Benefits, Recruitment, Organisational Development, Change Management and HR Generalist appointments.

Preferred method of contact Telephone for appointment

Minimum requirements HR experience of at least 12 months

Type of business Temporary and Permanent

Grade/Level of Appointments All levels

Bridge Human Resources Ltd

Head Office ✉ Second Floor, Montague Chambers, Montague Close, SE1 9DA
⊖ London Bridge
🚉 London Bridge
☎ T 020 7407 8080   F 020 7407 8070
@ hr@bhrl.co.uk
Market areas   HR

Website www.manleysummers.com

UK Offices 1

REC Member No

Brief Description Part of the Manley Summers Group, Bridge Human Resources is a specialist consultancy dedicated to providing HR personnel ranging from Consultants, Generalists through to HR Managing Directors.

Preferred method of contact Telephone for appointment

Minimum requirements Previous professional experience

Type of business Temporary and Permanent

Grade/Level of Appointments All levels

Carr-Lyons Search & Selection Ltd

See **Accountancy and Banking, page 8**

Courtenay HR

✉ 3 Hanover Sq, W1S 1HB
⊖ Oxford Circus
🚉 Charing Cross
☎ T 020 7491 4014   F 020 7493 3183
Market areas   HR

Website www.courtenayhr.com

UK Offices 1

REC Member Yes

Brief Description Courtenay is the UK's leading HR Search and Selection firm and, as their clients will testify, they are experts across all sectors and at every level within the HR profession.

Preferred method of contact Apply on line or telephone for an appointment

Minimum requirements Graduate, CIPD student

Type of business Contract and Permanent

Grade/Level of Appointments HR Advisor/HR Officer to HR Manager/Head of HR

EJ Group

Head Office ✉ Northumberland House, 303–306 High Holborn, WC1V 7JZ
⊖ Holborn
🚉 City Thameslink
☎ T 020 7400 2000   F 020 7404 8817
@ info@ejgroup.co.uk
Market areas   HR, Legal, Mergers, Taxation

Website www.ejgroup.co.uk

UK Offices 1

REC Member No

Brief Description EJ Group is divided into the following sectors: Human Resources, Legal, Mergers and Taxation. EJ Group are specialists in placing permanent staff ranging from Trainees to qualified Lawyers/HR Directors.

Preferred method of contact Telephone for appointment

Minimum requirements Ideally relevant industry exposure

Type of business Permanent

Grade/Level of Appointments Graduate to Fee Earners/Lawyers

Frazer Jones

Head Office ✉ Fleetway House, 25 Farringdon St, EC4A 4SR
　　　　　　⊖ St Pauls
　　　　　　🚉 City Thameslink
　　　　　　✆ T 020 7415 2815　F 020 7332 2495
　　　　　　@ markbrewer@thesrgroup.com
Market areas HR

Website www.thesrgroup.com

UK Offices 3

REC Member No

Brief Description A division of the SR Group, Frazer Jones is a specialist firm dedicating its activities to the Human Resources market. Their clients range from international Financial institutions and blue chip companies, to Music Publishers and Major Charities. Their activities cover all areas of Human Resources recruitment including Generalist HR, Management Development and Training, Resourcing, Compensation/Remuneration and Benefits, and ER/IR.

Preferred method of contact Apply on line or telephone for appointment

Minimum requirements None

Type of business Permanent and Interim

Grade/Level of Appointments Administrator to HR Director

Grove Recruitment Solutions

See Financial Services and Insurance, page 122

Hays HR Personnel

Head Office ✉ 141 Moorgate, EC2M 6TX
　　　　　　✆ T 020 7628 9999　F 020 7628 4698

　　　　　　✉ Mansfield House, 1st Floor, 1 Southampton St, WC2R 0LR
　　　　　　⊖ Covent Garden
　　　　　　🚉 Charing Cross
　　　　　　✆ T 020 7520 5995　F 020 7379 0357
　　　　　　@ london@hays-hrpersonnel.com
Market areas HR, Training

Website www.haysworks.com

UK Offices 16

REC Member No

Brief Description Hays Personnel Services is a division of Hays plc, the Business Services group listed in the FTSE 100. Hays Personnel Services is Europe's leading specialist professional recruitment group. Hays HR Personnel provide a specialist recruitment service in the areas of HR and Training.

Preferred method of contact Apply on line or telephone for an appointment

Minimum requirements Previous professional experience

Type of business Temporary, Permanent and Contract

Grade/Level of Appointments All levels

Headway Recruitment Specialists Ltd

See Secretarial, page 240

Interim Performers

Head Office ✉ Carpenter Hall, 1 Throgmorton Avenue, EC2N 2BY
　　　　　　⊖ Bank
　　　　　　🚉 Liverpool St
　　　　　　✆ T 020 7382 0680　F 020 7920 0861
　　　　　　@ mail@interimperformers.com
Market areas HR

Website www.rossgroup.co.uk

UK Offices 1

REC Member Yes

Brief Description Interim Performers has led the way in establishing Interim Management in Human Resources and is the only recruitment consultancy dedicated to providing Interim HR professionals to client organisations on a UK wide and international basis. Interims can expect professionalism and excellence in their service and they are committed to enhancing their development as an Interim Manager through their informative seminar programme.

Preferred method of contact Apply on line or telephone for an appointment

Minimum requirements Previous professional experience

Type of business Interim

Grade/Level of Appointments All levels

Jefferson Lloyd

Head Office ✉ 75 Cannon St, EC4N 5BN
　　　　　　⊖ Cannon St
　　　　　　🚉 Cannon St
　　　　　　✆ T 020 7329 5566　F 020 7649 9698
Market areas HR

Website www.jeffersonlloyd.co.uk

UK Offices 3

REC Member No

Brief Description Jefferson Lloyd is a consultancy specialising in the recruitment of Human Resources professionals throughout the UK. Operating from its addresses in London, York and its new administration centre in Guildford, the company provides a bespoke service to its network of clients across a range of market sectors.

Preferred method of contact Apply on line or telephone for an appointment

Minimum requirements None

Type of business Temporary and Permanent

Grade/Level of Appointments All levels

Resource Innovations

Head Office ✉ 16 Park St, W1K 2HZ
  ⊖ Marble Arch
  🚇 Paddington
  ☎ T 020 7495 5775   F 020 7495 5776
  @ info@riltd.co.uk
  Market areas HR

Website www.resourceinnovations.co.uk

UK Offices 1

REC Member No

Brief Description Resource Innovations is professional yet highly personalised. They were established to bridge a gap in the recruitment industry and return the focus to people. They're a close-knit team specialising in HR, and all share one important belief: that being totally in tune with all their clients — from blue-chip multinationals to small and funky start-ups — is the best way to get results.

Preferred method of contact Apply on line or telephone for an appointment

Minimum requirements Previous professional experience

Type of business Contract and Permanent

Grade/Level of Appointments All levels

Training Prospects

Head Office ✉ 45 Bloomsbury Sq, WC1A 1RA
  ⊖ Holborn
  🚇 City Thameslink
  ☎ T 020 7691 1939   F 020 7813 0500
  @ enquiries@training-prospects.co.uk
  Market areas Not for Profit, Training

Website www.prospect-us.co.uk

UK Offices 1

REC Member No

Brief Description Training Prospects is a division of ProspectUs, a London-based recruitment agency specialising in building careers and placing staff in Charities, Universities, NHS Trusts and other Not for Profit organisations. Candidates can expect an open and honest approach from them and they hope that they can make the search for work a positive experience.

Preferred method of contact Apply on line or telephone for an appointment

Minimum requirements None

Type of business Temporary and Permanent

Grade/Level of Appointments All levels

Industrial

Adecco

See **Secretarial, page 228**

Aptus Personnel

⊠ Warnford Ct, 29 Throgmorton St, EC2N 2AT
⊖ Bank
🚊 Cannon St
📞 T 020 7374 4298   F 020 7628 5878
@ info@aptus-personnel.com
Market areas Accountancy, care, Logistics, Retail, Catering, Public Services

Website www.aptus-personnel.com
UK Offices 40
REC Member Yes
Head Office Leicester

Brief Description Aptus Personnel is one of the UK's top 50 recruitment companies, with a pedigree stretching back to 1963. Operating through five specialist divisions and a nationwide network of 40 branches, they provide temporary, contract and permanent staff and innovative personnel services to more than 5,000 clients each year.

Preferred method of contact Apply on line or telephone for an appointment

Minimum requirements None

Type of business Temporary and Permanent

Grade/Level of Appointments All levels

Bligh Appointments Ltd

See **Secretarial, page 232**

Brook Street

See **Secretarial, page 232**

Crown Personnel

⊠ Suite 220, Princess House, 50–60 Eastcastle St, W1W 8EA
⊖ Oxford Circus
🚊 Charing Cross
📞 T 020 7436 6988   F 020 7436 6968
@ branch@westend.crownjobs.com
Market areas Secretarial, Industrial and Catering

⊠ Warwick House, 65–66 Queen St, EC4R 1EB
⊖ Mansion House
🚊 Blackfriars
📞 T 020 7236 7000   F 020 7236 7771
@ branch@city.crownjobs.com
Market areas Secretarial, Industrial and Catering

Website www.crownjobs.com
UK Offices 17
REC Member No
Head Office St Albans, Herts

Brief Description Crown offers a complete range of services across a variety of industries and professionals and is particularly strong in the Driving, Industrial and Commercial sectors.

Preferred method of contact Apply on line or telephone for appointment

Minimum requirements None

Type of business Temporary, Permanent and Contract

Grade/Level of Appointments All levels

Extraman Ltd

Head Office ⊠ 2 Hogarth Place, SW5 0QT
⊖ Earls Ct
🚊 Kensington (Olympia)
📞 T 020 7373 3045   F 020 7373 4651
@ extraman@extramanrecruitment.co.uk
Market areas Industrial, Unskilled

Website www.extramanrecruitment.co.uk
UK Offices 2
REC Member No

Brief Description Established over 30 years ago, Extraman Ltd has become the largest supplier of unskilled staff in London.

Preferred method of contact Telephone for appointment

Minimum requirements None

Type of business Temporary

Grade/Level of Appointments All levels

Hays Logistics Personnel

Head Office ⊠ 141 Moorgate, EC2M 6TX
📞 T 020 7628 9999   F 020 7628 4698

⊠ 1 Wilton Rd, Victoria, SW1V 1AB
⊖ Victoria
🚊 Victoria
📞 T 020 7630 1171   F 020 7931 8999

@ victorialog@hays-hps.com
Market areas Logistics and Distribution

Website www.haysworks.com

UK Offices 15

REC Member No

Brief Description Hays Personnel Services is a division of Hays plc, the Business Services group listed in the FTSE 100. Hays Personnel Services is Europe's leading specialist professional recruitment group. Hays Logistics Personnel specialises in the placement of temporary, permanent and contract staff in the Logistics and Distribution industries. All levels of personnel are catered for including Logistics Directors, Warehouse and Transport Managers, LGV Drivers, Fork-lift Truck Drivers, General Warehouse Staff and Order Pickers.

Preferred method of contact Apply on line or telephone for an appointment

Minimum requirements None

Type of business Temporary, Permanent and Contract

Grade/Level of Appointments Order Picker to Logistics Director

Hays Montrose Labour Hire Division

See **Construction and Property, page 50**

Julia Ross

See **Secretarial, page 243**

Kelly Scientific Resources

See **Secretarial, page 243**

Kelly Services

See **Secretarial, page 243**

Leopards Employment

See **Secretarial, page 246**

Manpower

See **Secretarial, page 247**

Randstad

See **Secretarial, page 253**

Ranmac Employment Agency

Head Office ✉ 801 Old Kent Rd, SE15 1NX
⊖ New Cross Gate
🚊 South Bermondsey
☎ T 020 7639 3900 F 020 7639 3005
Market areas Industrial, Domestic, Catering, Secretarial

Website www.ranmac.co.uk

UK Offices 1

REC Member Yes

Brief Description Established in early 1995, Ranmac Employment Agency is a specialist provider of trained and experienced staff in various industries. They have Consultants that specialise in the different sectors that they cover. Ranmac Employment Agency's main aim is to satisfy their clients and candidates and in doing so, achieve the highest standards possible.

Preferred method of contact Apply on line or telephone for an appointment

Minimum requirements None

Type of business Temporary and Permanent

Grade/Level of Appointments All levels

Recruit Employment Services

See **Secretarial, page 254**

Target Appointments

See **Secretarial, page 259**

TEMP-TEAM Ltd

See **Secretarial, page 260**

IT and Telecoms

Abraxas Plc

Head Office   ✉   47 Eastcastle St, W1W 8DY
  ⊖   Oxford Circus
  🚋   Charing Cross
  ☎   T 020 7255 5555   F 020 7636 0346
  @   contract@abraxas.com, perm@abraxas.com, graduate@abraxas.com

Market areas   IT

Website   www.abraxas.co.uk

UK Offices   1

REC Member   No

Brief Description   From its head office in London's West End, Abraxas' UK operations provide integrated recruitment solutions to a wide range of industry sectors within the UK and mainland Europe. As the Group's headquarters, the UK office is also a useful interface for the company's global operations. Abraxas offers a service portfolio ranging from the selection and recruitment of contract and permanent IT professionals to the provision of managed HR services and the co-ordination of Student and Graduate recruitment programmes.

Preferred method of contact   Apply on line or telephone for appointment

Minimum requirements   Previous professional experience

Type of business   Contract and Permanent

Grade/Level of Appointments   All levels up to Senior Management

Action First

See **Secretarial, page 227**

Adlam Consulting Ltd

Head Office   ✉   Alexander House, 9–11 Fulwood Place, WC1V 6HG
  ⊖   Chancery Lane
  🚋   City Thameslink
  ☎   T 020 7242 1234   F 020 7404 5279
  @   info@adlam.com

Market areas   IT/Project Management

Website   www.adlam.com

UK Offices   1

REC Member   No

Brief Description   Adlam consulting is a specialist niche provider of leading edge skills for Investment Banking, Financial Services and leading e-Commerce companies. The company's Managing Director has in excess of 13 years experience in the City market.

Preferred method of contact   Telephone for appointment

Minimum requirements   None

Type of business   Contract and Permanent

Grade/Level of Appointments   2nd Jobbers to Management

Advantage Group

Head Office   ✉   23 Fitzroy Sq, W1T 6EW
  ⊖   Great Portland St
  🚋   Euston
  ☎   T 020 7383 8100   F 020 7383 8101
  @   moreinfo@advantagexl.com

Market areas   IT

Website   www.theadvantagegroup.co.uk

UK Offices   1

REC Member   No

Brief Description   The Advantage Group specialises in providing leading IT solutions to European business and comprises of four divisions: Network Solutions, Business Systems, Managed Services and Resourcing. They deliver end to end web enabled solutions and address the key IT requirements for any organisation.

Preferred method of contact   Telephone for appointment

Minimum requirements   None

Type of business   Permanent and Contract

Grade/Level of Appointments   All levels

Ajilon Consulting Ltd

  ✉   12 Groveland Ct, Bow Lane, EC3M 9EH
  ⊖   Mansion House
  🚋   Cannon St
  ☎   T 020 7236 6732   F 020 7329 5916
  @   info@ajilion.co.uk

Market areas   IT

Website   www.ajilionconsulting.co.uk

UK Offices   5

REC Member   No

Head Office   Ajilion Services Limited, Apton House, 13 Apton Rd, Bishops Stortford, Herts, CM23 3SP

Brief Description   Part of the Adecco SA Group, Ajilion Consulting Ltd was founded in 1979 to address the need for customised professional Consulting services and Outsourcing in the Technology marketplace. Their main clients are commonly blue chip organisations within the Telecommunications, Manufacturing, Banking, Brokerage, Insurance, Computer and Utility concerns.

Preferred method of contact   Telephone for appointment

Minimum requirements   None

Type of business Contract and Permanent

Grade/Level of Appointments All levels

Alexander Mann Group

Head Office ✉ 1 Waterhouse Sq, 138–142 Holborn, EC1N 2ST
⊖ Holborn
🚄 Euston
☎ T 020 7242 9000   F 020 7405 6434
@ info@alexmann.com
Market areas IT and Banking

✉ Rodwell House, 100 Middlesex St, E1 7HD
⊖ Liverpool St
🚄 Liverpool St
☎ T 020 7984 4200   F 020 7984 4201
@ info@alexmann.com
Market areas IT and Banking

Website www.alexmann.com

UK Offices 4

REC Member No

Brief Description The Alexander Mann Group (AMG) is a leading international Outsourcing company and specialist solutions provider in the area of Human Capital Management. Founded in 1985, the other businesses in the group include Alexander Mann Solutions, Concise Group Ltd and Alexander Mann Technology and Global Markets.

Preferred method of contact Telephone for appointment

Minimum requirements None

Type of business Contract and Permanent

Grade/Level of Appointments All levels

Alexander McCann Ltd

See Accountancy and Banking, page 5

Amey Resource Management Solutions

✉ Amey Technology Services, 5th Floor, 1 Waterhouse Sq, Holborn, EC1N 2ST
⊖ Chancery Lane
🚄 City Thameslink
☎ T 020 7842 5950   F 020 7842 5951
@ it.recruitment@amey.co.uk
Market areas IT

Website www.ameyresources.co.uk

UK Offices 2

REC Member No

Head Office Athlestan House, St Clement St, Winchester, Hants, SO23 9DR

Brief Description Part of Amey Plc, Amey Resource Management Solutions was founded in 1976 to provide IT recruitment services to UK clients ranging from major national to international companies.

Preferred method of contact Telephone for appointment

Minimum requirements None

Type of business Contract

Grade/Level of Appointments All levels

Anderson Recruitment Ltd

Head Office ✉ 88 Kingsway, WC2B 6AA
⊖ Holborn
🚄 City Thameslink
☎ T 020 7681 6545   F 020 7861 6339
@ info@andersonrecruitment.co.uk
Market areas Telecoms and e-Commerce

Website www.andersonrecruitment.co.uk

UK Offices 1

REC Member No

Brief Description Established in 2000 and based in the heart of London, Anderson specialises in the four main areas of recruitment: Contingency Search, Agency Management, Advertising Management and Search and Selection within the Telecoms and e-Commerce market places.

Preferred method of contact Apply on line or telephone for appointment

Minimum requirements None

Type of business Permanent and Contract

Grade/Level of Appointments Graduates/Juniors to Systems Managers

Antal International

See Accountancy and Banking, page 6

ARC Recruitment

Head Office ✉ 15–16 New Burlington St, W1X 1FF
⊖ Oxford Circus
🚄 Charing Cross
☎ T 020 7287 2525   F 020 7287 9688
@ arc@itjobs.co.uk
Market areas IT for Investment Banking and Finance

Website www.itjobs.co.uk/arcrecruitment

UK Offices 1

REC Member No

Brief Description Founded in 1988, ARC was established to recruit for London's Investment Banking and Finance community. ARC consultants recruit permanent and contract staff, as well as offering market information and advice to clients and candidates alike.

Preferred method of contact Apply on line or telephone for appointment

Minimum requirements Previous professional experience

Type of business Permanent and Contract

Grade/Level of Appointments Systems Administrator to Senior Developer

Ark International

Head Office ✉ 1 Long Lane, SE1 4PG
　　　　　 ⊖ Borough
　　　　　 🚇 London Bridge
　　　　　 ✆ T 020 7407 6999　F 020 7407 6888
　　　　　 @ info@ark-int.com
　Market areas　IT, Telecoms

Website www.ark-int.com
UK Offices 1
REC Member Yes

Brief Description Ark International is an independent specialist IT recruitment consultancy, set up in response to the rapidly expanding markets of IT and Telecommunications.

Preferred method of contact Apply on line or telephone for appointment

Minimum requirements None

Type of business Permanent and Contract

Grade/Level of Appointments Graduate/Analyst to Project Manager/IT Director

Aston Carter

Head Office ✉ 123 Clifton St, EC2A 4LD
　　　　　 ⊖ Liverpool St
　　　　　 🚇 Liverpool St
　　　　　 ✆ T 020 7739 5500　F 020 7739 0020
　　　　　 @ info@astoncarter.co.uk
　Market areas　IT, Investment Banking, Finance, New Media, e-Commerce

Website www.astoncarter.co.uk
UK Offices 1
REC Member No

Brief Description Aston Carter was established in 1997 to address the lack of focus given to delivering a proactive based service in supplying qualified IT professionals to the Investment Banking market in London. Today the firm also supplies permanent staff to Finance and New Media/e-Commerce organisations.

Preferred method of contact Apply on line or telephone for appointment

Minimum requirements Previous IT exposure

Type of business Permanent

Grade/Level of Appointments Team Leader to Senior Developer

At mg

Head Office ✉ Venture House, 27–29 Glasshouse St, W1R 5RG
　　　　　 ⊖ Piccadilly Circus
　　　　　 🚇 Charing Cross
　　　　　 ✆ T 020 7494 6644　F 020 7494 6655
　　　　　 @ permanent@recruitment-mg.com,
　　　　　　　contract@recruitment-mg.com
　Market areas　IT

Website www.recruitment-mg.com
UK Offices 1
REC Member No

Brief Description At mg provides resource solutions and consultancy for high level international corporate business practices, with specialist knowledge of working in the following areas: ERP, RDBMS, CRM, Legacy Systems, e-Systems Development, SCM and Client Server.

Preferred method of contact Telephone for appointment

Minimum requirements None

Type of business Permanent and Contract

Grade/Level of Appointments All levels

BCL International

Head Office ✉ 18–20 Farringdon Lane, EC1R 3HG
　　　　　 ⊖ Farringdon
　　　　　 🚇 Farringdon
　　　　　 ✆ T 020 7295 6900　F 020 7257 4902
　　　　　 @ info@bcl.com
　Market areas　New Media, IT, Telecoms

Website www.bcl.com
UK Offices 2
REC Member No

Brief Description Over the last 18 years, BCL has provided recruitment solutions to organisations throughout the UK and internationally from three specialist divisions: IS&IT, New Media and Data and Telecoms.

Preferred method of contact Telephone for appointment

Minimum requirements None

Type of business Contract and Permanent

Grade/Level of Appointments All levels

Best International

Head Office ✉ Best Place, Bouverie St, EC4Y 8AX
　　　　　 ⊖ Blackfriars
　　　　　 🚇 Blackfriars

C T 020 7300 9000   F 020 7300 9090
@ mail@best-international.com

Market areas IT

Website www.best-international.com

UK Offices 5

REC Member Yes

Brief Description Founded in 1997, Best International's growth has been impressive during the last 5 years, operating from five locations in the UK and a number of offices worldwide, supplying IT staff to blue-chip and a variety of clients.

Preferred method of contact Telephone for appointment

Minimum requirements IT background

Type of business Contract and Permanent

Grade/Level of Appointments All levels

Blue Resource

Head Office ✉ 61 Southwark St, SE1 0HL
 ⊖ London Bridge
 ☒ London Bridge
 C T 020 7861 8900   F 020 7928 9900
 @ info@blueresource.co.uk

Market areas Telecoms

Website www.blueresource.com

UK Offices 1

REC Member No

Brief Description Established in 1999, Blue Resource has quickly become one of the market leaders in the placement of Telecoms personnel, providing an Interim Solution or Permanent Placement recruitment service for start-ups and international companies from offices in the UK, Europe, Asia and the US.

Preferred method of contact Telephone for appointment

Minimum requirements None

Type of business Permanent and Contract

Grade/Level of Appointments All levels

Bradfield Resourcing Ltd

 ✉ 2nd Floor, 64 Charlotte St, W1T 4QD
 ⊖ Goodge St
 ☒ Euston
 C T 020 7436 8851   F 020 7436 8852
 @ debbie@bradfield.co.uk

Market areas IT, Engineering, Technical, Financial

Website www.bradfield.co.uk

UK Offices 2

REC Member No

Head Office 47 High St, Melbourne, Cambs, SG8 6DZ

Brief Description Founded in 1989, Bradfield Consulting are a management consultancy specialising in all aspects of Human Resources. Able to apply its expertise across a wide range of industry sectors from Biotech, Telecoms, Computing and Software companies to engineering and financial services organisations.

Preferred method of contact Telephone for appointment

Minimum requirements Previous professional experience

Type of business Permanent

Grade/Level of Appointments Graduate/Junior to Management level

Cameron Kennedy

See **Financial Services and Insurance, page 120**

Campion Computer Recruitment Ltd

Head Office ✉ Africa House, 64–78 Kingsway, WC2B 6AH
 ⊖ Holborn
 ☒ City Thameslink
 C T 020 7831 6600   F 020 7831 6622
 @ campion@camco.demon.co.uk

Market areas Banking, IT, Legal, Financial

Website www.camco.demon.co.uk

UK Offices 1

REC Member No

Brief Description Established in 1990, Campion specialises in providing staff for the Banking, Financial, IT and Legal markets across the UK with a range of opportunities for Managing Directors, IT Directors, Project Managers, Business Analysts and System Developers.

Preferred method of contact Telephone for appointment

Minimum requirements Previous professional experience

Type of business Permanent

Grade/Level of Appointments Systems Developers to Managing Directors

Cantfield Charter Ltd

Head Office ✉ 99–101 Farringdon Rd, EC1R 3BT
 ⊖ Farringdon
 ☒ Farringdon
 C T 020 7689 1460   F 020 7689 0561
 @ enquiries@cantfield.com

Market areas IT

Website www.cantfield.com

UK Offices 1

REC Member No

THE LONDON JOBHUNTER'S GUIDE 2003/2004

Brief Description Founded in 1981, Cantfield Charter is an international Software consulting and recruitment company with offices in London, USA and France specialising in CRM, EAI, e-Business, ERP, Financial Services, Investment Management, Networks Infrastructure Design, Support Design and Telecommunications.

Preferred method of contact Telephone for appointment

Minimum requirements Previous professional experience

Type of business Permanent/Contract

Grade/Level of Appointments All levels

Central London Services

See *Accountancy and Banking, page 9*

Centric Consulting

Head Office   ✉ 81 Oxford St, W1D 2EU
          ⊖ Oxford Circus
          🚆 Charing Cross
          ✆ T 020 7903 5100   F 020 7903 5424
          @ mail@centric.co.uk
Market areas   IT

Website www.centric.co.uk

UK Offices 1

REC Member No

Brief Description Centric Consulting specialise in the recruitment of IT professionals.

Preferred method of contact Telephone for appointment

Minimum requirements Previous professional experience

Type of business Permanent and Contract

Grade/Level of Appointments All levels

Chess IT Solutions

Head Office   ✉ 62 The London Fruit Exchange, Brushfield St, E1 6EP
          ⊖ Liverpool St
          🚆 Liverpool St
          ✆ T 020 7655 0788   F 020 7375 0962
          @ info@chessitsolutions.com
Market areas   IT, Telecoms

Website www.chessitsolutions.com

UK Offices 1

REC Member Yes

Brief Description Due to the rapid growth of new technology and client organisations' increased demand for a flexible and motivated workforce, Chess IT Solutions realise there is an ever increasing demand for highly skilled professional personnel. By fully understanding their clients' and candidates' requirements, they are

able to provide a fast and effective recruitment solution. The company was founded by a group of industry-practised professionals, who have a total of 15 years experience in the recruitment marketplace.

Preferred method of contact Apply on line or telephone for appointment

Minimum requirements IT/Telecoms background

Type of business Contract and Permanent

Grade/Level of Appointments All levels

Citielite Resources Ltd

See *Accountancy and Banking, page 9*

Cititec Associates Ltd

Head Office   ✉ 70 Clifton St, EC2A 4HB
          ⊖ Liverpool St
          🚆 Liverpool St
          ✆ T 020 7422 7777   F 020 7422 7700
          @ info@cititec.com
Market areas   IT

Website www.cititec.com

UK Offices 1

REC Member Yes

Brief Description Founded in 1998, Cititec is a provider of specialist IT resource solutions and consulting services to the UK and European sectors for the Financial CRM/ERP and Telecommunications marketplaces.

Preferred method of contact Apply on line or telephone for appointment

Minimum requirements Previous professional experience

Type of business Permanent and Contract

Grade/Level of Appointments All levels

City People

Head Office   ✉ 7–8 Bell Ct House, 11 Blomfield St, EC2M 7AY
          ⊖ Liverpool St
          🚆 Liverpool St
          ✆ T 020 7256 2055   F 020 7256 2077
          @ permanent@citypeople.co.uk
Market areas   IT

Website www.permanent@citypeople.co.uk

UK Offices 1

REC Member Yes

Brief Description City People have been supplying quality personnel for over 20 years, from Helpdesk Assistants to IT Managers, their IT personnel have been despatched to international Law firms and Finance houses.

Preferred method of contact Apply on line or telephone for appointment

Minimum requirements Ideally IT exposure

Type of business Contract, Temporary and Permanent

Grade/Level of Appointments Helpdesk Assistants to IT Managers

City Software Consultants

Head Office ✉ Bucklersbury House, 3 Queen Victoria St, EC4 8NH
　　　　　　 ⊖ Blackfriars
　　　　　　 🚊 Blackfriars
　　　　　　 ☎ T 020 7329 9944　F 020 7329 3030
　　　　　　 @ email@cscstaff.com
Market areas　IT

Website www.citysoftware.co.uk

UK Offices 1

REC Member Yes

Brief Description City Software Consultants, trading since 1987, has grown to become one of the leading players in global IT resourcing, by offering clients, candidates and contractors a commitment to professionalism and ethical standards. They believe that business is about long term relationships and mutual understanding.

Preferred method of contact Apply on line or telephone for an appointment

Minimum requirements Previous professional experience

Type of business Contract and Permanent

Grade/Level of Appointments All levels

Comms 2000

Head Office ✉ 11 Harley St, W1G 9EQ
　　　　　　 ⊖ Regent's Park
　　　　　　 🚊 Marylebone
　　　　　　 ☎ T 020 7636 7584　F 020 7580 3734
　　　　　　 @ mail@2000group.co.uk
Market areas　IT, Telecoms, Communications

Website www.2000group.co.uk

UK Offices 1

REC Member Yes

Brief Description Comms 2000 is wholly committed to providing a totally professional service to the highly specialised Electronic and Electrical Engineering market. A group brand which has traded successfully in the PC and Communications marketplace since 1989, Comms 2000 was re-focused 2 years ago to concentrate exclusively on the rapidly expanding Mobile Communications market and can boast an impressive client base across the European and indeed global marketplace.

Preferred method of contact Apply on line or telephone for appointment

Minimum requirements Systems/Telecoms exposure

Type of business Permanent and Contract

Grade/Level of Appointments Consultant to Managerial level

Comms Futures

Head Office ✉ 2 Fouberts Place, W1F 7AD
　　　　　　 ⊖ Oxford Circus
　　　　　　 🚊 Charing Cross
　　　　　　 ☎ T 020 7446 6633　F 020 7446 6611
　　　　　　 @ perm@commsfutures.com,
　　　　　　　 contract@commsfutures.com
Market areas　IT

Website www.commsfutures.co.uk

UK Offices 6

REC Member No

Brief Description Comms Futures is a privately owned specialist Communications Technology recruitment consultancy. The company is part of the Computer Futures Group which is Europe's largest independent IT recruitment consultancy. On average the group secures a candidate a new permanent career opportunity approximately every 20 minutes of the working day, and has well in excess of 2000 contractors employed with over 600 clients every week.

Preferred method of contact Telephone for appointment

Minimum requirements Previous professional experience

Type of business Contract and Permanent

Grade/Level of Appointments All levels

Comms Liveware

Head Office ✉ 5th Floor, 145 Cannon St, EC4N 5BP
　　　　　　 ⊖ Cannon St
　　　　　　 🚊 Cannon St
　　　　　　 ☎ T 020 7886 9600　F 020 7886 9699
　　　　　　 @ cv@clw.co.uk
Market areas　IT, Telecoms

Website www.commsliveware.co.uk

UK Offices 1

REC Member Yes

Brief Description Comms Liveware was established in 1997 by two Directors who have jointly over 20 years experience within the LAN/WAN and Telecommunications recruitment area incorporated within their particular field of Systems Integration.

Preferred method of contact Apply on line or telephone for appointment

Minimum requirements Ideally IT/Telecoms Systems exposure

Type of business Contract and Permanent

Grade/Level of Appointments Help Desk Administrators to Communications Manager/Network Designers

Compucode Computer Recruitment Ltd

Head Office ✉ 14 London Fruit and Wool Exchange, Brushfield St, E1 6HB
⊖ Liverpool St
🚇 Liverpool St
📞 T 020 7247 2660   F 020 7247 9393
@ mail@compucode.co.uk
Market areas IT

Website www.compucode.co.uk

UK Offices 1

REC Member Yes

Brief Description Compucode was established in 1995 as a specialist staff agency for the provision of both contract and permanent IT professionals. Main areas of expertise are Systems Management/Administration, Technical Support, Computer Operations and Web Development but staff from all areas of IT are regularly provided, including Programmers, Data Comms Engineers and PC/Helpdesk Technicians.

Preferred method of contact Telephone for appointment

Minimum requirements None

Type of business Contract and Permanent

Grade/Level of Appointments Graduate/Technical Support to Systems Manager/Application Specialist

Computappoint Recruitment Services Ltd

Head Office ✉ Cepea House, 18 Noel St, W1F 8GN
⊖ Oxford Circus
🚇 Charing Cross
📞 T 020 7287 2550   F 020 7287 0717
@ mail@computappoint.co.uk
Market areas IT

Website www.computappoint.co.uk

UK Offices 2

REC Member No

Brief Description Computappoint was established in 1991 and originally focused on the recruitment of Technical Support Staff. Although they still specialise in the Technical Infrastructure arena, they have expanded into many other areas. As a quality provider of technical IT staff in the UK, they pride themselves in practising what they preach and their goal is to develop long term relationships with companies and individual IT professionals alike.

Preferred method of contact Apply on line or telephone for appointment

Minimum requirements None

Type of business Contract and Permanent

Grade/Level of Appointments Database Administrator to Business Analyst/Project Manager

Computer Connect Ltd

Head Office ✉ 68 Warwick Sq, SW1V 2AS
⊖ Pimlico
🚇 Victoria
📞 T 020 7233 6688   F 020 7233 6602
@ info@computerconnect.co.uk
Market areas IT

Website www.computerconnect.co.uk

UK Offices 1

REC Member No

Brief Description Computer Connect was established in 1988 and covers all areas of IT recruitment whilst providing a professional, honest and ethical solution.

Preferred method of contact Apply on line or telephone for appointment

Minimum requirements None

Type of business Contract and Permanent

Grade/Level of Appointments Bilingual Graduate/Customer Support to Programmer/Developer

Computer Futures Ltd

Head Office ✉ 2 Fouberts Place, W1F 7AD
⊖ Piccadilly Circus
🚇 Charing Cross
📞 T 020 7446 6666   F 020 7446 0095
@ permanent@compfutures.com, contract@compfutures.com
Market areas IT

Website www.compfutures.co.uk

UK Offices 8

REC Member Yes

Brief Description Computer Futures has achieved its success by providing the greatest possible choice for job seekers in both the permanent and contract markets. All of their consultants receive regular training in candidate and client care and have an in-depth understanding of their own technical and geographical markets. Their database of quality opportunities is second to none, and their network of 14 offices throughout eight countries ensures the best possible choice for candidates, wherever they are looking to work.

Preferred method of contact Apply on line or telephone for appointment

Minimum requirements None

Type of business Contract and Permanent

Grade/Level of Appointments Graduate/Technical Support to IT Management

Computer People

Head Office ✉ Piccadilly House, 33 Regent St, SW1Y 4NB
    ⊖ Piccadilly Circus
    🚉 Charing Cross
    ☎ T 020 7440 2000 F 020 7440 2120
    @ london@computerpeople.co.uk
  Market areas IT

Website www.computerpeople.com

UK Offices 12

REC Member Yes

Brief Description Part of the Adecco Group of companies, Computer People was established in 1972 and has expanded rapidly by organic growth and acquisition to become Europe's largest and most successful IT recruitment consultancy. Computer People work with a broad range of clients through their network of offices where experienced and knowledgeable consultants offer professional representation and advice at every stage of the recruitment process.

Preferred method of contact Apply on line or telephone for appointment

Minimum requirements IT Systems/Support exposure

Type of business Contract and Permanent

Grade/Level of Appointments Graduate/Helpdesk to Operations Manager/Senior Developer

Computer Personnel (UK) Ltd

Head Office ✉ 4th Floor, Waterman House, 41 Kingsway, WC2B 6TP
    ⊖ Holborn
    🚉 City Thameslink
    ☎ T 020 7240 7337 F 020 7240 0261
    @ info@computerpersonnel.com
  Market areas IT

Website www.computerpersonnel.com

UK Offices 1

REC Member No

Brief Description Established in 1997, Computer Personnel specialises in providing high calibre IT professionals ranging from Helpdesk to Systems Developers for a variety of clients.

Preferred method of contact Apply on line or telephone for appointment

Minimum requirements None

Type of business Contract and Permanent

Grade/Level of Appointments All levels

Computer Recruitment Services Ltd

Head Office ✉ 68 Leonard St, EC2A 4QY
    ⊖ Old St
    🚉 Old St
    ☎ T 020 7729 6999 F 020 7729 6111
    @ info@crs-ltd.co.uk
  Market areas IT

Website www.crs-ltd.co.uk

UK Offices 1

REC Member Yes

Brief Description CRS is a specialist recruitment business providing resource solutions to the Financial Markets. With a focused team of specialist recruitment consultants, they supply permanent and contract personnel at all levels. Their market expertise and established procedures have positioned them as the specialist of choice with many blue chip organisations.

Preferred method of contact Apply on line or telephone for appointment

Minimum requirements None

Type of business Contract and Permanent

Grade/Level of Appointments Graduate/Administration to Programmer/Project Manager

Connect Support Services Ltd

Head Office ✉ South Quay Plaza II, 183 Marsh Wall, E14 9SH
    ⊖ South Quay
    🚉 Limehouse
    ☎ T 020 7517 2000 F 020 7517 2099
  Market areas IT

Website www.connect.uk.com

UK Offices 1

REC Member Yes

Brief Description Connect is one of the UK's fastest growing IT Service companies.

Preferred method of contact Apply on line or telephone for an appointment

Minimum requirements Ideally IT/Helpdesk exposure

Type of business Contract and Permanent

Grade/Level of Appointments Helpdesk/Technical Support to Technical Specialists/Project Managers

Conspicuous

Head Office ✉ 119 Friars House, 157–168 Blackfriars Rd, SE1 8EZ
    ⊖ Blackfriars
    🚉 Blackfriars
    ☎ T 020 7620 0900 F 020 7928 5850

@ admin@conspic.com

Market areas   IT, Sales

Website www.conspicuous.com

UK Offices 1

REC Member No

Brief Description   Established in 2000, Conspicuous are a specialist IT and Sales recruitment agency built on a foundation of 14 years recruitment experience. Conspicuous specialise in providing effective recruitment solutions to the ever changing IT and Sales marketplace, successfully working with a variety of clients from established multinationals through to start ups and dot coms.

Preferred method of contact   Apply on line or telephone for appointment

Minimum requirements None

Type of business Contract and Permanent

Grade/Level of Appointments Helpdesk/Telesales to Project Manager/Director

Curtis Reed Associates Ltd

Head Office   ✉ 125 High Holborn, WC1V 6QA
              ⊖ Holborn
              🚇 City Thameslink
              ☎ T 020 7405 4480   F 020 7405 4481
              @ recruit@curtisreed.com

Market areas   IT

Website www.curtisreed.co.uk

UK Offices 1

REC Member No

Brief Description   Curtis Reed Associates is a specialist recruitment company providing resourcing solutions for the IT industry. Established in 1998, it is a young dynamic organisation with a highly professional approach.

Preferred method of contact   Telephone for appointment

Minimum requirements None

Type of business Contract and Permanent

Grade/Level of Appointments Graduates to Senior Managers/IT Directors

Datascope Recruitment

Head Office   ✉ 109–110 Bolsover St, W1W 5NT
              ⊖ Oxford Circus
              🚇 Charing Cross
              ☎ T 020 7580 6018   F 020 7580 6068
              @ info@datascope.co.uk

Market areas   New Media, Leisure Software

Website www.datascope.co.uk

UK Offices 1

REC Member No

Brief Description   Datascope Recruitment, based in central London, was established in 1991. Their consultants are recruitment specialists to the world of New Media and Leisure Software. The service covers Programmers, Artists, Designers, Developers, Sales, Marketing and PR staff at all levels, with clients ranging from small Software Developers to major international household names across the UK.

Preferred method of contact   Apply on line or telephone for appointment

Minimum requirements Ideally previous professional experience

Type of business Permanent

Grade/Level of Appointments Junior Account Executive to Business Development/Senior Programmer

Delta Personnel Ltd

              ✉ 5th Floor, New Zealand House, 80 Haymarket, SW1Y 4HW
              ⊖ Piccadilly Circus
              🚇 Charing Cross
              ☎ T 020 7930 4955   F 020 7930 9077
              @ info@delta-itrec.com

Market areas   IT - ERP/New Technology

Website www.delta-itrec.com

UK Offices 2

REC Member No

Head Office Albany Place, Hyde Way, Welwyn Garden City, Herts, AL7 3BG

Brief Description   Part of Carlisle Holdings, Delta was established in 1986, has grown steadily and today employs a team of highly trained consultants and support staff committed to service the ever-changing needs of their customers. As Carlisle's IT recruitment brand, Delta offer comprehensive contract and permanent recruitment services within their chosen technical markets.

Preferred method of contact   Apply on line or telephone for appointment

Minimum requirements Previous professional experience

Type of business Contract and Permanent

Grade/Level of Appointments All levels

Diamond Resourcing – Accountancy/IT/ Sales/Banking

See **Accountancy and Banking, page 11**

Elan Computing

Head Office   ✉ Elan House, 5–11 Fetter Lane, EC4A 1JB
              ⊖ Chancery Lane

🚉 City Thameslink
📞 **T** 020 7830 1300   **F** 020 7830 1333
@ info@elanit.co.uk
Market areas IT&Telecoms

Website www.elan.co.uk
UK Offices 8
REC Member No

Brief Description Part of Manpower Inc, Elan is one of Europe's leading IT&T recruitment consultancies, with a global network of offices and an annual turnover in excess of £250million. Their international presence allows them to meet the needs of their clients and candidates on a world-wide scale, because they have focused purely on IT&T since their inception in 1987, and have developed the technical understanding to truly match candidates' career aspirations to rewarding positions.

Preferred method of contact Apply on line or telephone for appointment

Minimum requirements None

Type of business Contract and Permanent

Grade/Level of Appointments Graduates/1st Jobbers to Management level

Euro Technique

Head Office ✉ 61 The London Fruit and Wool Exchange, Brushfield St, E1 6EX
⊖ Liverpool St
🚉 Liverpool St
📞 **T** 020 7422 0900   **F** 020 7247 9154
@ info@eurotechnique.co.uk
Market areas IT

Website www.eurotechnique.co.uk
UK Offices 1
REC Member No

Brief Description Eurotechnique specialises in the permanent and contract placements of IT personnel.

Preferred method of contact Apply on line or telephone for an appointment

Minimum requirements Previous professional experience

Type of business Contract and Permanent

Grade/Level of Appointments All levels

Farlow & Warren Search and Selection – Telecoms & IT

Head Office ✉ Unit 212–213 The Business Design Centre, 52 Upper St, N1 0QH
⊖ Highbury and Islington
🚉 Highbury and Islington
📞 **T** 020 7288 6211   **F** 020 7288 6208

@ telecoms@farlowandwarren.co.uk
Market areas IT and Telecoms

Website www.farlowandwarren.co.uk
UK Offices 1
REC Member No

Brief Description Farlow & Warren Search and Selection have been established for 10 years and have a wealth of experience of recruiting on a search and contingency basis to specialist niche market-places: Telecoms and IT including Customer Service, Engineering, Sales, Networking and Transmission; Financial including Life and Pensions and Financial Advisers; Construction including Interior Fit-out, Facilities Managers, Construction Services and Building Services; Commercial including Back Office, Secretarial, Administration, temporary and permanent.

Preferred method of contact Apply on line or telephone for an appointment

Minimum requirements None

Type of business Contract, Temporary and Permanent

Grade/Level of Appointments All levels

The Freshman Consultancy

See **Executive Search, page 89**

Glotel

Head Office ✉ The Quadrangle, 180 Wardour St, W1V 3AA
⊖ Oxford Circus
🚉 Charing Cross
📞 **T** 020 7734 7722   **F** 020 7734 6949
@ london@glotel.com
Market areas Telecommunications

✉ The Communications Building, 48 Leicester Sq, WC2H 7LT
⊖ Leicester Sq
🚉 Charing Cross
📞 **T** 020 7484 3000   **F** 020 7484 3001
@ london@glotel.com
Market areas Telecommunications

Website www.glotel.com
UK Offices 4
REC Member Yes

Brief Description Established in 1989, Glotel is one of the world's leading human capital solutions providers, focusing on the Telecommunications, Networking and Technology markets. In January 2001 the group's divisions (including Comms and PC People) were rebranded as Glotel in order to consolidate their global presence and to further increase opportunities for both clients and candidates.

Preferred method of contact Apply on line or telephone for appointment

Minimum requirements Previous professional experience

Type of business Contract and Permanent

Grade/Level of Appointments All levels

Greythorn Plc

Head Office ✉ 6 Southampton Place, WC1A 2DA
　　　　　　 ⊖ Holborn
　　　　　　 🚃 City Thameslink
　　　　　　 ☎ T 020 7576 6000   F 020 7831 2233
　　　　　　 @ careers@greythorn.com
Market areas Technology

Website www.greythorn.com

UK Offices 1

REC Member No

Brief Description Since 1977 Greythorn in London has set the pace in Technology recruitment. Their ability to cover a diverse range of skills whilst at the same time being able to offer a specialised service has meant that their name has become synonymous with high quality recruitment. As one of Europe's leading specialist agencies they have firmly established themselves as industry experts in areas such as Creative Design, IT Security, Telecommunications, Development, ERP, Networks and Audit and Risk.

Preferred method of contact Apply on line or telephone for appointment

Minimum requirements Previous professional experience

Type of business Contract and Permanent

Grade/Level of Appointments All levels

Guardian Appointments Ltd

Head Office ✉ 65 London Wall, EC2M 5TU
　　　　　　 ⊖ Moorgate
　　　　　　 🚃 Moorgate
　　　　　　 ☎ T 020 7638 5777   F 020 7638 5588
　　　　　　 @ info@it-guardian.com
Market areas IT, Financial, Insurance, Secretarial

Website www.it-guardian.com

UK Offices 1

REC Member Yes

Brief Description Guardian are a specialist recruitment consultancy covering all aspects of IT, Financial, Insurance and Secretarial for permanent, temporary and contract appointments. Their consultants are hand picked from relevant industry sectors for their in-depth knowledge, expertise and dedication, thus enabling them to achieve the best possible match.

Preferred method of contact Apply on line or telephone for appointment

Minimum requirements None

Type of business Temporary, Permanent and Contract

Grade/Level of Appointments All levels

Haigh Recruitment Consultants

See **Sales and Marketing, page 215**

Harrison Scott Associates

See **Media, page 198**

Harvard Associates

Head Office ✉ Dashwood House, 69 Old Broad St, EC2M 1NQ
　　　　　　 ⊖ Liverpool St
　　　　　　 🚃 Liverpool St
　　　　　　 ☎ T 020 7496 9633   F 020 7256 9898
　　　　　　 @ resource@harvard-it.com
Market areas IT

Website www.harvard-it.com

UK Offices 3

REC Member No

Brief Description Established in 1993, part of the CDI Corporation, Harvard Associates specialises in the supply of contractors and permanent staff to niche vertical markets within the IT industry. Their services range from IT recruitment to Contingency Search and Advertised Selection, through to Executive Search and Managed Staffing. Candidates are sourced from the following sectors: AS/400, Oracle, Sybase, IBM Mainframe, Internet, Intranet, ERP, PC Development, PC Lan and Comms, CRM, Real Time Software, Technical.

Preferred method of contact Apply on line or telephone for an appointment

Minimum requirements Previous professional experience

Type of business Contract and Permanent

Grade/Level of Appointments Project Manager to Programmer

Harvey Nash Contracts

Head Office ✉ 13 Bruton St, W1J 6QA
　　　　　　 ⊖ Green Park
　　　　　　 🚃 Victoria
　　　　　　 ☎ T 020 7071 6800   F 020 7071 6801
　　　　　　 @ londoninfo@harveynash.com
Market areas IT

Website www.harveynash.com

UK Offices 2

REC Member No

Brief Description Established in 1990, the contracting division of Harvey Nash places professional IT contractors on a pan-European basis across all skill sets and industry sectors. They are part of the Harvey Nash Group, an acknowledged market leader in IT, Telecoms and e-Business recruitment services with over 12 years experience in IT resourcing.

Preferred method of contact Apply on line or telephone for an appointment

Minimum requirements Previous professional experience

Type of business Contract

Grade/Level of Appointments All levels

Harvey Nash International Search & Selection

See **Executive Search, page 91**

Haymarket Consulting

Head Office ✉ Victory House, 14 Leicester Place, WC2H 7BZ
⊖ Leicester Sq
🚂 Charing Cross
☎ T 0871 871 1000   F 0871 871 1010
@ info@haymarket.com
Market areas   IT

Website www.haymarket.com
UK Offices 2
REC Member No

Brief Description Haymarket Consulting is an established professional IT recruitment consultancy with offices in London and Edinburgh.

Preferred method of contact Apply on line or telephone for an appointment

Minimum requirements Previous professional experience

Type of business Permanent and Contract

Grade/Level of Appointments All levels

Hays IT

Head Office ✉ 141 Moorgate, EC2M 6TX
⊖ Moorgate
🚂 Moorgate
☎ T 020 7588 7006   F 020 7588 7072
@ perm.london@hays-it.com
Market areas   IT

✉ Charter House, 13–15 Carteret St, SW1H 9DJ
⊖ St James's Park
🚂 Victoria
☎ T 020 7227 5000   F 020 7227 5005

@ london@hays-it.com
Market areas   IT

Website www.haysworks.com
UK Offices 14
REC Member No

Brief Description Hays Personnel Services is a division of Hays Plc, the Business Services group listed in the FTSE 100. Hays Personnel Services is Europe's leading specialist professional recruitment group. With 20 years at the forefront of IT recruitment, Hays IT has the strength to deliver heavyweight IT solutions. With a reputation for innovative, practical solutions and a fully resourced network of 16 offices across the UK, Ireland and Europe, they are ideally placed to meet the needs of both clients and candidates.

Preferred method of contact Apply on line or telephone for an appointment

Minimum requirements None

Type of business Permanent

Grade/Level of Appointments All levels

Huxley Associates

Head Office ✉ 75 King William St, EC4N 7BE
⊖ Monument
🚂 Cannon St
☎ T 020 7469 5000   F 020 7469 5001
@ jobs@huxley.co.uk
Market areas   IT, Communications and Financial

Website www.huxley.co.uk
UK Offices 5
REC Member No

Brief Description Huxley Associates are a well established recruitment consultancy, in all areas of IT, Financial, Communications, Engineering and Management Consultancy. Whether contract or permanent, UK or Europe, the combination of a strong market presence with intimate knowledge of the various industry and technical sectors enables them to present exactly the right portfolio of opportunities.

Preferred method of contact Apply on line or telephone for an appointment

Minimum requirements None

Type of business Temporary, Permanent and Contract

Grade/Level of Appointments All levels

Ibnix Ltd

Head Office ✉ 12–18 Paul St, EC2A 4NX
⊖ Liverpool St
🚂 Liverpool St
☎ T 020 7377 9995   F 020 7247 5471

@ london@ibnix.com

Market areas IT

Website www.ibnix.com

UK Offices 2

REC Member No

Brief Description Ibnix Services was established in 1991, having evolved from a successful technical consultancy. It is this inherent technical ability combined with extensive industry links that has led Ibnix to become one of the market leaders in the provision of IT personnel in the UK, Europe and the Asia-Pacific region.

Preferred method of contact Apply on line or telephone for an appointment

Minimum requirements Previous professional experience

Type of business Contract and Permanent

Grade/Level of Appointments All levels

Information Technology Services

Head Office ✉ Well Ct House, 5–7 Well Ct, EC4M 9DN
   🚇 Mansion House
   🚆 Cannon St
   ☎ T 020 7295 5999   F 020 7295 5939
   @ mail@infotechservices.co.uk

Market areas IT

Website www.infotechservices.co.uk

UK Offices 1

REC Member No

Brief Description Information Technology Services provides a recruitment service to people in all areas of IT from Helpdesk to Development to Senior Technical to Senior Management. They are a small, professional company with a client base consisting of leading small, medium and large companies.

Preferred method of contact Apply on line or telephone for an appointment

Minimum requirements None

Type of business Contract and Permanent

Grade/Level of Appointments Helpdesk to Senior Manager

Integral Personnel Ltd

Head Office ✉ 272–276 Pentonville Rd, N1 9JY
   ☎ T 020 7837 6444   F 020 7833 7783

   ✉ 176 Bishopsgate, EC2M 4NQ
   🚇 Liverpool St
   🚆 Liverpool St
   ☎ T 020 7444 4777   F 020 7444 4770

Market areas IT

Website www.keystone-recruitment.co.uk

UK Offices 4

REC Member Yes

Brief Description Integral Personnel Ltd is part of the Keystone Group. Keystone was originally formed in London in 1948. It was one of the first and largest privately owned employment agencies placing secretarial and general office staff. Their greatest assets are the people who work for them, they are the reason why clients and candidates are recommended to use the Keystone Group services – it is their ability to listen and understand people's needs, to work in partnership with them to achieve success, and more importantly client and candidate satisfaction.

Preferred method of contact Apply on line or telephone for an appointment

Minimum requirements None

Type of business Contract and Permanent

Grade/Level of Appointments All levels

Intelect Recruitment Ltd

Head Office ✉ Ingersoll House, 9 Kingsway, WC2B 6XF
   🚇 Holborn
   🚆 City Thameslink
   ☎ T 020 7759 4848   F 020 7759 4800
   @ londonperm@intelectplc.com, london@intelectplc.com

Market areas IT, Banking, Manufacturing

Website www.intelectplc.com

UK Offices 2

REC Member No

Brief Description Intelect Recruitment was established over 15 years ago and is a large independent consultancy with the stability and flexibility to compete with the challenges of the modern market. They deliver a complex service to clients across the UK and mainland Europe from their consultancy centres in London and Manchester in their specialist markets covering Banking, Telecommunications, Wireless Technology, Software Engineering, Manufacturing, IT Consultancy and Pharmaceuticals.

Preferred method of contact Apply on line or telephone for an appointment

Minimum requirements Previous professional experience

Type of business Contract and Permanent

Grade/Level of Appointments All levels

IT Human Resources

Head Office ✉ Victory House, 14 Leicester Place, WC2H 7BZ
   🚇 Leicester Sq
   🚆 Charing Cross
   ☎ T 020 7747 1000   F 020 7747 1010

Market areas IT

Website www.ithr.co.uk

UK Offices 1

REC Member Yes

Brief Description Established 4 years ago, IT Human Resources plc (ITHR) has rapidly built an unrivalled reputation for excellence in the IT recruitment solutions marketplace. As specialists, they provide a unique service based upon individual market awareness, building a complete picture of their clients' IT human resource needs for each Business and Technology sector, together with a matching portfolio of candidates to meet those needs. ITHR's management team comprises in excess of 70 years IT experience and the recruitment team in excess of 60 years IT contract and permanent recruitment experience – gained from some of the most high profile agencies in the UK.

Preferred method of contact Apply on line or telephone for an appointment

Minimum requirements Previous professional experience

Type of business Contract and Permanent

Grade/Level of Appointments All levels

James Rushmore

Head Office ✉ 32a Westminster Palace Gardens, Artillery Row, SW1P 1RR
⊖ St James's Park
🚇 Victoria
☎ T 020 7222 4900   F 0870 056 6249
@ mail@rushmore.co.uk
Market areas IT - SAP

Website www.sapjobs.com

UK Offices 1

REC Member No

Brief Description James Rushmore Ltd is directed by two senior project managers from the IT industry. Their careers span over 20 years and during this time they have managed and implemented many high profile IT systems. They have spent many years advising SAP candidates on successful career strategies for one of the most dynamic and fast moving markets in the world.

Preferred method of contact Telephone for appointment

Minimum requirements Previous professional experience

Type of business Permanent and Contract

Grade/Level of Appointments All levels

JM Recruitment

Head Office ✉ 12–14 Berry St, EC1V 0AQ
⊖ Barbican
🚇 Barbican
☎ T 020 7253 7172   F 020 7253 0420
Market areas IT

Website www.jmms.co.uk

UK Offices 1

REC Member No

Brief Description JM Recruitment are an independent IT consultancy who have been established for over 21 years. They have an enviable track record in IT recruitment and are constantly seeking areas where they can improve. They currently have 48 recruitment professionals working in JM and are able to bring a combined total of 200 years IT resourcing experience to their clients and candidates.

Preferred method of contact Apply on line or telephone for an appointment

Minimum requirements None

Type of business Temporary, Permanent and Contract

Grade/Level of Appointments All levels

KENDA Systems

Head Office ✉ 150 Minories, EC3N 1LS
⊖ Aldgate
🚇 Fenchurch St
☎ T 020 7264 2232   F 020 7264 2233
Market areas IT

Website www.kenda.com

UK Offices 1

REC Member Yes

Brief Description Founded in 1984, KENDA is a provider of IT talent to worldwide clients. From the beginning, they've earned an unrivalled reputation for outstanding personal service, professional integrity and ongoing client satisfaction. They pride themselves on their quality services, striving to obtain the best match possible between the needs of their clients and those of their IT professionals. Their representatives maintain regular contact with both the client and the IT professional throughout the contract period to ensure that there are no concerns or problems in the working environment.

Preferred method of contact Apply on line or telephone for an appointment

Minimum requirements Previous professional experience

Type of business Contract and Permanent

Grade/Level of Appointments All levels

The Kennedy Partnership

Head Office ✉ 15 St Helens Place, EC3A 6DE
⊖ Liverpool St
🚇 Liverpool St
☎ T 020 7860 2222   F 020 7860 2220
@ info@kennedy.com
Market areas IT

Website www.kennedy.com

UK Offices 1

REC Member No

Brief Description Since 1994 The Kennedy Partnership has provided IT professionals to some of the most prestigious companies worldwide. Experienced market coverage and in-depth knowledge of current and emerging technologies ensures that they tailor intelligent solutions to meet their clients' objectives. Whether this is Contract, Contingency, Search and Selection or a Managed Agency approach, they only commit to vacancies or projects where success can be assured.

Preferred method of contact Apply on line or telephone for an appointment

Minimum requirements Relevant systems exposure

Type of business Contract and Permanent

Grade/Level of Appointments All levels

Lawrence Allison Group

See **Secretarial, page 246**

Libra Consulting

Head Office ✉ 97 Mortimer St, W1W 7SU
⊖ Oxford Circus
🚋 Charing Cross
☎ T 020 7927 8362   F 020 7927 8363
@ enquiries@libranetwork.com
Market areas   IT

Website www.libranetwork.com
UK Offices 1
REC Member No

Brief Description Libra Consulting was established in 1996 by a team of leading SAP consultants. The business has evolved and broadened carefully to fit the service needs of their customers. By putting quality first they now enjoy 'business partner' level status with some of the leading management consultancies, IT enterprises and manufacturing companies, supplying them with key professionals in areas such as ERP, e-Commerce, and other emerging technologies, as well as traditional IT based skills.

Preferred method of contact Apply on line or telephone for an appointment

Minimum requirements Ideally relevant systems exposure

Type of business Permanent and Contract

Grade/Level of Appointments Junior to Senior level

Lorien Computer Recruitment Ltd

Head Office ✉ 80 Petty France, SW1H 9EX
⊖ Victoria
🚋 Victoria
☎ T 020 7654 1000   F 020 7654 1066
@ cvs@lorien.co.uk
Market areas   IT

Website www.lorien.co.uk
UK Offices 3
REC Member No

Brief Description Founded in 1977, Lorien provide IT resourcing and specialist services to organisations to help them to improve their performance. Their main activity is the provision of IT contract and permanent recruitment services as well as providing Training, Customer Management and Engineering services through their specialist business units.

Preferred method of contact Apply on line or telephone for an appointment

Minimum requirements Relevant systems exposure

Type of business Permanent and Contract

Grade/Level of Appointments Across all levels

MacAddicts International Group Ltd

Head Office ✉ 131 Middlesex St, E1 7JF
⊖ Aldgate
🚋 Fenchurch St
☎ T 020 7626 6686   F 020 7626 6685
@ recruit@macaddicts.co.uk
Market areas   IT, New Media

Website www.macaddicts.co.uk
UK Offices 1
REC Member No

Brief Description Established in 1989, MacAddicts is a leading recruitment company providing highly trained PC and Apple Macintosh based personnel for both temporary and permanent assignments. Their clients vary significantly in nature and size, from multinational organisations to smaller businesses. These businesses are found in many different industries from Management Consultancy to Travel to Advertising.

Preferred method of contact Apply on line or telephone for an appointment

Minimum requirements Ideally relevant systems exposure

Type of business Temporary and Permanent

Grade/Level of Appointments All levels

Major Players Ltd

See **Media, page 200**

Mayan International

Head Office ✉ 3rd Floor, 3 Golden Sq, W1F 9HR
⊖ Piccadilly Circus
🚋 Charing Cross
☎ T 020 7437 2947   F 020 7437 3744

@ info@maya.co.uk

Market areas   New Media

Website www.maya.co.uk

UK Offices 1

REC Member Yes

Brief Description Mayan International is one of London's first and leading Internet and New Technology recruitment consultancies, providing a one-stop shop for clients' Internet staffing needs. They deal in permanent, freelance, executive and consultancy positions, and place staff across the whole range of New Media and Internet jobs – from Junior Web Designers, Programmers, and Producers, right up to Chief Executive Officers, Directors and Chief Technology Officers. Companies such as BBC, Chello Broadband, Ogilvy Interactive, and Sportal regularly use Mayan International's services and they are recognised as one of London's leading Internet recruitment consultancies.

Preferred method of contact Apply on line or telephone for an appointment

Minimum requirements None

Type of business Contract and Permanent

Grade/Level of Appointments Junior Web Designers to Directors/Chief Executive Officers

McGregor Boyall Associates Ltd

Head Office   ✉ 114 Middlesex St, E1 7JH
　　　　　　 ⊖ Liverpool St
　　　　　　 🚆 Liverpool St
　　　　　　 ☎ T 020 7422 9000   F 020 7377 5338
　　　　　　 @ permanent@mcgregor-boyall.com, contract@mcgregor-boyall.com

Market areas   IT

Website www.mcgregor-boyall.com

UK Offices 1

REC Member Yes

Brief Description Founded in 1987, McGregor Boyall is an international IT recruitment firm focused on the Financial Markets/Services sector. They specialise in recruiting Information Technologists, Technology Managers and Business Analysts for Investment Banks, Securities Houses, On- and Off-line Brokerages, Investment/Asset Managers and Exchanges, as well as On- and Off-line Retail Banks. They also service suppliers to the Financial sector (Consulting firms, Applications Vendors, Software Houses, Systems Integrators) by recruiting Management, Consulting, Sales and Marketing professionals. The firm is divided functionally into two specialist areas, Permanent and Interim/Contract, which work closely together to deliver integrated solutions to clients' recruitment requirements.

Preferred method of contact Apply on line or telephone for an appointment

Minimum requirements Relevant systems exposure

Type of business Contract and Permanent

Grade/Level of Appointments Information Technologists/Business Analysts to Technology Managers

MECS Group

Head Office   ✉ 7 Heron Quay, E14 4JB
　　　　　　 ⊖ Heron Quay
　　　　　　 🚆 Limehouse
　　　　　　 ☎ T 020 7987 1001   F 020 7987 2002
　　　　　　 @ cvs@mecs.eu.com

Market areas   IT, Engineering, Communications, Sales

　　　　　　 ✉ 5 Ensign House, Admirals Way, E14 9XQ
　　　　　　 ⊖ South Quay
　　　　　　 🚆 Limehouse
　　　　　　 ☎ T 020 7510 2211   F 020 7538 3328
　　　　　　 @ cv@mecs.uk.net

Market areas   IT, Engineering, Communications, Sales

Website www.mecs.eu.com

UK Offices 2

REC Member No

Brief Description Established in 1999, MECS was founded to concentrate on recruiting within a number of different areas: Management, Engineering, Communications, Sales and IT.

Preferred method of contact Apply on line or telephone for an appointment

Minimum requirements Relevant industry exposure

Type of business Contract and Permanent

Grade/Level of Appointments Systems Administrator to Senior Systems Engineer

The Media Network

See **Media, page 200**

Michael Rothstein Ltd

Head Office   ✉ 9–12 Long Lane, EC1A 9HA
　　　　　　 ⊖ Barbican
　　　　　　 🚆 Barbican
　　　　　　 ☎ T 020 7600 7888   F 020 7600 7887
　　　　　　 @ web@rothstein.co.uk

Market areas   IT

Website www.rothstein.co.uk

UK Offices 1

REC Member Yes

Brief Description Established in 1985, Michael Rothstein Ltd has a large network of national and international contacts to ensure that the best people are matched to the right jobs, whether you're an IT professional looking for your next contract or for a permanent position.

Preferred method of contact Apply on line or telephone for an appointment

Minimum requirements None

Type of business Contract and Permanent

Grade/Level of Appointments All levels

Modis

Head Office ✉ 3rd Floor, 16–18 New Bridge St, EC4V 6HU
⊖ Blackfriars
🚆 Blackfriars
☎ T 020 7832 3888   F 020 7832 3801
@ info@modisintl.com
Market areas   IT

Website www.modisintl.com

UK Offices 1

REC Member Yes

Brief Description Modis, a subsidiary of the MPS Group, deals with the placement of both permanent and contract IT staff. They have a global presence and reach, serving the vast and growing IT needs of businesses worldwide.

Preferred method of contact Apply on line or telephone for an appointment

Minimum requirements Relevant systems exposure

Type of business Permanent and Contract

Grade/Level of Appointments All levels

Monarch Recruitment

Head Office ✉ Smithfield Business Centre, 5 St Johns Lane, EC1M 4BH
⊖ Farringdon
🚆 Farringdon
☎ T 0870 600 9079   F 0870 603 9077
@ contactus@monarchrecruitment.co.uk
Market areas   IT

Website www.monarch.co.uk

UK Offices 7

REC Member Yes

Brief Description Monarch is one of the UK's largest and most successful specialist recruitment consultancies. Formed in 1992, they aimed from the outset to deliver the highest possible standards and with offices in London, Windsor, Bristol, Birmingham, Edinburgh, Manchester, Leeds and Dublin, their phenomenal growth has been achieved on the back of this aim. As a company that has doubled in size every year, they have developed an unrivalled reputation within the IT industry, which allows them to attract the best companies, the most exciting roles and the most suitable candidates. Combined with their highly trained and motivated consultants and cutting edge IT

systems, the result is a company which is dynamic, focused and delivers the right result.

Preferred method of contact Apply on line or telephone for an appointment

Minimum requirements Relevant systems exposure

Type of business Permanent and Contract

Grade/Level of Appointments All levels

MSB Finance

✉ 90 Long Acre, WC2E 9RZ
⊖ Covent Garden
🚆 Charing Cross
☎ T 020 7849 3111   F 020 7849 3002
@ careers@msbfinance.com
Market areas   IT, Finance

Website www.msb.com

UK Offices 4

REC Member No

Head Office Hanover Place, 8 Ravensbourne Rd, Bromley, Kent, BR1 1HP

Brief Description Founded in 1984 as a specialist IT recruitment firm, MSB has long been regarded purely as a specialist contractor; however, this is no longer the case. The company was restructured in 1999 and now provides candidates and clients the services of an expanded human capital solutions provider. From their headquarters in London, MSB have embarked on a programme of geographic expansion with sizeable operations in Manchester, Glasgow and Dublin together with recently established offices in Holland and Germany.

Preferred method of contact Apply on line or telephone for an appointment

Minimum requirements Previous professional experience

Type of business Contract and Permanent

Grade/Level of Appointments All levels

Nash Direct

Head Office ✉ 13 Bruton St, W1J 6QA
⊖ Green Park
🚆 Victoria
☎ T 020 7071 6900   F 020 7071 6901
@ south@nashdirect.com
Market areas   IT

Website www.harveynash.com

UK Offices 2

REC Member No

Brief Description Nash Direct specialises in finding permanent positions for technically based IT professionals. They handle a broad range spectrum of assignments ranging from First Line Desktop

Support and Junior Developers to Senior Business Analysts and RDBMS Administrators across the following areas: Application Development, New Media, Internet, Desktop Support, Telecoms, RDBMS and Project Management. Each area is supported by a dedicated specialist resourcing team, known as vertical market teams. This means that whatever your skill or discipline, they will have a team that has a detailed understanding of both the technicalities and current climate of your particular market.

Preferred method of contact Apply on line or telephone for an appointment

Minimum requirements Previous professional experience

Type of business Permanent

Grade/Level of Appointments Junior Developer to Senior Business Analyst

---

Nationwider Technology Recruitment

Head Office   ✉   Bedford Chambers, The Piazza, WC2E 8HA
         ⊖   Covent Garden
         🚇   Charing Cross
         ℂ   T 020 7379 3939   F 020 7240 3934
         @   postmaster@nationwider.com
   Market areas   IT, Technical

Website www.nationwider.com

UK Offices 2

REC Member No

Brief Description Nationwider Technology Recruitment was established in 1991 as a Limited Company – now UK Plc status, with additional offices in The Netherlands. Currently, they recruit for clients throughout Europe (EU countries only), from their offices based in the UK and The Netherlands. Where citizenship allows, they work with suitable candidates from all around the world.

Preferred method of contact Apply on line or telephone for an appointment

Minimum requirements None

Type of business Contract and Permanent

Grade/Level of Appointments 1st Line Support to Systems Analysts

---

Net⁺Global Recruitment Ltd

Head Office   ✉   Chesham House, 150 Regent St, W1B 5SJ
         ⊖   Piccadilly Circus
         🚇   Charing Cross
         ℂ   T 020 7439 4600   F 020 7439 4601
         @   info@netglobalrecruitment.com
   Market areas   IT

Website www.netglobalrecruitment.com

UK Offices 1

REC Member No

Brief Description Since February 1999 NetGlobal have been providing IT recruitment solutions to large multi-national clients based in and around the European Union and overseas. NetGlobal can provide recruitment services to suit your needs. Their strength lies in efficiency – they keep in regular contact with the consultants and career-seekers registered with them and they are constantly searching for the industry's newest stars. They currently service some of the world's largest Network Service Providers and Consumers with contract and permanent placements in Europe, Africa, Asia and the United States.

Preferred method of contact Apply on line or telephone for an appointment

Minimum requirements Previous professional experience

Type of business Contract and Permanent

Grade/Level of Appointments All levels

Netsource Ltd

         ✉   61 Cheapside, EC2V 6AX
         ⊖   Mansion House
         🚇   Cannon St
         ℂ   T 020 7653 9100   F 020 7653 9106
         @   contracts@netsource.co.uk
   Market areas   IT

Website www.netsource.co.uk

UK Offices 2

REC Member Yes

Head Office St James' Building, Oxford St, Manchester, M1 6NT

Brief Description Netsource believe that recruitment is very much a people business and they firmly recognise people as individuals. Their individual and consultative approach, combined with their strong European alliances and vast wealth of experience, has made them one of the UK's fastest-growing specialist IT recruitment companies. Netsource originally specialised in recruiting technical staff with scarce skills in the Networking and Communications field. Now that traditional networks are being merged into one common corporate network and with their expertise in delivering leading edge skills in Networking and Communications, they have access to the following generic skill sets: LAN, WAN, ERP and CRM, Voice/VOIP, Mobile, Cellular, Wireless and 3G Comms, Telecoms, Call Centre Technologies, IT Design, Development and Implementation, e-Commerce and Web-based Technologies and Development, Storage/SAN/NAS and Unix.

Preferred method of contact Apply on line or telephone for an appointment

Minimum requirements Previous professional experience

Type of business Contract and Permanent

Grade/Level of Appointments All levels

Next Generation IT Recruitment

See **Executive Search, page 101**

Nicoll Curtin Ltd

Head Office ✉ 48 Gracechurch St, EC3V 0EJ
     ⊖ Bank
     🚋 Cannon St
     ☎ T 020 7397 0110   F 020 7397 0120
     @ enquiries@nicollcurtin.co.uk
Market areas IT

Website www.nicollcurtin.co.uk
UK Offices 1
REC Member No
Brief Description Founded in 2000, Nicoll Curtin is a young and vibrant organisation specialising in Operations and IT recruitment for the City. They run Executive Search and Contingency divisions and recruit for the world's largest and most prestigious Financial institutions.

Preferred method of contact Telephone for appointment
Minimum requirements Previous professional experience
Type of business Contract and Permanent
Grade/Level of Appointments All levels

Octad Plc

Head Office ✉ 14–22 Coleman Fields, N1 7AD
     ⊖ Angel
     🚋 Old St
     ☎ T 020 7688 6633   F 020 7688 6353
     @ info@octad.co.uk
Market areas IT

Website www.octad.co.uk
UK Offices 1
REC Member No
Brief Description Octad Plc was founded in 1999 to provide recruitment services to a number of niche IT sectors. Their mission is to provide high quality recruitment services to individuals and organisations which exceeds their expectations and ensures long term customer satisfaction and retention. They offer the same professional level of service to all their customers. Their experience shows that by maintaining high standards clients continue to use them and both clients and candidates recommend them.

Preferred method of contact Apply on line or telephone for an appointment
Minimum requirements Previous professional experience
Type of business Permanent and Contract
Grade/Level of Appointments All levels

Online Consultancy Services Ltd

Head Office ✉ 95A Rivington St, EC2A 3AY
     ⊖ Old St
     🚋 Old St
     ☎ T 020 7739 1113   F 020 7739 2228
     @ comms@onlineconsultancy.com
Market areas IT

Website www.onlineconsultancy.com
UK Offices 1
REC Member Yes
Brief Description Founded in 1998, Online Consultancy Services Ltd is an international IT recruitment firm focused on the Financial Markets/Services sector. They specialise in recruiting Information Technologists, Technology Managers and Business Analysts for Investment Banks, On-line Brokerages, Investment/Asset Managers and Exchanges, as well as On-line Retail Banks. They also service suppliers to the Financial sector (Consulting firms, Applications Vendors, Software Houses, Systems Integrators) by recruiting Management, Consulting, Sales and Marketing professionals. The firm is divided functionally into two specialist areas, permanent and contract, which work closely together to deliver integrated solutions to clients' recruitment requirements.

Preferred method of contact Apply on line or telephone for an appointment
Minimum requirements Previous professional experience
Type of business Contract and Permanent
Grade/Level of Appointments All levels

Optima Connections

Head Office ✉ 1st Floor, 63 Penfold St, NW8 8PQ
     ⊖ Marylebone
     🚋 Marylebone
     ☎ T 020 7723 0666   F 020 7724 1113
     @ enquiries@optima-connections.com
Market areas IT

Website www.optima-connections.com
UK Offices 1
REC Member Yes
Brief Description Optima Connections was founded in 1990 and is now established as a market leader in the provision of high-calibre IT professionals to the leading-edge Technology and Banking sectors. Fundamental to their success is the selection and development of recruitment consultants with a background in IT, creating a culture of genuine enthusiasm for the developments in Technology and a greater empathy with their market.

Preferred method of contact Apply on line or telephone for an appointment
Minimum requirements None

Type of business Contract and Permanent

Grade/Level of Appointments Graduate to Senior level

Type of business Contract

Grade/Level of Appointments All levels

OTC Computing Ltd

Head Office ✉ London Fruit Exchange, Brushfield St, E1 6EP
⊖ Liverpool St
🚇 Liverpool St
☎ T 020 7366 8100   F 020 7366 8200
@ info@otccomp.com

Market areas   IT

Website www.otccomp.com

UK Offices 1

REC Member No

Brief Description OTC Computing provide both permanent and contract posts in Financial IT. They provide a wide variety of rewarding and challenging opportunities with leading City companies. Partnerships with their clients help them identify the key factors within each job requirement to ensure only the right candidates are sourced. Specific technology areas include C++, Java (GUI and Server-side), Visual Basic, Scripting, CORBA, COM, XML, HTML, Power Builder, SQL Server, Sybase, Oracle, UNIX, NT, LANs and WANs. Positions vary through Front, Middle and Back Office, and they have experience of most Financial Market sectors. Specialist systems including SUMMIT, GLOSS, SWIFT, NEON, Fidessa, Triarch, TIB, MUREX and KONDOR+ are an integral part of many of their positions.

Preferred method of contact Apply on line or telephone for an appointment

Minimum requirements Previous professional experience

Type of business Contract and Permanent

Grade/Level of Appointments All levels

Oxford & Associates

Head Office ✉ Suite 11, Beaufort Ct, Admirals Way, E14 9XL
⊖ South Quay
🚇 Limehouse
☎ T 020 7531 6600   F 020 7531 6464
@ mail_london@oxfordcorp.com

Market areas   IT

Website www.oxfordcorp.com

UK Offices 1

REC Member Yes

Brief Description Oxford & Associates set the standards and the pace in fielding and developing hard-to-find, critical-skilled contractors, consultants and employee candidates in IT, Software and Hardware Engineering and Mechanical, Electrical and Telecommunications Engineering.

Preferred method of contact Telephone for appointment

Minimum requirements Previous professional experience

Paragon IT

Head Office ✉ Pride Ct, 80 White Lion St, N1 9PF
⊖ Angel
🚇 Old St
☎ T 020 7278 9444   F 020 7278 9446
@ london@paragon-it.com

Market areas   IT

Website www.paragon-it.com

UK Offices 4

REC Member Yes

Brief Description The industry respects Paragon IT for what it is – a company that excels in providing recruitment solutions to IT professionals and companies alike. Established in 1988, they've since grown into a team 120-strong. Now with offices in London, Leeds, Bristol, and Frankfurt, they've become one of the leading names in Europe's IT recruitment marketplace. An uncompromising commitment is at the heart of their success; realistic career guidance and targeted client services are extensions of that ethic. It all comes down to quality service and a reputation that attracts only the very best in the industry.

Preferred method of contact Apply on line or telephone for an appointment

Minimum requirements Previous professional experience

Type of business Contract and Permanent

Grade/Level of Appointments All levels

Parc Group

✉ 22 Queen Annes Gate, SW1H 9AA
⊖ St James's Park
🚇 Victoria
☎ T 020 7960 7600   F 020 7960 7601
@ london@parc-group.com

Market areas   IT/Telecoms, Aviation, Engineering, Technology

Website www.parc-group.com

UK Offices 3

REC Member No

Head Office Dublin

Brief Description Parc is a leading international staffing company providing human resource solutions to the Aviation, Engineering and Technology, and IT/Telecoms sectors. In business since 1975, they pride themselves on having an in-depth knowledge of the industry sectors and the skill sets which they serve.

Preferred method of contact Apply on line or telephone for an appointment

Minimum requirements Previous professional experience

Type of business Contract and Permanent
Grade/Level of Appointments All levels

Parity Resources Ltd

Head Office ✉ 4th Floor, 16 St Martins Le Grand, EC1A 4NA
⊖ St Pauls
🚊 City Thameslink
☎ T 020 7776 0876   F 020 7776 0801
@ london@parity-resources.co.uk
Market areas IT

✉ 12–18 Grosvenor Gardens, SW1W 0DH
⊖ Victoria
🚊 Victoria
☎ T 020 7881 2000   F 020 7259 0028
@ london@parity-resources.co.uk
Market areas IT

Website www.parity-resources.co.uk
UK Offices 8
REC Member Yes

Brief Description Parity Group is a leading provider of IT Services, Technology Staff, Training and Human Capital Management solutions operating from over 30 offices across the UK, mainland Europe and the USA.

Preferred method of contact Apply on line or telephone for an appointment

Minimum requirements Previous professional experience

Type of business Contract and Permanent
Grade/Level of Appointments All levels

Portland Resourcing Ltd

Head Office ✉ Edinburgh House, 40 Great Portland St, W1W 7LZ
⊖ Great Portland St
🚊 Euston
☎ T 020 7580 1837
@ info@portland-resourcing.com
Market areas IT

Website www.portland-resourcing.com
UK Offices 1
REC Member No

Brief Description Founded in 1996, Portland Resourcing is a leader in tightly-defined technical market niches. Specialising in SAP, Siebel, Ariba, CommerceOne, i2 and BroadVision only, Portland Resourcing offers effective and expert services for both contract and permanent recruitment.

Preferred method of contact Apply on line or telephone for an appointment

Minimum requirements Previous professional experience

Type of business Contract and Permanent
Grade/Level of Appointments All levels

Precision IT Recruitment Ltd

Head Office ✉ 3–5 Islington High St, N1 9LQ
⊖ Angel
🚊 Old St
☎ T 020 7745 2600   F 0870 135 0578
@ admin@precisionrecruitment.com
Market areas IT

Website www.precisionrecruitment.com
UK Offices 1
REC Member No

Brief Description Precision IT have gained an industry wide reputation for providing a quality recruitment service which is both professional and personable. Their dedicated consultants work in vertical markets, ensuring an accurate understanding of your skills and employment needs. Precision IT helps individuals to find the right opportunities in both the permanent and contract marketplaces.

Preferred method of contact Apply on line or telephone for an appointment

Minimum requirements Previous professional experience

Type of business Contract and Permanent
Grade/Level of Appointments All levels

Prime IT

Head Office ✉ 11 Blomfield St, EC2M 7AY
⊖ Holborn
🚊 City Thameslink
☎ T 020 7588 0174   F 020 7638 8421
@ roscoprime@euroitjobs.co.uk
Market areas IT

Website www.primeuk.com
UK Offices 1
REC Member No

Brief Description Part of the Prime Personnel Group, Prime-Euro IT Resourcing (Permanent and Contract) is focused on defined IT areas within the Banking, Financial, Insurance and Software/Hardware/Systems sectors. The Division is led by an ex IT professional (as are many of the staff) which means that they are able to not only better understand your requirements, but also provide comment, advice and assistance wherever needed. They provide a proactive IT staffing solution for their clients and candidates which results in a fast, responsive service.

Preferred method of contact Apply on line or telephone for an appointment

Minimum requirements None

Type of business Contract and Permanent

Grade/Level of Appointments Graduate/Desktop Support to Senior level

Project Partners Ltd

See Executive Search, page 104

Project People

    ✉ Suite 613, 150 Minories, EC3N 1LS
    ⊖ Aldgate
    🚃 Fenchurch St
    ✆ T 020 7709 9393   F 020 7709 9494
    @ all@projectpeople.com
Market areas IT

Website www.projectpeople.com

UK Offices 3

REC Member No

Head Office Whitefriars, Lewins Mead, Bristol, BS1 2NT

Brief Description Project People is a specialist recruitment consultancy. They provide highly effective permanent and contract recruitment solutions to clients across the UK and mainland Europe, primarily in the areas of IT and Telecommunications. Founded in Bristol in 1996, Project People now has additional offices in London and Maidenhead with consultants based in Italy and Sweden to service their pan-European client base. Project People is undoubtedly one of the UK's fastest growing independent consultancies.

Preferred method of contact Apply on line or telephone for an appointment

Minimum requirements Previous professional experience

Type of business Contract and Permanent

Grade/Level of Appointments All levels

Prospect

See Executive Search, page 104

PSD Group Plc

See Accountancy and Banking, page 23

The Purple Consultancy

See Media, page 203

RB Recruitment Services Ltd

See Sales and Marketing, page 217

Recruit First

Head Office ✉ 75 King William St, EC4N 7BE
        ⊖ Bank
        🚃 Cannon St
        ✆ T 020 7469 5678   F 020 7469 5601
        @ recruit@recruitfirst.com
Market areas IT

Website www.recruitfirst.com

UK Offices 1

REC Member No

Brief Description Recruit First's aim is to provide simple, fast and efficient solutions to permanent and contract recruitment needs. Employing industry experienced Recruitment Consultants with exceptional track records, and exploiting the latest technology allows them to provide a state of the art recruitment solution. They use the Internet and a simple four-stage process as tools to find the simplest and fastest solution to clients, recruitment needs and candidates' aspirations.

Preferred method of contact Telephone for appointment

Minimum requirements Previous professional experience

Type of business Contract and Permanent

Grade/Level of Appointments All levels

Recruit Media Ltd

See Media, page 203

The Recruitment Business Ltd

Head Office ✉ 10 Argyll St, W1F 4TF
        ⊖ Oxford Circus
        🚃 Charing Cross
        ✆ T 020 7287 2225   F 020 7287 2226
        @ jobs@macpeople.co.uk
Market areas Web Design, Creative Design

Website www.macpeople.co.uk

UK Offices 1

REC Member No

Brief Description The Recruitment Business Group is split into three sectors, MacPeople, WebPeople and Creative People, specialising respectively in Creativity, Creative Design and Web Design and Developers across temporary, permanent and contract opportunities.

Preferred method of contact Apply on line or telephone for an appointment

Minimum requirements Relevant industry exposure

Type of business Temporary, Permanent and Contract

Grade/Level of Appointments All levels

Red and Blue Ltd

Head Office ✉ Suite 12, Beaufort Ct, Admirals Way, E14 9XL
  ⊖ South Quay
  🚊 Limehouse
  ☎ T 020 7536 7900 F 020 7536 7890
  @ contact.us@redandblue.co.uk

Market areas IT

Website www.redandblue.co.uk

UK Offices 1

REC Member No

Brief Description Red and Blue recognises that today's IT professional expects a certain level of service. Their experienced consultants will endeavour to ensure you receive that service. Red and Blue can provide you with exciting permanent and contractual opportunities within leading corporate and financial organisations. Red and Blue was founded to provide permanent and contract IT recruitment solutions of the highest standard. They are dedicated to building long-term relationships that enable them to maximise the quality and integrity of their service.

Preferred method of contact Apply on line or telephone for an appointment

Minimum requirements Previous professional experience

Type of business Contract and Permanent

Grade/Level of Appointments All levels

Red Commerce Ltd

Head Office ✉ E9, 2 Michael Rd, SW6 2AD
  ⊖ Fulham Broadway
  🚊 Kensington (Olympia)
  ☎ T 020 7731 8877 F 020 7384 0194
  @ jobs@red-commerce.com

Market areas IT

Website www.red-commerce.com

UK Offices 1

REC Member No

Brief Description Red Commerce specialises in delivering tailored e-Commerce recruitment solutions to the new and emerging Technology marketplace. With a service that enables them to partner specific clients throughout Europe; they hold the capability to provide educated and effective delivery of resource in e-Business, B2B, B2C, Supply Chain Management, EAI, Integration and SAP.

Preferred method of contact Telephone for appointment

Minimum requirements Previous professional experience

Type of business Permanent

Grade/Level of Appointments All levels

Reed Technology Group

See Executive Search, page 105

Resolute Technology

Head Office ✉ 31 Angel Gate, EC1V 2PT
  ⊖ Angel
  🚊 Old St
  ☎ T 020 7278 1300 F 020 7278 3080
  @ resolute@resolutetechnology.com

Market areas IT

Website www.resolutetechnology.com

UK Offices 1

REC Member No

Brief Description At Resolute Technology all of their consultants have the experience to know that only a full understanding gets accurate solutions. Which is why close relationships form the basis of their work. It's because they respect individuality that they treat every assignment as essentially different from all others. They will give you the personal attention that your individual needs demand.

Preferred method of contact Apply on line or telephone for an appointment

Minimum requirements Previous professional experience

Type of business Contract and Permanent

Grade/Level of Appointments All levels

Resources Connection

See Accountancy and Banking, page 24

RGB Consultants Ltd

See Construction and Property, page 55

Roger Dimmock

Head Office ✉ New City Cloisters, 188–196 Old St, EC1V 9FR
  ⊖ Old St
  🚊 Old St
  ☎ T 020 7251 9494 F 020 7251 9031
  @ win@rda.uk.com

Market areas IT

Website www.rda.uk.com

UK Offices 1

REC Member Yes

Brief Description Roger Dimmock Associates was formed as a Limited Company in 1992 to provide IT consultancy and recruitment services.

Preferred method of contact Apply on line or telephone for an appointment

Minimum requirements Relevant systems exposure

Type of business Contract and Permanent

Grade/Level of Appointments All levels

S&H Consulting Ltd

Head Office ✉ 1a Carlisle Avenue, EC3N 2ES
⊖ Aldgate
🚋 Fenchurch St
📞 T 020 7481 1171   F 020 7481 1172
Market areas IT

Website www.shconsulting.co.uk

UK Offices 1

REC Member No

Brief Description S&H Consulting was established in 1992 and specialises in IT recruitment. They place high calibre staff within Investment Banks, Asset Management, Consultancy firms, Oil and Gas, Technology companies and Software Vendors.

Preferred method of contact Apply on line or telephone for an appointment

Minimum requirements Relevant systems exposure

Type of business Contract and Permanent

Grade/Level of Appointments All levels

SBS Group (UK) Ltd

Head Office ✉ 19th Floor, 103 New Oxford St, WC1A 1DY
⊖ Tottenham Court Rd
🚋 Euston
📞 T 020 7420 6700   F 020 7420 6767
@ london@sbsplc.com
Market areas IT

Website www.sbsplc.com

UK Offices 1

REC Member Yes

Brief Description As the UK arm of the international SBS Group plc, the specialist provider of IT staff, they support clients and provide contract opportunities across the length and breadth of the UK.

Preferred method of contact Apply on line or telephone for an appointment

Minimum requirements Relevant systems exposure

Type of business Contract and Permanent

Grade/Level of Appointments All levels

Selected Options

Head Office ✉ 6th Floor, 52–54 Gracechurch St, EC3V 0EH
⊖ Bank
🚋 Cannon St
📞 T 020 7929 0888   F 020 7929 0777
@ recruit@redtick.com
Market areas IT

Website www.redtick.com

UK Offices 1

REC Member Yes

Brief Description Redtick.com is the online presence of Selected Options Ltd. Founded in 1992, by 2001 Selected Options had established itself as a major player in the provision of IT contract and permanent personnel. Their client portfolio covers all industries, from Finance and Banking to Manufacturing and Telecoms.

Preferred method of contact Apply on line or telephone for an appointment

Minimum requirements Previous professional experience

Type of business Contract and Permanent

Grade/Level of Appointments All levels

Sheridan Associates

Head Office ✉ 2nd Floor, Bank Chambers, 30–31 Shoreditch High St, E1 6PJ
⊖ Liverpool St
🚋 Liverpool St
📞 T 020 7375 2016   F 020 7375 1096
@ info@sheridan-london.co.uk
Market areas IT, Technology, Aerospace

Website www.sheridan-associates.co.uk

UK Offices 2

REC Member Yes

Brief Description Sheridan Associates was established in response to the growing demand within industry for skilled IT, Communications and Technology personnel, to enable companies to meet their varied staffing requirements.

Preferred method of contact Apply on line or telephone for an appointment

Minimum requirements Relevant industry exposure

Type of business Contract and Permanent

Grade/Level of Appointments All levels

Smallworld

See **Media, page 205**

Spherion

See **Accountancy and Banking, page 26**

Spring Group Plc

See **Secretarial, page 257**

Square One

Head Office ✉ Earl Place, 15 Appold St, EC2A 2AD
⊖ Liverpool St
🚇 Liverpool St
☎ T 020 7208 2828
Market areas IT, Telecoms

Website www.square.co.uk
UK Offices 1
REC Member Yes

Brief Description Square One began trading in the UK as a limited company in November 1995. The company is wholly privately owned and funded. The principal activity of the organisation is as a provider of specialist IT&T recruitment services and resource consultancy. This covers contract recruitment, permanent recruitment, Executive Search & Selection, and Managed Services.

Preferred method of contact Apply on line or telephone for an appointment
Minimum requirements None
Type of business Contract and Permanent
Grade/Level of Appointments All levels

TCS Group

Head Office ✉ Ground Floor, The Media Centre, 131–151 Great Titchfield St, W1W 5BB
⊖ Great Portland St
🚇 Euston
☎ T 020 7664 5700   F 020 7664 5707
@ info@tcsr.co.uk
Market areas IT

Website www.tcsr.co.uk
UK Offices 1
REC Member No

Brief Description Founded in 1996, TCS Resources brought together a team with strong experience in IT contractor recruitment. From the start, the company was part of a network offering a broad selection of IT expertise solutions. In 1997, they added Interim IT

Management services and further extended this with the addition of permanent recruitment in 1998.

Preferred method of contact Applly on line or telephone for an appointment
Minimum requirements Relevant systems exposure
Type of business Contract and Permanent
Grade/Level of Appointments All levels

Techcentria

Head Office ✉ 114 Middlesex St, E1 7JH
⊖ Liverpool St
🚇 Liverpool St
☎ T 020 7422 9350   F 020 7375 3927
Market areas IT, Technology, Media, Communications

Website www.techcentria.com
UK Offices 1
REC Member No

Brief Description Techcentria is an autonomous trading division of McGregor Boyall Associates. Founded in 1987, McGregor Boyall has established its reputation as an international recruiting firm specialising in the Financial Markets/Services sector in London, New York and Frankfurt. Techcentria now brings to the TMT sector the same business principles and operating methods which have driven the success and growth of McGregor Boyall. Techcentria is divided functionally into three specialist teams: one which focuses primarily on Management and Sales positions for the Vendor/Consulting community; a permanent recruitment team which focuses primarily on Technical recruitment for Vendors, Consulting firms and End-users alike; a contract recruitment team provides contract Technical specialists to Vendors, Consulting firms and End-user organisations.

Preferred method of contact Apply on line or telephone for an appointment
Minimum requirements Relevant industry exposure
Type of business Permanent
Grade/Level of Appointments Mid to Senior Management level

Templeton & Partners Ltd

Head Office ✉ Templeton House, 33–34 Chiswell St, EC1Y 4SE
⊖ Moorgate
🚇 Moorgate
☎ T 020 7074 6000   F 020 7074 6001
@ mail@templeton-recruitment.com
Market areas IT

Website www.templeton-recruitment.com
UK Offices 1
REC Member No

Brief Description Templeton & Partners was established in August 1996 and is now highly regarded in the IT recruitment sector. They have secured many prestigious contracts through their reputation for speed and professionalism.

Preferred method of contact Apply on line or telephone for an appointment

Minimum requirements Relevant systems exposure

Type of business Contract and Permanent

Grade/Level of Appointments All levels

TRG Recruitment

Head Office ✉ 4 St Paul's Churchyard, EC4M 8AY
        ⊖ St Pauls
        🚊 City Thameslink
        📞 T 020 7236 2661   F 020 7236 8181
        @ info@trgresourcemanagement.co.uk
Market areas Telecoms

Website www.trgrecruitment.co.uk

UK Offices 1

REC Member Yes

Brief Description TRG Resource Management originated as a specialist Telecoms recruitment consultancy but recognising a changing market diversified into an outsourcing organisation capable of providing a wider range of call handling service offerings. TRG has adapted its service to reflect the ever changing marketplace in which they operate. Their portfolio has developed and expanded to offer clients a solution which may range from providing skilled staff for a particular resourcing need to the development of a total integrated programme of support.

Preferred method of contact Apply on line or telephone for an appointment

Minimum requirements None

Type of business Permanent

Grade/Level of Appointments All levels

TRS

Head Office ✉ Hanover House, 73–74 High Holborn, WC1V 6LS
        ⊖ Holborn
        🚊 City Thameslink
        📞 T 020 7419 5800   F 020 7419 5801
        @ trsuk@trs-staff.co.uk
Market areas IT

Website www.ambittechnology.co.uk

UK Offices 1

REC Member Yes

Brief Description TRS Staffing Solutions, Inc., headquartered in Salem, NH, is a global organisation providing staffing solutions through its branch locations in the United States and the United Kingdom. TRS specialises in IT, Technical, and Finance and Accounting staffing solutions. They succeed in these market segments through

temporary/contract, direct-hire, and contract-to-hire placements. Established in 1984, TRS is a subsidiary of Fluor Corporation. As a result of various acquisitions and mergers in the eighties and nineties, TRS exceeds 26 years of collective experience in the staffing industry.

Preferred method of contact Telephone for appointment

Minimum requirements Previous professional experience

Type of business Contract and Permanent

Grade/Level of Appointments All levels

Turner Human Resource Ltd

Head Office ✉ 29 Waterside, 44–48 Wharf Rd, N1 7UX
        ⊖ Angel
        🚊 Old St
        📞 T 020 7354 4444
Market areas IT, e-Commerce

Website www.turner.eu.com

UK Offices 1

REC Member No

Brief Description Turner are a permanent, contract and Executive Search recruitment company specialising in e-Commerce, Client/Server and New Media.

Preferred method of contact Apply on line or telephone for an appointment

Minimum requirements Relevant systems exposure

Type of business Contract and Permanent

Grade/Level of Appointments All levels

Universe Partners

Head Office ✉ 24 Lime St, EC3M 7HR
        ⊖ Bank
        🚊 Cannon St
        📞 T 020 7929 4114   F 020 7929 4224
        @ nina@universepartners.com
Market areas IT

Website www.universepartners.com

UK Offices 1

REC Member No

Brief Description Universe Partners is the IT recruitment company with the largest coverage of IT contract and permanent opportunities in the UK and Europe. A division of Universe Technology, the European market leader in SAP recruitment, Universe Partners provides a full recruitment service to the IT consultant and client. It employs specialist IT recruitment consultants who have in-depth experience of recruitment in each specialist area.

Preferred method of contact Apply on line or telephone for an appointment

Minimum requirements Relevant systems exposure

Type of business Contract and Permanent

Grade/Level of Appointments All levels

Universe Technology

Head Office ✉ 60 Mark Lane, EC3R 7ND
          ⊖ Aldgate
          🚊 Fenchurch St
          ✆ T 020 7480 7700   F 020 7480 7780
          @ pamela@utechnology.com
Market areas IT - SAP

Website www.utechnology.com

UK Offices 1

REC Member No

Brief Description Universe Technology supplies SAP professionals throughout Europe and beyond. It has extensive representation in the UK, Belgium, the Netherlands, Germany, France, Scandinavia, Spain, Italy, Portugal and South America.

Preferred method of contact Apply on line or telephone for an appointment

Minimum requirements Relevant systems exposure

Type of business Contract

Grade/Level of Appointments All levels

Venn Technology

Head Office ✉ 5 Langley St, WC2H 9JA
          ⊖ Covent Garden
          🚊 City Thameslink
          ✆ T 020 7557 7667   F 020 7557 7666
          @ info@venntec.com
Market areas IT

Website www.venntec.com

UK Offices 1

REC Member No

Brief Description Venn Technology is currently one of the UK's fastest growing and most exciting recruitment consultancies operating in the Technology arena. Specialising in building long-term relationships with their clients and candidates, they provide structured, proactive and creative recruitment solutions to market leading organisations. Their success is due to an innovative approach, delivering a high quality service based upon their commitment to building highly trained teams of consultants who are specialists in their fields, combining expertise from Technology, Recruitment, Telecoms and Management backgrounds.

Preferred method of contact Apply on line or telephone for an appointment

Minimum requirements Relevant systems exposure

Type of business Contract and Permanent

Grade/Level of Appointments All levels

Verity TMC

Head Office ✉ 10 South Molton St, W1K 5QJ
          ⊖ Bond St
          🚊 Paddington
          ✆ T 020 7495 7266   F 020 7355 2577
          @ cti@cix.co.uk
Market areas IT

Website www.verity-appointments.ltd.uk

UK Offices 2

REC Member Yes

Brief Description Verity TMC has a reputation for considered and creative career development within Emerging Technologies. They believe in developing close relationships with clients and candidates alike. A speedy response and careful attention to detail are elemental to their methodology; this is made possible by their enthusiasm and determination to keep abreast of this rapidly moving Research and Development world. They target individuals with talent and drive, offering them the opportunity to work with firms that want to push the boundaries of both the software and their own capability.

Preferred method of contact Apply on line or telephone for an appointment

Minimum requirements Previous professional experience

Type of business Contract and Permanent

Grade/Level of Appointments All levels

Virtual Purple

Head Office ✉ 85 Borough High St, SE1 1NH
          ⊖ London Bridge
          🚊 London Bridge
          ✆ T 020 7450 1111   F 020 7450 2255
          @ london@virtualpurple.com
Market areas IT, Engineering, Accountancy and Banking, Healthcare, Education

Website www.virtualpurple.co.uk

UK Offices 2

REC Member No

Brief Description Virtual Purple believes that as the global workforce moves to a more flexible, empowered way of working so their needs will change. They currently specialise in IT, Engineering, Financial (Banking and Accounting), Healthcare and Teaching recruitment, but plan to move into other employment sectors soon.

Preferred method of contact Apply on line or telephone for an appointment

Minimum requirements None

Type of business Temporary, Permanent and Contract

Grade/Level of Appointments All levels

Votive Systems Ltd

Head Office ✉ Polden House, Meridian Gate, 201 Marsh Wall,
E14 9YT
⊖ Heron Quay
🚊 Limehouse
☎ **T** 020 7515 0000 **F** 020 7515 0002
@ votive_systems@msn.com
Market areas IT - SAP

Website www.votive-sap.com

UK Offices 1

REC Member No

Brief Description Specialists in SAP jobs.

Preferred method of contact Apply on line or telephone for an appointment

Minimum requirements Previous professional experience

Type of business Contract and Permanent

Grade/Level of Appointments All levels

Way Forward

Head Office ✉ 4th Floor, 18 Broadwick St, W1F 8HS
⊖ Tottenham Court Rd
🚊 Euston
☎ **T** 020 7734 4664 **F** 020 7439 2582
@ info@way-forward.com
Market areas New Media

Website www.wayforward.com

UK Offices 1

REC Member No

Brief Description Way Forward are specialists in New Media recruitment, based in the West End of London, and they pride themselves on a mature and professional approach. They actively recruit in all areas of the New Media industry from Designers/Developers through to Senior Management – if you are in the digital economy they can help you. Way Forward's team has many years of recruitment experience, which guarantees a fast and efficient service as either a candidate or a recruiter.

Preferred method of contact Apply on line or telephone for an appointment

Minimum requirements Previous professional experience

Type of business Temporary and Permanent

Grade/Level of Appointments Designer/Developer to Senior level

Web Career Consultants Ltd

Head Office ✉ 309 Coppergate, 16 Brune St, E1 7NJ
⊖ Liverpool St
🚊 Liverpool St
☎ **T** 020 7496 9955 **F** 020 7448 5212
@ sales@webcareer.co.uk
Market areas New Media, Secretarial

Website www.webcareer.co.uk

UK Offices 1

REC Member No

Brief Description Web was formed in 1998 in response to a rapidly changing market, with new and unknown opportunities available to both candidates and clients. They believe in candid conversations with honest advice and guidance with a simple philosophy – they want to find the right person for the right job. They have a vast portfolio of clients ranging from dot.coms and New Media to International Banks.

Preferred method of contact Apply on line or telephone for an appointment

Minimum requirements None

Type of business Temporary and Permanent

Grade/Level of Appointments All levels

Wiremelts Ltd

Head Office ✉ 43–45 Portman Sq, W1H 6HN
⊖ Marble Arch
🚊 Paddington
☎ **T** 020 7333 0660 **F** 020 7333 0990
@ info@wiremelts.com
Market areas IT

Website www.wiremelts.com

UK Offices 1

REC Member No

Brief Description Wiremelts is a fast-paced, rapidly growing company located in Central London. With strong financial backing and industry-leading experience, they have the flexibility and culture of a start-up backed by the decisive and streamlined execution of an established corporation. They partner with their clients to identify innovative approaches to solving their technology needs, be it development of solutions that improve business impact or new approaches to resourcing and staffing IT projects. They believe in long-term relationships delivering 100% quality and 100% customer satisfaction.

Preferred method of contact Apply on line or telephone for an appointment

Minimum requirements Previous professional experience

Type of business Contract and Permanent

Grade/Level of Appointments All levels

Workstation Solutions Ltd

Head Office ✉ 421 New Kings Rd, SW6 4RN
⊖ Putney Bridge
🚃 Wimbledon
☎ T 020 7371 7161   F 020 7371 7181
@ info@workstation.co.uk
Market areas New Media, Media

Website www.workstation.co.uk

UK Offices 1

REC Member Yes

Brief Description Founded in 1989, Workstation Solutions is a successful recruitment agency with divisions specialising in different aspects of Creative Services: Design and Production, Freelance, DTP, New Media, Editorial, Reprographics, Sales, Conferencing and Events.

Preferred method of contact Apply on line or telephone for an appointment

Minimum requirements Previous professional experience

Type of business Temporary and Permanent

Grade/Level of Appointments All levels

Xtra IT Resources

Head Office ✉ 59–61 Hatton Garden, EC1N 8LS
⊖ Chancery Lane
🚃 City Thameslink
☎ T 020 7242 2929   F 020 7242 2901
@ post@xtra-it.com
Market areas IT

Website www.xtra-it.com

UK Offices 1

REC Member Yes

Brief Description Specialists in all areas of IT recruitment.

Preferred method of contact Apply on line or telephone for an appointment

Minimum requirements Previous professional experience

Type of business Contract and Permanent

Grade/Level of Appointments All levels

Zarak Group

See **Secretarial, page 262**

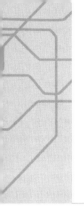

Look before you leap

What to do before the interview and how to survive on the day

This chapter is taken from "Brilliant Answers to Tough Interview Questions" by Susan Hodgson, published by Prentice Hall, an imprint of Pearson Education. © Pearson Education Ltd 2002.

Never was the motto 'be prepared' more appropriate than when you have been invited to an interview. Researching appropriate information, preparing yourself mentally and anticipating the questions you are likely to be asked are the key elements to success.

You will have to prepare for every eventuality. You are unlikely to be asked everything for which you have prepared, but it does not have to be like a written examination where you have revised the wrong bits of the syllabus, it is possible to prepare for whatever is in your interviewer's armoury.

Remind yourself that almost all the questions you will be asked are designed to find out more about you and, above everything else, your suitability for a particular position and the likelihood of you fitting in well with the organisation, its ethos, its staff and its work style. Whatever range of questions you encounter and in whatever form they are asked, all interviewers are seeking the answers to three absolutely fundamental questions.

Can you do the job? Do you have the appropriate mix of qualifications and/or experience to provide you with the basic skills and knowledge to do the job?

Will you do the job? A quite different question from 'can you' – this question is all about your willingness to do the work. Are you keen and eager, how can you demonstrate your motivation?

Will you fit in? This is all about your suitability to work in that particular set up. Part of the answer to this question is hard to put into formal questions and answers; it is something you put over and the interviewer takes in at a more intuitive level. There are, however, whole sets of questions that do relate to this area – those questions about teamwork, dealing with difficult situations with other members of staff, being adaptable, flexible and friendly.

Tip

Don't waste your time working out which of these three themes your interviewer is exploring as he or she questions you, simply be aware that you want them to be thinking 'yes, yes, yes' to these most fundamental questions as you prepare and deliver all your answers.

Given that the interviewer wants to know about you, make sure this is a topic with which you are comfortable and familiar. You may have come to take yourself for granted by now, so take time to really sit down and think about what your qualities and your strengths are, and also any weak spots you have that an interviewer may pick up on. Beware of doing yourself down. Many people are far quicker at listing their drawbacks than their plus points. It is essential that you do this as part of your interview preparation and the short questionnaire that follows will help you to focus clearly on your main selling points.

It is true that different jobs require different portfolios of skills and experience, but there is a hard core of skills and abilities that feature in many job adverts and on many job descriptions regardless of the position being sought. Your own common sense and knowledge of the particular field of employment concerned will help you work out what combination of these skills is most important for the kind of work for which you are applying. A psychotherapist probably needs greater listening skills than a chartered accountant, for example, and the creativity of an advertising copy-writer is not the same as the creativity of a food technologist.

Work through the questionnaire on the next page and rate which of the skills you possess. Be as honest as you can, but beware of being too hard on yourself.

Now look carefully at your list and where you rated yourself as possessing any selling point, then think of an occasion or situation when you have demonstrated this quality. It is irritating to interviewers when a candidate reels off a long list of what sound like very desirable characteristics, but when asked to give an example of where they have used or developed a certain ability, the candidate is left floundering – struggling to give an example and revealing the fact that they are good at reading adverts and job descriptions rather than that they are well qualified for the post. Be really rigorous about these concrete examples, but be flexible in the aspects of your life that you use to demonstrate these – work, school, college, voluntary activities, interests, home and family are all a valuable resource for this exercise and it is less boring for the interviewer if your examples are drawn from a variety of situations.

Tip

For jobs where you have a detailed job description that sets out specific selection criteria or a person specification, ensure that you have relevant material to talk about against each criterion mentioned. Interviews based on these often require the interviewer to score candidates against each criterion, so don't miss any out.

Ensure that you can demonstrate all your good points with examples. This is not only for the reason mentioned above but also because if you consider that if most interviews only last for 30 minutes maximum, they provide a brief snapshot of you. The greater the amount of evidence of your suitability you can draw from describing real situations in your past, the greater is the opportunity for the interviewer to make an informed decision. Research shows that despite the effort selectors and candidates put into interviews, they are actually rather a fallible tool for measuring future performance – past performance provides a more accurate measure. Unfortunately,

Key:

0 = You do not possess the skill

1 = You possess the skill to a limited degree

2 = You possess the skill to a high level of competence

Selling point	Score
Good with numbers	
Good at writing business letters, reports, etc	
Good at creative writing	
Good at talking to people face to face	
Good at talking to people on the telephone	
Good at taking decisions	
Good at listening to other people's problems	
Good at advising and helping people	
Good at persuading people around to your point of view	
Good at solving intellectual problems	
Good at solving practical problems	
Good at organising your time and prioritising your workload	
Good at meeting deadlines	
Good at designing on paper, with your hands or with the aid of computers	
Good at building things to someone else's specifications	
Good level of IT literacy – knowledge of software/hardware	
Good at working flexibly within a team	
Good at taking responsibility for your own actions and your own work	
Able to work on your own without supervision	
Able to follow instructions given by others	
Able to delegate work to others	
Good at explaining things to other people, teaching skills to others	
Able to pay attention to detail	
Able to work under pressure	
Able to motivate other people	
Able to use your own initiative	
Able to think on your feet	
Able to learn new tasks or assimilate new information quickly	

the fact that interviews are fallible does not mean you can take your preparation any less seriously because they are still a major selection tool used by most employers.

In preparing your answers remind yourself never to answer with a single 'yes' or 'no'. Experienced interviewers will encourage you to avoid this by asking open questions that oblige you to give a fuller answer. 'Do you like your current job?' is a closed question whereas 'Tell me what you enjoy about your current job?' is open. Always behave as if you have been asked a question in this second fashion, so that you don't slip into monosyllabic answers. There are exceptions – if you are asked whether you would prefer tea or coffee there is no need to offer a lengthy explanation on the relative caffeine contents and possible medical benefits or drawbacks of either beverage; a straightforward 'coffee please' will suffice.

Tip

If you know what you can offer and you can put it across effectively, you are well on the way to giving a convincing interview performance.

In anticipating potential questions and planning brilliant answers, don't forget that some of your answers will automatically lead to a follow-up question from the interviewer. Don't be disconcerted by this, it usually means you have said something of interest and they want to know more. If it is simply that they want something clarified, they will say so. The key to success is to rehearse what you want to say, but not learn it off by heart. Recall all your relevant experience, your unique selling points, your personal qualities and strengths and any problem areas you might encounter. Become so familiar with this material that if someone stopped you in the street and asked you to tell them everything about yourself in the next 60 seconds, you could do so with ease.

If the time is right

Plan your journey carefully, taking into account all the worst possibilities that public transport, traffic jams or limited parking facilities might conjure up to thwart your good intentions. Inevitably, there will be those occasions when even if you have done everything within your power to ensure arriving in plenty of time, something will happen to disrupt your journey. If this happens, telephone the company/organisation immediately. There is a world of difference for them between sitting there wondering whether someone will appear or having the opportunity to reschedule the interviews and knowing that you took the most sensible action you could by contacting them.

You will find it disconcerting if you arrive too early, so have a cup of coffee, go for a walk and do some deep breathing to calm your pre-interview nerves. Once you have arrived at the offices where your interview is to take place, use the few spare minutes constructively, but not frantically. Make a little bit of an assessment of the place. Do the staff you meet seem friendly, relaxed, busy, disorganised? What kind of atmosphere pervades the whole place? Do they have literature about the organisation, its products and services lying around for the browsing visitor? What information can you glean that you have not found out before?

Nerves are natural

It is a very unusual person who does not suffer from some pre-interview nerves and a limited amount of adrenaline in the system can enhance performance. Interviewers are used to dealing with nerves, but they don't all possess the skill to discern the difference between a slight attack of interview nerves and an overall nervous temperament. Above all, you want to avoid nerves reaching the stage where they interfere with your performance. How each of us deals with pre-interview tension is to some extent an individual matter, but deep breathing really does help and knowing that you have prepared thoroughly and carefully makes a real difference. It may be extremely useful to get a friend or trusted colleague (provided that they are not applying for the same position) to ask you some of the questions to which you have prepared answers, so that you can become more at ease with your subject matter.

Say it without words

A good, well-constructed answer to any question loses its impact if that answer is given in a diffident, lacklustre sort of way that doesn't really match up to the content of what is being said. The non-verbal clues that you give during an interview say a great deal about you. This starts from the minute you enter the interview room (or even the building) – staff you meet there may be giving informal feedback to the interviewer or interview panel. Be pleasant to everyone you meet. Clichés are sometimes truths and a smile really does cost nothing, even if your stomach is churning and your palms feel sticky. It is always a good idea to rinse your hands just before your interview, so that you don't have a clammy handshake. If your file or briefcase is in your left hand, you are ready to shake hands without suddenly having to shuffle everything around. Make sure you use a good, firm, handshake without trying to convince the interviewer that you were the national arm wrestling champion for the past three years.

Nightmare to avoid

One candidate was greatly surprised when a lady dressed in a flowery skirt and cardigan who was offering tea to candidates actually turned out to be the chair of the interview panel later in the day. How glad the candidate was that she had accepted her tea graciously and had not made a pig of herself with the biscuits.

Seating arrangements in interview rooms vary – in part depending on whether you are being interviewed by one person or by a panel and also according to what your interviewer(s) prefer. Don't take a seat until you are invited to do so, then remember to thank your interviewer. You may find yourself in an easy chair with perhaps a coffee table between you and your interviewer, or you may find yourself on one side of a formal table facing your interview panel across an expanse of desk top and note pads. Don't be daunted – the questions will not be any more or less difficult because of the seating arrangements. When interviewers are taking extensive notes, a more formal set-up is easier for them. It is difficult if you are sitting in an easy chair, but best to sit forward – this makes you look interested and not too casual. Look at the interviewer when you answer your questions and if you are being interviewed by a panel look mainly at the person who has asked you the question – occasionally glancing in the direction of the others to ensure that they feel included in the conversation. If interview panels feel daunting, then bear in mind that you will only be asked the same range of questions as you would be by one person and that they are likely to have arranged in advance who will ask you what questions.

If you know that you have nervous habits like twiddling your watchstrap or earrings, remind yourself to cut these out. Similarly, if you tend to make extravagant hand movements while talking, try to cut these back a little, but you don't need to sit on your hands in a desperate bid to eliminate all evidence of your usual communication style.

Listen carefully before you say anything at all

Think about the answers that you should give to interview questions and anticipate, as best you can, all the likely questions in the various forms in which they arise. Before you can answer any questions at all you must make sure that you have really listened to what is being asked.

→ Concentrate – don't let nerves stop you hearing what is being said.

→ Listen carefully to what you are being asked – rather like reading an exam question before you put pen to paper.

→ Don't interrupt your questioner.

→ Show that you are listening actively, but ask appropriate questions to help the conversation along.

→ Understand your interviewer's point of view – preferably without suggesting that they would benefit from counselling or therapy.

Nightmare to avoid

A candidate who was asked if she had any weaknesses was not sure if she had heard correctly, but thought she had been asked if she had any witnesses. This resulted in a very confused conversation where it sounded to the interviewer as if she was summoning everyone she had ever known to state that of course she was of good character – the inference being of course that no, she did not have any weaknesses. It was only in a rare interview feedback discussion that this muddle was unpicked.

Research suggests that the outcome of many interviews is decided by interviewers within the first two or three minutes of an interview and that these decisions are made at an intuitive level, being dependent on the rapport that builds up between selector and candidate. If this is true, then it means that those early aspects of non-verbal communication – smile, handshake, general demeanour – are important. There is no mystery to this and the same rules of courtesy and common sense apply as with any other aspect of life. What is different is that you probably think about it a great deal more than you would on other occasions. It is dangerous to become too paranoid about these aspects of your interview, to worry about whether you have just blown your chances because your handshake wasn't quite right or that you sat down in your chair a nano-second too soon. So long as you remain friendly, warm and enthusiastic you can't go far wrong.

Final tips for preparation

1. Double check your interview date and time.

2. Read through your application form and/or CV, or the notes you made during a telephone call.

3. Ensure that you have read any instructions about your interview. Sometimes you are asked to bring something with you or arrive early for a tour of the department or production site.

4. Check your travel plans.

5. Make sure your interview wardrobe is in good order.

6. Complete any research you need to do about the job/organisation.

7. Remind yourself of your key selling points.

8. Switch your mobile phone off - no interviewer wants to know which of your friends is on a train at the moment, or even that you are just about to clinch a highly successful sales deal; there is a time and a place for everything.

9. Be positive.

Legal

Absolute Recruitment Ltd

Head Office ✉ Staple Inn Building (North), WC1V 7PZ
🚇 Chancery Lane
🚆 City Thameslink
☎ T 020 7404 6292   F 020 7404 6275
@ info@absolute-recruitment.com
Market areas Legal Secretarial, Banking and Investment, Fitness and Health

Website www.absolute-recruitment.com

UK Offices 2

REC Member No

Brief Description Established in 1992, Absolute Recruitment specialises in Legal Secretarial and Support Staff. Their Banking and Investment Management Division came into force in July 1993 with all divisions focused on offering both clients and applicants an honest, respectable service, restoring a positive attitude to recruitment with no pressure sales techniques and only sound career advice and genuine opportunities. In January 2000 they launched the Fitness Division offering a full recruitment and selection service ranging from Operational to Sales and Marketing level for the Recreation industry.

Preferred method of contact Interviews are by appointment only - please make initial contact by telephone or email

Minimum requirements None

Type of business Contract, Temporary and Permanent

Grade/Level of Appointments All levels up to Senior Management

Allegro Solutions Ltd

Head Office ✉ New City Cloisters,196 Old St, EC1V 9FR
🚇 Old St
🚆 Liverpool St
☎ T 020 7253 8275   F 020 7253 8278
@ people@allegrosolutions.co.uk
Market areas Legal, Finance, Secretarial

Website www.allegrosolutions.co.uk

UK Offices 1

REC Member No

Brief Description Allegro Solutions was established in 1999 and trades from offices in the City of London to provide a finely tuned recruitment service to Legal and Accountancy practices as well as the Commercial sector.

Preferred method of contact Telephone for appointment

Minimum requirements None

Type of business Temporary and Permanent

Grade/Level of Appointments All levels

Artemis Recruitment Ltd

See **Secretarial, page 230**

ASA Law Professional

Head Office ✉ 52–54 Carter Lane, EC4V 5EA
🚇 Blackfriars
🚆 Blackfriars
☎ T 020 7236 4625   F 020 7246 4745
@ law@asagroup.co.uk
Market areas Legal

Website www.asagroup.co.uk

UK Offices 1

REC Member Yes

Brief Description ASA was founded in 1973 to deal specifically with Legal Secretarial positions, expanding into Professional Legal recruitment, contract Locums, Education, Banking, IT and Medical sectors.

Preferred method of contact Telephone for appointment

Minimum requirements None

Type of business Permanent, Temporary and Contract

Grade/Level of Appointments All levels

ASA Law Secretarial

Head Office ✉ 52–54 Carter Lane, EC4V 5EA
🚇 Blackfriars
🚆 Blackfriars
☎ T 020 7236 4624   F 020 7246 4746
@ lawsecs@asagroup.co.uk
Market areas Legal Secretarial

Website www.asagroup.co.uk

UK Offices 1

REC Member Yes

Brief Description ASA was founded in 1973 to deal specifically with Legal Secretarial positions, expanding into Professional Legal recruitment, contract Locums, Education, Banking, IT and Medical sectors.

Preferred method of contact Telephone for appointment

Minimum requirements None

Type of business Permanent, Temporary and Contract

Grade/Level of Appointments All levels

Capital Legal

Head Office ✉ 40 Lime St, EC3M 7AW
  ⊖ Bank
  ☒ Cannon St
  ☎ T 020 7458 2760   F 020 7458 2728
  @ mail@capitallegal.co.uk
Market areas Legal Secretarial

Website www.capitallegal.co.uk

UK Offices 1

REC Member No

Brief Description Established in 1996, Capital Legal is a division of the Carlisle Group. Dedicated to the recruitment of Legal Secretaries, with an office based in the centre of London's Legal industry and an associate office in Sydney, they provide a specialist recruitment service to the Legal and Finance community.

Preferred method of contact Apply on line or telephone for appointment

Minimum requirements Previous professional experience

Type of business Permanent/Temporary

Grade/Level of Appointments Legal Secretary to PA for Managing Partner

Career Legal

Head Office ✉ Broad St House, 55 Old Broad St, EC2M 1RX
  ⊖ Bank
  ☒ Cannon St
  ☎ T 020 7628 7117   F 020 7638 4300
  @ info@careerlegal.co.uk
Market areas Legal Secretarial / Professionals

Website www.careerlegal.co.uk

UK Offices 1

REC Member Yes

Brief Description Established in 1991, Career Legal is an independent recruitment consultancy providing specialist services to the Legal sector, ranging from Secretarial to Legal Professionals. They supply a significant majority of London's prominent Legal practices.

Preferred method of contact Telephone for appointment

Minimum requirements None

Type of business Permanent, Temporary and Contract

Grade/Level of Appointments Administration/Secretarial to Trade Mark Attorneys/Partners

Cavendish Personnel

See Secretarial, page 234

Chadwick Nott

Head Office ✉ 9 Carmelite St, EC4Y 0DR
  ⊖ Temple
  ☒ Charing Cross
  ☎ T 020 7072 8484   F 020 7072 8493
  @ enquiries@chadwicknott.co.uk
Market areas Legal

Website www.chadwicknott.co.uk

UK Offices 2

REC Member No

Brief Description Part of Matrix Human Resources, Chadwick Nott specialise in the placement of Partners, Lawyers and Fee Earners within some of the world's best known Law firms, Banks and blue chip companies including private practice and in-house recruitment across Europe, Asia, US, Middle and Far East.

Preferred method of contact Telephone for appointment

Minimum requirements Previous professional experience

Type of business Permanent

Grade/Level of Appointments Partners, Lawyers and Fee Earners

Chambers & Partners

Head Office ✉ Saville House, 23 Long Lane, EC1A 9HL
  ⊖ Barbican
  ☒ Barbican
  ☎ T 020 7606 8844   F 020 7606 0906
  @ recruitment@chambersandpartners.co.uk
Market areas Legal

Website www.chambersandpartners.com

UK Offices 1

REC Member No

Brief Description Founded in 1973, Chambers & Partners specialise in placing Lawyers in industry and private practice, Company Secretaries and Legal Marketers within various industries including Banking, Commerce and Industry, UK and international Law firms.

Preferred method of contact Telephone for appointment

Minimum requirements Previous professional experience

Type of business Permanent

Grade/Level of Appointments Legal Secretarial, Paralegals, Lawyers, Partners

Chancery Lane Legal Secretaries

Head Office ✉ 30 Chancery Lane, WC2A 1LB
⊖ Chancery Lane
🚆 City Thameslink
☏ T 020 7242 1301   F 020 7405 2220
@ info@legal-secretaries.co.uk
Market areas Legal Secretarial

Website www.legal-secretaries.co.uk
UK Offices 1
REC Member Yes

Brief Description Established in 1973, Chancery Lane Legal Secretaries are a privately owned specialist employment consultancy placing permanent and temporary Legal Secretaries in well established firms throughout London and surrounding areas.

Preferred method of contact Telephone for appointment

Minimum requirements Secretarial background

Type of business Permanent and Temporary

Grade/Level of Appointments 2nd Jobber Legal Secretary to Conveyancing/PA

Dawn Ellmore

See Secretarial, page 236

Deacon Search

See Executive Search, page 85

EJ Group

See Human Resources, page 147

Fox Rodney Search

See Executive Search, page 88

Garfield Robbins International

Head Office ✉ 5 Wormwood St, EC2M 1RQ
⊖ Liverpool St
🚆 Liverpool St
☏ T 020 7417 1400   F 020 7417 1444
@ info@garfieldrobbins.com
Market areas Legal

Website www.garfieldrobbins.com
UK Offices 1
REC Member No

Brief Description Established in 1989, Garfield Robbins International specialises in the placement of Lawyers, Paralegals and Legal Executives, and has offices in London, Hong Kong, Sydney and Melbourne.

Preferred method of contact Telephone for appointment

Minimum requirements Previous professional experience

Type of business Permanent

Grade/Level of Appointments Newly Qualified to Senior level

Garrett McCarroll Knowles Ltd

Head Office ✉ 125 High Holborn, WC1V 6QA
⊖ Holborn
🚆 City Thameslink
☏ T 020 7405 6464   F 020 7405 6476
@ info@gmk-legal.co.uk
Market areas Legal

Website www.gmk-legal.co.uk
UK Offices 1
REC Member No

Brief Description Established in 1998, Garrett McCarroll Knowles Ltd place Lawyers in London and the South East, as well as other major cities in the UK, Europe, and the Middle East. With a wealth of experience in the Legal recruitment market, they can offer those seeking a career move outstanding opportunities. All consultants are qualified Lawyers, and are committed to the company's ethos of partnership, trust, and communication — core values that deliver the complete recruitment solution you can rely on.

Preferred method of contact Apply on line or telephone for appointment

Minimum requirements Previous professional experience

Type of business Permanent

Grade/Level of Appointments Newly Qualified to Partner

GR Law Ltd

See Secretarial, page 239

Graham Gill

Head Office ✉ 46 Kingsway, WC2B 6EN
⊖ Holborn
🚆 City Thameslink
☏ T 020 7430 1711   F 020 7831 4186
@ recruit@grahamgill.com
Market areas Legal

Website www.grahamgill.com
UK Offices 1
REC Member No

Brief Description Established in 1988, for over a decade Graham Gill have been providing a cutting edge Legal recruitment service with their fundamental commitment to personal service, absolute integrity and confidentiality. They specialise in UK and international positions for Solicitors, Barristers and Legal Executives in private practice and in-house.

Preferred method of contact Apply on line or telephone for appointment

Minimum requirements Previous professional experience

Type of business Permanent

Grade/Level of Appointments All levels

Harvey Sutton Ltd

See **Accountancy and Banking, page 14**

Hays ZMB

Head Office ✉ 37 Sun St, EC2M 2PL
🚇 Liverpool St
🚆 Liverpool St
✆ T 020 7523 3838   F 020 7523 3881
@ london@zmb.co.uk
Market areas   Legal, Legal Secretarial

Website www.haysworks.com

UK Offices 4

REC Member No

Brief Description A market leader in the legal sector, Hays ZMB sources Lawyers on a permanent and temporary basis at all levels for Law firms, In House Legal Departments, Banks and Finance Houses. The result of a high profile Hays acquisition in autumn 2000, this division is at the very forefront of developments in the niche Legal sector and complements this expertise with specialist teams recruiting Company Secretaries, Human Resources, Business Development and Finance professionals.

Preferred method of contact Apply on line or telephone for an appointment

Minimum requirements Previous professional experience

Type of business Temporary and Permanent

Grade/Level of Appointments All levels

HD+L Selection

See **Financial Services and Insurance, page 123**

Hughes Castell

Head Office ✉ 87 Chancery Lane, WC2A 1BD
🚇 Chancery Lane

🚆 City Thameslink
✆ T 020 7242 0303   F 020 7242 7111
@ help@hughescastell.com
Market areas   Legal

Website www.hughescastell.com

UK Offices 1

REC Member No

Brief Description Hughes Castell is one of the world's leading Legal recruiters. Their highly experienced consultants have built their reputations on the quality of service and advice they deliver to clients and candidates. Local expertise is combined with global reach and an international approach.

Preferred method of contact Apply on line or telephone for an appointment

Minimum requirements Previous professional experience

Type of business Permanent

Grade/Level of Appointments All levels

HW Search & Selection

See **Executive Search, page 94**

JCL Search

See **Executive Search, page 95**

JM Legal Ltd

See **Secretarial, page 242**

Laurence Simons

Head Office ✉ Craven House, 121 Kingsway, WC2B 6PA
🚇 Holborn
🚆 City Thameslink
✆ T 020 7831 3270   F 020 7831 4429
@ info@laurencesimons.com
Market areas   Legal

Website www.laurencesimons.com

UK Offices 1

REC Member No

Brief Description Laurence Simons specialises in the recruitment of Legal professionals globally.

Preferred method of contact Apply on line or telephone for an appointment

Minimum requirements Qualified Legal professionals

Type of business Permanent

Grade/Level of Appointments Newly Qualified to Partner

Law & Finance International

See Financial Services and Insurance, page 125

Law Choice Recruitment Ltd

See Secretarial, page 245

Law Professionals

Head Office ✉ 26–28 Bedford Row, WC1R 4HE
 ⊖ Chancery Lane
 🚇 City Thameslink
 ☎ T 020 7845 4200   F 020 7845 4249
Market areas Legal

Website www.pro-rec-org.com

UK Offices 2

REC Member No

Brief Description Law Professionals specialises in recruitment for the Legal profession.

Preferred method of contact Apply on line or telephone for an appointment

Minimum requirements Previous professional experience

Type of business Temporary, Permanent and Contract

Grade/Level of Appointments All levels

Law Support Services Ltd

See Secretarial, page 245

Lawson Clark

See Secretarial, page 246

Learned Friends Group

See Secretarial, page 246

Lipson Lloyd-Jones

Head Office ✉ 127 Cheapside, EC2V 6BT
 ⊖ St Pauls
 🚇 City Thameslink
 ☎ T 020 7600 1690   F 020 7600 1972

 @ info@ll-j.com
Market areas Legal

Website www.ll-j.com

UK Offices 2

REC Member Yes

Brief Description Lipson Lloyd-Jones (LLJ) was established in 1987 and now operates out of its offices in the City and Manchester providing coverage for the South, North and Midlands. The company also has associate offices in Paris, Australia and New York with strong links throughout the Far East. LLJ provides comprehensive coverage of the Legal marketplace. They handle private practice and in-house vacancies throughout England, whilst their international network gives them access to vacancies in the Far East, Australasia, USA and Europe.

Preferred method of contact Apply on line or telephone for an appointment

Minimum requirements Relevant legal exposure

Type of business Permanent

Grade/Level of Appointments Newly Qualified to Partner/Senior appointments

LPA Legal Recruitment

Head Office ✉ 7 Gray's Inn Sq, WC1R 5AZ
 ⊖ Chancery Lane
 🚇 City Thameslink
 ☎ T 020 7430 1199   F 020 7831 1001
 @ info@the-lpa.co.uk
Market areas Legal - Lawyers, Solicitors

Website www.the-lpa.co.uk

UK Offices 1

REC Member No

Brief Description LPA Legal Recruitment was established in 1996 and has since become one of the major players in the Legal recruitment market. Based in the heart of Legal London (Gray's Inn), their professionally trained consultants operate through three divisions – LPA Private Practice, LPA In-House & Banking, and LPA Partners & Teams – and draw on their extensive contacts and market knowledge to offer a level of service considered by many to be unrivalled. Their clients include UK, US and international Law firms and industry clients in a diverse range of sectors from Investment Banking to Media. They are also instructed by Law firms and industry clients overseas, covering the Asia Pacific region, Middle East, emerging markets countries, off-shore jurisdictions and mainland Europe.

Preferred method of contact Apply on line or telephone for an appointment

Minimum requirements Qualified Legal professionals

Type of business Permanent

Grade/Level of Appointments Newly Qualified to Senior level

MacDonald & Company

See **Construction and Property, page 53**

Maine-Tucker Recruitment

See **Secretarial, page 247**

Opus Personnel Ltd

See **Secretarial, page 251**

Perry Clayman Employment Agency Ltd

See **Secretarial, page 252**

Prolaw

Head Office   ✉   87 Chancery Lane, WC2A 1BD
  ⊖   Chancery Lane
  🚆   City Thameslink
  ☎ T 020 7242 6633   F 020 7242 6677
  @ info@prolaw.co.uk
Market areas   Legal

Website www.prolaw.co.uk
UK Offices 1
REC Member No

Brief Description Established in 1987, Prolaw is one of the leading Paralegal and Locum Solicitor agencies in the UK. Their team of consultants focuses exclusively on the Paralegal and Locum Solicitor market – enabling them to concentrate their energy entirely on that sector. They advise on all aspects of temporary, contract and permanent Legal staffing options across a wide range of industry sectors, from Private Practice Law firms to In-house Corporate and Banking clients, to Central and Local Government Departments.

Preferred method of contact Apply on line or telephone for an appointment
Minimum requirements Previous professional experience
Type of business Temporary and Permanent
Grade/Level of Appointments Paralegals to Locum Solicitors

Robinson Owen

Head Office   ✉   1 Temple Avenue, EC4Y 0HA
  ⊖   Temple
  🚆   Victoria
  ☎ T 020 7583 1200   F 020 7353 8090
  @ seemakapoor@robinsonowen.co.uk
Market areas   Legal - Lawyers, Solicitors

Website www.robinsonowen.co.uk
UK Offices 2
REC Member No

Brief Description Part of the Chadwick Knott Group, Robinson Owen was established in 1992 and specialises solely in the Legal recruitment marketplace.

Preferred method of contact Apply on line or telephone for an appointment
Minimum requirements Relevant legal exposure
Type of business Permanent
Grade/Level of Appointments Qualified Staff to Partner level

S&G Recruitment

See **Secretarial, page 256**

Stanford Resourcing Ltd

See **Executive Search, page 108**

Taylor Root

Head Office   ✉   Fleetway House, 25 Farringdon St, EC4A 4SR
  ⊖   Chancery Lane
  🚆   City Thameslink
  ☎ T 020 7415 2828   F 020 7332 2494
  @ nickroot@taylorroot.com
Market areas   Legal

Website www.taylor-root.com
UK Offices 2
REC Member No

Brief Description Part of the SR Group, Taylor Root is one of the world's leading Legal recruitment organisations. Based in London, Leeds, Hong Kong and Sydney, Taylor Root sources Lawyers within the Commercial areas of Law around the world for international and local Law firms, multinational corporations and major Banking groups.

Preferred method of contact Apply on line or telephone for an appointment
Minimum requirements Relevant legal exposure
Type of business Contract and Permanent
Grade/Level of Appointments Paralegals to Lawyers

Tully International Group

Head Office   ✉   121 Salisbury House, London Wall, EC2M 5QQ
  ⊖   Moorgate
  🚆   Moorgate
  ☎ T 020 7628 1828   F 020 7628 2328

@ london@tullyrecruitment.com
Market areas Legal - Lawyers, Solicitors

Website www.tullyrecruit.com

UK Offices 3

REC Member No

Brief Description Tully International is a Legal recruitment consultancy with offices in London, Hong Kong, Glasgow and Edinburgh. It is also the founding member of the Tully International Group of Legal recruiters which is an integrated network of Legal recruiters covering Europe, Asia and Australia. They specialise in providing high-quality personalised consultancy services for clients and candidates, both on a domestic and an international basis.

Preferred method of contact Apply on line or telephone for an appointment

Minimum requirements Qualified Legal professionals

Type of business Permanent

Grade/Level of Appointments Newly Qualified to Partner

Media

42nd Street Recruitment

Head Office ✉ Room 228, The Linen Hall, Regent St, W1R 5TB
⊖ Oxford Circus
🚊 Charing Cross
☎ T 020 7734 4422   F 020 7287 5481
@ info@42ndstreetrecruitment.com
Market areas Television/Music and related media industries

Website www.42ndstreetrecruitment.com

UK Offices 1

REC Member No

Brief Description Established in 1995 in order to provide a specialist service to the Television/Music and related Media industries, 42nd Street Recruitment has now expanded and provides Office personnel i.e. Administration, Sales, Marketing and Secretarial staff.

Preferred method of contact Apply on line or telephone for appointment

Minimum requirements Ideally previous TV/Film exposure, Bi-lingual

Type of business Temporary, Permanent and Contract

Grade/Level of Appointments Junior/Graduate to Management

Albany Appointments

Head Office ✉ 5 Dering St, W1S 1AA
⊖ Bond St
🚊 Paddington
☎ T 020 7493 8611   F 020 7495 0119
@ careers@albany-appointments.co.uk
Market areas Media, Conferencing and Events

Website www.albany-appointments.co.uk

UK Offices 1

REC Member No

Brief Description Albany Appointments is the leading Media and Conference recruitment consultancy in London. Established over 25 years ago the Media and Communications sector was expanded to enable a Conference division being set up 10 years ago to provide recruitment services to the most successful companies.

Preferred method of contact Telephone for appointment

Minimum requirements PC Literate

Type of business Temporary and Permanent

Grade/Level of Appointments Graduate/Junior to Management

Aquarius Employment Bureau

See **Secretarial, page 230**

Aquent

Head Office ✉ 1 Bedford St, WC2E 9HD
⊖ Covent Garden
🚊 Charing Cross
☎ T 020 7836 8200   F 020 7836 4034
@ shutson@aquent.com
Market areas Creative Design

Website www.aquent.com

UK Offices 3

REC Member No

Brief Description Founded in 1987, Aquent has led the staffing industry through innovation and a commitment to providing unequalled customer/client value, placing highly skilled professionals in a variety of Creative fields, with nearly 70 offices across the US, Europe and Far East.

Preferred method of contact Telephone for appointment

Minimum requirements Previous professional experience

Type of business Temporary, Permanent and Contract

Grade/Level of Appointments All levels

Astron Ltd

Head Office ✉ 4th Floor, 55 Conduit St, W1R 9TG
⊖ Oxford Circus
🚊 Charing Cross
☎ T 020 7734 4940   F 020 7494 0023
@ goastron@globalnet.co.uk
Market areas Book Publishing

Website www.bookcareers.com

UK Offices 1

REC Member No

Brief Description Specialising in Book Publishing opportunities and, based in the West End, Astron supplies staff ranging from 2nd Jobbers to Executive and Director level roles.

Preferred method of contact Telephone for appointment

Minimum requirements 2nd Jobber upwards

Type of business Permanent

Grade/Level of Appointments 2nd Jobbers to Senior Management level

BDG Recruitment

Head Office   ✉   13 Goodwins Ct, WC2N 4LL
    ⊖   Leicester Sq
    🚊   Charing Cross
    ✆   T 020 7379 6650   F 020 7379 4436
    @   bdg@bdgrecruitment.co.uk
Market areas   Design, Advertising and New Media

Website   www.bdgrecruitment.co.uk

UK Offices   1

REC Member   No

Brief Description   Based in Covent Garden, BDG is one of the UK's leading specialist recruitment companies for Design and Advertising people, with a reputation built during the last 20 years. Their consultants have worked in the Front Line, Creative or Account Management providing clients with expertise in the marketplace.

Preferred method of contact   Apply on line or telephone for appointment

Minimum requirements   Previous professional experience

Type of business   Permanent

Grade/Level of Appointments   All levels

Bohman's Network

Head Office   ✉   262a Fulham Rd, SW10 9EL
    ⊖   Earls Ct
    🚊   Kensington (Olympia)
    ✆   T 020 7849 3928   F 020 7849 3926
    @   recruit@bohmans.com
Market areas   Media, PR, Marketing, Advertising

Website   www.bohmans-network.co.uk

UK Offices   1

REC Member   Yes

Brief Description   Established in 1993, Bohman's Network is uniquely placed to offer a competent and effective resourcing service tailored to the Media, Marketing, Marketing/Communication, Advertising and Public Relations arenas.

Preferred method of contact   Apply on line or telephone for appointment

Minimum requirements   Ideally relevant industry exposure

Type of business   Permanent

Grade/Level of Appointments   Assistant to Managing Director level

Bond Accountancy

See Accountancy and Banking, page 8

Career Moves

Head Office   ✉   Sutherland House, 5–6 Argyll St, W1V 1AD
    ⊖   Oxford Circus
    🚊   Charing Cross
    ✆   T 020 7292 2900   F 020 7434 0297
    @   careermoves@cmoves.co.uk
Market areas   Media

Website   www.cmoves.co.uk

UK Offices   1

REC Member   Yes

Brief Description   Career Moves are an established recruitment consultancy with a comprehensive Media client database, supplying many of the industry's top names ranging from Television, Production, PR, Advertising, Music, Publishing to New Media.

Preferred method of contact   Apply on line or telephone for appointment

Minimum requirements   None

Type of business   Temporary and Permanent

Grade/Level of Appointments   PR Administrators/Receptionists to HR Officers/Product Managers

Carreras Lathane Associates

Head Office   ✉   4 Golden Sq, W1R 3AE
    ⊖   Piccadilly Circus
    🚊   Charing Cross
    ✆   T 020 7439 9634   F 020 7434 9150
    @   info@carresaslathane.com
Market areas   Media, Sales

Website   www.carreraslathane.com

UK Offices   1

REC Member   No

Brief Description   Carreras Lathane was established in 1981 as a Media Sales recruitment consultancy and since then has expanded into related fields such as Direct Marketing and Exhibitions, operating from offices in London, Singapore and Sydney.

Preferred method of contact   Apply on line or telephone for appointment

Minimum requirements   None

Type of business   Permanent

Grade/Level of Appointments   Graduate to Sales/Managing Director

Christopher Keats

Head Office   ✉   3rd Floor, Kenilworth House, 79–80 Margaret St, W1N 7HB
    ⊖   Oxford Circus
    🚊   Charing Cross

☎ T 020 7637 7555   F 020 7637 8777
@ recruitment@keats.co.uk
Market areas   Media

Website www.christopherkeats.co.uk
UK Offices 1
REC Member Yes

Brief Description   Established in 1987, Christopher Keats is an independent consultancy specialising in the Media sector ranging from Broadcast/Entertainment, Advertising, Publishing, Public Relations, Marketing and Design, providing high calibre professionals to many established names in the industry.

Preferred method of contact   Apply on line or telephone for appointment
Minimum requirements   None
Type of business   Permanent
Grade/Level of Appointments   Graduate/Creative Junior to Editor/Chairman's PA

Creative Career Partnership Ltd

Head Office ✉ 5 Green Dragon Ct, SE1 9AW
⊖ London Bridge
🚉 London Bridge
☎ T 0870 901 7001   F 0870 901 7009
@ info@ccp.uk.com
Market areas   New Media, Creative and Production

Website www.ccp.uk.com
UK Offices 1
REC Member No

Brief Description   Based in London SE1, the Creative Career Partnership (CCP) are one of the leading suppliers of Creative staff to the Advertising, Design and Corporate industries.

Preferred method of contact   Apply on line or telephone for appointment
Minimum requirements   1 year's relevant commercial exposure
Type of business   Permanent and and Contract
Grade/Level of Appointments   Typesetters/Interior Designers to Web Designers/Studio Managers

Creative Recruitment Ltd

Head Office ✉ 17 Devonshire Sq, EC2M 4SQ
⊖ Liverpool St
🚉 Liverpool St
☎ T 020 7247 3458   F 020 7375 0096
@ info@creativerecruitment.co.uk
Market areas   New Media, Publishing, Design, PR, Marketing

Website www.creativerecruitment.co.uk
UK Offices 1

REC Member   No

Brief Description   Creative Recruitment was established in 1995 as a purist within the Creative field, recruiting permanent and freelance Print and New Media staff – from Designers, Art Directors, Copywriters, Traffickers, Account/Project Managers, Programmers/Coders through to DTP and Presentation Operators. They deliver integrated solutions within the following markets: Advertising, Design, Marketing, PR, blue chip, Financial, New Media and Publishing.

Preferred method of contact   Apply on line or telephone for appointment
Minimum requirements   None
Type of business   Temporary, Permanent and Contract
Grade/Level of Appointments   Copywriters/Coders to Art Directors/Project Managers

Dagmar Tara

Head Office ✉ 48 Chandos Place, WC2N 4HS
⊖ Charing Cross
🚉 Charing Cross
☎ T 020 7379 4141   F 020 7836 9406
@ recruit@dagmar-tara.com
Market areas   Printing, Reprographics, DTP

Website www.dagmar-tara.com
UK Offices 1
REC Member No

Brief Description   Established in 1948, Dagmar Tara was the first agency to service exclusively the needs of Print and associated markets ranging from Publishing to Printing sectors.

Preferred method of contact   Telephone for appointment
Minimum requirements   Ideally exposure to print or associated sectors
Type of business   Temporary and Permanent
Grade/Level of Appointments   Receptionist/Administrator to Designer/Proof Reader

Datascope Recruitment

See **IT and Telecoms, page 160**

The Davis Co Ltd

See **Executive Search, page 84**

Direct Recruitment Ltd

See **Sales and Marketing, page 214**

Folio Personnel Ltd (Graphic Design Division)

Head Office ✉ Dorland House, 14–16 Regent St, SW1Y 4PH
⊖ Piccadilly Circus
🚊 Charing Cross
☎ T 020 7484 0603   F 020 7484 0601
@ jatherton@foliopersonnel.com
Market areas Graphic Design

Website www.foliopersonnel.com
UK Offices 1
REC Member No
Brief Description Established in 1994, Folio Personnel was founded to provide a professional service to the industry it serves. They offer a complete recruitment service for both temporary and permanent staff at all levels.
Preferred method of contact Apply on line or telephone for appointment
Minimum requirements None
Type of business Contract and Permanent
Grade/Level of Appointments All levels

The Foundry

See Executive Search, page 88

G Solution

See Accountancy and Banking, page 13

Graduate Recruitment Company

See Graduates, page 127

Hamblyn Selection

See Sales and Marketing, page 215

Handle Recruitment

See Secretarial, page 239

Harrison Pursey

See Secretarial, page 240

Harrison Scott Associates

Head Office ✉ 21–24 Chesham Place, SW1X 8HG
⊖ Victoria
🚊 Victoria
☎ T 020 7838 9695
@ graham@harrison-scott.co.uk
Market areas Printing, Packaging, IT, Pharmaceutical

Website www.harrison-scott.co.uk
UK Offices 4
REC Member No
Brief Description Although many candidates deal with them because they are the largest in the UK within most of their specialist sectors, most work with them because their focus is on candidates' needs. Their teams of highly trained consultants are passionately committed to specialist areas of the market, and as a company they never lose sight of the fact that it is a person's career and livelihood they are dealing with and as such they will never compromise on the quality of advice they give on the many opportunities they handle nationally.
Preferred method of contact Apply on line or telephone for an appointment
Minimum requirements None
Type of business Permanent
Grade/Level of Appointments All levels

Hills Flower Strong Ltd

See Sales and Marketing, page 216

Instant Library Recruitment

Head Office ✉ 104b St John St, EC1M 4EH
⊖ Angel
🚊 City Thameslink
☎ T 020 7608 1414   F 020 7608 1038
@ recruitment@instant-library.com
Market areas Librarian, Archivists, Information Services

Website www.instant-library.com
UK Offices 2
REC Member No
Brief Description Instant Library Recruitment provides a professional employment consultancy service specialising in career opportunities for Librarians, Information Specialists, Records Managers and Archivists. They handle temporary and permanent, full time and part time positions, nationwide and overseas.
Preferred method of contact Telephone for appointment
Minimum requirements Previous professional experience

Type of business Temporary, Permanent and Contract

Grade/Level of Appointments All levels

Irene Anderson Associates

Head Office ✉ 12 Charlotte Place, W1P 1AP
      ⊖ Goodge St
      ☻ Euston
      ☎ T 020 7580 5060 F 020 7631 1404
      @ enquiry@iaa.co.uk
    Market areas Media, Secretarial

Website www.iaa.co.uk

UK Offices 1

REC Member No

Brief Description Established in 1993, Irene Anderson Associates specialises in the Media industry, predominately Advertising and Public Relations, but also within the ancillary support areas of Marketing, Design, Broadcast, Sponsorship and Publishing.

Preferred method of contact Apply on line or telephone for an appointment

Minimum requirements None

Type of business Temporary, Permanent and Contract

Grade/Level of Appointments All levels

JFL

Head Office ✉ 47 New Bond St, W1S 1DJ
      ⊖ Bond St
      ☻ Paddington
      ☎ T 020 7493 8824 F 020 7493 7161
      @ info@jflrecruit.com
    Market areas Communications, PR, Marketing, Publishing, Secretarial

Website www.jflrecruit.com

UK Offices 1

REC Member No

Brief Description JFL was founded in 1972 as a specialist Search and Selection consultancy for the Communications sector, working primarily in PR, Marketing, Communications and Publishing. They offer candidates an individual service tailored to their own aims and aspirations.

Preferred method of contact Telephone for appointment

Minimum requirements None

Type of business Temporary and Permanent

Grade/Level of Appointments Graduates to Board level

Joyce Guiness Partnership

See Secretarial, page 242

Judy Fisher Associates

See Secretarial, page 243

Keystone Employment Group – Printing & Design

Head Office ✉ 272–276 Pentonville Rd, N1 9JY
      ⊖ Kings Cross
      ☻ Kings Cross
      ☎ T 020 7833 7780 F 020 7833 7783
    Market areas Print

Website www.keystone-recruitment.co.uk

UK Offices 4

REC Member Yes

Brief Description Keystone was originally formed in London in 1948. It was one of the first and largest privately owned employment agencies placing Secretarial and General Office Staff. Their greatest assets are the people who work for them, they are the reason why clients and candidates are recommended to use the Keystone Group services – it is their ability to listen and understand people's needs, to work in partnership with them to achieve success, and more importantly client and candidate satisfaction.

Preferred method of contact Apply on line or telephone for an appointment

Minimum requirements None

Type of business Temporary and Permanent

Grade/Level of Appointments All levels

KP Publishing Personnel

      ✉ 10 Argyll St, W1V 1AB
      ⊖ Oxford Circus
      ☻ Charing Cross
      ☎ T 020 7734 7823 F 020 7437 0105
      @ info@kp-group.co.uk
    Market areas Publishing, Secretarial, Sales

Website www.kp-group.co.uk

UK Offices 1

REC Member No

Head Office KP Group, Kingsland House, 43 Dane St, Bishops Stortford, Herts, CM23 3BT

Brief Description Established over 25 years, KP Publishing has built their reputation on honesty, reliability and proficiency. KP Publishing has always exceeded in the recruitment of the very best in Media recruitment, with a long established relationship with clients who rely on them to recruit resourceful personnel tailored to individual needs. This relationship with clients has proved to be fundamental to their success and continues to further enhance their long established reputation for providing high calibre candidates.

Preferred method of contact Apply on line or telephone for an appointment

Minimum requirements None

Type of business Temporary and Permanent

Grade/Level of Appointments All levels

Lipton Fleming Appointments Ltd

Head Office ✉ Northumberland House, 155–157 Great Portland St, W1W 6QP
⊖ Great Portland St
🚇 Euston
☏ T 020 7636 0303   F 020 7255 1584
Market areas Media, Creative, Research, Marketing, New Media and Design, Secretarial

Website www.liptonfleming.co.uk

UK Offices 1

REC Member Yes

Brief Description Established in 1987, Lipton Fleming have cultivated a loyal client and candidate base through their specialist knowledge of Media and recruitment. They believe that the single most important factor in driving a business forward is people, and that choosing the right recruitment consultancy is crucial to both candidates and clients. Through their specialist divisions they are able to offer many clients a 'one-stop' recruitment solution.

Preferred method of contact Apply on line or telephone for an appointment

Minimum requirements None

Type of business Temporary and Permanent

Grade/Level of Appointments All levels

Major Players Ltd

Head Office ✉ 73–75 Endell St, WC2H 9AJ
⊖ Covent Garden
🚇 Charing Cross
☏ T 020 7836 4041   F 020 7836 4009
@ helen.allen@majorplayers.co.uk
Market areas Marketing, New Media, IT, PR, Creative

Website www.majorplayers.co.uk

UK Offices 1

REC Member No

Brief Description Major Players was established in 1992 to focus on providing staff ranging from Graduates/1st Jobbers through to

Management level for the Marketing, New Media, IT, Public Relations and Creative industries across the UK.

Preferred method of contact Apply on line or telephone for an appointment

Minimum requirements None

Type of business Permanent

Grade/Level of Appointments Graduates/1st Jobbers to Management level

---

Management Personnel

See **Sales and Marketing, page 216**

Management Selection Consultants

See **Accountancy and Banking, page 19**

Media Contacts Ltd

Head Office ✉ The Windsor Centre, Windsor St, N1 8QG
⊖ Angel
🚇 Barbican
☏ T 020 7359 8244   F 020 7226 9121
@ careers@media-contacts.co.uk
Market areas Media, New Media, PR, Sales, Events, Publishing

Website www.media-contacts.co.uk

UK Offices 1

REC Member No

Brief Description Established in 1993, Media Contacts was founded with the aim of being the premier recruiter of high calibre Sales Executives to the Media industry. Since then they have established an outstanding track record of recruiting at all levels from Graduate Trainee to Board level. They have also broadened their horizons to recruit Sales, Marketing, Editorial, Design, Production, Support and Operations Executives for a much wider range of clients. They have consultants specifically recruiting for New and Traditional Media, Recruitment Consultancies, Conferences, Exhibitions and blue chip organisations.

Preferred method of contact Apply on line or telephone for an appointment

Minimum requirements None

Type of business Permanent

Grade/Level of Appointments Graduate Trainees to Board level

The Media Network

Head Office ✉ 28 Mortimer St, W1W 7RD
⊖ Oxford Circus
🚇 Marylebone

℃ T 020 7637 9227   F 020 7323 3903
@ across@tmn.co.uk
Market areas   Print and Web Publishing

Website   www.tmn.co.uk
UK Offices   1
REC Member   No

Brief Description   The Media Network specialises in Editorial recruitment for Print and Web Publishing. Established in 1989, they have become the UK's leaders in the field of Magazine Journalism recruitment. Today, they are equally known for recruiting Content Editors, Writers and Producers for both mainstream and corporate Internet sites and Intranets

Preferred method of contact   Apply on line or telephone for an appointment

Minimum requirements   Relevant industry exposure

Type of business   Permanent

Grade/Level of Appointments   All levels

The Media Partnership

Head Office   ✉ Garden Studios, 11–15 Betterton St, WC2H 9BP
   ⊖ Covent Garden
   ⊟ Charing Cross
   ℃ T 020 7470 8781   F 020 7470 8782
Market areas   Media, New Media, Sales

Website   www.the-media-partnership.com
UK Offices   1
REC Member   No

Brief Description   Formed in May 1998, The Media Partnership (UK) Ltd quickly became established as one of the key players on the Media recruitment scene. The company specialises in Media Sales positions from Graduate Trainee level through to General Management roles, and works across the entire Media spectrum, including Business Publishing, Consumer Magazines, National Press, New Media, Exhibitions, Radio Sales, Television and Outdoor Media.

Preferred method of contact   Apply on line or telephone for an appointment

Minimum requirements   None

Type of business   Permanent

Grade/Level of Appointments   All levels

The Media Place

Head Office   ✉ 21 South Molton St, W1K 5QZ
   ⊖ Bond St
   ⊟ Paddington
   ℃ T 020 7408 0575
   @ shirley@themediaplace.co.uk
Market areas   PR and Marketing

Website   www.themediaplace.co.uk
UK Offices   1
REC Member   No

Brief Description   The Media Place is an established agency specialising in recruitment for the Public Relations and Marketing industry. Established in 1999 and located in the West End, their recruitment specialists have over 20 years experience in the Media industry.

Preferred method of contact   Apply on line or telephone for an appointment

Minimum requirements   None

Type of business   Permanent

Grade/Level of Appointments   All levels

The Meridian Consultancy Group

Head Office   ✉ 27 Adam and Eve Mews, W8 6UG
   ⊖ High St Kensington
   ⊟ Kensington (Olympia)
   ℃ T 020 7795 6633   F 020 7795 6644
   @ search@meridian-recruit.com
Market areas   Publishing, Media, Music, Broadcasting, e-commerce, direct selling

Website   www.meridian-recruit.co.uk
UK Offices   1
REC Member   No

Brief Description   Established in 1994, The Meridian Consultancy Group provides a specialist recruitment and HR service to the Publishing and Media industries. It has forged a reputation as Publishing's leading recruitment organisation and now extends its activities to related industries such as Music, Broadcasting and e-Commerce.

Preferred method of contact   Apply on line or telephone for an appointment

Minimum requirements   Relevant industry management exposure

Type of business   Contract and Permanent

Grade/Level of Appointments   Marketing/Publishing Manager to Vice President

Network Design

See **Construction and Property, page 54**

Pathfinders Media Recruitment

Head Office   ✉ 37–38 Golden Sq, W1F 9LA
   ⊖ Piccadilly Circus
   ⊟ Charing Cross
   ℃ T 020 7434 3511
Market areas   Media, Secretarial, Sales

Website www.pathfindersrecruitment.com

UK Offices 1

REC Member No

Brief Description Pathfinders Support has specialised in recruiting Secretarial Support Staff for Media and Marketing related companies for over 35 years. No-one can boast more experience in this sector or more knowledge of it. Their depth of experience is matched by the breadth of positions they cover, from the most Junior to the most Senior Support roles, on a permanent, temporary or contract basis. Pathfinders Mainstream has been a leading Executive consultancy in the PR, Marcomms and Marketing industries for over 20 years. Their candidates range from Graduates through to Senior Managers and Directors.

Preferred method of contact Apply on line or telephone for an appointment

Minimum requirements None

Type of business Temporary and Permanent

Grade/Level of Appointments Graduate to Senior level

Peter Childs Associates

Head Office ✉ 8–9 Berkeley St, W1J 8DW
⊖ Green Park
🚆 Victoria
📞 T 020 7659 9966   F 020 7659 9965
@ pca@peterchilds.co.uk
Market areas Public Affairs, Public Relations

Website www.peterchilds.co.uk

UK Offices 1

REC Member No

Brief Description Established in 1986, Peter Childs Ltd offers a recruitment service that is both discreet and personal. They believe that the excellent reputation that they have earned is based upon their knowledge of Public Relations and Political Communications and those who work within them. They favour an individual approach to clients and candidates, offering thoughtful, relevant suggestions and ensuring that they attract the best of both.

Preferred method of contact Apply on line or telephone for an appointment

Minimum requirements Previous professional experience

Type of business Contract and Permanent

Grade/Level of Appointments All levels

Price Trace & Hawes Ltd

Head Office ✉ 299 Oxford St, W1R 1LA
⊖ Bond St
🚆 Paddington
📞 T 020 7529 6020   F 020 7499 9259
@ inbox@pthrecruit.co.uk
Market areas Public Relations

Website www.pthrecruit.co.uk

UK Offices 1

REC Member Yes

Brief Description PTH specialises exclusively in Corporate Communications recruitment. Their success spans almost 20 years, and their consultants are all experienced recruitment or PR professionals. So whether you are a client or a candidate you can be certain that your requirements are in expert hands.

Preferred method of contact Apply on line or telephone for an appointment

Minimum requirements Previous professional experience

Type of business Contract and Permanent

Grade/Level of Appointments Account Executives to Senior Board level

pricejamieson

Head Office ✉ Paramount House, 104–108 Oxford St, W1D 1LP
⊖ Oxford Circus
🚆 Charing Cross
📞 T 020 7580 7702   F 020 7436 4789
@ recruit@pricejam.com
Market areas Digital and Marketing Communications, PR

Website www.pricejam.com

UK Offices 1

REC Member Yes

Brief Description pricejamieson is a London based privately owned recruitment company. They specialise in recruitment for clients in the Digital and Marketing Communications sectors. They are also the UK partner of an international network. Areas they continuously recruit for include: New Media, Telecommunications, Print and Outdoor Media, Research, Marketing Services, Direct Marketing, IT, Broadcast, Wireless and Mobile, Design, Professional Services and Database Management.

Preferred method of contact Apply on line or telephone for an appointment

Minimum requirements Previous professional experience

Type of business Permanent

Grade/Level of Appointments All levels

prjobs.net

Head Office ✉ 53 New Oxford St, WC1A 1BL
⊖ Tottenham Court Rd
🚆 Euston
📞 T 020 7240 6373   F 020 7240 6374
Market areas Public Relations

Website www.prjobs.net

UK Offices 1

REC Member No

Media

Brief Description With prjobs.net you get a round the clock, round the calendar service – 24 hours a day, 365 days a year – that's personal to you and tailored to your requirements. They ensure that each of their candidates has a personal recruitment consultant looking after their needs. They have a personal home page on their website dedicated to them. They offer comprehensive on and off-line search facilities, giving people the opportunity to find exactly what or whom they're looking for. At prjobs.net, they take the uncertainty out of the recruitment process. If you're actively looking for a career move, they offer up-to-date and comprehensive information about what's available, enabling you to make an informed choice about the opportunities that are right for you.

Preferred method of contact Apply on line or telephone for an appointment

Minimum requirements Previous professional experience

Type of business Permanent

Grade/Level of Appointments All levels

PRMoves

Head Office ✉ Sutherland House, 5–6 Argyll St, W1F 7TE
🚇 Oxford Circus
🚂 Charing Cross
📞 T 020 7292 2926
@ info@prmoves.com
Market areas Public Relations

Website www.prmoves.com
UK Offices 1
REC Member No

Brief Description PRMoves Ltd successfully launched in 2001 offering a fresh, flexible approach to Public Relations recruitment. Their genuine approach to both clients and candidates combined with their tried and tested vetting procedures ensures they don't waste their client's or candidate's time. PRMoves is a division of the leading media recruitment consultancy Career Moves. Career Moves has been providing recruitment solutions to a wide range of clients in Media across Broadcasting, Advertising, Marketing, Publishing and Music since 1987.

Preferred method of contact Apply on line or telephone for an appointment

Minimum requirements Previous professional experience

Type of business Contract and Permanent

Grade/Level of Appointments All levels

promopromo

Head Office ✉ 1–6 Falconberg Ct, W1D 3AB
🚇 Tottenham Court Rd
🚂 Euston
📞 T 020 7440 1090 F 020 7440 1099

@ enquiries@promopromo.com
Market areas Broadcasting

Website www.promopromo.com
UK Offices 1
REC Member Yes

Brief Description promopromo is a unique employment agency with over 600 Creatives on board, run by people from the Broadcasting industry for people in the Broadcasting industry. Established in 1999, promopromo was set up in response to the changing needs of Television Production to harness the power of TV Creatives. promopromo specialises in providing experienced and reliable freelance and permanent Promo Producers, Directors, Promotion Managers, Creative Directors, Production Managers, Schedulers, Linear and Non-linear Editors, TV Designers and Special Effects Operators to meet the needs of a growing global list of clients.

Preferred method of contact Apply on line or telephone for an appointment

Minimum requirements Previous professional experience

Type of business Contract and Permanent

Grade/Level of Appointments All levels

The Purple Consultancy

Head Office ✉ Business Design Centre, 52 Upper St, N1 0QH
🚇 Angel
🚂 Old St
📞 T 020 7288 6700 F 020 7288 6730
@ purple@purple-consultancy.com
Market areas Advertising, Design, New Media

Website www.purple-consultancy.com
UK Offices 1
REC Member No

Brief Description The Purple Consultancy specialises in the fields of Advertising, Design and New Media. Their aim is to offer an unrivalled service to clients on both sides of the recruitment fence.

Preferred method of contact Telephone for appointment
Minimum requirements None
Type of business Permanent
Grade/Level of Appointments All levels

Rainbow Recruitment

See **Secretarial, page 253**

Recruit Media Ltd

Head Office ✉ 20 Colebrooke Row, N1 8AP
🚇 Angel
🚂 Old St

C T 020 7704 1227   F 020 7704 1370
@ info@recruitmedia.co.uk
Market areas New Media, Editorial, DFP and Business Information

Website www.recruitmedia.co.uk
UK Offices 1
REC Member Yes

Brief Description Recruit Media are specialists in Creative, Media and Information-based industries. From Print and CD-ROM to Internet and Digital Broadcast, they provide permanent and temporary staff solutions to clients.

Preferred method of contact Apply on line or telephone for an appointment

Minimum requirements Previous professional experience

Type of business Contract and Permanent

Grade/Level of Appointments All levels

The Recruitment Business Ltd

See IT and Telecoms, page 173

Regan & Dean

Head Office   23 Old Bond St, W1X 3DA
Green Park
Victoria
C T 020 7409 3244   F 020 7409 7430
@ info@reganonddean.co.uk
Market areas Media, Secretarial

Website www.reagananddean.co.uk
UK Offices 1
REC Member Yes

Brief Description Regan & Dean Recruitment has been recruiting in the Media, Advertising, Conferences, Exhibitions and Communications business for over 10 years. During that time they have built up an enviable reputation among clients and job-seekers alike for placing the right people in the right jobs at the right time. Their clients include leading Advertising agencies, PR consultancies, Design companies, Entertainment groups and New Media companies.

Preferred method of contact Apply on line or telephone for an appointment

Minimum requirements None

Type of business Contract and Permanent

Grade/Level of Appointments All levels

Reilly Recruitment

Head Office   Dudley House, 36–38 Southampton St, WC2E 7HE
Holborn
City Thameslink

C T 020 7240 8080   F 020 7240 8082
@ careers@reillyrecruitment.co.uk
Market areas Media and Advertising, Sales

Website www.reillyrecruitment.co.uk
UK Offices 1
REC Member No

Brief Description Reilly Recruitment is a firm of recruiters established in 1993 specialising in Media and Advertising. They recruit Salespeople and Planners/Buyers of Advertising Space and Time, Quantitative Media Researchers, Conference Producers, New Media personnel, Media Managers and Advertising Account people.

Preferred method of contact Apply on line or telephone for an appointment

Minimum requirements None

Type of business Permanent

Grade/Level of Appointments All levels

Rose Associates

Head Office   1st Floor, 27 Phipp St, EC2A 4NP
Old St
Old St
C T 020 7613 5401   F 020 7739 7343
Market areas Secretarial, Media, TV/Film

Website www.rose-inc-co.uk
UK Offices 1
REC Member No

Brief Description Rose Inc was founded in 1995. They specialise in providing professional staff for Creative businesses, offering their clients an insightful and positive approach to recruitment. They focus on understanding the varying cultures and particular 'people needs' of Advertising, PR, Design, Brand Consultancy, TV and New Media companies. Within these fields, they recruit at all levels from the most Junior Receptionists through to Executive PAs, from Junior Account Executives to the most Senior Managers.

Preferred method of contact Apply on line or telephone for an appointment

Minimum requirements None

Type of business Temporary and Permanent

Grade/Level of Appointments All levels

Sales Associates

Head Office   Southbank House, Black Prince Rd, SE1 7SJ
Vauxhall
Victoria
C T 020 7587 1802   F 020 7582 8399
@ info@salesassociates.co.uk
Market areas Media

Website www.salesassociates.co.uk
UK Offices 1
REC Member No
Brief Description Sales Associates is a highly motivated company specialising in Sales Training and Media recruitment. Since they were established in 1995 they have delivered tailor-made solutions and superior service to the Media Sales market
Preferred method of contact Apply on line or telephone for an appointment
Minimum requirements None
Type of business Permanent
Grade/Level of Appointments Graduate Trainees to Board level

Smallworld

Head Office ✉ 9 Berkeley St, W1J 8DW
⊖ Green Park
🚊 Victoria
☎ T 020 7659 9964   F 020 7659 9965
@ info@thesmallworld.co.uk
Market areas   Creative, Print and New Media

Website www.thesmallworld.co.uk
UK Offices 1
REC Member No
Brief Description Smallworld is a recruitment consultancy representing Middle and Senior level appointments within Creative, Print and New Media for clients across the London area.
Preferred method of contact Apply on line or telephone for an appointment
Minimum requirements Relevant industry exposure
Type of business Temporary and Permanent
Grade/Level of Appointments Mid to Senior Management level

Spectrum Specialist Recruitment

See **Sales and Marketing, page 218**

Techcentria

See **IT and Telecoms, page 176**

TFPL Ltd

Head Office ✉ 17–18 Britton St, EC1M 5TL
⊖ Farringdon
🚊 Farringdon
☎ T 020 7251 5522   F 020 7251 8318
@ central@tfpl.com
Market areas   Information Management, Research, Executive Search

Website www.tfpl.com
UK Offices 1
REC Member Yes
Brief Description TFPL was founded in 1987 to provide a range of professional services to the rapidly expanding and changing Corporate Information market. They are now the leading international organisation providing specialist Consultancy, Research, Recruitment, Executive Search, Training and Conferences. They have gained a reputation for innovation, style and quality in creating new products and services to meet the changing needs of the Information and Knowledge Management market. Headquartered in London and with an office in New York they work with clients across Europe, North America and other regions of the world.
Preferred method of contact Apply on line or telephone for an appointment
Minimum requirements None
Type of business Temporary and Permanent
Grade/Level of Appointments All levels

Tiro Resource Solutions Ltd

Head Office ✉ 6 Long Lane, EC1A 9HF
⊖ Barbican
🚊 Barbican
☎ T 020 7759 8000   F 020 7759 8001
Market areas   Media, Retail, Leisure, Public Practice

Website www.tiro.co.uk
UK Offices 1
REC Member No
Brief Description Tiro was established in 1999 by a team of Search Specialists from a service sector giant, TMP, and a Non-executive Chairman with a 20 year background in Recruitment Advertising. The business was established to provide delivery of people, speed of response and a cost-effective pricing structure to the Media, Retail and Leisure industries, Public Practice and the companies that invest in those markets
Preferred method of contact Apply on line or telephone for an appointment
Minimum requirements None
Type of business Permanent
Grade/Level of Appointments All levels

TMP Worldwide Advertising and Communications

Head Office ✉ Chancery House, 53–64 Chancery Lane, WC2A 1QU
☎ T 020 7406 5000
✉ 53–64 Chancery Lane, WC2A 1QS
⊖ Chancery Lane
🚊 City Thameslink

℃ T 020 7406 5000

Market areas Advertising and Communication

Website www.tmp.com

UK Offices 30+

REC Member No

Brief Description Human capital has become the most critical component of any organization. Meeting these challenges off- and online is TMP Worldwide, an interactive company with a unique suite of Global Career Solutions and a client base that includes more than 90 of the Fortune 100 and more than 490 of the Fortune 500. Expertise in this area is one reason why TMP is the largest Recruitment Advertising Agency in the world. They sell, market, and brand employers to talent on a global scale. This is accomplished through product offerings such as: Media Research/Planning/Buying, Strategic Hiring Plans, Creative Services, On-campus Recruiting, the Web-based Intern Center, and Interactive.

Preferred method of contact Apply on line or telephone for an appointment

Minimum requirements None

Type of business Temporary and Permanent

Grade/Level of Appointments All levels

TMP Worldwide Directional Marketing

Head Office ✉ Chancery House, 53–64 Chancery Lane, WC2A 1QU
⊖ Chancery Lane
🚊 City Thameslink
℃ T 020 7406 5000
Market areas Advertising and Communication

Website www.tmp.com

UK Offices 30+

REC Member No

Brief Description Human capital has become the most critical component of any organization. Meeting these challenges off- and online is TMP Worldwide, an interactive company with a unique suite of Global Career Solutions and a client base that includes more than 90 of the Fortune 100 and more than 490 of the Fortune 500. Expertise in this area is one reason why TMP is the largest recruitment advertising agency in the world. They sell, market, and brand employers to talent on a global scale. This is accomplished through product offerings such as: Media Research/Planning/Buying, Strategic Hiring Plans, Creative Services, On-campus Recruiting, the Web-based Intern Center, and Interactive.

Preferred method of contact Apply on line or telephone for an appointment

Minimum requirements None

Type of business Temporary and Permanent

Grade/Level of Appointments All levels

VPS Ltd

See **Secretarial, page 261**

Warren Recruitment Print Specialists Ltd

Head Office ✉ Unit 6, 17 Pepper St, E14 9RP
⊖ South Quay
🚊 Limehouse
℃ T 020 7512 0443   F 020 7512 0442
@ wrs@print-recruitment.com
Market areas Printing

Website www.print-recruitment.com

UK Offices 1

REC Member Yes

Brief Description Established over 5 years ago, WRS has grown to become the UK Print industry's premier recruitment specialist. At any one time they have around 400 Printing staff working for them at client locations. They bring together more than 25 years' experience in recruitment with expert understanding of the Print and Reprographics industry.

Preferred method of contact Apply on line or telephone for an appointment

Minimum requirements None

Type of business Temporary and Permanent

Grade/Level of Appointments Mailroom Assistant to Senior level

WayGoose Selection

Head Office ✉ 45 Skylines Village, Limeharbour, E14 9TS
⊖ Crossharbour
🚊 Limehouse
℃ T 020 7537 0700   F 020 7515 4545
@ info@waygoose.com
Market areas Design, Reprographics and Printing

Website www.waygoose.com

UK Offices 1

REC Member No

Brief Description WayGoose Selection is the leading specialist recruitment consultancy for the Design, Reprographics and Printing industries, with operations covering the UK, Europe and North America.

Preferred method of contact Apply on line or telephone for an appointment

Minimum requirements None

Type of business Temporary and Permanent

Grade/Level of Appointments All levels

Witan Jardine

See **Accountancy and Banking, page 27**

The Works

Head Office ✉ Hedges House, 153–155 Regent St, W1B 4JE
⊖ Piccadilly Circus
🚆 Charing Cross
☎ T 020 7494 0207 F 020 7439 4522
@ jobs@the-works.co.uk
Market areas PR

Website www.the-works.co.uk

UK Offices 1

REC Member Yes

Brief Description Established in 1996, The Works specialises in the Public Relations industry, providing permanent staff to clients across London.

Preferred method of contact Apply on line or telephone for an appointment

Minimum requirements None

Type of business Permanent

Grade/Level of Appointments All levels

Workstation Solutions Ltd

See **IT and Telecoms, page 180**

Xchangeteam

Head Office ✉ 32–34 Danbury St, N1 8JU
⊖ Angel
🚆 Old St
☎ T 020 7354 0814 F 020 7704 3148
@ info@xchangeteam.com
Market areas Communications, PR, Marketing, Events, Copywriting and Journalism

Website www.xchangeteam.com

UK Offices 1

REC Member No

Brief Description Run by industry experts, Xchangeteam is the leading freelance resource company in Communications and PR, Marketing, Events, Copywriting and Journalism. Their pioneering approach enables companies and freelance consultants to embrace freelancing as their preferred way of working. They are renowned for attracting the best, the most talented, freelance consultants who appreciate their personal, professional service and the investment they make in their freelance community.

Preferred method of contact Apply on line or telephone for an appointment

Minimum requirements Previous professional experience

Type of business Contract

Grade/Level of Appointments All levels

Not for Profit

Beaumont Leslie Thomas (BLT)

See **Financial Services and Insurance, page 119**

Charity Action Recruitment (LWTS)

Head Office ✉ 207 Waterloo Rd, SE18 8XD
     ⊖ Waterloo
     🚆 Waterloo
     ☎ T 020 7928 2843   F 020 7928 3868
     @ carerecruitment@lwts.org.uk
Market areas Charity and Non-Profit

Website www.lwts.org.uk
UK Offices 1
REC Member No

Brief Description Part of London West Training Services (LWTS), Charity Action Recruitment was established in 1997 to provide temporary and permanent staff to Non-profit/Volunteer organisations.

Preferred method of contact Telephone for appointment
Minimum requirements None
Type of business Temporary, Permanent and Contract
Grade/Level of Appointments 1st Jobber to Management level

Charity Connections

Head Office ✉ The Chandry 311, 50 Westminster Bridge Rd, SE1 7QY
     ⊖ Waterloo
     🚆 Waterloo
     ☎ T 020 7721 7606   F 020 7721 7608/7605
     @ info@charityconnections.co.uk
Market areas Charity and Non-Profit

Website www.charityconnections.co.uk
UK Offices 1
REC Member No

Brief Description Charity Connections specialises in placing temporary, permanent and contract personnel both in the UK and overseas. Its clients include some of the most established Charities with opportunities from Junior to Executive level.

Preferred method of contact Telephone for appointment
Minimum requirements None
Type of business Temporary, Permanent and Contract
Grade/Level of Appointments 1st Jobber to Management level

Charity People

Head Office ✉ 38 Bedford Place, WC1B 5JH
     ⊖ Holborn
     🚆 City Thameslink
     ☎ T 020 7636 3900   F 020 7636 3331
     @ alisonw@charitypeople.co.uk
Market areas Charity and Non-Profit

Website www.charitypeople.co.uk
UK Offices 1
REC Member Yes

Brief Description Established in 1990, Charity People has worked to promote the Charity/Non-profit sector as a natural career choice for high calibre professionals with opportunities ranging from Secretarial to Junior/Middle and Executive appointments for Art, Education, Housing, Health and Sports organisations.

Preferred method of contact Apply on line or telephone for appointment
Minimum requirements None
Type of business Temporary, Permanent and Contract
Grade/Level of Appointments 1st Jobber to Management level

Charity Recruitment

Head Office ✉ 40 Rosebery Avenue, EC1R 4RX
     ⊖ Chancery Lane
     🚆 City Thameslink
     ☎ T 020 7833 0770   F 020 7833 0188
     @ enquiries@charityrecruitment.co.uk
Market areas Charity and Non-Profit

Website www.charityrecruitment.co.uk
UK Offices 1
REC Member Yes

Brief Description Established in 1986, Charity Recruitment is one of the leading agencies in the recruitment sector for the Non-profit market. Its clients cover a range of disciplines including Schools, Colleges, Housing Associations, International Aid, Arts and Medical Research organisations.

Preferred method of contact Apply on line or telephone for appointment
Minimum requirements Previous professional experience
Type of business Permanent
Grade/Level of Appointments Executive Assistant to Chief Executive

Execucare

Head Office ✉ 34 Edbury St, SW1W 0LU
     ⊖ Victoria
     🚊 Victoria
     ☎ T 020 7761 0700   F 020 7761 0707
     @ info@execucare.com
Market areas   Not for Profit

Website www.execucare.com
UK Offices 1
REC Member No

Brief Description Established in 1990, Execucare are a modern, open and professional Search and Selection consultancy working in the Not for Profit sector.

Preferred method of contact Apply on line or telephone for appointment

Minimum requirements None

Type of business Permanent

Grade/Level of Appointments All levels

Management Prospects

Head Office ✉ 45 Bloomsbury Sq, WC1A 1RA
     ⊖ Holborn
     🚊 City Thameslink
     ☎ T 020 7813 0101   F 020 7813 0500
     @ ross.anderson@permanent-prospects.co.uk
Market areas   Not for Profit, Charities, Secretarial, IT

Website www.prospect-us.co.uk
UK Offices 1
REC Member No

Brief Description Management Prospects is a division of ProspectUs, a London-based recruitment agency specialising in building careers and placing staff in Charities, Universities, NHS Trusts and other Not for Profit organisations. Candidates can expect an open and honest approach from them and they hope that they can make the search for work a positive experience.

Preferred method of contact Apply on line or telephone for an appointment

Minimum requirements Previous managerial exposure

Type of business Permanent

Grade/Level of Appointments Management level

Part-time Prospects

Head Office ✉ 45 Bloomsbury Sq, WC1A 1RA
     ⊖ Holborn
     🚊 City Thameslink
     ☎ T 020 7691 1933   F 020 7813 0500

     @ enquiries@flexible-prospects.co.uk
Market areas Not for Profit, Charities, Secretarial, IT

Website www.prospect-us.co.uk
UK Offices 1
REC Member No

Brief Description Part-time Prospects is a division of ProspectUs, a London-based recruitment agency specialising in building careers and placing staff in Charities, Universities, NHS Trusts and other Not for Profit organisations. Candidates can expect an open and honest approach from them and they hope that they can make the search for work a positive experience.

Preferred method of contact Apply on line or telephone for an appointment

Minimum requirements None

Type of business Temporary and Permanent

Grade/Level of Appointments All levels

Permanent Prospects

Head Office ✉ 45 Bloomsbury Sq, WC1A 1RA
     ⊖ Holborn
     🚊 City Thameslink
     ☎ T 020 7813 0101   F 020 7813 0500
     @ enquiries@permanent-prospects.co.uk
Market areas Not for Profit, Charities, Secretarial, IT

Website www.prospect-us.co.uk
UK Offices 1
REC Member No

Brief Description Permanent Prospects is a division of ProspectUs, a London-based recruitment agency specialising in building careers and placing staff in Charities, Universities, NHS Trusts and other Not for Profit organisations. Candidates can expect an open and honest approach from them and they hope that they can make the search for work a positive experience.

Preferred method of contact Apply on line or telephone for an appointment

Minimum requirements None

Type of business Permanent

Grade/Level of Appointments All levels

ProspectUs

Head Office ✉ 45 Bloomsbury Sq, WC1A 1RA
     ⊖ Holborn
     🚊 City Thameslink
     ☎ T 020 7691 1925   F 020 7691 1930
     @ enquiries@prospect-us.co.uk
Market areas Not for Profit, Charities, Secretarial, IT

Website www.prospect-us.co.uk

UK Offices 1

REC Member Yes

Brief Description ProspectUs is a London-based recruitment agency specialising in building careers and placing staff in Charities, Universities, NHS Trusts and other Not for Profit organisations. Candidates can expect an open and honest approach from them and they hope that they can make the search for work a positive experience.

Preferred method of contact Apply on line or telephone for an appointment

Minimum requirements None

Type of business Temporary and Permanent

Grade/Level of Appointments All levels

Step Ahead

Head Office ✉ 47 Islington Park St, N1 1QB
⊖ Highbury and Islington
🚊 Highbury and Islington
☎ T 020 7359 0963   F 020 7359 8415
@ info@stepahead.co.uk
Market areas Not for Profit, Charities

✉ 239 High Holborn, WC1V 7EW
⊖ Holborn
🚊 City Thameslink
☎ T 020 7404 5180   F 020 7404 5181
@ info@stepahead.co.uk
Market areas Not for Profit, Charities

Website www.stepahead.co.uk

UK Offices 2

REC Member Yes

Brief Description Step Ahead is a division of Credentials Ltd, a company which has built its reputation on the provision of quality yet cost-effective recruitment solutions. Their aim is to deliver a service which is directly in accordance with the needs and requirements of the customer. Step Ahead's philosophy is based upon listening to and learning from the customer (both candidates and clients) in order to provide bespoke recruitment and placement solutions. They pride themselves on the supply of bespoke quality services and currently

have contracts with a wide range of organisations specialising in the Charitable and Not for Profit and Public sectors.

Preferred method of contact Apply on line or telephone for an appointment

Minimum requirements None

Type of business Permanent and Contract

Grade/Level of Appointments All levels

Technical Prospects

See **Technical, page 270**

Temporary Prospects

Head Office ✉ 45 Bloomsbury Sq, WC1A 1RA
⊖ Holborn
🚊 City Thameslink
☎ T 020 7405 4999   F 020 7405 5996
@ enquiries@temporary-prospects.co.uk
Market areas Not for Profit, Charities, Secretarial, IT

Website www.prospect-us.co.uk

UK Offices 1

REC Member No

Brief Description Temporary Prospects is a division of ProspectUs, a London-based recruitment agency specialising in building careers and placing staff in Charities, Universities, NHS Trusts and other Not for Profit organisations. Candidates can expect an open and honest approach from them and they hope that they can make the search for work a positive experience.

Preferred method of contact Apply on line or telephone for an appointment

Minimum requirements None

Type of business Temporary

Grade/Level of Appointments All levels

Training Prospects

See **Human Resources, page 149**

Public Sector

Hays Executive Search – Public Sector Practice

See Executive Search, page 92

Hays Montrose Public Sector DLO Division

See Construction and Property, page 51

Hays Montrose Public Sector DSO Division

See Construction and Property, page 52

Hays Montrose Social Housing Division

See Construction and Property, page 52

Wren Care

See Social Care, page 265

Sales and Marketing

Adecco Sales Recruitment

⊠ Atlantic House, 351 Oxford St, W1R 1FA
⊖ Oxford Circus
🚊 Charing Cross
📞 T 020 7629 2912   F 020 7629 1098
@ 163.asr@adecco.co.uk
Market areas   Sales and Marketing

Website www.adecco.co.uk
UK Offices 358
REC Member No
Head Office Adecco House, Elstree Way, Borehamwood, Herts, WD6 1HY
Brief Description Adecco is the only personnel services company in the world to offer such a comprehensive range of services with such a geographic reach, from general to highly specialised staffing, temporary and permanent placement, Human Resource consulting and Career Management. Formed from the merger of Adia Alfred Marks and Ecco Employment in 1997, its group companies include Office Angels, Computer People, Ajilon, Accountants on Call (AOC) and Jonathan Wren.
Preferred method of contact Interviews are by appointment only - please make initial contact by telephone or email
Minimum requirements Previous professional experience
Type of business Temporary and Permanent
Grade/Level of Appointments All levels up to Senior Management

Ashley Stewart Ltd

See **Secretarial, page 230**

Ball and Hoolahan

Head Office ⊠ 75–77 Margaret St, W1N 7HB
⊖ Oxford Circus
🚊 Charing Cross
📞 T 020 7323 4041   F 020 7323 2163
@ info@ballandhoolahan.co.uk
Market areas   Marketing/New Media

Website www.ballandhoolahan.co.uk
UK Offices 2
REC Member No
Brief Description Ball and Hoolahan was established in 1988 as a specialist in Marketing recruitment. The company is privately owned with offices in Central London and Richmond, Surrey, covering all Marketing roles from Branch and Retail Marketing to Category/ Management, PR, Market Research and Sales Promotion.

Preferred method of contact Telephone for appointment
Minimum requirements Previous professional experience
Type of business Permanent
Grade/Level of Appointments Junior Executive to Director

Bartlett Scott Edgar

See **Executive Search, page 78**

Beauty Consultants Bureau

Head Office ⊠ Crown House, 143–147 Regent St, W1B 4NR
⊖ Piccadilly Circus
🚊 Charing Cross
📞 T 020 7287 8060   F 020 7287 7118
@ postmaster@beauty-consultants-bureau.co.uk
Market areas   Sales and Promotional

Website www.beauty-consultants-bureau.co.uk
UK Offices 1
REC Member No
Brief Description BCB has been providing Sales and Promotional consultants to a wide variety of clients since 1968. Based in Central London, BCB supply temporary staff throughout the UK to major Department Stores, PR and Marketing Houses, Fashion Houses and Cosmetic Houses.

Preferred method of contact Telephone for appointment
Minimum requirements None
Type of business Temporary
Grade/Level of Appointments All levels

Bruzas & Graves Ltd

Head Office ⊠ 72 Wardour St, W1F OTD
⊖ Oxford Circus
🚊 Charing Cross
📞 T 020 7434 2818   F 020 7434 2848
@ info@bruzasgraves.co.uk
Market areas   Direct Marketing, Sales Promotion, Advertising, New Media

Website www.bruzasgraves.co.uk
UK Offices 1
REC Member No
Brief Description Established in 1988, Bruzas & Graves specialise in Direct Marketing, Sales Promotion, Advertising and New Media.

Preferred method of contact Apply on line or telephone for appointment

Minimum requirements None

Type of business Permanent

Grade/Level of Appointments All levels

Call Centre Placements

See **Customer Services, page 68**

Campbell Johnston Associates

Head Office ✉ 2 London Wall Buildings, EC2M 5UX
      ⊖ Moorgate
      ☒ Moorgate
      ☏ T 020 7588 3588   F 020 7256 8501
      @ cja@cjagroup.com
Market areas Recruitment Advertising

Website www.cjagroup.com

UK Offices 1

REC Member No

Brief Description Campbell Johnson Associates, established in 1969, is committed to recruiting through press advertising. It is the effective alternative to Head Hunting since it provides the widest choice of candidates. The CJA Group's six specialist companies are: CJA – full interviewing and selection service for Senior Management appointments; ALPS – Advisory and integrated interviewing service for Financial Management, Accountancy and Legal Staff; MMR – Interviewing and selection for Middle/Junior management, as well as Graduate entry positions; CJES – Screening, testing and selection service for experienced Secretaries and Personal Assistants for permanent or temporary positions; CJRA – full service recruitment consultancy; CJPA – corporate communications and advertising division.

Preferred method of contact Apply on line or telephone for appointment

Minimum requirements None

Type of business Temporary and Permanent

Grade/Level of Appointments All levels

Carreras Lathane Associates

See **Media, page 196**

Chambeau

See **Secretarial, page 234**

Chambers Communications

Head Office ✉ 2nd Floor, 29–30 High Holborn, WC1V 6BE
      ⊖ Chancery Lane
      ☒ City Thameslink
      ☏ T 020 7440 9455   F 020 7405 5457
      @ day.s@chamberscomms.com
Market areas IT Sales

Website www.chamberscomms.com

UK Offices 1

REC Member Yes

Brief Description Established for over 32 years, Chambers Communications Ltd is a specialist agency measured by the number of clients who use their service and the number of candidates they place in temporary and permanent jobs.

Preferred method of contact Apply on line or telephone for appointment

Minimum requirements Ideally Sales exposure

Type of business Permanent and Temporary

Grade/Level of Appointments Sales Executive/Account Manager to Senior Sales/Business Development Manager

Compton Associates

Head Office ✉ 9 Orme Ct, W2 4RL
      ⊖ Bayswater
      ☒ Paddington
      ☏ T 020 7229 9272   F 020 7229 9255
      @ info@jobsindirectmarketing.com
Market areas Direct Marketing, Telesales

Website www.jobsindirectmarketing.com

UK Offices 1

REC Member No

Brief Description As specialists in Direct Marketing recruitment, Compton Associates offer a comprehensive portfolio of vacancies and work in partnership with their clients to match them with the most appropriate candidates at Senior, Middle and Junior levels.

Preferred method of contact Apply on line or telephone for appointment

Minimum requirements None

Type of business Permanent

Grade/Level of Appointments Account Handler to Business Development Manager

Conspicuous

See **IT and Telecoms, page 159**

Diamond Resourcing Plc

Head Office   ✉   62–74 Leadenhall Market, EC3V 1LT
      ⊖   Bank
      🚃   Cannon St
      ☎   T 020 7929 2976   F 020 7929 5395
      @   info@diamondresourcing.com
Market areas   IT, Banking, Accountancy and Finance, Secretarial, Sales and Insurance

Website   www.diamondresourcing.com

UK Offices   3

REC Member   Yes

Brief Description   Established in 1988, Diamond Resourcing is located in the heart of the City of London. Their broad client base ranges from many small and medium business enterprises to large and well known blue chip organisations throughout the UK and Europe. They have a proven track record in the placement of key personnel in IT, Accountancy, Secretarial, Banking/Finance, Insurance, Telecoms and Sales. Each division is an independent business ensuring that their consultants have the extensive expertise that their clients and candidates expect from a leading recruitment consultancy.

Preferred method of contact   Apply on line or telephone for appointment

Minimum requirements   None

Type of business   Temporary, Permanent and Contract

Grade/Level of Appointments   Office Junior to Finance Director/Analyst

Direct Recruitment Ltd

Head Office   ✉   21a Noel St, W1F 8GR
      ⊖   Oxford Circus
      🚃   Charing Cross
      ☎   T 020 7287 1171   F 020 7494 3696
      @   info@direct-recruitment.co.uk
Market areas   Direct Marketing, Sales Promotion, PR

Website   www.direct-recruitment.co.uk

UK Offices   1

REC Member   No

Brief Description   For almost 13 years Direct Recruitment has been at the forefront of below the line Marketing recruitment. They enjoy an enviable success rate with the candidates they introduce and clients include an impressive range of blue chip companies, Direct Marketing agencies, Sales Promotion/Integrated agencies, Public Relations agencies, Event Management, New Media, Data Analysis, Data Processing and Database Marketing consultancies, Telemarketing companies, List Brokers and Mailing/Fulfilment specialists.

Preferred method of contact   Apply on line or telephone for appointment

Minimum requirements   Previous professional experience

Type of business   Permanent

Grade/Level of Appointments   Account Executive to Account Supervisor/Director

Elizabeth Norman International

Head Office   ✉   Sussex House, 143 Long Acre, WC2E 9AD
      ⊖   Covent Garden
      🚃   Charing Cross
      ☎   T 020 7836 3311   F 020 7836 8146
      @   recruitment@elizabethnorman.com
Market areas   Market Research, Pharmaceutical

Website   www.elizabethnorman.com

UK Offices   1

REC Member   Yes

Brief Description   Established in 1984, Elizabeth Norman has recruited for Marketing Insight positions on both a temporary and contractual basis. Their international business has been built on long term partnerships with candidates and clients. Today they recruit in Research, Field, Advertising Planning, Database Analysis and Pharmaceutical sectors.

Preferred method of contact   Apply on line or telephone for appointment

Minimum requirements   None

Type of business   Contract and Temporary

Grade/Level of Appointments   Graduate/Research Executive to Chief Executive Officer

The EMR Group

Head Office   ✉   33 Sloane St, SW1X 9NR
      ⊖   Knightsbridge
      🚃   Victoria
      ☎   T 020 7823 1300   F 020 7823 1400
      @   london@theemrgroup.com
Market areas   Sales and Marketing

Website   www.theemrgroup.com

UK Offices   2

REC Member   Yes

Brief Description   Established in 1994, The EMR Group is one of the leading recruiters of Marketing professionals within the UK. They have built long term relationships with some of the most highly regarded companies in the UK. Primarily they operate in Marketing covering a diverse number of sectors including FMCG, Retail, Research, Professional Services, Financial Services, Agency, Leisure, Travel and Entertainment. More recently they have moved into National Accounts Management within FMCG and Consumer Products.

Preferred method of contact   Apply on line or telephone for an appointment

Minimum requirements   Relevant industry exposure

Type of business Permanent

Grade/Level of Appointments Graduate to Senior level

Eurecruit

See Secretarial, page 237

Folio Personnel Ltd (Sales and Marketing Division)

Head Office ✉ Dorland House, 14–16 Regent St, SW1Y 4PH
        ⊖ Piccadilly Circus
        🚊 Charing Cross
        ☎ T 020 7484 0608   F 020 7484 0601
        @ acurtis@foliopersonnel.com
Market areas Sales and Marketing

Website www.foliopersonnel.com

UK Offices 1

REC Member No

Brief Description Established in 1994, Folio Personnel was founded to provide a professional service to the industry it serves. They offer a complete recruitment service for both temporary and permanent staff at all levels.

Preferred method of contact Apply on line or telephone for appointment

Minimum requirements None

Type of business Temporary and Permanent

Grade/Level of Appointments All levels

Haigh Recruitment Consultants

Head Office ✉ 115 Crawford St, W1H 2JH
        ⊖ Edgeware Rd
        🚊 Marylebone
        ☎ T 020 7487 4844   F 020 7487 4833
        @ recruit@haigh-recruitment.com
Market areas Marketing, Healthcare, Technology, IT, Telecoms

Website www.haigh-recruitment.com

UK Offices 1

REC Member No

Brief Description Haigh are an independent recruitment company, engaged primarily in permanent placements where the emphasis is on providing a high quality and innovative consultancy service based on their expertise in the vertical markets in which they specialise: Marketing, Healthcare, IT, Telecoms, Technology.

Preferred method of contact Apply on line or telephone for appointment

Minimum requirements None

Type of business Permanent

Grade/Level of Appointments Helpdesk/Web Developer to Director

Hamblyn Selection

Head Office ✉ Victor House, 81 Oxford St, W1D 2EU
        ⊖ Oxford Circus
        🚊 Charing Cross
        ☎ T 020 7903 5121   F 020 7903 5125
        @ media@hamblynselection.com
Market areas Media, Advertising, Sales, Marketing

Website www.hamblynselection.com

UK Offices 2

REC Member No

Brief Description Hamblyn Selection was originally formulated through what is now the parent company – Christopher Hamblyn Associates Ltd. The company was established in 1987 with a mission to provide clients with an extremely high quality of service and support throughout the recruitment process. In 1999 the company was reformulated with the creation of the Executive and Media Divisions, along with Strategic Development, Training etc.

Preferred method of contact Apply on line or telephone for appointment

Minimum requirements None

Type of business Permanent

Grade/Level of Appointments Graduates to Board level

Hays Marketing Personnel

Head Office ✉ 141 Moorgate, EC2M 6TX
        ☎ T 020 7628 9999   F 020 7628 4698

        ✉ 172 Tottenham Ct Rd, W1T 7NR
        ⊖ Tottenham Court Rd
        🚊 Euston
        ☎ T 020 7387 9037   F 020 7387 3928
        @ london.mk@hays-marketing.com
Market areas Marketing

Website www.haysworks.com

UK Offices 1

REC Member No

Brief Description Hays Personnel Services is a division of Hays Plc, the Business Services group listed in the FTSE 100. Hays Personnel Services is Europe's leading specialist professional recruitment group. Hays Marketing Personnel is one of the UK's leading specialist Marketing, Sales and Creative Services recruitment consultancies, offering Database Selection, Recruitment Campaign Advertising and Executive Search.

Preferred method of contact Apply on line or telephone for an appointment

Minimum requirements None

Type of business Permanent

Grade/Level of Appointments All levels

Hills Flower Strong Ltd

Head Office ✉ 4 Great James St, WC1N 7AD
- ⊖ Holborn
- 🚇 City Thameslink
- ☎ T 020 7404 6664   F 020 7404 6662
- @ hfscons@globalnet.co.uk

Market areas Sales

Website www.hillsflowerstrong.co.uk

UK Offices 1

REC Member No

Brief Description Established in 1989, Hills Flower Strong has been successful in placing Graduate Trainees and experienced Sales professionals in some of the most coveted jobs in Media, Recruitment and Retail. Hills Flower Strong is a recruitment consultancy which has built up an enviable reputation for perfectly pairing the expectations of candidates with the requirements of clients.

Preferred method of contact Apply on line or telephone for an appointment

Minimum requirements None

Type of business Permanent

Grade/Level of Appointments Graduate to Senior level

Hodge Recruitment Consultants

See Secretarial, page 241

Hollis Personnel Ltd

See Secretarial, page 241

JPA Graduates

See Graduates, page 127

JPA Recruitment

Head Office ✉ 14–15 Lower Grosvenor Place, SW1W 0EX
- ⊖ Victoria
- 🚇 Victoria
- ☎ T 020 7828 8520   F 020 7828 8522
- @ temps@j-p-a.co.uk

Market areas Sales

Website www.j-p-a.co.uk

UK Offices 1

REC Member Yes

Brief Description JPA was established in 1998 with the aim of providing companies with the highest calibre of employee covering a wide range of Sales sector jobs.

Preferred method of contact Apply on line or telephone for an appointment

Minimum requirements None

Type of business Temporary and Permanent

Grade/Level of Appointments Graduate to Senior level

KD Consulting

Head Office ✉ 22–28 Shepherd St, W1J 7LJ
- ⊖ Green Park
- 🚇 Victoria
- ☎ T 020 7518 6060   F 020 7499 6355
- @ mail@kdconsulting.co.uk

Market areas Market Research

Website www.kdconsulting.co.uk

UK Offices 1

REC Member Yes

Brief Description Established in 1989, KD Consulting have earned a reputation for providing a top quality service to their clients and candidates alike.

Preferred method of contact Telephone for appointment

Minimum requirements None

Type of business Permanent

Grade/Level of Appointments All levels

Management Personnel

Head Office ✉ Suite 130–131, The Business Design Centre, 52 Upper St, N1 0QH
- ⊖ Angel
- 🚇 Kings Cross
- ☎ T 020 7226 8889   F 020 7226 9963
- @ webresponse@managementpersonnel.co.uk

Market areas Creative, IT Sales, Publishing, New Media, Advertising Marketing

Website www.managementpersonnel.co.uk

UK Offices 3

REC Member No

Brief Description Part of the Opera Group of Recruitment Companies, Management Personnel is divided into two sectors: Creative – specialising in New Media, Publishing, Advertising and Marketing; and IT Sales – supplying Sales professionals to organisations ranging from FTSE 100 companies to niche Software houses.

Preferred method of contact Apply on line or telephone for an appointment

Minimum requirements None

Type of business Temporary, Permanent and Contract

Grade/Level of Appointments Graduates/1st Jobbers to Board level

The Media Partnership

See **Media, page 201**

Ortus Interim Solutions

Head Office   ✉   33 Sloane St, SW1X 9NR
      ⊖   Knightsbridge
      🚇   Victoria
      ✆   T 020 7556 2980   F 020 7245 6711
      @   info@ortusinterim.com
Market areas   Sales and Marketing

Website www.ortusinterim.com

UK Offices 1

REC Member Yes

Brief Description Ortus Interim Solutions specialise in the provision of Interim Sales and Marketing Executives on a national and international level. As an associate of the EMR Group they benefit from not just the several years of accumulated industry knowledge and recruitment experience of the group but also from a substantial network of contacts. They work across many industry sectors including FMCG, Retail, Consumer Durables, Financial Services, Business Services, Leisure and Travel, Entertainment, IT, Telecommunications, Agency, Consultancy and Public Services. Ortus Interim Solutions make simple a process that is often over complicated and guarantee a fast, seamless, cost effective and honest approach across all levels of interim work.

Preferred method of contact Apply on line or telephone for an appointment

Minimum requirements Relevant industry exposure

Type of business Contract and Temporary

Grade/Level of Appointments All levels

Paul James Associates

See **Technical, page 268**

Personnel Resources Recruitment Ltd

See **Executive Search, page 103**

Primat Recruitment

See **Technical, page 269**

Profile Management

See **Hospitality and Leisure, page 144**

RB Recruitment Services Ltd

Head Office   ✉   Unicorn House, 3 Plough Yard, EC2A 3LP
      ⊖   Liverpool St
      🚇   Liverpool St
      ✆   T 020 7247 4560   F 020 7247 1675
      @   sales@rbrecruitment.co.uk
Market areas   Sales, IT Sales, Technical

Website www.rbrecruitment.co.uk

UK Offices 1

REC Member No

Brief Description RB Recruitment Services Ltd is an independent company specialising in the recruitment of Business-to-Business, IT Sales, Telesales and Technical personnel. Located in the City of London, 6 minutes walk from Liverpool Street Station, they cater for the full range of appointments from Junior to Director level. They specialise in all Sales and IT Technical positions but have a particular affinity with the following areas: Internet Services, IT, Telecommunications, On-line Information, Workflow Management, Document Storage /Imaging Media Sales, including New Media.

Preferred method of contact Apply on line or telephone for an appointment

Minimum requirements None

Type of business Permanent

Grade/Level of Appointments Junior to Senior level

Reilly Recruitment

See **Media, page 204**

Robert Walters

See **Accountancy and Banking, page 25**

Sales Professionals

Head Office   ✉   26–28 Bedford Row, WC1R 4HE
      ⊖   Chancery Lane
      🚇   City Thameslink
      ✆   T 020 7845 4200   F 020 7845 4249
Market areas   Sales

Website www.pro-rec-org.com

UK Offices 2

REC Member No

Brief Description Established in the early part of 2000, Sales Professionals is a specialist division within the Professional Recruitment Organisation. It has already shown considerable success within a highly competitive marketplace and is set to continue its growth. Sales Professionals has a specialist team of highly trained and focused consultants who are dedicated to finding and advising the best Sales candidates in the marketplace. These candidates will already be high achievers looking to either find out more about the market or make their next step upwards in their career. They recruit for a variety of different roles within Sales including: Managing Directors, Sales Directors, Account Managers, Marketing Sales, Field Sales Executives, Investor Relations, Telesales Managers, Business Development Managers.

Preferred method of contact Apply on line or telephone for an appointment

Minimum requirements Previous professional experience

Type of business Temporary, Permanent and Contract

Grade/Level of Appointments Account Managers to Managing Directors

Spalding Smith Associates

Head Office ✉ 235–241 Regent St, W1R 8JU
  ⊖ Oxford Circus
  🚆 Charing Cross
  ☎ T 020 7499 7499   F 020 7499 7477
  @ ssa@spalding-smith.co.uk
Market areas Market Research

Website www.spalding-smith.co.uk

UK Offices 1

REC Member No

Brief Description Established in 1992, Spalding Smith Associates specialise in the recruitment of Market Research professionals at all levels from Graduate to Senior Management, placing individuals into a broad range of clients ranging from blue chip to Telecoms, IT, Finance and Retail.

Preferred method of contact Apply on line or telephone for an appointment

Minimum requirements None

Type of business Permanent

Grade/Level of Appointments Graduate Trainees to Board level

Spectrum Specialist Recruitment

Head Office ✉ Capital House, 20–22 Craven Rd, W2 3PX
  ⊖ Lancaster Gate
  🚆 Paddington

☎ T 020 7724 0211   F 020 7724 9332
@ enquiries@spectrumrecruitment.co.uk
Market areas Sales and Marketing, PR, Events, Retail

Website www.spectrumrecruit.co.uk

UK Offices 1

REC Member No

Brief Description Spectrum is a highly successful Marketing recruitment agency run by a specialist team of experienced and committed professionals, with Marketing industry backgrounds. Founded in 1988, Spectrum's three partners have worked together in Marketing recruitment since 1983.

Preferred method of contact Apply on line or telephone for an appointment

Minimum requirements None

Type of business Permanent

Grade/Level of Appointments All levels

SSC Staff Consultants

Head Office ✉ Ormond House, 26–27 Boswell St, WC1N 3JZ
  ⊖ Holborn
  🚆 City Thameslink
  ☎ T 020 7242 4266   F 020 7404 4148
Market areas Sales and Marketing to the Healthcare, Pharmaceutical, Laboratory supply industries

Website www.scientificstaff.com

UK Offices 1

REC Member No

Brief Description SSC is the UK's longest established agency dedicated to the recruitment of Sales and Marketing personnel for the Medical, Healthcare and scientifically related industries. Established since 1974, SSC is a recognised leader in its field. Their enviable client list built over 26 years is testimony to their excellent reputation for both quality and personal service.

Preferred method of contact Apply on line or telephone for an appointment

Minimum requirements None

Type of business Permanent

Grade/Level of Appointments All levels

Success Appointments

See **Fashion and Retail, page 114**

Technical Aid International

See **Technical, page 269**

Sales and Marketing

Tele Temps Ltd

Head Office   ✉   65 London Wall, EC2M 5TU
      ⊖   Moorgate
      🚆   Moorgate
      ☎   T 020 7588 4012   F 020 7628 8443
      @   consultants@tele-temps.co.uk
Market areas   Telestaff, Helpdesk, Receptionists

Website   www.tele-temps.co.uk

UK Offices   1

REC Member   Yes

Brief Description   Tele Temps is a high calibre company renowned for assisting companies throughout London and the South East with selective staff for permanent, contract and temporary positions. Areas within Communications which Tele Temps cover include: Telex/Message Switch/Swift/Fax Operators.

Preferred method of contact   Apply on line or telephone for an appointment

Minimum requirements   None

Type of business   Temporary and Permanent

Grade/Level of Appointments   All levels

Teleresources

      ✉   99 Mansell St, E1 8AX
      ⊖   Tower Hill
      🚆   Fenchurch St
      ☎   T 020 7481 4814   F 020 7481 4121
      @   london@teleresources.co.uk
Market areas   Telestaff

Website   www.teleresources.co.uk

UK Offices   5

REC Member   No

Head Office   Edgeware

Brief Description   Working nationally with operations in the Midlands, North West, North, London and the Home Counties, Teleresources understand the idiosyncrasies of Telebusiness recruitment at every level from temporary Telesales Agent through to Call Centre Director.

Preferred method of contact   Apply on line or telephone for an appointment

Minimum requirements   None

Type of business   Temporary and Permanent

Grade/Level of Appointments   Telesales Agent to Call Centre Director

Accepting the offer and clinching the deal

This chapter is taken from "The Graduate Career Handbook" by Shirley Jenner, published by Financial Times Prentice Hall, an imprint of Pearson Education. © Pearson Education Ltd 2000

Congratulations – you have got the job! Before you accept, though, ask yourself:

→ are any strings attached?

→ is there scope for negotiating better terms and conditions?

In this chapter, you will:

→ find out about accepting a job offer;

→ see how you can clinch the deal, negotiating to your advantage;

→ see how to then accept the job;

→ come to understand the 'psychological contract';

→ find out about sources of further information, including websites.

A heavier than usual thud

The long-awaited moment has arrived, and the envelope lands with a heavier than usual thud on the doormat. You open it to read that your application has been successful. Your job offer is a reality at last! You may, of course, receive the news by telephone – for many jobs an employer wants a quick decision. If you turn it down, they may want to move on quickly and offer the job to their second reserve.

Here, I outline key issues and the formal procedures involved in making and receiving job offers. I shall also help you think about the 'package' you are being offered and the scope you may have to negotiate the best deal possible.

It is important to state at the outset that this material cannot provide comprehensive and detailed coverage of all aspects of contemporary employment law. European and UK employment legislation is a highly complicated and specialist field, but, more pertinently, it is changing so fast that information included here would soon be out of date. However, I do include signposts to regularly updated sources of employment law information below and in the companion website for anyone interested.

Receiving a job offer

Once you have recovered from the initial euphoria, there are several issues to consider. You will be interested in key aspects of the job offer, such as starting salary, holidays and any perks in the package being offered. First, though, take a moment to find out if the offer has any strings attached.

'Offer subject to...'

The offer is likely to be conditional. The following are the six areas that your prospective employer will be concerned about.

References

Many job offers are conditional on receiving satisfactory references. Not all employers bother to follow up references, but many do. Those that don't would probably agree with the following comment made by leading human resources management writer and consultant, Michael Armstrong in his book *A Handbook of Personnel Management Practice* (Kogan Page, 1996):

> 'Personal referees are, of course, entirely useless. All they prove is that the applicant has at least one or two friends.'

You are entitled to ask about the timescale involved and can get in touch with referees and ask them to reply quickly.

Health

You may be asked to complete a self-report questionnaire about your health. Some organisations go a step further and require you to have a medical examination with their own doctor or by arrangement with a local GP. Under the Data Protection Act 1998, you are entitled to see the medical report if you wish, subject to certain procedures being followed.

Medical examinations involve varying degrees of thoroughness. Your prospective employer will probably send you a form outlining the type of examination they wish you to be given. You should ask for details from the organisation if you want to know more. The medical examination is often linked to pension and life assurance arrangements. An increasing number of UK companies include pre-employment urine screening to test for drug or alcohol use.

Security

Some jobs, such as those that involve working with children, require a police check by law. Jobs with the Civil Service, government bodies and some private-sector organisations (especially involving military equipment) may also require more in-depth security clearance.

If your role involves responsibility for money, you may be investigated for creditworthiness. The past few years have seen a rise in private investigation and 'fidelity bonding' agencies, which specialise in pre-employment checks.

Exam results

If you are applying prior to graduation, your job offer may be subject to your exam grade. Do not despair, though – even if you fail to reach the usual 2:1 standard, the employer may still be interested in you. You can contact them with your results to see. Some employers may require you to pass your driving test as a condition of employment, though.

Relocation

The job offer may be dependent on your agreeing to relocate. This can mean a one-off relocation to work at a given operational site, office or service centre. You may receive a 'disturbance allowance' – the ultimate irony if you are moving from college to live in London, which is the aspired work destination of most students in the most recent survey by High Fliers Research Ltd (1999).

Eligibility for employment

Your offer of employment will be subject to your eligibility. This may be clear-cut if you are either a UK citizen or citizen of an EU member state. Work permits and a visa may be necessary – depending on your status, you may need to check this out.

Accepting a job offer

An employer will usually confirm the offer of employment after satisfactory references have been obtained and other conditions, such as passing the medical, have been met.

You should not rush to formally accept a job offer. Instead, check it carefully. Once accepted, this forms your contract of employment and is binding. It is far better to ask questions about the job and terms and conditions now than after acceptance.

> 'Employers will be flexible in the setting of deadlines for the acceptance of offers. Short deadlines may limit the ability of students to make informed decisions and prejudice the recruitment activities of other employers. This in turn may lead to students accepting offers and then reneging on them.'
>
> (Code of Practice 1995, AGR, AgCAS and NUS)

I think it is perfectly reasonable to write a letter of personal acceptance subject to discussion about the details of the contract of employment.

An important factor to remember about the employment relationship is that, generally, it is the employer who has the power to dictate the contractual terms. However, in many cases it is possible to 'talk up' your package.

Negotiating the best deal you can

Conventional wisdom suggests that you must accept the offer as it stands. In practice, many employers are flexible and will listen to your requests seriously. Some aspects of the employment contract may not be open to negotiation, especially if the organisation operates a rigid reward system with salary and holiday linked to pay scales. Read through the terms and conditions listed below to see if you have any scope for negotiating your package.

Starting date

This may be flexible. Many organisations recruit all year round and may be able to delay your start date. Some employers are willing to consider substantial deferrals – of months or even up to a year. You will need to present a compelling case, though, or compromise and cut down on your time out.

Scale, rate and method of calculating pay

Your starting scale may be fixed or within a band of possibilities. Ask! The design and operation of pay scales is very complicated, often including an element related to your individual performance or, in the private sector, to company profitability.

It is also important to find out how often your pay is assessed. One job may have a lower starting salary than another, but have greater prospects for speedy increases if you do well. Is there any possibility of overtime payments for going beyond the contracted hours of working or are you just expected to work as long as it takes to get the job done?

Hours

These may be fixed across the organisation or relate to your role. You may want to negotiate starting earlier, or finishing later (don't worry, in most graduate jobs it will be both anyway!).

Holidays

There may be an organisational pecking order of holidays, starting with the least senior or most recent recruit having, for example, 20 days (plus the eight statutory bank holidays), only rising to 25 with promotion or long service. In such cases, an organisation won't offer flexibility. You may be able to negotiate 'hidden holidays' by agreeing 'time in lieu' of long hours (say up to a day or so a month).

Personally tailored packages

Many organisations now offer a graduate package, which includes salary, holidays and often other perks, such as car leasing schemes, private health care, health or sports club membership and discounts on company products. You may be able to negotiate a personally tailored package – sometimes regarded as 'cafeteria benefits'. This is because you pick and mix the package to your own preferences within a certain pre-set 'value'.

Training and personal development

The graduate training scheme may be a set programme or tailor-made according to the specific job. In addition, you may be able to gain agreement to study for externally accredited professional membership, Diploma in Management or even for an MBA. It's worth discussing your aspirations early and finding out what the possibilities are. Some organisations agree to fund your studies and offer reasonable paid release for study and exams.

'Special' terms, conditions and restrictions

Increasing numbers of employers include special clauses or restrictions. Try to find out if any of these apply to you.

On joining the organisation

'A friend of mine has just been offered "serious money" to join a small local IT firm writing tailor-made software programs.'

'Golden hellos' or 'golden handshakes' are a means of attracting you to accept a particular post, especially in sectors such as IT, where there is a shortage of candidates with the necessary skills.

Many organisations will offer incoming employees financial and practical help, finding accommodation and so on. If the move is expected within four weeks or so of accepting the job, this would often include a package of hotel accommodation, meals and other expenses.

To stop you leaving . . .

Some organisations also attach 'golden handcuffs', which are usually a lump sum or other inducement to stay for a specified period or complete a project. Given the highly mobile nature of some jobs and the lucrative benefits of career hopping, this is becoming an increasingly common practice.

'Opt out' clauses

'I have been offered a job with a leading management consultancy in London, but they want me to agree to "opt out" of my right not to work more than 48 hours in the average week.'

Some employers ask employees to 'opt out' of their statutory rights, as given under the Working Time Directive. The employer may want you to be available to respond to customers or cover for colleagues. This is very common in many fast-moving customer service sectors, such as management consultancy. The employer is entitled to ask you to opt out but you do not have to agree. Even if you sign the opt out clause, you can change your mind, provided that you give your employer three months' notice.

'Mobility clauses'

Certain graduate trainee schemes involve a rotational system where you move between sites to gain experience. In some cases, the requirement to be mobile is included in express terms, but in many it is implied in the promotional material and job adverts. Employers must act reasonably, and it may be seen as reasonable if you are warned beforehand! There may be scope to reduce the number of hours you do if you can demonstrate prior knowledge or experience.

Leaving the organisation and beyond

'I have just been offered a job in a local advertising/PR agency, but my contract includes a clause that I cannot work for their competitors if I leave.'

Get legal advice. This sounds like a 'restraint of trade' clause and the courts tend to look on them with disfavour. Your employer would have to demonstrate that the clause is reasonable – many such clauses are invalid. Check it out as such clauses could have a detrimental effect on your future career.

Some organisations require you to sign a clause that you will not take clients with you if you leave (for example, management consultants, accountancy firms and solicitors' practices). Again, take care to read the small print – these clauses can restrict your future career options. If in doubt, seek legal advice.

The psychological contract

The psychological contract is the set of unwritten expectations that operates between employees and employers. In an ideal world, the contract of employment would give room to include the expectations and assumptions being made on both sides. Problems can occur when there is a mismatch between your expectations and the reality of the job and/or organisational life.

You can do a lot to ensure your expectations are realistic by researching the organisation and job as thoroughly as you can and asking detailed, probing questions throughout the selection process and after you have been offered the job. Make sure you use the information provided here to your advantage!

Summary

→   Fantastic – you have a job offer! First, check there are no strings attached. If there are conditions, can you fulfil them?

→   Your contract of employment is at the heart of your relationship with your future employer, so be sure you have as much information as possible before accepting the offer. This will help you to avoid disappointment and nasty surprises later on.

→   Some aspects of the employment contract may be negotiable. You may have to respect existing pay scales and holiday allowances, but nothing ventured, nothing gained! Many aspects of the overall package can be individually tailored.

→   Watch out for special terms and conditions that may have financial penalties or commercial restrictions attached if you leave.

Signposts to more help

Factsheets

There are useful DTI factsheets on terms and conditions, sex discrimination and equal pay, maternity rights, the national minimum wage and many more.

Many university student union offices produce their own information leaflets and update them annually.

ɔok

Rousseau, D. (1995) *Psychological Contracts in Organizations: Understanding written and unwritten agreements*, Sage, Newbury Park, California.

Websites

www.dti.gov.uk/guidance.htm

A government site with comprehensive, up-to-date information and contacts.

www.tuc.org.uk

The Trades Union Congress site has regularly updated information on employment rights, plus details of a telephone advice service.

www.eoc.org.uk

The Equal Opportunities Commission site has data, contacts and telephone advice details.

www.incomesdata.co.uk

Incomes Data Services is an organisation that produces a range of surveys of interest, including the *Directory of Salary Surveys*, *Pay in the Public Services* and *Company Car Policies*.

Secretarial

42nd Street Recruitment

See **Media, page 195**

AA Appointments

Head Office ✉ 6th Floor, St Claire House, 30–33 Minories, EC3N 1PQ
⊖ Aldgate
🚆 Fenchurch St
☎ T 020 7480 7506   F 020 7480 5467
@ london@aaappointments.com
Market areas   Accountancy, Secretarial, Banking, Hospitality

✉ 72 Wells St, W1P 3RD
⊖ Tottenham Court Rd
🚆 Charing Cross
☎ T 020 7323 2237   F 020 7323 2245
@ westendtravel@aaappointments.com
Market areas   Travel, Secretarial

Website www.aaappointments.com
UK Offices 7
REC Member No

Brief Description Established in 1982, AA Appointments operate from UK locations in London, Glasgow, Crawley, Manchester, Birmingham and Woking. They deal with a variety of market sectors including Accounts, Travel, Banking, Secretarial, Customer Services, Hospitality and e-Business.

Preferred method of contact Apply on line or telephone for appointment

Minimum requirements None

Type of business Temporary, Permanent and Contract

Grade/Level of Appointments Graduate 1st Jobbers to Senior Management

Abbatt Recruitment Consultants

Head Office ✉ New Penderel House, 283–287 High Holborn, WC1V 7HF
⊖ Chancery Lane
🚆 City Thameslink
☎ T 020 7404 7890   F 020 7242 4620
@ natalie.ac@abbatt.co.uk
Market areas   Secretarial

Website www.abbatt.co.uk
UK Offices 1
REC Member No

Brief Description Abbatt Recruitment specialises in the temporary, contract and permanent recruitment of Secretarial and Administration staff.

Preferred method of contact Apply on line or telephone for appointment

Minimum requirements None

Type of business Contract and Permanent

Grade/Level of Appointments All levels

Abbey Exec/AES Contract Services

See **Healthcare, page 129**

Acme Appointments

See **Accountancy and Banking, page 5**

Action First

Head Office ✉ 8 Canfield Place, NW6 3BT
⊖ Finchley Rd
🚆 West Hampstead
☎ T 020 7625 5222   F 020 7625 5252
@ recruit@actionfirstplc.com
Market areas   IT, Secretarial, Accountancy and Finance, Housing, Social Work

Website www.actionfirstplc.com
UK Offices 1
REC Member Yes

Brief Description Established in 1982, Action First specialise in temporary and permanent positions across Central London and, for IT, across Europe, ranging from 1st Jobbers/Office Administrators to Managerial appointments for Project Managers/Account Directors. They are a single branch providing an extensive service in IT, Administration and Secretarial, Housing, Social Work and Finance and have enjoyed steady growth since their inception.

Preferred method of contact Apply on line or telephone for appointment

Minimum requirements None

Type of business Permanent and Temporary

Grade/Level of Appointments Graduate/1st Jobber to Account Director/Project Manager

Adecco

✉ 133 Victoria St, SW1 6RD
⊖ Westminster
🚃 Charing Cross
☎ T 020 7828 6886   F 020 7821 7208
@ 278.westminster@adecco.co.uk
Market areas Secretarial and Industrial

✉ Unit 2, 129 Finchley Rd, Cresta House, NW3 6HY
⊖ Swiss Cottage
🚃 West Hampstead
☎ T 020 7722 2298   F 020 7722 1384
@ 737.swiss.cottage@adecco.co.uk
Market areas Secretarial and Industrial

✉ 410 The Strand, WC2R ONS
⊖ Charing Cross
🚃 Charing Cross
☎ T 020 7539 7500   F 020 7497 2149
@ 470.strand@adecco.co.uk
Market areas Secretarial and Industrial

✉ 230 Edgeware Rd, W2 1DW
⊖ Paddington
🚃 Paddington
☎ T 020 7402 6651   F 020 7706 3724
@ 728.paddington@adecco.co.uk
Market areas Secretarial and Industrial

✉ Century House, 100–102 Oxford St, W1D 1LN
⊖ Oxford Circus
🚃 Charing Cross
☎ T 020 7631 5262   F 020 7631 4355
@ 486.oxford.street@adecco.co.uk
Market areas Secretarial and Industrial

✉ Bridge House, 4 Borough High St, SE1 9QQ
⊖ London Bridge
🚃 London Bridge
☎ T 020 7403 0978   F 020 7407 5317
@ 489.london.bridge@adecco.co.uk
Market areas Secretarial and Industrial

✉ 3rd Floor, 150 Brompton Rd, SW3 1HX
⊖ Knightsbridge
🚃 Victoria
☎ T 020 7590 5580   F 020 7590 5581
@ 239.knightsbridge@adecco.co.uk
Market areas Secretarial and Industrial

✉ 383 Euston Rd, NW1 3AU
⊖ Gt Portland St
🚃 Euston
☎ T 020 7380 3890   F 020 7380 3891
@ 768.euston@adecco.co.uk
Market areas Secretarial and Industrial

✉ 12–14 Devonshire Row, EC2M 5RH
⊖ Moorgate
🚃 Moorgate
☎ T 020 7247 4244   F 020 7247 8456

@ 476.devonshire.row@adecco.co.uk
Market areas Secretarial and Industrial

✉ 46 St John's Rd, SW11 1PW
⊖ Clapham Common
🚃 Clapham High St
☎ T 020 7978 4797   F 020 7978 5707
@ 110.clapham@adecco.co.uk
Market areas Secretarial and Industrial

✉ Bolsa House, 80 Cheapside, EC2V 6EE
⊖ Bank
🚃 Cannon St
☎ T 020 7236 6832   F 020 7236 9832
@ 482.cheapside@adecco.co.uk
Market areas Secretarial and Industrial

✉ 4th Floor, Alliance House, 29–30 High Holborn, WC1V 6AZ
⊖ Chancery Lane
🚃 City Thameslink
☎ T 020 7831 5400   F 020 7404 4601
@ chancery.lane.620@adecco.co.uk
Market areas Secretarial and Industrial

✉ 160 Camden High St, NW1 ONE
⊖ Camden Town
🚃 Kentish Town
☎ T 020 7485 5855   F 020 7267 0094
@ 768.camden@adecco.co.uk
Market areas Secretarial and Industrial

Website www.adecco.co.uk

UK Offices 358

REC Member No

Head Office Adecco House, Elstree Way, Borehamwood, Herts, WD6 1HY

Brief Description Adecco is the only personnel services company in the world to offer such a comprehensive range of services with such a geographic reach, from general to highly specialised staffing, temporary and permanent placement, Human Resource consulting and Career Management. Formed from the merger of Adia Alfred Marks and Ecco Employment in 1997, its group companies include Office Angels, Computer People, Ajilon, Accountants on Call (AOC) and Jonathan Wren.

Preferred method of contact Walk in, telephone or e-mail – candidates will normally be required to make an appointment for interview

Minimum requirements None

Type of business Temporary and Permanent

Grade/Level of Appointments All levels up to Senior Management

Aldrich & Co

See **Financial Services and Insurance, page 119**

Allegis Group Ltd

Head Office	✉	1st Floor, Therese House, 29–30 Glass House Yard, EC1A 4JN
	⊖	Barbican
	▣	Barbican
	☏	T 020 7608 8300 F 020 7608 8302
	@	london@allegisgroup.co.uk
Market areas		IT, Education, Secretarial, Financial Services, Outsourcing

Website www.allegisgroup.co.uk

UK Offices 13

REC Member No

Brief Description Founded in 1983, Allegis Group is one of the largest International Staffing Service firms currently supplying over 4,000 companies. Allegis pride themselves on delivering an unparalleled level of customer service to both client managers and contractors from strategic staffing to consulting.

Preferred method of contact Telephone for appointment

Minimum requirements None

Type of business Contract and Permanent

Grade/Level of Appointments All levels

Andersen Leigh Associates Plc

See **Accountancy and Banking, page 5**

Anderson Hoare Associates

Head Office	✉	56 Sloan Sq, SW1W 8AX
	⊖	Sloane Sq
	▣	Victoria
	☏	T 020 7824 8821 F 020 7730 2700
	@	mail@andersonhoare.co.uk
Market areas		Secretarial

Website www.andersonhoare.co.uk

UK Offices 1

REC Member No

Brief Description Anderson Hoare specialises in the recruitment of the highest calibre Secretaries, Personal Assistants and Senior Executive Assistants for many of the country's most successful organisations and individuals, as well as Non-profit Making organisations and Charities.

Preferred method of contact Telephone for appointment

Minimum requirements None

Type of business Permanent and Contract

Grade/Level of Appointments All levels

Angel Human Resources Plc

Head Office	✉	Angel House, 4 Union St, SE1 1SZ
	☏	T 020 7940 2000 F 020 7940 2018
	✉	4 Union St, SE1 1SZ
	⊖	London Bridge
	▣	London Bridge
	☏	T 020 7940 2000 F 020 8749 4950
	@	west@angelhr.org
Market areas		Secretarial, Hospitality, Events, Industrial, Construction, Agriculture, Nursing and Care

Website www.angelhr.org

UK Offices 5

REC Member No

Brief Description Founded in 1965, Angel Human Resources provides personnel services to a variety of sectors.

Preferred method of contact Telephone for appointment

Minimum requirements None

Type of business Temporary and Permanent

Grade/Level of Appointments All levels

Angela Mortimer Plc

Head Office	✉	37–38 Golden Sq, W1F 9LA
	⊖	Piccadilly Circus
	▣	Charing Cross
	☏	T 020 7287 7788 F 020 7499 5378
	@	cv@angelamortimer.com
Market areas		Secretarial
	✉	11 Old Jewry, EC2R 8DU
	⊖	Bank
	▣	Cannon St
	☏	T 020 7814 0800 F 020 7814 0801
	@	cv@angelamortimer.com
Market areas		Secretarial
	✉	1 Fredericks Place, EC2R 8AB
	⊖	Bank
	▣	Cannon St
	☏	T 020 7600 0286 F 020 7606 2010
	@	cv@angelamortimer.com
Market areas		Secretarial

Website www.angelamortimer.com

UK Offices 3

REC Member No

Brief Description Angela Mortimer Plc is Britain's leading quality Secretarial recruitment consultancy specialising in Office Staff for London and key support roles across the UK.

Preferred method of contact Apply on line or telephone for appointment

Minimum requirements None

Type of business Temporary and Permanent

Grade/Level of Appointments All levels

Appointments Bi-Language

See **Bilingual, page 38**

Aquarius Employment Bureau

Head Office   ✉   Aquarius House, Archway Corner, N19 3TD

     ⊖   Archway

     🚊   Kentish Town

     ☎   T 020 7272 6252   F 020 7263 2485

     @   rp@aquarius-employment.com

Market areas   Media, Banking, Medical, Secretarial, Industrial, Catering

Website   www.aquarius-employment.com

UK Offices   1

REC Member   Yes

Brief Description   Established in 1971, Aquarious Employment Bureau (London) Ltd is one of North London's most successful independent agencies supplying temporary and permanent staff to various business sectors.

Preferred method of contact   Apply on line or telephone for appointment

Minimum requirements   None

Type of business   Temporary and Permanent

Grade/Level of Appointments   Researchers/Administrators to Management level

Artemis Recruitment Ltd

Head Office   ✉   36 Langham St, W1W 7AP

     ⊖   Oxford Circus

     🚊   Charing Cross

     ☎   T 020 7436 5004   F 020 7637 0316

     @   caroline@artemis-recruitment.co.uk

Market areas   Secretarial, Legal Secretarial

Website   www.artemis-recruitment.co.uk

REC Member   Yes

Brief Description   Founded in 2000, Artemis Recruitment offers a refreshing alternative to the traditional recruitment service. They are an independent agency specialising in the recruitment of temporary and permanent personnel to a variety of companies, throughout London.

Preferred method of contact   Apply on line or telephone for appointment

Minimum requirements   None

Type of business Temporary and Permanent

Grade/Level of Appointments All levels

ASA Law Secretarial

See **Legal, page 188**

Ashford Associates

See **Bilingual, page 38**

Ashley Stewart Ltd

Head Office   ✉   4 Margaret St, W1N 7LG

     ⊖   Oxford Circus

     🚊   Charing Cross

     ☎   T 020 7580 9103   F 020 7580 9104

     @   asl@ashleystewart.co.uk

Market areas   Retail, Promotional Personnel, Secretarial

Website   www.ashleystewart.co.uk

UK Offices   1

REC Member   No

Brief Description   Ashley Stewart specialises in the recruitment of permanent and temporary Secretarial and Retail personnel and the provision of Promotional personnel and skilled Artistes for all Promotional situations throughout the UK.

Preferred method of contact   Apply on line or telephone for appointment

Minimum requirements   None

Type of business   Permanent and Temporary

Grade/Level of Appointments   All levels

Austen Smythe

Head Office   ✉   12 Groveland Ct, EC4M 9EH

     ⊖   Mansion House

     🚊   Cannon St

     ☎   T 020 7248 2288   F 020 7248 8833

     @   mail@austensmythe.com

Market areas   Banking and Secretarial staff to the Banking and Financial Sector

Website   www.austensmythe.com

UK Offices   1

REC Member   No

Brief Description   Established in 1989, Austen Smythe is a privately owned recruitment consultancy who specialise in providing Support and Secretarial staff for the Banking and Financial sector including Credit Risk Analysts, Project Finance, Receptionists and Office Management.

Preferred method of contact Telephone for appointment

Minimum requirements None

Type of business Permanent and Temporary

Grade/Level of Appointments All levels

Barbara Houghton Associates Ltd

See **Accountancy and Banking, page 7**

Barnett Personnel Ltd

Head Office ✉ 28 South Molton St, W1K 5RG
⊖ Bond St
🚇 Paddington
☎ T 020 7629 7838   F 020 7495 6234
@ dad@dial.pipex.com
Market areas Secretarial, Medical Secretarial

Website www.barnettpersonnel.com

UK Offices 1

REC Member No

Brief Description Founded in 1980, Barnett Personnel has gained an enviable reputation for providing a fast and efficient quality service in both temporary and permanent personnel.

Preferred method of contact Apply on line or telephone for appointment

Minimum requirements None

Type of business Temporary and Permanent

Grade/Level of Appointments All levels

Beauchamp Bureau

See **Domestic, page 69**

Beavers Ltd

Head Office ✉ Holden House, 57 Rathbone Place, W1P 1AW
⊖ Tottenham Court Rd
🚇 Euston
☎ T 020 7636 3424   F 020 7255 1237
@ dam@beavers.co.uk
Market areas Secretarial

Website www.beavers.co.uk

UK Offices 1

REC Member No

Brief Description Beavers specialises in Secretarial and Administration staff across all levels.

Preferred method of contact Telephone for appointment

Minimum requirements None

Type of business Permanent, Temporary and Contract

Grade/Level of Appointments All levels

Belle Recruitment Ltd

Head Office ✉ 8 Staple Inn, WC1V 7QH
⊖ Chancery Lane
🚇 City Thameslink
☎ T 020 7404 4655   F 020 7831 7581
@ marta@bellerecruitment.co.uk
Market areas Secretarial

Website www.hrgo.co.uk

UK Offices 1

REC Member No

Brief Description Established over 15 years ago, Belle Recruitment is part of the HR Group Plc and works with large and small companies including those from the Commercial sector, Medical and Law as well as retaining close links with the Charitable sector.

Preferred method of contact Telephone for appointment

Minimum requirements None

Type of business Temporary and Permanent

Grade/Level of Appointments All levels

Bilinguagroup

See **Bilingual, page 38**

Bilingual People Ltd

See **Bilingual, page 39**

BJ Crawfords Ltd

Head Office ✉ 69 Wigmore St, W1U 1PZ
⊖ Bond St
🚇 Paddington
☎ T 020 7935 9692   F 020 7487 2930
@ permjobs@bjcrawfords.co.uk, tempjobs@bjcrawfords.co.uk
Market areas Secretarial

Website www.bjcrawfords.co.uk

UK Offices 1

REC Member Yes

Brief Description Established in 1985, BJ Crawfords services the London area from the West End with temporary and permanent Secretarial and Office staff for the Advertising, Media, PR, Legal, Banking, Fashion, Financial Services and Interior Design sectors.

Preferred method of contact Telephone for appointment

Minimum requirements None

Type of business Permanent and Temporary

Grade/Level of Appointments All levels

Bligh Appointments Ltd

Head Office ✉ 70 North End Rd, W14 9EP
⊖ West Kensington
🚉 Kensington (Olympia)
☎ T 020 7603 6123   F 020 7371 6898
@ info@bligh.co.uk

Market areas Secretarial, Industrial, Nannies

Website www.bligh.co.uk

UK Offices 1

REC Member Yes

Brief Description Bligh Appointments specialise in Industrial, Secretarial and Nanny recruitment.

Preferred method of contact Telephone for appointment

Minimum requirements None

Type of business Permanent and Temporary

Grade/Level of Appointments All levels

Blue Arrow Personnel

✉ 9 Fenchurch Place, EC3M 4AJ
⊖ Tower Hill
🚉 Fenchurch St
☎ T 020 7702 1591   F 020 7480 6355
@ staff@bluearrow.co.uk

Market areas Secretarial

Website www.bluearrow.co.uk

UK Offices 250

REC Member Yes

Head Office 800 The Boulevard, Capability Green, Luton, LU1 3BA

Brief Description Part of the Corporate Services Group (CSG), Blue Arrow was founded over 40 years ago to become one of the UK's largest recruitment businesses with a network of over 250 locations in the UK, providing temporary, permanent and contract staff across Office, Catering, Construction, Healthcare, Technical and Industrial sectors.

Preferred method of contact Telephone for appointment

Minimum requirements None

Type of business Temporary, Permanent and Contract

Grade/Level of Appointments All levels

Bond Street Personnel Ltd

Head Office ✉ 22 South Molton St, W1Y 1DD
⊖ Bond St

🚉 Paddington
☎ T 020 7629 3692   F 020 7409 1524
@ enquiries@bondstreetpersonnel.co.uk

Market areas Secretarial

Website www.bondstreetpersonnel.co.uk

UK Offices 1

REC Member No

Brief Description London based Bond Street Personnel Ltd is a long established recruitment company specialising in the supply of Office Managers, Secretarial, Reception and all Office Support staff on a temporary, permanent or contract basis.

Preferred method of contact Apply on line or telephone for appointment

Minimum requirements None

Type of business Temporary, Permanent and Contract

Grade/Level of Appointments Administration Staff to Office Manager

Boyce Recruitment

See **Bilingual, page 39**

Brook Street

✉ 139 Victoria St, SW1E 6RD
⊖ Victoria
🚉 Victoria
☎ T 020 7630 6112   F 020 7834 2316
@ london_victoriastreet@brookstreet.co.uk

Market areas Secretarial, Industrial

✉ 32 Strand, WC2N 5HY
⊖ Charing Cross
🚉 Charing Cross
☎ T 020 7930 7399   F 020 7839 2274
@ london_strand@brookstreet.co.uk

Market areas Secretarial, Industrial

✉ 230 High Holborn, WC1V 7DA
⊖ Holborn
🚉 City Thameslink
☎ T 020 7242 6991   F 020 7405 3889
@ london_holborn@brookstreet.co.uk

Market areas Secretarial, Industrial

✉ 108 Fenchurch St, EC3M 5JJ
⊖ Tower Hill
🚉 Fenchurch St
☎ T 020 7481 8441   F 020 7702 3069
@ london_fenchurchstreet@brookstreet.co.uk

Market areas Secretarial, Industrial

✉ 6–6a South Quay Plaza, 185 Marsh Wall, E14 9SH
⊖ South Quay
🚉 Limehouse

C T 020 7515 8118   F 020 7515 8315
@ docklands@brookstreet.co.uk
Market areas   Secretarial, Industrial

✉ 131–133 Cannon St, EC4N 5AX
⊖ Cannon St
🚆 Cannon St
C T 020 7623 3966   F 020 7623 1401
@ london_cannonstreet@brookstreet.co.uk
Market areas   Secretarial, Industrial

✉ 136 Baker St, W1U 6PL
⊖ Baker St
🚆 Marylebone
C T 020 7486 6144   F 020 7935 7600
@ london_bakerstreet@brookstreet.co.uk
Market areas   Secretarial, Industrial

✉ 353 Oxford St, W1R 1FA
⊖ Oxford Circus
🚆 Charing Cross
C T 020 7493 8531   F 020 7629 3614
@ london_oxfordstreet@brookstreet.co.uk
Market areas   Secretarial, Industrial

Website www.brookstreet.co.uk

UK Offices 120+

REC Member No

Head Office Clarence House, 134 Hatfield Rd, St Albans, Herts, AL1 4JB

Brief Description Part of Manpower Inc and established in 1946, Brook Street Bureau Plc specialises in providing Commercial, Secretarial and Light Industrial staff for both temporary and permanent positions.

Preferred method of contact Apply on line or telephone for appointment

Minimum requirements None

Type of business Temporary, Permanent and Contract

Grade/Level of Appointments All levels

Cannon Persona International Recruitment

See **Bilingual, page 39**

Capital Legal

See **Legal, page 189**

The Career Factor Ltd

Head Office **✉** Linen Hall, 162–168 Regent St, W1R 5TE
⊖ Oxford Circus
🚆 Charing Cross
C T 020 7306 3196   F 020 7306 3198

@ perms@careerfactor.com
Market areas   Secretarial

Website www.careerfactor.com

UK Offices 1

REC Member No

Brief Description The Career Factor was established in 1994 to supply London organisations including Banks, Charities, PR/Advertising, Property Consultants and Publishing Houses with all levels of Support staff.

Preferred method of contact Telephone for appointment

Minimum requirements None

Type of business Permanent and Temporary

Grade/Level of Appointments All levels

Career Legal

See **Legal, page 189**

Career Moves

See **Media, page 196**

Carousel Consultancy

Head Office **✉** 2nd Floor, Russell Chambers, The Piazza, WC2E 8AA
⊖ Covent Garden
🚆 Charing Cross
C T 020 7240 2833   F 020 7240 7300
@ infoCG@carousel.co.uk
Market areas   Secretarial

✉ 2nd Floor, 1 Gracechurch St, EC3V 0DD
⊖ Monument
🚆 London Bridge
C T 020 7220 9700   F 020 7220 9711
@ infoCITY@carousel.co.uk
Market areas   Secretarial

✉ Ramillies Buildings, 1–9 Hills Place, W1F 7SA
⊖ Oxford Circus
🚆 Charing Cross
C T 020 7734 7277   F 020 7240 7300
@ info@carousel.co.uk
Market areas   Secretarial

Website www.carousel.co.uk

UK Offices 3

REC Member Yes

Brief Description Carousel Consultancy specialise in placing Secretarial and Administrative Support staff to companies within the Finance, Media, Law and Retail sectors from three offices in London. They provide permanent, temporary and contract opportunities.

‹›4‹›‹›3‹›‹›2‹›‹›2‹›

Preferred method of contact Apply on line or telephone for appointment

Minimum requirements None

Type of business Temporary, Permanent and Contract

Grade/Level of Appointments Receptionist/Administrator to Personnel Professionals, Sales and Marketing Executives

Catch 22 Facilities Support Services

See Construction and Property, page 44

Cavendish Personnel

Head Office ✉ 113 Gloucester Place, W1U 6JR
⊖ Baker St
🚇 Marylebone
☎ T 020 7486 1777   F 020 7486 2802
@ info@netsites.co.uk
Market areas Secretarial, Legal Secretarial

Website www.cavendish-personnel.co.uk
UK Offices 1
REC Member No

Brief Description Cavendish Personnel is a privately owned recruitment consultancy established in 1976 providing an efficient and reliable service to clients across all levels from Accountancy, Banking, Charities, Engineering, IT, Property and Publishing.

Preferred method of contact Telephone for appointment

Minimum requirements None

Type of business Permanent

Grade/Level of Appointments Graduate/1st Jobbers to Office Managers, Legal Secretaries

Centre People Appointments Ltd

See Bilingual, page 39

Centrepoint Group (CPG)

Head Office ✉ 16 St Helen's Place, EC3A 6DP
⊖ Liverpool St
🚇 Liverpool St
☎ T 020 7562 1600   F 020 7588 8010
@ secretarial@centrepointgroup.co.uk
Market areas Secretarial

Website www.centrepointgroup.co.uk
UK Offices 1
REC Member No

Brief Description Centrepoint Group was founded over 20 years ago to specialise in permanent and contract Operations and Support staff

within the Commercial and Public sectors including prestigious City Financial Institutions, Government Bodies and leading blue chip organisations.

Preferred method of contact Apply on line or telephone for appointment

Minimum requirements None

Type of business Permanent and Contract

Grade/Level of Appointments Graduate/1st Jobber to Management level

Chambeau

Head Office ✉ 75 Chancery Lane, WC2A 1AA
⊖ Chancery Lane
🚇 City Thameslink
☎ T 020 7404 7314   F 020 7404 7399
@ jobs@chambeau.com
Market areas HR, Sales, Secretarial, Finance

Website www.chambeau.com
UK Offices 1
REC Member No

Brief Description Chambeau specialise in the recruitment of Secretarial, Sales, HR and Finance professionals.

Preferred method of contact Telephone for appointment

Minimum requirements None

Type of business Permanent

Grade/Level of Appointments Graduate/Receptionist to Management level

Chancery Lane Legal Secretaries

See Legal, page 190

Changes Recruitment

Head Office ✉ 14 South Molton St, W1K 5QP
⊖ New Bond St
🚇 Paddington
☎ T 020 7491 1255   F 020 7493 2621
@ admin@changesrecruitment.com
Market areas Secretarial

Website www.changesrecruitment.com
UK Offices 1
REC Member Yes

Brief Description Established in 1982, Changes Recruitment specialises in providing temporary and permanent personnel including Secretaries, Receptionists, PAs, Juniors and Account Co-ordinators to a range of clients including Advertising Agencies, PR, Design companies, Publishing and Sales Promotion organisations.

Preferred method of contact Apply on line or telephone for appointment

Minimum requirements None

Type of business Temporary and Permanent

Grade/Level of Appointments Graduate/Junior to PAs/ Management

Charity Action Recruitment (LWTS)

See **Not for Profit**, page 208

Charity Connections

See **Not for Profit**, page 208

Charity People

See **Not for Profit**, page 208

Charity Recruitment

See **Not for Profit**, page 208

Charles Birch Recruitment Ltd

See **Construction and Property, page 45**

City Centre Group

Head Office ✉ 133 Oxford St, W1R 1TD
☎ **T** 020 7287 0055   **F** 020 7287 3137

✉ Oxford Circus House, 245 Oxford St, W1D 2LX
⊖ Oxford Circus
🚆 Charing Cross
☎ **T** 020 7287 0055   **F** 020 7287 3137
@ tempstaff@city-centre.co.uk
Market areas   Secretarial, Catering, IT, Sales

Website www.city-centre.co.uk

UK Offices 2

REC Member Yes

Brief Description Based in the West End, the City Centre Group has been supplying temporary and permanent staff to clients across London and the UK for over 25 years, covering Office, Catering, IT and Sales recruitment.

Preferred method of contact Telephone for appointment

Minimum requirements Word processing skills

Type of business Temporary and Permanent

Grade/Level of Appointments All levels

City Quest Recruitment Ltd

See **Accountancy and Banking, page 10**

Coby Phillips

Head Office ✉ 82 Wigmore St, W1U 2SN
⊖ Bond St
🚆 Paddington
☎ **T** 020 7487 3355   **F** 020 7487 3955
@ info@cobyphillips.co.uk
Market areas   Secretarial

Website www.cobyphillips.co.uk

UK Offices 1

REC Member No

Brief Description Coby Phillips specialise in the recruitment of Secretarial and Administrative Support staff to a wide range of industry sectors.

Preferred method of contact Telephone for appointment

Minimum requirements None

Type of business Temporary, Permanent and Contract

Grade/Level of Appointments Graduate/Junior to PAs/ Management

Crone Corkill Group Plc

Head Office ✉ 5 Queen St, EC4N 1SW
⊖ Mansion House
🚆 Blackfriars
☎ **T** 020 7390 7000   **F** 020 7390 2997
@ cvlegal@cronecorkill.co.uk
Market areas   Legal Secretarial

✉ 1 Stratton St, W1J 8LA
⊖ Green Park
🚆 Victoria
☎ **T** 020 7636 0800   **F** 020 7499 4300
@ emmacameron@cronecorkill.co.uk
Market areas   Secretarial

Website www.cronecorkill.co.uk

REC Member Yes

Brief Description Part of the Spherion Corporation, Crone Corkill specialise in placing both temporary and permanent Secretaries, PAs, Legal Secretaries, Paralegals and Bi-linguists in many major national and international clients.

Preferred method of contact Apply on line or telephone for appointment

Minimum requirements None

Type of business Temporary and Permanent

Grade/Level of Appointments All levels

Cross Selection

Head Office ✉ 154 Bishopsgate, EC2M 4LN
⊖ Liverpool St
🚇 Liverpool St
☎ T 020 7377 5500   F 020 7377 5599
@ info@crossselection.co.uk
Market areas Secretarial

Website www.crossselection.co.uk

UK Offices 1

REC Member Yes

Brief Description Cross Selection is a top flight specialist consultancy which has focused on PA, Secretarial and Administrative recruitment for over 10 years, placing permanent staff within a broad range of clients across London and the surrounding areas.

Preferred method of contact Telephone for appointment

Minimum requirements None

Type of business Permanent

Grade/Level of Appointments Graduate/Office Junior to Team Secretary/PA

Crown Personnel

See Industrial, page 150

David Alan Associates

Head Office ✉ 88 Kingsway, WC2B 6AA
⊖ Holborn
🚇 City Thameslink
☎ T 020 7681 6170   F 020 7681 6179
@ mail@david-alan.com
Market areas Secretarial

Website www.david-alan.com

UK Offices 1

REC Member No

Brief Description David Alan Associates is a fast expanding recruitment consultancy, specialising in Secretarial, Administrative and Office Support staff. Situated in Central London, they are ideally placed for staffing City, West End and Docklands organisations. Their team of dedicated professionals bring over 30 years experience to clients' personal requirements.

Preferred method of contact Apply on line or telephone for appointment

Minimum requirements None

Type of business Temporary, Permanent and Contract

Grade/Level of Appointments Graduate/1st Jobber to PA/Legal Secretary

Dawn Ellmore

Head Office ✉ 26 Gray's Inn Rd, WC1X 8HP
⊖ Chancery Lane
🚇 City Thameslink
☎ T 020 7405 5039   F 020 7405 5065
@ office@dawnellmore.co.uk
Market areas Patents, Trademark, Legal, Medical, Marketing, IT, Secretarial

Website www.dawnellmore.co.uk

UK Offices 1

REC Member No

Brief Description With over 25 years experience in recruitment, Dawn Ellmore's trained consultants can offer professional advice for permanent and temporary requirements, especially within the Patents, Trademarks, Legal, Medical, Marketing, IT, Secretarial and General Office sectors.

Preferred method of contact Telephone for appointment

Minimum requirements Ideally relevant industry exposure

Type of business Temporary and Permanent

Grade/Level of Appointments Legal Secretary/Administrator to Lawyer/Account Manager

Diamond Resourcing – Secretarial

Head Office ✉ 62–74 Leadenhall Market, EC3V 1LT
☎ T 020 7929 2976   F 020 7929 5395
✉ 29–30 Leadenhall Market, EC3V 1LR
⊖ Bank
🚇 Cannon St
☎ T 020 7929 2977   F 020 7929 2980
@ info@diamondresourcing.com
Market areas IT, Banking, Accountancy and Finance, Secretarial, Sales and Insurance

Website www.diamondresourcing.com

UK Offices 3

REC Member Yes

Brief Description Established in 1988, Diamond Resourcing is located in the heart of the City of London. Their broad client base ranges from many small and medium business enterprises to large and well known blue chip organisations throughout the UK and Europe. They have a proven track record in the placement of key personnel in IT, Accountancy, Secretarial, Banking/Finance, Insurance, Telecoms and Sales. Each division is an independent business ensuring that their consultants have the extensive expertise that their clients and candidates expect from a leading recruitment consultancy.

Preferred method of contact Apply on line or telephone for appointment

Minimum requirements None

Type of business Temporary, Permanent and Contract

Grade/Level of Appointments Office Junior to Finance Director/Analyst

DISCO International Ltd

See **Bilingual, page 40**

Drake International Ltd

Head Office ✉ 20 Regent St, SW1Y 4PH
🚇 Piccadilly Circus
🚆 Charing Cross
☎ T 020 7484 0800   F 020 7484 0808
@ info@drakeintl.co.uk
Market areas Industrial, Nursing, Secretarial, Occupational Health

Website www.drakeintl.com

UK Offices 19

REC Member No

Brief Description Established over 50 years ago, Drake specialises across a range of specialist areas including Secretarial, Industrial, Call Centre, Occupational Health and Nursing recruitment.

Preferred method of contact Apply on line or telephone for appointment

Minimum requirements None

Type of business Temporary, Permanent and Contract

Grade/Level of Appointments All levels

DSA Bilingual Ltd

See **Bilingual, page 40**

Eden Brown Recruitment Ltd

See **Construction and Property, page 46**

Elan Recruitment

Head Office ✉ Grampian House, Meridian Gate, Marsh Wall, E14 9YT
🚇 Crossharbour
🚆 Limehouse
☎ T 020 7537 4114   F 020 7537 3927
Market areas Secretarial, Support, Accountancy, IT/Telecoms

Website www.elanrecruitment.com

UK Offices 1

REC Member Yes

Brief Description Part of Courtland Holdings, Elan Recruitment was established in 1986 to supply Administration and Back Office Support staff.

Preferred method of contact Apply on line or telephone for an appointment

Minimum requirements None

Type of business Temporary and Permanent

Grade/Level of Appointments All levels

Elizabeth Hunt Recruitment Consultants

Head Office ✉ Warnford Ct, 29 Throgmorton St, EC2N 2AT
🚇 Bank
🚆 Cannon St
☎ T 020 7330 8200   F 020 7920 0641
@ ehcity@spring.com
Market areas Secretarial

✉ Coin House, 2 Gees Ct, St Christophers Place, W1U 1JA
🚇 Bond St
🚆 Paddington
☎ T 020 7535 5050   F 020 7535 5053
@ ehwestend@spring.com
Market areas Secretarial

Website www.spring.com

UK Offices 2

REC Member Yes

Brief Description Part of the Spring Group, Elizabeth Hunt has over 23 years of experience in placing candidates in temporary, permanent, part or full time positions. Based in the heart of London, with offices in the West End and City, their expertise lies in their ability to match you to work that complements your skills. Wherever your strengths lie, whatever your background, their helpful and experienced consultants will take the time and attention to establish the type of role you require.

Preferred method of contact Apply on line or telephone for appointment

Minimum requirements None

Type of business Temporary and Permanent

Grade/Level of Appointments Junior Secretaries to PAs/Managerial

Eurecruit

Head Office ✉ 27 Holywell Row, EC2A 4JB
🚇 Liverpool St
🚆 Liverpool St
☎ T 020 7247 1407   F 020 7247 1408
@ eurecruit@eurecruit.com
Market areas Marketing, Sales, Secretarial, Languages

Website www.eurecruit.com

UK Offices 1

REC Member No

Brief Description Eurecruit Ltd is renowned for its professionalism, attention to detail and exemplary levels of service to both clients and candidates alike. They pride themselves on their personalised service to their candidates, taking time to listen to their requirements and needs, and providing them with a professional consultation.

Preferred method of contact Telephone for appointment

Minimum requirements None

Type of business Temporary and Permanent

Grade/Level of Appointments Junior to Senior Executive

Euro London Appointments

See **Bilingual, page 40**

Euro London Appointments (Temporaries Division)

See **Bilingual, page 41**

Exclusive Recruitment

See **Hospitality and Leisure, page 140**

Fairstaff Agency Ltd

See **Healthcare, page 132**

Forties People

Head Office ✉ 11–13 Dowgate Hill, EC4R 2ST
⊖ Monument
🚊 Cannon St
📞 T 020 7329 4044   F 020 7329 4540
@ info@fortiespeople.net
Market areas Secretarial

Website www.fortiespeople.net

UK Offices 1

REC Member Yes

Brief Description Forties People are committed to equal opportunity for all and their selection criteria depend totally on skills. They employ a friendly and well trained team of recruitment consultants who will carefully listen to your needs and will provide you with a tailored service that is only possible when the company works together for the benefit of all.

Preferred method of contact Apply on line or telephone for appointment

Minimum requirements None

Type of business Temporary and Permanent

Grade/Level of Appointments Mature individuals

Freedom Recruitment

See **Fashion and Retail, page 112**

Gel Appointments

Head Office ✉ Ground Floor, 65 London Wall, EC2M 5TU
⊖ Moorgate
🚊 Moorgate
📞 T 020 7256 2345   F 020 7256 2255
@ info@gel-appointments.co.uk
Market areas Secretarial, Accountancy

Website www.changing-jobs.com

UK Offices 1

REC Member No

Brief Description Established in 1988, Gel Appointments is a substantial independent supplier of temporary, contract and permanent staff in the City, West End and nationally. They have earned an excellent reputation through their unique approach to recruitment. They are well known for having an excellent range of Secretarial, Accounts and Administration positions, but their expertise as professional recruiters enables them to provide a comprehensive service, supplying virtually any category of staff.

Preferred method of contact Apply on line or telephone for appointment

Minimum requirements None

Type of business Temporary, Permanent and Contract

Grade/Level of Appointments All levels

Gordon Yates

Head Office ✉ Candlewick House, 120 Cannon St, EC4N 6AS
⊖ Cannon St
🚊 Cannon St
📞 T 020 7283 4664   F 020 7283 4994
@ online@gycity.co.uk
Market areas Secretarial

✉ Palladium House, 1–4 Argyll St, W1V 1AD
⊖ Oxford Circus
🚊 Charing Cross
📞 T 020 7494 4466   F 020 7494 4499
@ online@gywestend.co.uk
Market areas Secretarial

Website www.gordonyates.co.uk

UK Offices 2

REC Member Yes

Brief Description Founded in 1947, Gordon Yates is the first name in London for Secretarial and skilled staff recruitment. Their purpose is to help their clients recruit outstanding people. Their approach is to try always to see things from the perspective of what they term their '3Cs' – their clients, candidates and colleagues.

Preferred method of contact Apply on line or telephone for an appointment

Minimum requirements None

Type of business Temporary and Permanent

Grade/Level of Appointments All levels

GR Law Ltd

Head Office ✉ 5 Wormwood St, EC2M 1RQ
⊖ Liverpool St
🚊 Liverpool St
✆ T 020 7216 8787   F 020 7417 1444
@ register@grlaw.co.uk
Market areas   Secretarial, Legal Secretarial

Website www.grlaw.co.uk

UK Offices 1

REC Member No

Brief Description GR Law specialises in recruiting temporary and permanent Secretarial and Legal Support staff. They've been a major player in the UK for over 7 years and set up an office in Sydney in 2000.

Preferred method of contact Apply on line or telephone for appointment

Minimum requirements None

Type of business Temporary and Permanent

Grade/Level of Appointments Junior to PA/Managerial

Gray & Associates

Head Office ✉ 21 Ironmonger Lane, EC2V 8EY
⊖ Bank
🚊 Cannon St
✆ T 020 7600 6220   F 020 7600 6221
@ recruitment@grayagency.com
Market areas   Secretarial

Website www.grayagency.com

UK Offices 1

REC Member Yes

Brief Description Established in 1994 to offer a truly personal service to clients and candidates, Gray & Associates offer private interviewing facilities and will advise you on all aspects of Secretarial,

Administrative, Reception, Accounting and Clerical work and will actively seek the right vacancy to suit your requirements.

Preferred method of contact Apply on line or telephone for appointment

Minimum requirements None

Type of business Temporary and Permanent

Grade/Level of Appointments All levels

Grosvenor Bureau

Head Office ✉ 3 Old Garden House, The Lanterns, Bridge Lane,
SW11 3AD
⊖ Vauxhall
🚊 Clapham Junction
✆ T 020 7223 6768   F 020 7978 7384
@ gb@grosvenorbureau.co.uk
Market areas   Secretarial

Website www.grosvenorbureau.co.uk

UK Offices 1

REC Member Yes

Brief Description Grosvenor Bureau has remained at the forefront of the recruitment industry for over 50 years. This longevity has been achieved by their commitment to quality and professionalism. They have gained a reputation for providing accomplished professional Secretarial and Administrative staff to a wide range of Creative industries.

Preferred method of contact Apply on line or telephone for appointment

Minimum requirements None

Type of business Temporary, Permanent and Contract

Grade/Level of Appointments All levels

Handle Recruitment

Head Office ✉ 4 Gees Ct, W1U 1JD
⊖ Bond St
🚊 Paddington
✆ T 020 7569 9999   F 020 7569 9988
@ info@handle.co.uk
Market areas   Media, Music, Entertainment, Secretarial, Accounts

Website www.handle.co.uk

UK Offices 1

REC Member Yes

Brief Description Handle Recruitment has been providing a path into the most exciting roles in the Music, Entertainment and Media industries since 1978. Their Secretarial Division is the cornerstone of their recruitment business, placing Support staff at all levels within the areas of the Media industry. The Executive Division specialises in sourcing Senior-level Executives within the Media, Music and

Communications industries. They have a team of specialist consultants placing Accounts people from Purchase Ledger to Financial Director.

Preferred method of contact Apply on line or telephone for appointment

Minimum requirements None

Type of business Temporary and Permanent

Grade/Level of Appointments Accounts Clerk/Administrator to Senior Management

Harrison Pursey

Head Office ✉ Noland House, 12–13 Poland St, W1F 8QB
             ⊖ Oxford Circus
             🚊 Charing Cross
             ✆ T 020 7287 3008   F 020 7287 3009
             @ info@harrisonpursey.co.uk
Market areas Secretarial, Media

Website www.harrisonpursey.co.uk

UK Offices 1

REC Member No

Brief Description Harrison Pursey has been leading the way in Media recruitment since 1987, providing support staff at all levels, both temporary and permanent, to the Media, Advertising, Creative and Design industries.

Preferred method of contact Apply on line or telephone for an appointment

Minimum requirements None

Type of business Temporary and Permanent

Grade/Level of Appointments Office Junior/1st Jobber to Team Secretary/Office Manager

Hays Accountancy Personnel

See **Accountancy and Banking, page 15**

Hays Banking Personnel

See **Accountancy and Banking, page 15**

Hays Personnel

Head Office ✉ 141 Moorgate, EC2M 6TX
             ✆ T 020 7628 9999   F 020 7628 4698

             ✉ 4th Floor, 1 Wilton St, SW1V 1AB
             ⊖ Victoria
             🚊 Victoria
             ✆ T 020 7630 5080   F 020 7828 7059
             @ victoria@hays-ap.co.uk
Market areas Secretarial, Purchasing

Website www.haysworks.com

UK Offices 111

REC Member No

Brief Description Hays Personnel Services is a division of Hays Plc, the Business Services group listed in the FTSE 100. Hays Personnel Services is Europe's leading specialist professional recruitment group. Hays Personnel provide a specialist recruitment service in the areas of Administration, PA and Secretarial , Management and Purchasing.

Preferred method of contact Apply on line or telephone for an appointment

Minimum requirements None

Type of business Temporary and Permanent

Grade/Level of Appointments All levels

Hays Taxation Personnel

See **Financial Services and Insurance, page 123**

Hays ZMB

See **Legal, page 191**

Headway Recruitment Specialists Ltd

Head Office ✉ 113–117 Wardour St, W1V 3TD
             ⊖ Oxford Circus
             🚊 Charing Cross
             ✆ T 020 7494 0448   F 020 7494 0321
             @ info@headwayrecruitment.com
Market areas HR, Financial, Secretarial

Website www.headwayrecruitment.com

UK Offices 1

REC Member Yes

Brief Description Headway is a young and innovative recruitment agency dealing in the following sectors: HR, Financial and Secretarial Support staff.

Preferred method of contact Telephone for appointment

Minimum requirements None

Type of business Temporary and Permanent

Grade/Level of Appointments All levels

Hendersons Recruitment

Head Office ✉ 20–21 Jockey's Fields, WC1R 4BW
             ⊖ Chancery Lane
             🚊 City Thameslink
             ✆ T 020 7864 6290   F 020 7864 6291
             @ jobs@hendersons-recruitment.co.uk
Market areas Secretarial

Website www.hendersons-recruitment.co.uk

UK Offices 1

REC Member Yes

Brief Description Since 1960, Hendersons Recruitment has been placing temporary, permanent and contract staff into both commercial and non-commercial organisations and has developed a reputation for providing a professional and personal service to both clients and candidates. Their clients cover a broad range of industries including the Luxury Goods market, Fashion, Design, Museums and Galleries as well as HR, Charities, Medical Colleges and blue chip companies. All of their positions are based in Central London.

Preferred method of contact Apply on line or telephone for an appointment

Minimum requirements None

Type of business Temporary, Permanent and Contract

Grade/Level of Appointments Junior to PA/Managerial

Hillman Saunders

See **Financial Services and Insurance, page 123**

Hodge Recruitment Consultants

Head Office   ✉ 22 Henrietta St, WC2E 8ND
              ⊖ Covent Garden
              🚊 Charing Cross
              ☎ **T** 020 7420 3950   **F** 020 7379 8030
              @ eng@hodge.co.uk
Market areas   Secretarial

Website www.hodge.co.uk

UK Offices 1

REC Member Yes

Brief Description Hodge Recruitment was established over 21 years ago, and specialises in finding permanent and temporary positions for all levels of Secretarial work including: Personal and Executive Assistants, Office Managers, HR personnel, Marketing personnel, Sales Administrators, Receptionists and General Administration staff.

Preferred method of contact Apply on line or telephone for an appointment

Minimum requirements None

Type of business Temporary and Permanent

Grade/Level of Appointments Junior to PA/Managerial

Hollis Personnel Ltd

Head Office   ✉ 258 Linen Hall, 162–168 Regent St, W1R 5TB
              ⊖ Piccadilly Circus
              🚊 Charing Cross
              ☎ **T** 020 7434 4389   **F** 020 7434 4112

              @ hollispersonnel@aol.com
Market areas   Secretarial, Sales, Logistics

Website www.hollispersonnel.co.uk

UK Offices 1

REC Member No

Brief Description Established in 1997, Hollis Personnel are an independent recruitment consultancy specialising in Secretarial, Sales, Logistics, Marketing, Accounts and General Administration positions.

Preferred method of contact Telephone for appointment

Minimum requirements None

Type of business Permanent

Grade/Level of Appointments All levels

Hudson York Farrell

Head Office   ✉ Broad St House, 55 Old Broad St, EC2M 1RX
              ⊖ Liverpool St
              🚊 Liverpool St
              ☎ **T** 020 7638 0303   **F** 020 7638 4300
              @ info@hyf.co.uk
Market areas   Secretarial, Facilities, Procurement

Website www.hyf.co.uk

UK Offices 1

REC Member No

Brief Description Established in 1994, Hudson York Farrell is an independent consultancy situated in the heart of the City of London. They provide specialist recruitment services to the Financial sector covering a wide range of disciplines with both temporary and permanent staff.

Preferred method of contact Apply on line or telephone for an appointment

Minimum requirements None

Type of business Temporary and Permanent

Grade/Level of Appointments All levels

Irene Anderson Associates

See **Media, page 199**

JAC

See **Bilingual, page 41**

JFL

See **Media, page 199**

JHA Recruitment

Head Office ✉ 37–39 Eastcheap, EC3M 1DP
⊖ Bank
🚊 Cannon St
☎ T 020 7621 1269   F 020 7626 2262
@ mail@jha-recruitment.co.uk
Market areas   Secretarial

Website www.jha-recruitment.co.uk
UK Offices 1
REC Member No

Brief Description Established for over 14 years, JHA have gained a solid reputation in recruitment for understanding their clients' business and culture and placing candidates in sought after positions in major blue chip organisations in and around London.

Preferred method of contact Apply on line or telephone for an appointment

Minimum requirements None

Type of business Temporary and Permanent

Grade/Level of Appointments All levels

JHW Ltd

See **Accountancy and Banking, page 18**

Jigsaw Recruitment

Head Office ✉ 17 Red Lion Sq, WC1R 4QH
⊖ Holborn
🚊 City Thameslink
☎ T 020 7831 2496   F 020 7831 3080
@ jobs@jigsawrecruitment.co.uk
Market areas   Secretarial

Website www.jigsawrecruitment.co.uk
UK Offices 1
REC Member Yes

Brief Description Established in 1986, Jigsaw Recruitment specialise in the Secretarial market throughout London.

Preferred method of contact Apply on line or telephone for an appointment

Minimum requirements None

Type of business Temporary and Permanent

Grade/Level of Appointments All levels

JM Legal Ltd

Head Office ✉ Ground Floor, Totara Park House, 34–36 Grays Inn Rd, WC1X 8HR
⊖ Chancery Lane

🚊 City Thameslink
☎ T 020 7430 2408   F 020 7430 2432
@ recruitment@jmlegal.co.uk
Market areas   Legal, Secretarial, IT

Website www.jmlegal.co.uk
UK Offices 1
REC Member No

Brief Description JM Legal are regarded as one of the leading Secretarial, Support and IT recruitment consultants to the Legal profession. Based in the heart of London with over 25 years experience, their client base numbers the vast majority of leading international and national practices along with the smaller practice and Legal departments of 'quoted' organisations and many blue chip companies.

Preferred method of contact Apply on line or telephone for an appointment

Minimum requirements None

Type of business Temporary and Permanent

Grade/Level of Appointments All levels

Josephine Sammons Ltd

Head Office ✉ 46 Fish St Hill, EC3R 6BR
⊖ Monument
🚊 Cannon St
☎ T 020 7293 7000   F 020 7626 5759
Market areas   Secretarial

Website www.sammons.co.uk
UK Offices 1
REC Member No

Brief Description Part of the Sammons Group, Josephine Sammons provides the highest quality employment service for organisations needing permanent, contract or temporary Secretarial, Clerical and General Office staff. Their consultants are leading providers for companies in all Industrial and Commercial sectors, Central and Local Government organisations, Trade Unions and Professional Bodies, and Charities.

Preferred method of contact Apply on line or telephone for an appointment

Minimum requirements None

Type of business Temporary, Permanent and Contract

Grade/Level of Appointments All levels

Joyce Guiness Partnership

Head Office ✉ Suite 102 Collier House, 163–169 Brompton Rd, SW3 1PY
⊖ South Kensington
🚊 Victoria
☎ T 020 7589 8807   F 020 7584 3520

@ perm@joyceguiness.co.uk, temp@joyceguiness.co.uk

Market areas Communications, PR, Marketing, Finance, Property, Secretarial

Website www.joyceguiness.co.uk

UK Offices 1

REC Member No

Brief Description Established for over 30 years, Joyce Guiness has celebrated countless successful appointments with the foremost companies in London and Europe, many of them marking the start of long term and rewarding relationships. They commit to taking the time to get to know candidates rather than simply matching CVs to vacancies. They can also help candidates wanting to travel and work in Australia, through their affiliation with Kinsman Reynolds Consulting, a Sydney based recruitment agency.

Preferred method of contact Apply on line or telephone for an appointment

Minimum requirements None

Type of business Temporary and Permanent

Grade/Level of Appointments All levels

Judy Fisher Associates

Head Office ✉ 7 Swallow St, W1B 4DE
⊖ Piccadilly Circus
🚇 Charing Cross
☎ T 020 7437 2277   F 020 7434 2696

Market areas Media, Secretarial

Website www.judyfisher.co.uk

UK Offices 1

REC Member No

Brief Description Established in 1986, Judy Fisher Associates is one of London's leading Media recruitment consultancies. Effectively and efficiently managing their clients' recruitment needs, they are dedicated to finding accomplished temporary and permanent Administrative staff for the Media industry.

Preferred method of contact Apply on line or telephone for an appointment

Minimum requirements None

Type of business Temporary and Permanent

Grade/Level of Appointments Receptionists to Executive Assistants

Julia Ross

Head Office ✉ Walter House, 418–422 Strand, WC2R 0PT
⊖ Charing Cross
🚇 Charing Cross
☎ T 020 7836 5666   F 020 7836 5566

Market areas Secretarial, Industrial, Accounting, IT, Finance

Website www.juliaross.com.au

UK Offices 1

REC Member No

Brief Description Established in London for over 5 years, Julia Ross is an acknowledged market leader in the provision of Office Support, Call Centre and Industrial staff.

Preferred method of contact Apply on line or telephone for an appointment

Minimum requirements None

Type of business Temporary and Permanent

Grade/Level of Appointments All levels

Kelly Scientific Resources

✉ 1st Floor, 82–83 Strand, WC2R 0DW
⊖ Charing Cross
🚇 Charing Cross
☎ T 020 7836 7598   F 020 7836 7973
@ ksr.london@kellyservices.co.uk

Market areas Secretarial, Industrial

Website www.kellyservices.co.uk

UK Offices 100+

REC Member Yes

Head Office Apple Market House, 17 Union St, Kingston Upon Thames, Surrey, KT1 1RR

Brief Description Established in Detroit, USA, in 1946, Kelly Services is one of the world's largest recruitment and human resource specialists with a global network spanning more than 25 countries and a turnover in excess of £4.5 billion per year. With 900 staff in over 100 High Street locations across the UK, Kelly Services places 10,000 people in permanent work every year and more than 21,000 people in temporary placements every week.

Preferred method of contact Apply on line or telephone for an appointment

Minimum requirements None

Type of business Temporary, Permanent and Contract

Grade/Level of Appointments All levels

Kelly Services

✉ 49 Oxford St, W1R 1RD
⊖ Tottenham Court Rd
🚇 Euston
☎ T 020 7494 1133   F 020 7287 1646
@ 49oxfordstreet@kellyservices.co.uk

Market areas Secretarial, Industrial

✉ 82–83 Strand, WC2R 0DW
⊖ Charing Cross
🚇 Charing Cross
☎ T 020 7836 3856   F 020 7497 0495
@ strandbranch@kellyservices.co.uk

Market areas Secretarial, Industrial

✉ 411 Oxford St, W1R 1FG
⊖ Marble Arch
🚊 Paddington
☎ T 020 7495 1320   F 020 7495 3528
@ 411oxfordstreet@kellyservices.co.uk
Market areas Secretarial, Industrial

✉ 163 New Bond St, W1S 2UQ
⊖ Bond St
🚊 Paddington
☎ T 020 7493 3051   F 020 7495 3527
@ mayfairbranch@kellyservices.co.uk
Market areas Secretarial, Industrial

✉ 12 Kensington Church St, W8 4EP
⊖ Notting Hill Gate
🚊 Paddington
☎ T 020 7376 1300   F 020 7376 1311
@ kensingtonbranch@kellyservices.co.uk
Market areas Secretarial, Industrial

✉ 275 Holborn, WC1V 7EE
⊖ Chancery Lane
🚊 City Thameslink
☎ T 020 7242 1832   F 020 7430 1318
@ holbornbranch@kellyservices.co.uk
Market areas Secretarial, Industrial

✉ 108 Fenchurch St, EC3M 5JR
⊖ Tower Hill
🚊 Fenchurch St
☎ T 020 7480 6367   F 020 7488 1583
@ fenchurchstreet@kellyservices.co.uk
Market areas Secretarial, Industrial

✉ West India House, 30 Marsh Wall, E14 9TP
⊖ South Quay
🚊 Limehouse
☎ T 020 7512 0220   F 020 7512 0240
@ dockinst@kellyservices.co.uk
Market areas Secretarial, Industrial

✉ 128–140 Bishopsgate, EC2M 4HX
⊖ Liverpool St
🚊 Liverpool St
☎ T 020 7377 9898   F 020 7247 9849
@ bishopsgatebranch@kellyservices.co.uk
Market areas Secretarial, Industrial

Website www.kellyservices.co.uk

UK Offices 100+

REC Member Yes

Head Office Apple Market House, 17 Union St, Kingston Upon Thames, Surrey, KT1 1RR

Brief Description Established in Detroit, USA, in 1946, Kelly Services is one of the world's largest recruitment and human resource specialists with a global network spanning more than 25 countries and a turnover in excess of £4.5 billion per year. With 900 staff in over 100 High Street locations across the UK, Kelly Services places 10,000 people in permanent work every year and more than 21,000 people in temporary placements every week.

Preferred method of contact Apply on line or telephone for an appointment

Minimum requirements None

Type of business Temporary, Permanent and Contract

Grade/Level of Appointments All levels

Keystone Employment Group – Secretarial & Office

Head Office ✉ 272–276 Pentonville Rd, N1 9JY
⊖ Kings Cross
🚊 Kings Cross
☎ T 020 7833 7788   F 020 7833 7783
Market areas Secretarial

Website www.keystone-recruitment.co.uk

UK Offices 4

REC Member Yes

Brief Description Keystone was originally formed in London in 1948. It was one of the first and largest privately owned employment agencies placing Secretarial and General Office staff. Their greatest assets are the people who work for them, they are the reason why clients and candidates are recommended to use the Keystone Group services – it is their ability to listen and understand people's needs, to work in partnership with them to achieve success, and more importantly client and candidate satisfaction.

Preferred method of contact Apply on line or telephone for an appointment

Minimum requirements None

Type of business Temporary and Permanent

Grade/Level of Appointments All levels

King & Toben

Head Office ✉ Foxglove House, 166 Piccadilly, W1J 9EF
⊖ Piccadilly Circus
🚊 Charing Cross
☎ T 020 7629 9648   F 020 7408 0579
@ team@kandt.co.uk
Market areas Secretarial

Website www.kandt.co.uk

UK Offices 1

REC Member No

Brief Description Established in 1988, King & Toben pride themselves on providing London businesses with a truly professional and personal recruitment consultancy.

Preferred method of contact Apply on line or telephone for an appointment

Minimum requirements None

Type of business Temporary and Permanent

Grade/Level of Appointments Junior to PA/Managerial

Knightsbridge Secretaries

Head Office   132–135 Sloane St, SW1X 9AX
 Sloane Sq
 Victoria
 T 020 7468 0400   **F** 020 7468 0009
 @ mail@knightsbridgesecretaries.co.uk
Market areas Secretarial

Website www.knightsbridgesecretaries.co.uk
UK Offices 1
REC Member No

Brief Description Knightsbridge Secretaries have a reputation for providing challenging, high profile, unusual and well paid jobs. Their clients cover a range of sectors from Advertising, Art Galleries and Auction Houses to Management Consultancies and PR. Specialist divisions include Business Assistants, Languages, Receptionists and Part Time.

Preferred method of contact Apply on line or telephone for an appointment

Minimum requirements None

Type of business Temporary and Permanent

Grade/Level of Appointments College Leavers to Executive Pas

KP Publishing Personnel

See **Media, page 199**

Lancaster Associates

Head Office   65 London Wall, EC2M 5TU
 Moorgate
 Moorgate
 T 020 7628 6971   **F** 020 7628 0497
 @ info@lancasterassociates.co.uk
Market areas Secretarial

Website www.lancasterassociates.co.uk
UK Offices 1
REC Member Yes

Brief Description Established in 1985, Lancaster Associates is an efficient recruitment practice servicing the permanent and temporary Support staffing needs of London based organisations within the Banking and Finance sectors.

Preferred method of contact Apply on line or telephone for an appointment

Minimum requirements Ideally relevant office exposure

Type of business Permanent, Temporary and Contract

Grade/Level of Appointments Accounts Clerk/Portfolio Administrator to Group PA

The Language Business

See **Bilingual, page 41**

Language Matters

See **Bilingual, page 42**

Language Recruitment Services Ltd

See **Bilingual, page 42**

Law Choice Recruitment Ltd

Head Office   Hanging Sword House, 21 Whitefriars St, EC4Y 8JJ
 Blackfriars
 Blackfriars
 T 020 7379 0550   **F** 020 7583 2906
 @ mike@law-choice.com
Market areas Legal Secretarial, Legal Support

Website www.law-choice.com
UK Offices 4
REC Member Yes

Brief Description With offices in London, Leeds, Birmingham and Manchester, Law Choice specialise in the supply of permanent, temporary and contract staff to UK, international and US Law firms ranging from Legal Cashiers, Support staff to Legal Secretaries and Account Managers.

Preferred method of contact Apply on line or telephone for appointment

Minimum requirements Relevant legal exposure

Type of business Temporary, Permanent and Contract

Grade/Level of Appointments Junior to Management level

Law Support Services Ltd

Head Office ✉ 240 High Holborn, WC1V 7DN
 Holborn
 City Thameslink
 T 020 7405 7397   **F** 020 7831 2051
 @ christina@lawsupportservices.co.uk
Market areas Legal Secretarial, Legal Support

Website www.lawsupportservices.co.uk
UK Offices 1

REC Member No

Brief Description Law Support Services was established in 1968 in response to a need for an agency with the knowledge and resources to meet the specific demands of Law firms. The aim of the group is to supply a specialist tailored service to the Legal profession under their three specialist divisions: Law Temps, Law Staff and Law Secretaries.

Preferred method of contact Apply on line or telephone for appointment

Minimum requirements Ideally relevant legal exposure

Type of business Temporary and Permanent

Grade/Level of Appointments Juniors to Office Managers

Lawrence Allison Group

Head Office   ✉   20 Eastbourne Terrace, W2 6LE
  ⊖   Paddington
  🚃   Paddington
  ☎   T 020 7957 4344   F 020 7957 4333
  @   info@lawrenceallison.com
Market areas   IT, Secretarial, Accountancy, Sales and Marketing

Website www.lawrenceallison.com

UK Offices 5

REC Member Yes

Brief Description Lawrence Allison has a proven track record in supplying professional recruitment services to industry for over 25 years. It has recently expanded its operations to include a specialist IT recruitment operation, Commercial sector dealing with Secretarial and Support staff, as well as Accountancy and Sales and Marketing.

Preferred method of contact Apply on line or telephone for appointment

Minimum requirements None

Type of business Temporary and Permanent

Grade/Level of Appointments Customer Service/Accounts Clerk to Account Manager/Project Manager

Lawson Clark

Head Office   ✉   Bell Ct House, 11 Blomfield St, EC2M 7AY
  ⊖   Liverpool St
  🚃   Liverpool St
  ☎   T 020 7256 6666   F 020 7256 2266
  @   admin@lawson-clark.co.uk
Market areas   Legal Secretarial, Legal Support

Website www.lawson-clark.co.uk

UK Offices 1

REC Member No

Brief Description Established in 1993, Lawson Clark specialises in the recruitment of Legal Secretaries and Support staff. They have built a reputation for the breadth of their client list and the sheer variety of

openings they can offer, with clients who range from the world's top Law firms to London's sole practitioners.

Preferred method of contact Telephone for appointment

Minimum requirements Ideally relevant legal exposure

Type of business Temporary, Permanent and Contract

Grade/Level of Appointments Accounts Clerk/Legal Cashier to PA

Learned Friends Group

  ✉   6th Floor, 72 Cannon St, EC4N 6AE
  ⊖   Cannon St
  🚃   Cannon St
  ☎   T 020 7248 6180   F 020 7248 5415
  @   recruitment@learnedfriends.co.uk
Market areas   Legal, Legal Secretarial, Legal Support

Website www.learnedfriends.com

UK Offices 1

REC Member Yes

Head Office Australia

Brief Description Established in 1984, Learned Friends assist clients with great staff and candidates to find great jobs. The Learned Friends Group is the premier legal recruitment consultancy in Australia, with offices in Sydney, Melbourne, London and Hong Kong and affiliates worldwide. They provide a professional, reliable and friendly service to both their candidates and clients and pride themselves on being at the forefront of their profession.

Preferred method of contact Apply on line or telephone for an appointment

Minimum requirements Ideally relevant legal exposure

Type of business Temporary, Permanent and Contract

Grade/Level of Appointments Accounts Clerk/Receptionist to Paralegal/Solicitor

Leopards Employment

Head Office   ✉   250 Kilburn High Rd, NW6 2BS
  ⊖   Kilburn
  🚃   West Hampstead
  ☎   T 020 7624 0777   F 020 7372 8376
  @   leopardgm@yahoo.co.uk
Market areas   Secretarial, Industrial, Catering, IT, Domestic, Sales and Marketing

Website www.leopardgm.co.uk

UK Offices 1

REC Member No

Brief Description Established in 1989, Leopards Employment specialise in providing temporary and permanent professionals to various industry sectors for clients across London.

Preferred method of contact Apply on line or telephone for an appointment

Minimum requirements None

Type of business Temporary and Permanent

Grade/Level of Appointments Graduate/1st Jobber to Management level

Lifeline Personnel

Head Office ✉ 122 Great Portland St, W1W 6LN
⊖ Great Portland St
🚇 Euston
✆ T 020 7637 3737   F 020 7637 7337
@ lifeline@lifeline-personnel.com
Market areas Healthcare, Charity, Secretarial

Website www.lifeline-personnel.com

UK Offices 1

REC Member Yes

Brief Description Lifeline Personnel provides top quality temporary and permanent Office staff to the Healthcare and Charitable sectors. Established by a renowned hospital in 1989, Lifeline quickly emerged as an independent company and has evolved into a highly successful quality driven organisation, having won several prestigious contracts to supply substantial NHS Trusts.

Preferred method of contact Apply on line or telephone for an appointment

Minimum requirements None

Type of business Temporary and Permanent

Grade/Level of Appointments Administrators to Charity Managers

Lindsey Morgan Associates

Head Office ✉ Prince Rupert House, 64 Queen St, EC4R 1AD
⊖ Mansion House
🚇 Cannon St
✆ T 020 7236 4999   F 020 7236 5999
@ progress@lmassoc.com
Market areas Secretarial, Accountancy

Website www.lmassoc.com

UK Offices 1

REC Member No

Brief Description Lindsey Morgan Associates place permanent and temporary staff in Accountancy, Operations and Secretarial roles at all levels, from Junior Clerks to Senior Managers.

Preferred method of contact Apply on line or telephone for an appointment

Minimum requirements None

Type of business Permanent and Temporary

Grade/Level of Appointments Accounts Clerks/VDU Operators to Credit Managers/Senior Managers

Lipson Lloyd-Jones

See Legal, page 192

Lipton Fleming Appointments Ltd

See Media, page 200

LJC Banking

See Accountancy and Banking, page 19

Maine-Tucker Recruitment

Head Office ✉ 18–21 Jermyn St, SW1Y 6HP
⊖ Piccadilly Circus
🚇 Charing Cross
✆ T 020 7734 7341   F 020 7734 3260
@ info@maine-tucker.co.uk
Market areas Secretarial, Legal Secretarial

Website www.maine-tucker.co.uk

UK Offices 1

REC Member No

Brief Description Maine-Tucker Recruitment was established in 1987 to specialise in recruiting high calibre Secretarial and Administrative Support staff into companies based mainly in and around London. The firm is now widely recognised as one of London's leading recruitment companies with consultant teams specialising in temporary and permanent recruitment for the West End, the City and Canary Wharf. MTR Legal meanwhile, is a specialist division which concentrates on recruiting Legal Secretarial, Marketing and Administrative Support staff into London's Law firms.

Preferred method of contact Apply on line or telephone for an appointment

Minimum requirements None

Type of business Temporary, Permanent and Contract

Grade/Level of Appointments Graduate/Office Junior to Team Secretary/PA

Management Prospects

See Not for Profit , page 209

Manpower

Head Office ✉ International House, 66 Chiltern St, W1M 4JT
✆ T 020 7224 6688   F 020 7224 5267
✉ 7 Butler Place, SW1H 0QD
⊖ Victoria

🚇 Victoria
☎ T 020 7222 4554   F 020 7233 4232
@ victoria.branch.manager@manpower.co.uk
Market areas Secretarial, Industrial, IT, Technical

✉ 1 Pudding Lane, EC3R 8AB
⊖ Monument
🚇 Cannon St
☎ T 020 7929 5284   F 020 7283 7727
@ pudding.lane.branch.manager@manpower.co.uk
Market areas Secretarial, Industrial, IT, Technical

✉ 1 Harewood Place, W1S 1BU
⊖ Oxford Circus
🚇 Charing Cross
☎ T 020 7493 8668   F 020 7629 1029
@ oxford.street.branch.manager@manpower.co.uk
Market areas Secretarial, Industrial, IT, Technical

✉ 46 Moorgate, EC2R 6EH
⊖ Moorgate
🚇 Moorgate
☎ T 020 7628 4134   F 020 7628 8758
@ moorgate.branch.manager@manpower.co.uk
Market areas Secretarial, Industrial, IT, Technical

✉ 13–15 Brompton Rd, SW3 1ED
⊖ Knightsbridge
🚇 Victoria
☎ T 020 7589 2446   F 020 7584 9244
@ knightsbridgebranchmanager@manpower.co.uk
Market areas Secretarial, Industrial, IT, Technical

✉ 52 High Holborn, WC1V 6RL
⊖ Chancery Lane
🚇 City Thameslink
☎ T 020 7831 6868   F 020 7404 1351
@ holborn.branch.manager@manpower.co.uk
Market areas Secretarial, Industrial, IT, Technical

✉ 8 Hammersmith Broadway, W6 7AL
⊖ Hammersmith
🚇 Kensington (Olympia)
☎ T 020 7741 1192   F 020 7748 4387
@ hammersmith.branch.manager@manpower.co.uk
Market areas Secretarial, Industrial, IT, Technical

✉ 78 Fenchurch St, EC3M 4BT
⊖ Monument
🚇 Cannon St
☎ T 020 7481 1455   F 020 7481 4166
@ fenchurchstreet.branch.manager@manpower.co.uk
Market areas Secretarial, Industrial, IT, Technical

✉ Unit 2, South Quay, Marsh Wall, E14 9SH
⊖ South Quay
🚇 Limehouse
☎ T 020 7987 6944   F 020 7628 8758
@ london.docklands@manpower.co.uk
Market areas Secretarial, Industrial, IT, Technical

Website www.manpower.co.uk

UK Offices 300+

REC Member Yes

Brief Description Part of Manpower Inc, Manpower is a leading recruiter of specialist, flexible and contract workforces and a respected authority in employment. They employ over 100,000 people each year, through a network of over 300 UK offices, making it easy for people to find interesting and flexible employment opportunities and for companies to recruit staff with the skills and experience they need.

Preferred method of contact Apply on line or telephone for an appointment

Minimum requirements None

Type of business Temporary, Permanent and Contract

Grade/Level of Appointments All levels

Masterlock

Head Office ✉ McMillan House, 96 Kensington High St, W8 4SG
⊖ High St Kensington
🚇 Kensington (Olympia)
☎ T 020 7938 1718   F 020 7937 3164
@ westend@masterlock.co.uk
Market areas Secretarial, Teaching, Support Staff

Website www.masterlock.co.uk

UK Offices 3

REC Member Yes

Brief Description Masterlock Recruitment was established in 1983 and is a specialist division supplying Secretarial and Support staff throughout London and the M25 ring. Masterlock Education was established in Kensington in 1993 to provide Teaching and Non-teaching staff to schools throughout the London area, and since then have opened additional offices in St Albans and Bristol.

Preferred method of contact Apply on line or telephone for an appointment

Minimum requirements None

Type of business Temporary, Permanent and Contract

Grade/Level of Appointments All levels

Milkround

See **Graduates, page 128**

Mison Recruitment

Head Office ✉ St Bartholomew House, 92 Fleet St, EC4Y 1DH
⊖ Blackfriars
🚇 Blackfriars
☎ T 020 7583 4749   F 020 7353 6443
@ office@misonrecruitment.co.uk
Market areas Secretarial

Website www.misonrecruitment.co.uk

UK Offices 1

REC Member Yes

Brief Description Mison Recruitment specialises in placing temporary, permanent and contract staff ranging from Graduates/ 2nd Jobbers to PAs in a variety of Banking and Financial clients across the London market.

Preferred method of contact Apply on line or telephone for an appointment

Minimum requirements None

Type of business Temporary, Permanent and Contract

Grade/Level of Appointments Reception/Administration to Director PA

Mitchell Young

Head Office ✉ 25 Wormwood St, EC2M 1RP
⊖ Liverpool St
🚇 Liverpool St
☎ T 020 7588 3055   F 020 7588 3066
@ enquiries@mitchellyoung.co.uk
Market areas Secretarial

Website www.mitchellyoung.co.uk

UK Offices 1

REC Member Yes

Brief Description Mitchell Young Associates specialises in the recruitment of Executive Secretaries and PAs into permanent jobs, principally from Director to Chairman/Chief Executive level. In addition to this top level, they have successfully expanded into the recruitment of Secretaries who may not yet be quite so advanced in their career.

Preferred method of contact Apply on line or telephone for an appointment

Minimum requirements Ideally secretarial exposure

Type of business Permanent

Grade/Level of Appointments Secretaries to PA/Executive Secretary

Monument Recruitment

Head Office ✉ Forum House, 15–18 Lime St, EC3M 7AP
⊖ Bank
🚇 Cannon St
☎ T 020 7929 1281   F 020 7621 0985
@ enquiries@monumentrecruitment.co.uk
Market areas Secretarial, Banking, Fund Management, Human Resources

Website www.monumentrecruitment.co.uk

UK Offices 1

REC Member No

Brief Description Monument Recruitment has been established since 1980 and successfully recruits both permanent and contract staff within the Financial sector's most prestigious and high profile organisations.

Preferred method of contact Apply on line or telephone for an appointment

Minimum requirements None

Type of business Temporary and Permanent

Grade/Level of Appointments Administrators to Technical Banking and Fund Management

Mortgage Recruitment

See Financial Services and Insurance, page 125

Newman Personnel

Head Office ✉ 100 New Bridge St, EC4V 6JJ
⊖ Blackfriars
🚇 Blackfriars
☎ T 020 7489 0111   F 020 7248 4747
@ admin@newmanpersonnel.co.uk
Market areas Secretarial

✉ 123 Houndsditch, EC3A 7BU
⊖ Aldgate
🚇 Liverpool St
☎ T 020 7929 1263   F 020 7623 6165
@ admin@newmanpersonnel.co.uk
Market areas Secretarial

Website www.newmanpersonnel.co.uk

UK Offices 2

REC Member No

Brief Description Established in 1983, Newman Personnel is a privately owned recruitment consultancy group, specialising in both temporary and permanent staff in the City and West End areas of London.

Preferred method of contact Telephone for appointment

Minimum requirements None

Type of business Temporary and Permanent

Grade/Level of Appointments All levels

next4GRADS

See Graduates, page 128

Nice People Employment Bureau

Head Office ✉ 1–3 Leadenhall Market, EC3V 1LR
⊖ Bank

🚊 Cannon St
☎ T 020 7626 8886   F 020 7626 8887
@ nicepeople@btconnect.com
Market areas   Secretarial

Website www.nice-people-empl.com

UK Offices 1

REC Member No

Brief Description Nice People Employment Bureau is a small privately owned recruitment bureau, formed in 1990, and located in the heart of the City of London. Their objective is to provide Secretarial and Administrative Support for the professional companies within the boundaries of the City.

Preferred method of contact Apply on line or telephone for an appointment

Minimum requirements None

Type of business Temporary

Grade/Level of Appointments All levels

Nicholas Andrews & Temps Financial

See Accountancy and Banking, page 21

Norma Skemp Recruitment Ltd

Head Office ✉ 65 New Bond St, W1S 1RN
⊖ Bond St
🚊 Paddington
☎ T 020 7491 0707   F 020 7491 1121
@ info@normaskemp-recruitment.co.uk
Market areas   Secretarial

Website www.normaskemp-recruitment.co.uk

UK Offices 1

REC Member Yes

Brief Description For over 50 years the consultants at Norma Skemp Recruitment have upheld an enviable reputation. They are acknowledged for their individuality, honesty and the unique service that lies at the very heart of their consultancy. The company is privately owned and this makes an enormous impact on the performance of the team in general. The consultants take a pride in their work and are committed to finding tailor-made solutions to your recruitment needs.

Preferred method of contact Apply on line or telephone for an appointment

Minimum requirements None

Type of business Temporary and Permanent

Grade/Level of Appointments College Leavers to Executive Pas

Office Angels

Head Office ✉ 96–98 King St, W6 0QW
☎ T 020 8741 8080   F 020 8741 9212

✉ 71–75 Buckingham Palace Rd, SW1W 0QU
⊖ Victoria
🚊 Victoria
☎ T 020 7630 0844   F 020 7828 9387
@ victoria@office-angels.com
Market areas   Secretarial

✉ 25 Oxford St, W1R 1RF
⊖ Tottenham Court Rd
🚊 Euston
☎ T 020 7434 9545   F 020 7494 2668
@ oxfordstreet@office-angels.com
Market areas   Secretarial

✉ 76–78 Mortimer St, W1N 7DE
⊖ Oxford Circus
🚊 Charing Cross
☎ T 020 7580 0777   F 020 7436 7241
@ oxfordcircus@office-angels.com
Market areas   Secretarial

✉ 20 Moorfields High Walk, EC2Y 9DP
⊖ Moorgate
🚊 Moorgate
☎ T 020 7638 0055   F 020 7920 9280
@ moorgate@office-angels.com
Market areas   Secretarial

✉ Hays Galleria, 56 Tooley St, SE1 2QN
⊖ London Bridge
🚊 London Bridge
☎ T 020 7403 2424   F 020 7403 8977
@ londonbridge@office-angels.com
Market areas   Secretarial

✉ 115 High Holborn, WC1V 6JJ
⊖ Holborn
🚊 City Thameslink
☎ T 020 7430 2531   F 020 7831 6544
@ holborn@office-angels.com
Market areas   Secretarial

✉ Ground Floor East, 40 Marsh Wall, E14 9TP
⊖ South Quay
🚊 Limehouse
☎ T 020 7512 2333   F 020 7512 2193
@ docklands@office-angels.com
Market areas   Secretarial

✉ 12 Groveland Ct, EC4M 9EH
⊖ Mansion House
🚊 Cannon St
☎ T 020 7606 0011   F 020 7489 9282
@ bowlane@office-angels.com
Market areas   Secretarial

✉ 67–69 George St, W1H 5PJ
⊖ Baker St

🚇 Marylebone
☎ T 020 7935 7248   F 020 7487 5352
@ bakerstreet@office-angels.com
Market areas Secretarial

Website www.officeangels.co.uk
UK Offices 59
REC Member No

Brief Description Office Angels is the UK's leading Secretarial and Office Support recruitment consultancy. Established in 1986, Office Angels have expanded to 59 branches across the country, employing over 550 people. They supply temporary and permanent staff to tens of thousands of prestigious UK companies and have an annual turnover in excess of £125 million. Within the past 14 years, Office Angels has established itself as a major force in the personnel and recruitment industry.

Preferred method of contact Apply on line or telephone for an appointment

Minimum requirements None

Type of business Temporary and Permanent

Grade/Level of Appointments All levels

Office Team

Head Office ✉ Rex House, 10 Regent St, SW1Y 4PE
🚇 Piccadilly Circus
🚆 Charing Cross
☎ T 020 7389 6900   F 020 7389 6999
@ westend@officeteam.com
Market areas Secretarial

✉ 10–11 Austin Friars, EC2P 2JD
🚇 Bank
🚆 Cannon St
☎ T 020 7562 6500   F 020 7588 2959
@ city@officeteamuk.com
Market areas Secretarial

Website www.officeteam.net
UK Offices 18
REC Member Yes

Brief Description Office Team in the United Kingdom is the specialist for all administrative recruitment needs. Specialisation and a rigorous selection procedure, designed to meet specific needs through a dynamic but ever flexible approach, have made them the name of reference — and the world leader — in the field of administrative recruitment. Office Team is a Robert Half International Company.

Preferred method of contact Apply on line or telephone for an appointment

Minimum requirements None

Type of business Temporary and Permanent

Grade/Level of Appointments All levels

Opus Personnel Ltd

Head Office ✉ 106 Baker St, W1U 6TW
🚇 Baker St
🚇 Marylebone
☎ T 020 7486 7921   F 020 7486 2111
@ jobs@opuspersonnel.co.uk
Market areas Secretarial, Legal Secretarial

✉ 154 Bishopsgate, EC2M 4LN
🚇 Liverpool St
🚆 Liverpool St
☎ T 020 7247 6111   F 020 7375 3060
@ jobs@opuspersonnel.co.uk
Market areas Secretarial, Legal Secretarial

Website www.opuspersonnel.co.uk
UK Offices 2
REC Member Yes

Brief Description Opus Personnel was founded in 1976 by Valerie Selman, who remains at the helm today. Opus concentrate on the whole spectrum of Office personnel with an emphasis on Secretarial staff. Opus has steadily grown to include a dedicated Legal division, in addition to their busy temporary and permanent Commercial teams. Central to the policy of Opus Personnel has always been its excellence of service to both client and candidate.

Preferred method of contact Apply on line or telephone for an appointment

Minimum requirements None

Type of business Temporary and Permanent

Grade/Level of Appointments All levels

Parkway Recruitment

Head Office ✉ Warwick House, 25–27 Buckingham Palace Rd, SW1W 0PP
🚇 Victoria
🚆 Victoria
☎ T 020 7828 3838   F 020 7828 3888
@ info@parkwayrecruit.com
Market areas Secretarial

Website www.parkwayrecruit.co.uk
UK Offices 1
REC Member No

Brief Description Formerly known as Harriet Gabb Recruitment, Parkway Recruitment specialise in the recruitment of temporary and permanent Office staff from Junior to Management level.

Preferred method of contact Apply on line or telephone for an appointment

Minimum requirements None

Type of business Temporary and Permanent

Grade/Level of Appointments Junior to PA/Managerial

Part-time Prospects

See Not for Profit , page 209

Pathfinders Media Recruitment

See Media, page 201

People First Recruitment Ltd

See Bilingual, page 42

Permanent Prospects

See Not for Profit , page 209

Perry Clayman Employment Agency Ltd

Head Office ✉ 31–33 High Holborn, WC1V 6AX
⊖ Chancery Lane
🚊 City Thameslink
☎ T 020 7831 7622   F 020 7831 4664
@ jobs@pclayman.com

Market areas Secretarial, Legal Secretarial, Accounts, IT, Shipping, Patents

Website www.pclayman.com

UK Offices 1

REC Member Yes

Brief Description Perry Clayman pride themselves on offering a complete recruitment service, with specialised expertise and knowledge in each of the following key areas for supplying permanent and temporary Staff: Patents and Trademarks, Shipping, Secretarial, Legal Secretarial, Accountancy, IT.

Preferred method of contact Apply on line or telephone for an appointment

Minimum requirements None

Type of business Temporary and Permanent

Grade/Level of Appointments All levels

Premiere People

Head Office ✉ 219 Kensington High St, W8 6BD
⊖ High St Kensington
🚊 Kensington (Olympia)
☎ T 020 7937 9026

@ enquiries@premierepeople.com

Market areas Healthcare, Industrial, Engineering, Sales and Marketing, Customer Services, Secretarial

Website www.premierepeople.com

UK Offices 1

REC Member No

Brief Description Premiere People is a member of the MATCH Group of companies, one of the UK's leading and most innovative recruitment specialists. With over 25 years experience, they aim to set the standards in recruitment and flexible staffing solutions. By joining Premiere People, you can take advantage of their benefits like holiday pay, an exclusive reward scheme and their simply exceptional rates of pay. They can help whatever type of work you're after across the whole spectrum from Healthcare to Accountancy, Customer Services to Driving, from Factory work to Management – they'll be delighted to help you.

Preferred method of contact Apply on line or telephone for an appointment

Minimum requirements None

Type of business Temporary and Permanent

Grade/Level of Appointments All levels

Prime Secretarial

Head Office ✉ 11 Blomfield St, EC2M 7AY
⊖ Holborn
🚊 City Thameslink
☎ T 020 7588 0174   F 020 7638 8421
@ dacosta@primeuk.com

Market areas Secretarial

Website www.primeuk.com

UK Offices 1

REC Member No

Brief Description Part of the Prime Personnel Group, Prime Secretarial is committed to providing high calibre permanent personnel in all areas including Management, General and Specialist Administration, Human Resources, IT and Secretarial Support. Facilities for further training on Access, Excel, PowerPoint and Word are available in their dedicated suites in the City.

Preferred method of contact Apply on line or telephone for an appointment

Minimum requirements None

Type of business Permanent

Grade/Level of Appointments 2nd Jobber to Senior PA

Prime Temps

See Accountancy and Banking, page 23

The Principle Partnership

Head Office   ✉   6 Junction Mews, W2 1PN
  ⊖   Edgeware Rd
  🚇   Paddington
  ☎   T 020 7706 7887   F 020 7706 7889
  @   admin@tpp.co.uk
Market areas   Secretarial, PR, Accountancy

Website www.tpp.co.uk

UK Offices 1

REC Member Yes

Brief Description The Principle Partnership specialises in placing permanent and temporary staff within the Accountancy, Marketing, Secretarial, PR and Fundraising sectors.

Preferred method of contact Apply on line or telephone for an appointment

Minimum requirements None

Type of business Temporary and Permanent

Grade/Level of Appointments All levels

ProspectUs

See **Not for Profit** , page 209

PS Recruitment Ltd

Head Office   ✉   35–37 Ludgate Hill, EC4M 7JN
  ⊖   Blackfriars
  🚇   City Thameslink
  ☎   T 020 7329 2262   F 020 7329 2264
  @   info@psrecruitment.co.uk
Market areas   Secretarial

Website www.psrecruitment.co.uk

UK Offices 1

REC Member Yes

Brief Description PS Recruitment offer a focused, yet flexible, and fundamentally people-centred approach to Office staff recruitment. Drawing both on the wealth of skills and experience brought by their candidates, and on the store of rewarding opportunities offered by their clients, PS Recruitment consultants create dynamic, effective combinations of people and positions to meet all their placement targets.

Preferred method of contact Telephone for appointment

Minimum requirements None

Type of business Temporary and Permanent

Grade/Level of Appointments All levels

Rainbow Recruitment

Head Office   ✉   12 South Molton St, W1K 5QN
  ⊖   Bond St
  🚇   Paddington
  ☎   T 020 7491 7252   F 020 7491 2887
  @   enquiries@rainbowrecruitment.co.uk
Market areas   Secretarial, Legal Secretarial, Public Relations, Telecoms, IT

Website www.rainbowrecruitment.co.uk

UK Offices 1

REC Member Yes

Brief Description Rainbow Recruitment was founded in 1990 by HR professionals who felt that they could provide a more comprehensive service than many of the consultancies that were available at that time. This philosophy continues as Rainbow strives to provide unique recruitment solutions, forming partnerships with their clients and candidates and ensuring that they have a complete understanding of the variety of disciplines in which they work. Over the years they have successfully placed thousands of candidates, many of whom are still in contact with Rainbow and recommend them to clients and friends. On this basis Rainbow is still growing and succeeding. Their aim is to continue to provide an accountable and tailored service to clients and candidates alike. They listen to your needs and work to your goals and aspirations.

Preferred method of contact Apply on line or telephone for an appointment

Minimum requirements None

Type of business Temporary and Permanent

Grade/Level of Appointments All levels

Randstad

  ✉   67 Borough High St, SE1 1NF
  ⊖   London Bridge
  🚇   London Bridge
  ☎   T 020 7407 0313   F 020 7407 0117
  @   londonbridge@mail.uk.randstad.com
Market areas   Secretarial, Office, Industrial

  ✉   44–46 Kingsway, WC2B 6EN
  ⊖   Holborn
  🚇   City Thameslink
  ☎   T 020 7831 4339   F 020 7831 6610
  @   kingsway@uk.randstad.com
Market areas   Secretarial, Office, Industrial

  ✉   Bedford Chambers, The Piazza, WC2E 8HA
  ⊖   Covent Garden
  🚇   Charing Cross
  ☎   T 020 7257 2600   F 020 7251 2700
  @   covent.garden@uk.randstad.com
Market areas   Secretarial, Office, Industrial

✉ 154 Bishopsgate, EC2M 4LN
⊖ Liverpool St
🚇 Liverpool St
📞 T 020 7247 7035   F 020 7426 0194
@ londoncity.branch@mail.uk.randstad.com
Market areas Secretarial, Office, Industrial

Website www.randstad.co.uk
UK Offices 71
REC Member Yes
Head Office Newbury
Brief Description With a wealth of experience, Randstad is part of the international Randstad Group. Established in 1960, the Group now operates in over 2000 branches in Europe, Canada and the US, making it one of the world's largest and most experienced specialist employment businesses. In the UK, with a growing network of 71 branches located nationwide, Randstad leads the market as an attractive employer. With a strong portfolio of benefits engineered for all parties involved (clients, flex-workers and corporate staff) they expect to keep the pace of their development – bringing the service to more clients and flex-workers in the UK.

Preferred method of contact Telephone for appointment
Minimum requirements None
Type of business Temporary and Permanent
Grade/Level of Appointments All levels

Ranfurly Recruitment

See **Accountancy and Banking, page 23**

Ranmac Employment Agency

See **Industrial, page 151**

Recruit Employment Services

✉ 6–8 James St, W1U 1ED
⊖ Bond St
🚇 Paddington
📞 T 020 7499 8112   F 020 7499 8115
@ westend@recruitgroup.co.uk
Market areas Secretarial, Industrial, Catering, Care, Driving

✉ 10 Lloyd's Avenue, EC3N 3AX
⊖ Aldgate
🚇 Fenchurch St
📞 T 020 7480 7400   F 020 7480 7411
@ city@recruitgroup.co.uk
Market areas Secretarial, Industrial, Catering, Care, Driving

Website www.recruitemployment.co.uk
UK Offices 31
REC Member Yes

Head Office Albany Place, Hyde Way, Welwyn Garden City, Herts, AL7 3BG

Brief Description Part of the Carlisle Group, Recruit Employment Services, formed in 1993, is now firmly established as one of the UK's leading multi-disciplinary Support Service businesses, with 31 branches across England, Scotland, and Wales. They provide both temporary staffing solutions and permanent staff, in the Commercial, Industrial, Driving, Catering and Care sectors.

Preferred method of contact Apply on line or telephone for an appointment
Minimum requirements None
Type of business Temporary and Permanent
Grade/Level of Appointments All levels

Reed Employment Services

Head Office ✉ Reed Executive Plc, 145 Kensington High St, W8 7LP
📞 T 020 7313 7450   F 020 7313 7451

✉ 22 Harbour Exchange Sq, E14 9GE
⊖ Crossharbour
🚇 Limehouse
📞 T 020 7538 9696
Market areas Secretarial

✉ Unit 3, Marsh Wall, E14 9GE
⊖ South Quay
🚇 Limehouse
📞 T 020 7538 9797
Market areas Secretarial

✉ 402 The Strand, WC2R 0NE
⊖ Charing Cross
🚇 Charing Cross
📞 T 020 7379 4767
Market areas Secretarial

✉ 143 Victoria St, SW1E 5NH
⊖ Victoria
🚇 Victoria
📞 T 020 7834 1801
Market areas Secretarial

✉ 19 Borough High St, SE1 9SE
⊖ London Bridge
🚇 London Bridge
📞 T 020 7939 7303
Market areas Secretarial

✉ 87 Moorgate, EC2M 6SA
⊖ Moorgate
🚇 Moorgate
📞 T 020 7638 1666
Market areas Secretarial

✉ Unit 4 , Cannon St Station, EC4N 6AP
⊖ Cannon St
🚇 Cannon St
📞 T 020 7337 9950

Market areas	Secretarial
✉	1st Floor, 148 Leadenhall St, EC3V 4QT
⊖	Bank
🚇	Cannon St
☎	T 020 7481 2661
Market areas	Secretarial
✉	402 The Strand, WC2R ONE
⊖	Charing Cross
🚇	Charing Cross
☎	T 020 7379 4767
Market areas	Secretarial
✉	5th Floor, Fairgate House, 78 New Oxford St, WC1A 1HB
⊖	Holborn
🚇	City Thameslink
☎	T 020 7255 1005
Market areas	Secretarial
✉	159 Charing Cross Rd, WC2H 0EN
⊖	Charing Cross
🚇	Charing Cross
☎	T 020 7734 8694
Market areas	Secretarial
✉	94 Baker St, W1M 1LA
⊖	Baker St
🚇	Marylebone
☎	T 020 7224 2820
Market areas	Secretarial

Website www.reed.co.uk

UK Offices 250+

REC Member No

Brief Description A subsidiary of Reed Executive Plc established in 1960, Reed's growth has been dramatic and the company's stated ambition is to grow the business substantially. Reed has been organised into a number of separate operating companies to make this happen. Reed Employment Services concentrates in the Office/Secretarial/Support sectors.

Preferred method of contact Apply on line or telephone for an appointment

Minimum requirements None

Type of business Temporary and Permanent

Grade/Level of Appointments All levels

Reed Employment Services – City Solutions

Head Office	✉	Reed Executive Plc, 145 Kensington High St, W8 7LP
	☎	T 020 7313 7450 F 020 7313 7451
	✉	5–10 Bury St, EC3A 5AT
	⊖	Aldgate
	🚇	Fenchurch St

	☎	T 020 7220 4740
Market areas		Secretarial

Website www.reed.co.uk

UK Offices 250+

REC Member No

Brief Description A subsidiary of Reed Executive Plc established in 1960, Reed's growth has been dramatic and the company's stated ambition is to grow the business substantially. Reed has been organised into a number of separate operating companies to make this happen. Reed Employment Services concentrates in the Office/Secretarial/Support sectors.

Preferred method of contact Apply on line or telephone for an appointment

Minimum requirements None

Type of business Temporary and Permanent

Grade/Level of Appointments All levels

Reed Employment Services – International

Head Office	✉	Reed Executive Plc, 145 Kensington High St, W8 7LP
	☎	T 020 7313 7450 F 020 7313 7451
	✉	78 New Oxford St, WC1A 1HB
	⊖	Holborn
	🚇	City Thameslink
	☎	T 020 7580 3801
Market areas		Secretarial

Website www.reed.co.uk

UK Offices 250+

REC Member No

Brief Description A subsidiary of Reed Executive Plc established in 1960, Reed's growth has been dramatic and the company's stated ambition is to grow the business substantially. Reed has been organised into a number of separate operating companies to make this happen. Reed Employment Services concentrates in the Office/Secretarial/Support sectors.

Preferred method of contact Apply on line or telephone for an appointment

Minimum requirements None

Type of business Temporary and Permanent

Grade/Level of Appointments All levels

Regan & Dean

See **Media, page 204**

Ritz Recruitment

Head Office	✉	133 Middlesex St, E1 7JF
	⊖	Liverpool St

🚊 Liverpool St
☎ T 020 7929 5850   F 020 7929 1370
@ ritzcity@ritzrec.com
Market areas Secretarial

✉ 2–3 Conduit St, W1R 9TG
🚇 Oxford Circus
🚉 Charing Cross
☎ T 020 7629 4343   F 020 7491 2972
@ ritzwestend@ritzrec.com
Market areas Secretarial

Website www.ritzrec.com

UK Offices 4

REC Member No

Brief Description Ritz Recruitment are committed to assisting clients in the development and execution of cost effective recruiting programmes. Established since 1980, they have built a considerable reputation for their expertise in the Secretarial, Word Processing and Office Support sectors of the market. They operate from seven prime locations in London, Leeds and Manchester.

Preferred method of contact Apply on line or telephone for an appointment

Minimum requirements None

Type of business Temporary and Permanent

Grade/Level of Appointments All levels

Rose Associates

See **Media**, page 204

S&G Recruitment

Head Office ✉ Diamond House, 37–38 Hatton Garden, EC1N 8EB
🚇 Chancery Lane
🚉 City Thameslink
☎ T 020 7831 4546   F 020 7831 0353
@ jobs@sandg.co.uk
Market areas Secretarial and Admin, IT, Legal Support Staff

Website www.sandg.co.uk

UK Offices 1

REC Member No

Brief Description S&G are an independent privately owned employment agency established in 1989. They specialise in placing Administrative and Support staff (Legal and Commercial) into a variety of clients ranging from Law firms to blue chip organisations.

Preferred method of contact Apply on line or telephone for an appointment

Minimum requirements None

Type of business Temporary and Permanent

Grade/Level of Appointments All levels

Secretaries Plus

Head Office ✉ Devonshire House, 146 Bishopsgate, EC2M 4JX
🚇 Liverpool St
🚉 Liverpool St
☎ T 020 7377 8600   F 020 7375 1950
@ city@secretariesplus.co.uk
Market areas Secretarial

✉ 70 New Bond St, W1Y 9DE
🚇 Bond St
🚉 Paddington
☎ T 020 7493 7001   F 020 7493 7002
@ west@secretariesplus.co.uk
Market areas Secretarial

Website www.ljcgroup.co.uk

UK Offices 2

REC Member Yes

Brief Description Secretaries Plus is part of the LJC Group. The LJC Group is split into two separate companies: LJC Banking specialises in Back and Middle Office operations, including Risk, Treasury, Derivatives, Trade Finance and Securities; and Secretaries Plus which deals with permanent, temporary and contract Secretarial and Support staff for a range of clients.

Preferred method of contact Apply on line or telephone for an appointment

Minimum requirements None

Type of business Temporary, Permanent and Contract

Grade/Level of Appointments 1st Jobber to Management level

Select Appointments

✉ Unit 2, 300–310 Vauxhall Bridge Rd, SW1V 1AA
🚇 Victoria
🚉 Victoria
☎ T 020 7233 5433   F 020 7233 8175
@ victoria@select.co.uk
Market areas Secretarial, Customer Services

✉ 28 South Molton St, W1K 5RF
🚇 Bond St
🚉 Paddington
☎ T 020 7491 8133   F 020 7493 8456
@ mayfair@select.co.uk
Market areas Secretarial, Customer Services

✉ 31 High Holborn, WC1V 6AX
🚇 Holborn
🚉 City Thameslink
☎ T 020 7405 5467   F 020 7405 5468
@ holborn@select.co.uk
Market areas Secretarial, Customer Services

✉ 13–14 King St, EC2V 8LB
🚇 Mansion House
🚉 Cannon St

Secretarial

C T 020 7600 8582   F 020 7374 2704
@ city@select.co.uk
Market areas Secretarial, Customer Services

Website www. selectgroup.com

UK Offices 60+

REC Member Yes

Head Office 7th Floor, Ziggurat, Grosvenor Rd, St Albans, Hertfordshire, AL1 3HW

Brief Description Established in 1980, Select Appointments has over 60 offices throughout the UK and Ireland and is recognised as a leading national staffing services company. They find office-based jobs for people and people for jobs, specialising in all areas of Secretarial and Administration, Call and Contact Centres, Corporate Travel and Legal and Medical Secretarial.

Preferred method of contact Apply on line or telephone for an appointment

Minimum requirements None

Type of business Temporary and Permanent

Grade/Level of Appointments All levels

Sharon Gay Associates

Head Office ✉ 3 Cavendish Ct, EC3A 7GA
⊖ Aldgate
🚊 Fenchurch St
C T 020 7422 0036   F 020 7247 1686
@ info@sga-ltd.com
Market areas Secretarial and Admin

Website www.sharongayassociates.ltd.uk

UK Offices 1

REC Member Yes

Brief Description Established in 1991, The Sharon Gay Group consists of Sharon Gay Associates covering Stockbroking and Commercial divisions, SGA Legal supplying temporary and permanent Administrative Support personnel.

Preferred method of contact Apply on line or telephone for an appointment

Minimum requirements None

Type of business Temporary and Permanent

Grade/Level of Appointments All levels

Shearer Darnell Recruitment Ltd

Head Office ✉ 4 Sloane St, SW1X 9LA
⊖ Tower Hill
🚊 Fenchurch St
C T 020 7680 0000   F 020 7680 0012
@ careers@sdrecruitment.com
Market areas Property, Financial Services, Sales and Marketing, Secretarial

Website www.sdrecruitment.com

UK Offices 2

REC Member No

Brief Description Established in 1998, Shearer Darnell specialises in Property, Financial Services, Sales and Marketing and Secretarial opportunities across London and nationally.

Preferred method of contact Apply on line or telephone for an appointment

Minimum requirements None

Type of business Permanent

Grade/Level of Appointments All levels

Southern Cross Employment Agency Ltd

See **Healthcare, page 135**

Spencerbull

Head Office ✉ 54 Poland St, W1F 7NJ
⊖ Oxford Circus
🚊 Charing Cross
C T 020 7432 0532   F 020 7432 0531
@ spencerbull@ukgateway.net
Market areas Secretarial and Support Staff

Website www.spencerbull.com

UK Offices 1

REC Member No

Brief Description Spencerbull was established in 1999 and specialises in permanent secretarial Support staff recruitment. Their main aim is to give a professional, honest and personal service.

Preferred method of contact Apply on line or telephone for an appointment

Minimum requirements None

Type of business Permanent

Grade/Level of Appointments All levels

Spring Group Plc

Head Office ✉ 80 Bishopsgate, EC2N 4AG
C T 020 7655 8610   F 020 7655 8649
✉ 388 Oxford St, W1C 1ND
⊖ Bond St
🚊 Paddington
C T 020 7317 6200   F 020 7317 6293
@ corp@spring.com
Market areas Secretarial, IT, Support Staff

Website www.spring.com

UK Offices 30+

REC Member Yes

Brief Description Spring Personnel is the recruitment 'partner of choice' for SMEs, as well as blue chip companies across all sectors of industry. With 250 staff and 27 branches, the division annually fulfils 3,000 vacancies for permanent staff on behalf of employers, and manages temporary assignments for a weekly workforce of 3,600. No one client, industry or skill set dominates the division's business which splits equally between white and blue-collar sectors. Spring Personnel is established in a range of staffing markets including Commercial, Call Centre, Telecoms, Financial, Industrial, Technical and Data Entry.

Preferred method of contact Apply on line or telephone for an appointment

Minimum requirements None

Type of business Temporary and Permanent

Grade/Level of Appointments All levels

St James's Consultancy

Head Office ✉ 35 Thurloe St, SW7 2LQ
🚇 South Kensington
🚉 Victoria
☎ T 020 7589 1866   F 020 7589 8142
@ recruit@stjc.co.uk
Market areas Secretarial and Support Staff

Website www.stjamessconsultancy.co.uk
UK Offices 1
REC Member Yes

Brief Description St James's Consultancy is an extremely successful and well established recruitment specialist with over 17 years experience of placing Secretarial and Administrative staff in Central London.

Preferred method of contact Apply on line or telephone for an appointment

Minimum requirements None

Type of business Temporary and Permanent

Grade/Level of Appointments All levels

Sugarman Group

Head Office ✉ Northumbrian House, 14 Devonshire Sq, EC2M 4YT
🚇 Liverpool St
🚉 Liverpool St
☎ T 020 7456 8780   F 020 7456 8781
@ medical@sugarman.co.uk,
secretarial@sugarman.co.uk
Market areas Secretarial , Medical

Website www.sugarman.co.uk
UK Offices 1
REC Member Yes

Brief Description Sugarman Associates was established in 1986. From those early beginnings their organisation has gone from strength to strength and proudly states that as a direct result of their success and continued demand from clients, the Sugarman Group of Companies is now structured to provide specialist recruitment in the fields of Secretarial and Medical staff. They pride themselves on providing their clients with high calibre applicants and a service based in honesty, efficiency and expediency. They enjoy placing a broad spectrum of Operations and Support staff ranging from Trainee Support Personnel through to Middle Management.

Preferred method of contact Apply on line or telephone for an appointment

Minimum requirements None

Type of business Temporary and Permanent

Grade/Level of Appointments Trainee Support Personnel to Middle Management

Summers By Two Ltd

Head Office ✉ Walmer House, 296 Regent St, W1B 3AW
🚇 Oxford Circus
🚉 Charing Cross
☎ T 020 7637 3212   F 020 7637 3168
@ info@summersbytwo.com
Market areas Secretarial

Website www.summersbytwo.com
UK Offices 1
REC Member Yes

Brief Description Established in 1993, Summers By Two is a family owned recruitment consultancy that specialises in the provision of high quality skilled Office Support staff including all levels of Secretaries, Receptionists and Administrators.

Preferred method of contact Apply on line or telephone for an appointment

Minimum requirements None

Type of business Temporary and Permanent

Grade/Level of Appointments All levels

Susan Hamilton Personnel Services

Head Office ✉ 13–14 Upper St, N1 0PQ
☎ T 020 7704 9034   F 020 7704 1427

✉ 2nd Floor, York House, 78 Queen Victoria St, EC4N 4SJ
🚇 Blackfriars
🚉 Blackfriars
☎ T 020 7246 7999   F 020 7246 7900
@ catering@susanhamilton.co.uk
Market areas Secretarial, Catering

✉ 72 Cannon St, EC4N 6AE
🚇 Cannon St
🚉 Cannon St

C T 020 7236 9696   F 020 7236 9292

@ city@susanhamilton.co.uk

Market areas Secretarial, Catering

✉ 43—44 Albemarle St, W1S 4JJ

⊖ Green Park

🚆 Charing Cross

C T 020 7499 5406   F 020 7499 4878

@ mayfair@susanhamilton.co.uk

Market areas Secretarial, Catering

Website www.susanhamilton.co.uk

UK Offices 8

REC Member Yes

Brief Description Over the years many candidates have become clients in many market sectors, others have had children who are now our next generation of job seekers. So from a 1st Jobber to Chief Executive Officer, Manufacturing to Media, Parliamentary to Publishing, Training to Tourism, Entrepreneur, blue chip or international conglomerate; you can be sure that someone within the Group will have a current assignment, contact or an idea that will benefit you and your particular needs.

Preferred method of contact Apply on line or telephone for an appointment

Minimum requirements None

Type of business Temporary and Permanent

Grade/Level of Appointments All levels

The Synergy Group

Head Office ✉ 77 Cornhill, EC3V 3QQ

⊖ Bank

🚆 Cannon St

C T 020 7556 1122   F 020 7556 1133

@ enquiries@synergygroup.co.uk

Market areas Commercial, Education, Facilities Management, Housing, Information Technology, Revenues & Benefits, Sales, Support Services and Social Care

Website www.synergygroup.co.uk

UK Offices 3

REC Member Yes

Brief Description The Synergy Group was launched in 1997 and is an established nationwide organisation with a reputation for providing high quality human resources solutions to specialist sectors across the UK and mainland Europe. The three main areas in which they provide resource solutions are: Recruitment, Training and Consultancy. The group consists of 10 specialist divisions: Commercial, Education, Facilities Management, Housing, IT, Revenues and Benefits, Sales, Support Services and Social Care. Each division is made up of industry experienced consultants and recruitment experts.

Preferred method of contact Apply on line or telephone for an appointment

Minimum requirements None

Type of business Temporary and Permanent

Grade/Level of Appointments All levels

T&T Recruitment & Resourcing Ltd

See **Hospitality and Leisure, page 145**

Target Appointments

Head Office ✉ MWB Business Exchange, 88 Kingsway, WC2B 6AA

⊖ Holborn

🚆 City Thameslink

C T 020 7242 1183   F 020 7405 5542

@ jobs@targetappointments.com

Market areas Office, Retail, Horticulture, Warehouse, Landscaping

Website www.targetappointments.com

UK Offices 1

REC Member Yes

Brief Description Target Appointments was established in 1991 and supplies temporary and permanent staff to the London employment market. They source their staff for short and long term assignments — predominantly Commonwealth travellers. In 11 years the business has grown four fold. Recommendation is the cornerstone of the company's success, covering Office, Retail, Warehouse, Horticulture and Landscaping.

Preferred method of contact Apply on line or telephone for an appointment

Minimum requirements None

Type of business Temporary and Permanent

Grade/Level of Appointments All levels

Tate

Head Office ✉ 7 Hanover Sq, W1S 1HQ

⊖ Oxford Circus

🚆 Charing Cross

C T 020 7408 0424   F 020 7493 8790

@ temps@tate.co.uk

Market areas Office and Secretarial

✉ 2nd Floor, 40 Lime St, EC3M 7AW

⊖ Bank

🚆 Cannon St

C T 020 7458 2727   F 020 7493 8790

@ perms@tate.co.uk

Market areas Office and Secretarial

Website www.tate.co.uk

UK Offices 2

REC Member Yes

Brief Description Tate specialises in the recruitment and placement of high quality office support staff in London. Tate offers a complete

259

portfolio of recruitment solutions and opportunities spanning temporary, contract and permanent work.

Preferred method of contact Apply on line or telephone for an appointment

Minimum requirements None

Type of business Temporary and Permanent

Grade/Level of Appointments All levels

Tele Temps Ltd

See **Sales and Marketing**, page 219

TEMP-TEAM Ltd

Head Office ✉ Meridian Gate, 203 Marsh Wall, E14 9YT
⊖ South Quay
🚊 Limehouse
☎ T 020 7531 1128   F 020 7537 7707
@ london@temp-team.com
Market areas Secretarial, Warehouse, Construction, M&E, Catering, IT, Manufacturing

Website www.temp-team.co.uk

UK Offices 6

REC Member No

Brief Description TEMP-TEAM, one of Scandinavia's most successful suppliers of permanent and temporary staff, now offer the same high standard of service throughout the UK, continental Europe, Singapore and Australia. Together with Active Selection, Professional and Executive recruitment, the company continues to expand and strengthen its UK network. With 20 years experience, they are certain TEMP-TEAM can offer you the best practical and flexible solutions, maintaining close contact to ensure that all of your requirements are met and your expectations exceeded. They are able to offer a network of UK offices, all with regional appeal, committed to servicing the temporary staffing requirements of local Public and Private Sector employees.

Preferred method of contact Apply on line or telephone for an appointment

Minimum requirements None

Type of business Temporary and Permanent

Grade/Level of Appointments All levels

Temporary Prospects

See **Not for Profit**, page 210

Thirty Plus Ltd

Head Office ✉ 92–93 Great Russell St, WC1B 3PS
⊖ Tottenham Court Rd

🚊 Euston
☎ T 020 7323 4155   F 020 7323 9397
@ info@thirtyplus-recruitment.com
Market areas Secretarial

Website www.thirtyplus-recruitment.com

UK Offices 1

REC Member Yes

Brief Description Thirty Plus Recruitment Ltd specialises in the recruitment of more mature personnel – 30 to retiring age, within the Greater London area only. They believe in the skills, experience, and professionalism that mature employees can provide an employer.

Preferred method of contact Apply on line or telephone for an appointment

Minimum requirements Age 30+

Type of business Permanent

Grade/Level of Appointments All levels

THS Resourcing

Head Office ✉ 99–100 Turnmill St, EC1M 5QP
⊖ Farringdon
🚊 Farringdon
☎ T 020 7251 5544   F 020 7251 4545
@ contact@thsresourcing.co.uk
Market areas Secretarial, Office Support

Website www.thsresourcing.co.uk

UK Offices 2

REC Member Yes

Brief Description THS Resourcing Ltd was founded in October 1998 by six dedicated individuals with over 35 years combined experience within the Office recruitment, Training and Personnel industries.

Preferred method of contact Apply on line or telephone for an appointment

Minimum requirements None

Type of business Temporary and Permanent

Grade/Level of Appointments All levels

Tiger Recruitment Ltd

Head Office ✉ 211 Piccadilly, W1J 9HF
⊖ Piccadilly Circus
🚊 Charing Cross
☎ T 020 7917 1801   F 020 7917 1802
@ info@tiger-recruitment.co.uk
Market areas Secretarial, Office Support

Website www.tiger-recruitment.co.uk

UK Offices 1

REC Member Yes

Brief Description Tiger recruit for jobs covering a broad salary range, from £15,000–£60,000, and have the resources in place to recruit for a number of other positions, e.g. Marketing Assistant, Account Administrator, Desk Assistant etc.

Preferred method of contact Apply on line or telephone for an appointment

Minimum requirements None

Type of business Temporary, Permanent and Contract

Grade/Level of Appointments All levels

Verity Appointments

Head Office	✉	10 South Molton St, W1K 5QJ
	⊖	Bond St
	🚇	Paddington
	✆	T 020 7493 0437 F 020 7493 0647
Market areas		Secretarial, Lingual
	✉	68 Lombard St, EC3V 9LJ
	⊖	Bank
	🚇	Cannon St
	✆	T 020 7868 2375 F 020 7477 6768
Market areas		Legal Secretarial

Website www.verityappointments.com

UK Offices 2

REC Member Yes

Brief Description At Verity, they want the very best Legal, Commercial and Multilingual people. If you have the skills, experience and approach they look for in their temporary and permanent candidates, you can count on them to find you the top jobs with the best companies – and take good care of you every step of the way.

Preferred method of contact Apply on line or telephone for an appointment

Minimum requirements None

Type of business Temporary and Permanent

Grade/Level of Appointments All levels

Victoria Wall Associates Ltd

Head Office	✉	3 Cromwell Place, SW7 2JE
	⊖	South Kensington
	🚇	Victoria
	✆	T 020 7225 1888 F 020 7225 2013
Market areas		Secretarial

Website www.vwa.com

UK Offices 1

REC Member Yes

Brief Description Victoria Wall Associates Ltd was established in 1989 with the commitment to create a new standard of excellence in the level of service provided by recruitment consultancies. Due to the fulfilment of this commitment Victoria Wall Associates are now recognised for providing one of the most professional services in the recruitment industry. The VWA philosophy is different from other selection consultancies, due to the emphasis they place on truly understanding a candidate's personality and skills.

Preferred method of contact Apply on line or telephone for an appointment

Minimum requirements None

Type of business Temporary and Permanent

Grade/Level of Appointments All levels

VPS Ltd

Head Office	✉	20–22 Maddox St, W1R 9PG
	⊖	Oxford Circus
	🚇	Charing Cross
	✆	T 020 7491 8553 F 020 7493 2090
	@	info@vpsrecruitment.com
Market areas		Secretarial, Media

Website www.vpsrecruitment.com

UK Offices 1

REC Member Yes

Brief Description Part of the Empressaria Group, VPS are an agency specialising in the permanent and temporary recruitment of Secretarial/Administrative staff covering all sectors to include Media, Corporate and Finance. They are friendly, dedicated and approachable. Every applicant who walks through their doors will be provided with support and advice about their job search.

Preferred method of contact Apply on line or telephone for an appointment

Minimum requirements None

Type of business Temporary and Permanent

Grade/Level of Appointments All levels

Walker & Kutner

Head Office	✉	2 London Wall Buildings, EC2M 5UU
	⊖	Moorgate
	🚇	Moorgate
	✆	T 020 7448 5174 F 020 7448 5179
	@	sara.kutner@walkerkutner.co.uk
Market areas		Equity Support Staff

Website www.walkerkutner.co.uk

UK Offices 1

REC Member No

Brief Description Walker & Kutner specialise in providing Equities Support staff to London's Investment Banks/Financial Institutions. They cover roles within Equities Research, Sales and Trading, Desk/Team Assistants, Secretaries, PAs, Research Assistants, DTP/Presentation Support staff.

Preferred method of contact Apply on line or telephone for an appointment

Minimum requirements None

Type of business Temporary and Permanent

Grade/Level of Appointments All levels

Web Career Consultants Ltd

See IT and Telecoms, page 179

Wise Owls Ltd

Head Office	✉	18 Ashwin St, E8 3DL
	⊖	Highbury and Islington
	🚇	Dalston Kingsland
	☎	T 020 7923 7771 F 020 7923 9320
	@	webmaster@wiseowls.co.uk
Market areas		Secretarial, Hospitality, Financial, Retail

Website www.wiseowls.co.uk

UK Offices 1

REC Member No

Brief Description Funded by LSCLE, Wise Owls is a recruitment organisation specifically aimed at finding employment for the over 45 age range.

Preferred method of contact Apply on line or telephone for an appointment

Minimum requirements Over 45s

Type of business Temporary and Permanent

Grade/Level of Appointments All levels

Zarak Group

Head Office	✉	4 Crown Place, EC2A 4BT
	⊖	Liverpool St
	🚇	Liverpool St
	☎	T 020 7539 0000 F 020 7539 0001
	@	london@zarakgroup.com
Market areas		Legal, HR, IT Sales, IT, Marketing, Financial Services, Secretarial

Website www.zarakgroup.com

UK Offices 2

REC Member Yes

Brief Description Established in 1984, The Zarak Group is a high quality consultancy encompassing specialist divisions providing Secretaries, Administrators, Human Resources, Training and Marketing professionals, IT Sales, Pre-sales and Technical staff as well as Finance and Banking personnel. At the Zarak Group, they pride themselves on their customised service. This service is tailored to each of their client's needs and their ability to source both permanent and temporary staff.

Preferred method of contact Apply on line or telephone for an appointment

Minimum requirements None

Type of business Temporary and Permanent

Grade/Level of Appointments All levels

Social Care

Capita Social Care Resourcing

Head Office   ✉   New Loom House, 101 Backchurch Lane, E1 1LU
          ⊖   Aldgate East
          🚊   Fenchurch St
          ℂ   T 020 7481 8383   F 020 7481 8900
          @   london@capitascr.co.uk
  Market areas   Social Care, Care Workers

Website www.capitascr.co.uk
UK Offices 5
REC Member No
Brief Description Vacancies within the Social Work, Social Care and Supported Housing sectors need to be filled with care and sensitivity. With over 14 years of experience in this area, Capita Social Care Resourcing and Capita Social Work Resourcing have the experience and resources to find high quality staff from basic grade RSWs, Support and Social Workers right through to Senior Management level posts. Their range of disciplines covers: Qualified Social Workers, Social Work Assistants, Residential Support Workers, Care Workers, Relief Wardens, Project Workers, Sheltered Housing Officers and Supported Housing Officers.
Preferred method of contact Telephone for appointment
Minimum requirements Previous professional experience
Type of business Temporary and Permanent
Grade/Level of Appointments RSWs to Senior Management level

Capita Social Work Resourcing

Head Office   ✉   New Loom House, 101 Backchurch Lane, E1 1LU
          ⊖   Aldgate East
          🚊   Fenchurch St
          ℂ   T 0800 358 8202   F 020 7481 0303
          @   swr.info@capita.co.uk
  Market areas   Social Work

Website www.capitaswr.co.uk
UK Offices 1
REC Member No
Brief Description Through their extensive experience, Capita Social Work Resourcing can offer you the ultimate solution to your Social Work recruitment needs. They have over 15 years experience in providing candidates with the best in temporary and permanent recruitment solutions. Experienced, suitably qualified candidates are available to cover sickness, maternity, annual leave, permanent posts and special projects. They are part of the Capita Group Plc, which is one of the largest and fastest growing professional support organisations in the UK. Capita provides a nationwide range of integrated professional support services across the Public Sector, Local and Central Government, and Education.

Preferred method of contact Apply on line or telephone for an appointment
Minimum requirements Previous professional experience
Type of business Temporary and Permanent
Grade/Level of Appointments Social Work Assistants to Senior Social Workers

Celsian Group – Social Care

          ✉   5th Floor, New Zealand House, 80 Haymarket, SW1Y 4TE
          ⊖   Piccadilly Circus
          🚊   Charing Cross
          ℂ   T 020 7930 4945   F 020 7930 4937
          @   enquiries@celsiangroup.co.uk
  Market areas   Social Care

Website www.celsiangroup.co.uk
UK Offices 24
REC Member Yes
Head Office Albany Place, Hyde Way, Welwyn Garden City, Herts, AL7 3BG
Brief Description Part of Carlisle Group UK, Celsian is the new collective brand name unveiled in 2002 for the following divisions: Recruit Education Services, Recruit Employment Care, Agency Cover and First Call.
Preferred method of contact Apply on line or telephone for appointment
Minimum requirements None
Type of business Permanent, Temporary and Contract
Grade/Level of Appointments All levels

Central Recruitment Services

Head Office   ✉   81 Holloway Rd, N7 8LT
          ⊖   Highbury and Islington
          🚊   Highbury and Islington
          ℂ   T 020 7619 6200   F 020 7697 0661
          @   work@centralcare.co.uk
  Market areas   Social Workers, Home Care, Domincilary

Website www.centralcare.co.uk
UK Offices 1
REC Member Yes
Brief Description Central Care is a specialist recruitment facility for Local Authorities, Housing Associations, Charities and Private organisations. They recruit and place the following staff: Outreach and

Support Workers, Qualified Social Workers, Residential and Day Care Workers, Home Care and Domiciliary Workers.

Preferred method of contact Apply on line or telephone for an appointment

Minimum requirements Previous professional experience

Type of business Permanent

Grade/Level of Appointments All levels

City Qualified Social Workers

Head Office ✉ 1 Blandford St, W1U 3DA
⊖ Marble Arch
🚃 Marylebone
☎ T 020 7486 1334   F 020 7486 1414
@ cityqualifeduk@aol.com
Market areas Social Workers

Website www.c-q-s-w.co.uk

UK Offices 1

REC Member No

Brief Description City Qualified Social Workers specialise in the permanent recruitment of Social Workers.

Preferred method of contact Apply on line or telephone for appointment

Minimum requirements Qualified Social Worker

Type of business Permanent

Grade/Level of Appointments Newly Qualified to Manager level

Cooper Stanley

Head Office ✉ 60 Grays Inn Rd, WC1X 8LT
⊖ Chancery Lane
🚃 City Thameslink
☎ T 020 7430 6600   F 020 7242 6928
@ info@cs-careers.com
Market areas Social Workers

Website www.cs-careers.com

UK Offices 1

REC Member No

Brief Description Cooper Stanley is a leading well established recruitment consultancy based in Central London, a few minutes walk from Chancery Lane tube station. They have been successfully recruiting and placing Qualified Social Workers and Social Work Managers in the UK since 1992. They provide temporary locum and permanent staff at all levels to Social Services departments and Voluntary organisations nationwide.

Preferred method of contact Apply on line or telephone for an appointment

Minimum requirements Qualified Social Worker

Type of business Temporary and Permanent

Grade/Level of Appointments All levels

Reed Healthcare International

See **Healthcare, page 135**

Reliance Care

Head Office ✉ 67–69 Cowcross St, EC1M 6BP
⊖ Farringdon
🚃 Farringdon
☎ T 020 7549 4000   F 020 7253 9100
@ farringdon@reliancecare.com
Market areas Social Care, Social Workers

✉ 199 Holloway Rd, N7 8DJ
⊖ Holloway Rd
🚃 Finsbury Park
☎ T 020 7607 5472   F 020 7700 4575
@ hollowayroad@reliancecare.com
Market areas Social Care, Social Workers

Website www.reliancecare.com

UK Offices 15

REC Member Yes

Brief Description Reliance was established in 1967, the first agency to supply locum Care staff to Social Services and is today the largest Social Care recruitment specialist. The consistently high standards set by Reliance are sought by an increasing number of Local Authorities and Private organisations and has resulted in their continued expansion throughout the UK. Reliance Care is the leading specialist recruitment agency for the Social Care sector.

Preferred method of contact Apply on line or telephone for an appointment

Minimum requirements Previous professional experience

Type of business Temporary and Permanent

Grade/Level of Appointments All levels

Smile Healthcare

See **Healthcare, page 135**

Social Work Associates

Head Office ✉ Wickham House, Cleveland Way, E1 4TR
⊖ Stepney Green
🚃 Fenchurch St
☎ T 020 7790 4448
@ colette@socialworkassociates.co.uk
Market areas Social Workers

Website www.socialworkassociates.co.uk

UK Offices 1

REC Member Yes

Brief Description Social Work Associates is a specialist recruitment consultancy providing Qualified Social Workers up to Senior level to fill temporary and permanent positions. The company was set up by a group of individuals with substantial experience of Social Work recruitment.

Preferred method of contact Apply on line or telephone for an appointment

Minimum requirements Qualified Social Worker

Type of business Temporary and Permanent

Grade/Level of Appointments All levels

Social Workline

Head Office ✉ Social Workline House, 329 Euston Rd, NW1 3AD
⊖ Great Portland St
🚃 Euston
✆ T 020 7383 3939 F 020 7383 3262
@ hi@socialworkline.com
Market areas Social Workers

Website www.socialworkline.com

UK Offices 1

REC Member Yes

Brief Description Social Workline is the largest specialist agency for Social Workers in Britain, providing temporary and contract opportunities for Qualified and Non-qualified Social Workers.

Preferred method of contact Apply on line or telephone for an appointment

Minimum requirements None

Type of business Temporary and Contract

Grade/Level of Appointments All levels

Stafflink

See **Education, page 74**

Wren Care

Head Office ✉ 4th Floor, Cloister Ct, 22–26 Farringdon Lane, EC1R 3AU
⊖ Farringdon
🚃 City Thameslink
✆ T 020 7253 6742 F 020 7253 6743
@ wren.care@virgin.net
Market areas Public Sector, Social Work

Website www.wrencare.co.uk

UK Offices 1

REC Member Yes

Brief Description Wren Care is part of the Wren Group established in 1972 and has enjoyed a growth from a generic Social Work agency to providing specialised innovative and customised staffing solutions to the Public, Private and Voluntary sectors. Wren Care is accredited by many of the London Boroughs' inspection departments. Wren Care are also approved suppliers to a large number of organisations in the Public, Voluntary and Independent sectors.

Preferred method of contact Apply on line or telephone for an appointment

Minimum requirements None

Type of business Temporary and Permanent

Grade/Level of Appointments All levels

Technical

A1-Cliveden

✉ 27 Old Gloucester St, WC1N 3XX
⊖ Holborn
🚊 City Thameslink
☎ T 020 7831 2434   F 0845 702 3495
@ wc@a1-cliveden.co.uk
Market areas IT, Engineering, Telecoms, Electronics, Rail

Website www.a1-cliveden.co.uk
UK Offices 12
REC Member No
Head Office 92 The Broadway, Bracknell, RG12 1AR
Brief Description Established in 1977, A1-Cliveden supply qualified and experienced Technical staff who work on a temporary, contract or permanent basis for clients in the Electronics, IT, Telecoms and Engineering sectors with clients ranging from large multi-nationals to small specialist firms in the UK, Europe and worldwide.
Preferred method of contact Apply on line or telephone for appointment
Minimum requirements None
Type of business Temporary, Permanent and Contract
Grade/Level of Appointments Graduate 1st Jobbers to Senior Management

AMSA Ltd

See **Construction and Property, page 43**

Anders Elite

See **Construction and Property, page 43**

Anglo Technical

See **Construction and Property, page 43**

Anthony Moss & Associates Ltd

See **Construction and Property, page 44**

Asdem Ltd

Head Office ✉ Colette House, 52–55 Piccadilly, W1J 0DX
⊖ Piccadilly Circus
🚊 Charing Cross
☎ T 020 7493 0973   F 020 7499 5270
@ info@asdem.co.uk
Market areas Oil

Website www.asdem.co.uk
UK Offices 1
REC Member Yes
Brief Description Established in 1988, Asdem is an independent Oil Industry consultancy whose clients include major Oil and Chemical companies, International Traders, Tanker Owners and Lawyers. Asdem can call upon the services of a wide range of experts and regularly supplies experienced Claims Analysts to work in client companies on long or short term contracts.
Preferred method of contact Telephone for appointment
Minimum requirements Ideally oil related exposure
Type of business Permanent and Contract
Grade/Level of Appointments Trainee Oil Broker to Demurrage Analyst

Avery Associates Ltd

See **Construction and Property, page 44**

Beresford Blake Thomas Ltd

Head Office ✉ 14 Buckingham Palace Rd, SW1W 0QP
☎ T 020 7233 8999   F 020 7233 8004
✉ 59 Buckingham Gate, SW1E 6AJ
⊖ St James's Park
🚊 Victoria
☎ T 020 7828 1555   F 020 7828 1941
@ technical@bbt.co.uk
Market areas Technical, Logistics, Construction and Surveying

Website www.bbt.co.uk
UK Offices 15
REC Member Yes
Brief Description Part of the Select Group BBT were founded in 1990. BBT is established as a truly international specialist recruitment company, providing temporary and permanent staff to the Technical, Health and Social Care sectors with offices across the UK and worldwide.
Preferred method of contact Apply on line or telephone for appointment
Minimum requirements None

Type of business Temporary and Permanent
Grade/Level of Appointments All levels

Bluetec Recruitment
See Construction and Property, page 44

Bradfield Resourcing Ltd
See IT and Telecoms, page 155

Computappoint Recruitment Services Ltd
See IT and Telecoms, page 158

Daniel Owen Associates
See Construction and Property, page 45

Facilities Management Recruitment
See Construction and Property, page 46

Facilities Recruitment Ltd
See Construction and Property, page 47

Folio Personnel Ltd (Shell and Core Division)
See Construction and Property, page 48

Hays Montrose Civil and Structural Division
See Construction and Property, page 49

Hays Montrose Communications Division
See Construction and Property, page 49

Hays Montrose Liftstaff Division
See Construction and Property, page 50

Hays Montrose Maintenance Division
See Construction and Property, page 51

Hays Montrose Process and Production Engineering Division

Head Office ✉ 141 Moorgate, EC2M 6TX
℡ T 020 7628 9999 F 020 7628 4698
✉ Abford House, 15 Wilton Rd, SW1V 1LT
⊖ Victoria
🚆 Victoria
℡ T 020 7931 8953 F 01226 720724
@ victoria.ppe@hays-montrose.com
Market areas Construction, Property, Architecture

Website www.haysworks.com
UK Offices 40
REC Member No

Brief Description Hays Personnel Services is a division of Hays Plc, the Business Services group listed in the FTSE 100. Hays Personnel Services is Europe's leading specialist professional recruitment group. Hays Montrose is the largest supplier of staff to the Construction, Property and Maintenance sector with over 40 offices in the UK, Ireland, Portugal and Australia. Exclusive recruitment agreements with the Chartered Institute of Building Services Engineers illustrates the reputation of Hays Montrose in this field.

Preferred method of contact Apply on line or telephone for an appointment
Minimum requirements None
Type of business Temporary and Permanent
Grade/Level of Appointments All levels

Hays Montrose Property and Surveying Division
See Construction and Property, page 51

Hays Montrose Rail Division
See Construction and Property, page 52

Hays Montrose Technical Admin Division
See Construction and Property, page 52

267

Heyman Woodworth Search and Selection Ltd

See Executive Search, page 92

Keystone Employment Group – Defence & Aerospace

Head Office ✉ 272–276 Pentonville Rd, N1 9JY
🚇 Kings Cross
🚊 Kings Cross
☎ T 020 7833 7788   F 020 7833 7783
Market areas   Defence and Aerospace

Website www.keystone-recruitment.co.uk

UK Offices 4

REC Member Yes

Brief Description Keystone was originally formed in London in 1948. It was one of the first and largest privately owned employment agencies placing Secretarial and General Office staff. Their greatest assets are the people who work for them, they are the reason why clients and candidates are recommended to use the Keystone Group services – it is their ability to listen and understand people's needs, to work in partnership with them to achieve success, and more importantly client and candidate satisfaction.

Preferred method of contact Apply on line or telephone for an appointment

Minimum requirements None

Type of business Temporary and Permanent

Grade/Level of Appointments All levels

Malla

See Construction and Property, page 54

MECS Group

See IT and Telecoms, page 167

Morson Group

See Construction and Property, page 54

Nationwider Technology Recruitment

See IT and Telecoms, page 169

Parc Group

See IT and Telecoms, page 171

Paul James Associates

Head Office ✉ 27 Little Russell St, WC1A 2HN
🚇 Holborn
🚊 City Thameslink
☎ T 020 7404 9990   F 020 7404 9992
@ bsmart@pauljamesassociates.com
Market areas   Technical, Construction and Property, Industrial

Website www.pauljamesassociates.com

UK Offices 1

REC Member Yes

Brief Description Paul James Associates is a highly motivated, focused Technical recruitment services organisation, operating across a wide range of disciplines and countries. The company has been steadily expanding mainly as a result of growing client demand. Paul James Associates aims to build long-term relationships with both clients and candidates whilst consistently using new practices and technologies to improve their services – they recognise the role their clients and candidates play in their success.

Preferred method of contact Apply on line or telephone for an appointment

Minimum requirements None

Type of business Contract and Permanent

Grade/Level of Appointments All levels

Precision Resources Ltd

Head Office ✉ 100 New Kings Rd, SW6 4LX
🚇 Putney Bridge
🚊 Wimbledon
☎ T 020 7731 8199   F 020 7371 7200
@ precision@iofm.net
Market areas   Engineering, Technical

Website www.precisionresources.co.uk

UK Offices 1

REC Member No

Brief Description Precision Resources Ltd is an employment business specialising in the permanent placement and contract hire of Engineering, Technical and Project personnel to multi-national clients worldwide. Their head office is based in London, UK, plus they have associate offices in France and Germany with whom they share vacancies and candidates, which greatly enhances their capability to offer some great prospects.

Preferred method of contact Apply on line or telephone for an appointment

Minimum requirements Previous professional experience

Type of business Contract and Permanent
Grade/Level of Appointments All levels

Premiere People
See Secretarial, page 252

Primat Recruitment

Head Office ✉ 28–30 Trinity St, SE1 4JE
  ⊖ Borough
  ⊞ London Bridge
  ☎ T 020 7539 5877   F 020 7539 6959
  @ primat.sales@amec.com
Market areas Oil& Gas, Sales and Marketing

Website www.primat.co.uk
UK Offices 10
REC Member Yes

Brief Description Primat Recruitment has been established since 1965 offering a whole host of recruitment solutions to a wide variety of industry sectors within the UK and overseas. Their tailor made service offers more to their customers and candidates than the more traditional High Street companies. Their specialist teams operate throughout their UK network of offices, offering innovative and inspiring recruitment solutions.

Preferred method of contact Apply on line or telephone for an appointment
Minimum requirements Previous professional experience
Type of business Temporary and Permanent
Grade/Level of Appointments All levels

Rail Personnel

Head Office ✉ 3rd Floor, Nutmeg House, 60 Gainsford St, SE1 2NY
  ⊖ London Bridge
  ⊞ London Bridge
  ☎ T 020 7403 8966   F 020 7403 8869
  @ info@railpersonnel.com
Market areas Rail

Website www.railpersonnel.com
UK Offices 1
REC Member No

Brief Description Rail Personnel is an organisation of dedicated Rail experts who have extensive world-wide industry experience. With offices in Australia, Hong Kong, Malaysia, Singapore, Canada, New Zealand, Spain and the UK, they know the world's Rail industry and the people who work in it. Simply put, they match the best people to the best jobs. They're always on the lookout for people who want challenging jobs to help broaden their experience.

Preferred method of contact Apply on line or telephone for an appointment

Minimum requirements None
Type of business Contract and Permanent
Grade/Level of Appointments All levels

Robert Giles

Head Office ✉ 11 Bruton St, W1J 6PY
  ⊖ Piccadilly Circus
  ⊞ Charing Cross
  ☎ T 020 7491 4491   F 020 7491 3311
  @ info@robertgilesagencies.com
Market areas Technical, Engineering, Architecture, Building Services

Website www.robertgilesagencies.com
UK Offices 1
REC Member Yes

Brief Description Robert Giles Agencies recruit permanent and temporary staff, all of whom are fully trained, widely experienced and ready for work the moment they arrive.

Preferred method of contact Apply on line or telephone for an appointment
Minimum requirements None
Type of business Temporary and Permanent
Grade/Level of Appointments All levels

Sheridan Associates
See IT and Telecoms, page 175

Technical Aid International

  ✉ 55 Grosvenor St, W1K 3HY
  ⊖ Green Park
  ⊞ Victoria
  ☎ T 020 7659 9800   F 020 7659 9820
  @ ict@1taceurope.com
Market areas Engineering, IT, Sales and Marketing

Website www.1taceurope.com
UK Offices 2
REC Member Yes
Head Office Basingstoke

Brief Description Established in 1994, TAC Europe has gained extensive experience and knowledge across a variety of industries and business areas. As a result, the company's core vision to develop the most innovative and flexible professional recruitment solutions and services has enabled the company to establish strong partnerships with some of the foremost organisations in a number of market sectors. Through its 'macro' understanding of its customers' and candidates' needs, TAC Europe strives to enhance its recruitment, consultancy and outsourcing services to bring quality, value and growth to its customers and candidates alike throughout Europe. As part of TAC Worldwide Companies, a US based organisation established in 1969, TAC Europe forms part of one of the largest privately owned companies supplying contract professionals and human resource management solutions in the world.

Preferred method of contact Apply on line or telephone for an appointment

Minimum requirements None

Type of business Temporary and Permanent

Grade/Level of Appointments All levels

Technical Prospects

Head Office ✉ 45 Bloomsbury Sq, WC1A 1RA
        ⊖ Holborn
        🚊 City Thameslink
        ☎ T 020 7691 1931   F 020 7813 0500
        @ enquiries@tech-prospects.co.uk
  Market areas Not for Profit, Technical

Website www.prospect-us.co.uk

UK Offices 1

REC Member No

Brief Description Technical Prospects is a division of ProspectUs, a London-based recruitment agency specialising in building careers and placing staff in Charities, Universities, NHS Trusts and other Not for Profit organisations. Candidates can expect an open and honest approach from them and they hope that they can make the search for work a positive experience.

Preferred method of contact Apply on line or telephone for an appointment

Minimum requirements None

Type of business Temporary and Permanent

Grade/Level of Appointments All levels

Technology Project Services

Head Office ✉ 1 Warwick Row, SW1E 5ER
        ⊖ Victoria
        🚊 Victoria
        ☎ T 020 7963 1212   F 020 7963 1299
  Market areas Advanced Engineering, Technical, IT, Aerospace

Website www.tps.co.uk

UK Offices 4

REC Member Yes

Brief Description TPS is a recruitment agency specialising in Advanced Engineering, Technical, IT and related professionals. With access to 1200 offices in 146 countries TPS has a truly global reach. TPS can provide a shortlist of suitable candidates for contract and permanent positions at all levels within a suitable timescale anywhere in the world. It also offers Management Agency Services, providing a totally outsourced recruitment package. Thirty years experience in providing effective solutions for all Technical recruitment requirements has given TPS a cutting edge in HR Management, one that guarantees customer satisfaction.

Preferred method of contact Apply on line or telephone for an appointment

Minimum requirements Previous professional experience

Type of business Contract and Permanent

Grade/Level of Appointments All levels

TED Recruitment Ltd

See **Construction and Property, page 56**

Bring it on

Making the web work for you

This chapter is taken from "The Monster Guide to Jobhunting" by Andrew Chapman, published by Prentice Hall, an imprint of Pearson Education, © Pearson Education Ltd 2001

One of the all-out best things with the internet is how you can let things come to you rather than constantly having to solicit the information and the opportunities you're looking for. This is very much the way things are developing: the technology is already powerful enough to make the jobs come to you for a change. While no employer is going to want to encourage you to be lazy, it's nevertheless in their interests as much as yours to speed up the recruitment process, and this is one way of doing it.

Looking at the figures

The whole premise of most major jobsites on the internet, as you've probably discovered already, is that they offer a database of current vacancies which you can search by:

→ category
→ keyword
→ employer
→ location
→ salary
→ level.

Not all sites offer the same search mechanisms by any means, and few offer all of the above. That doesn't matter – it's how you use the facilities that is most important.

Being able to search the listings is all very well, but if you don't find what you're looking for, it can be frustrating. There may be a number of reasons for this:

→ limited number of opportunities listed;
→ your particular type of job is not featured;
→ your search criteria are too broad or too narrow.

In general, the more opportunities you are exposed to the better, of course. A number of the bigger sites in the UK already have more than 10 000 job vacancies on their books, and in general the figures are rising. Every time you go to a site, the vacancies will have changed – and if the numbers have gone down for any reason, you might well ask yourself why. If a site doesn't publish the size of its database somewhere obvious, usually on the home page, that is a good reason to be suspicious.

As ever, though, numbers can be misleading. In some cases, the number of jobs on offer that you see is not limited to the UK but might include partner sites overseas. If the astonishing 123 000 vacancies available include those in the States, the figure might not mean very much to you as a UK jobseeker. PlanetRecruit, for example, advertises itself specifically as an *international* jobsite, and the number of vacancies shown on the home page reflects that.

The number of vacancies is not the only statistic that might be useful to you – or, inevitably, the only one that might be misleading. Treat all data with circumspection, and remember that it's results that count. Having said that, it's also worth bearing in mind:

→   the number of visitors or hits;
→   the number of companies featured;
→   the number of CVs stored.

The first and last of these give an indication of how many people like yourself are actually using the site in question. Monthly visitors/hits is a statistic not often displayed, though, and is an inherently confusing term. 'Hits' in the web world can mean many things, including:

→   number of different people using the site;
→   number of times each page has been accessed;
→   number of times the overall site has been accessed.

It's a minefield, so maybe you should focus more on the number of CVs listed. That figure is probably there to impress potential employers, but it also reveals how many people have found the site worth spending enough time with to go as far as creating a CV on it. Some of those will inevitably have gone stale long ago, but it's still a good indication of the site's quality. What's going to reassure you is some sign that other people like yourself are bothering with this site.

Number of companies is also a useful piece of information (although again, not often displayed): if all the vacancies are coming from a handful of major firms, then the market is not truly being represented. The greater the diversity of employers using the site, the wider the variety of jobs on offer. There's no reason why you shouldn't e-mail the jobsite in question and ask for this sort of information.

As ever, there's a caveat: 'employers' in internet recruitment terms can often include agencies. There are many recruitment consultants that use jobsites to post up the vacancies on their books. For you as a committed jobseeker, this needn't be a problem, as it's jobs you're looking for, but don't be surprised if you come across a lot of agencies rather than being led directly to the heart of a particular firm when you click on a link to find more details about a job.

It's all very well listing thousands of jobs, but at the end of the day what counts is whether any of those are what you are looking for. It's difficult to assess the value of a particular site in this respect, especially given that the listings change from day to day; the only way to get a feel is to give it a go and try a site on a few occasions over a period of time before you decide what you really think about it.

But visiting a dozen websites over and over again is where things really start to become a bore. You need to get on with your life, and you can't spend all day every day trawling through huge databases. After all, the internet is supposed to be making this whole business more convenient – otherwise you might just as well not bother with it. And another thing: if you're doing this at home, you don't want an epic phone bill; if you're at work, you don't want to get sacked from the job you're trying to leave by spending all your time there trying to leave it.

Don't despair. What you need are search *agents*, and plenty of the better sites now offer them.

Cut out the legwork

In the infamous *Harry Potter* books, messages are delivered by owls which will track you down wherever you happen to be and drop a letter or parcel into your lap. For anyone disappointed that real life can't be more like that of the wizards created by J. K. Rowling, the good news is that we have e-mail, which can do all this and more.

You may well have already set up various job search agents to do your bidding. Either way, in this chapter you'll find useful advice on how to make them more effective. If you're not sure what they are yet, this section is for you.

Put simply, search agents automate the process of looking through a database so that you only have to do it once. In the same way that you enter search details such as keywords or job type, you set up the same criteria and save them on the website in question as a personal 'agent'. You can then forget about visiting the site every day or whatever, and whenever suitable matches are found, the site will e-mail you to let you know.

There are variations within this model. Some sites, such as *www.topjobs.com*, will only send you an e-mail when a match has come up. Others will contact you on a regular basis – daily or weekly, say – and present the matches in one go.

And the way the matches are presented varies significantly, too. In some cases, fairly full details of each match will be mailed to you; in others, just a one-line summary with a link to follow that will take you straight to the full information on the website in question. Others still may tell you that there have been some matches (perhaps saying how many), but you have to visit the site to find out anything about what they are.

You're after an easy life here, and in an ideal world you would probably want perfect matches, with full details (including contacts for applying) e-mailed to you on the spot. But life isn't as simple as that, even on the internet – and there are reasons for it. It's rare for a site to give away quite that much: however grateful you are to it for finding the jobs you want, you are not actually going to bother returning to the site. All of these jobsites thrive on traffic, and they need you to come back.

The deal is that they should make it worth you coming back – if you find it pure inconvenience to return to them, and they do not bring anything new to the experience, then more fool them. The best sites create a culture where you *want* to go back – for job listings, of course, but also for advice and support throughout all stages of the process.

Once you've accepted that you may well have to go back to the site to see full details of the job you're interested in, you can still demand certain levels of service within that model. For example, e-mails from some sites actually say how many matches have been found in the subject line. This gives you some idea – and indeed warning – of what to expect. You'll be amazed: some sites can send you two vacancies on one day, and 72 on the next. If you know that the e-mail you're about to open is enormous, you can then save it for a coffee break.

What's more annoying still is that you often find the same vacancies coming up over and over again. To some extent this is simply because the same employers post them over and over again, and it's next to impossible for the site to filter them, especially if each new posting does something sneaky like change the wording slightly – it's a bit like being spammed by e-mail.

Other issues to consider include the possibility of setting up more than one agent at the same site. We all know that submitting search criteria to forms on the internet is not always entirely satisfying, and you may feel you are being forced into certain keywords that do not entirely cover what you're looking for. If you could just send out another agent, with slightly different details…

Often, you can. At *www.monster.co.uk*, for example, you can save up to five different search agents as part of your personal profile on the site ('My Monster'). They can be wildly different from each other or vary in only the smallest detail. If you really want to keep your options open, you could search for astronaut jobs with one and commis chef posts with another.

This technique is a bit like compiling different CVs tailored to different jobs you're hankering after, only much less time-consuming – and you can set up different online CVs in a similar way. You might well be advised to avoid setting up *too* many agents, however, or information overload will set in and you'll never find the real job offers lost in the endless forest of opportunities that your e-mail inbox has become. What you want to do is make a few agents work really effectively.

If you're going to set an agent on the trail of a killer job, you'd rather it were Sherlock Holmes than Inspector Clouseau. You don't want it dragging back any old job like the cat bringing half-eaten birds to your doormat and expecting praise for it.

The quality of the results you get will depend on three things:

→ the quality of the jobs;
→ the quality of the agent;
→ the quality of the way you use it.

There's nothing you can do about the first of these, apart from exercise your judgement in choosing which sites to use. The same applies to the quality of the agent, i.e.

the criteria by which you are able to search a particular database or the way in which its mechanisms actually work. Of the possible options listed at the beginning of this chapter, some are obviously more useful than others, and it will depend upon your priorities. If you don't mind where you work, then the location factor obviously loses importance.

The main area of concern for anyone lies with categories and keywords. Categorising a database of jobs by type offers clear benefits, but also disadvantages in that different people sometimes refer to the same job by different titles. To take a media example, most magazines and newspapers employ people known as sub-editors who take the writers' copy and either ruin it or make it readable, according to which side of the fence you fall. The job of a 'sub' can also involve laying out pages and doing design work, but not necessarily. And the titles given to people who undertake these tasks can be any of the following and more: sub-editor, production editor, production assistant, editorial assistant, assistant editor, editor, copy editor, etc. That's not even taking into account the fact that some employers have large teams of such people, with chiefs, deputy chiefs and so on. So if you're looking for a job as a sub, are you sunk from the start?

Well no, as most sites invoke more general categories: you'll probably find these jobs under 'media', for example. 'Media' itself, however, can be lumped with 'marketing', say, or with 'arts'. Every site does it differently, and this is one reason why having the option of saving several agents can be a great benefit to you. The main thing is to be alert, and consider being broader-minded in terms of categories than you think you might need to include.

Keywords are more complex still, yet ultimately your most powerful tool. Again, different sites mean different things. In the case of Monster, for example, the agent will search the full text of relevant jobs (i.e. ones that match your other criteria) for the occurrence of whatever words you have chosen. Other sites, however, will predefine keywords for a particular post, and you may be restricted in your choice; or the search will be applied only to the keyword list for a job rather than to the whole text of the job description.

It's actually very similar to the way different search engines work. Some just trawl through the <META> tags of sites on the web (i.e. the keywords put into the code by whoever designed the site), while others look through absolutely everything, and then either pick out keywords for themselves or store the actual text of the site.

Using keywords effectively takes a certain amount of experience, and although the aim here is to make internet jobhunting as painless as possible, you will have to be prepared for a little trial and error at the start to get the feel of things. Sometimes you need to make your search more specific, especially if you're being inundated with dross, and sometimes less so. It won't take long to get the hang of it, though – take a look at the box on the next page to find out exactly what the sites' experts say.

How long can you expect all this to take? Most search agents will start e-mailing you matches, if they have any, within 24 hours; if it takes more than a week, there's definitely call for changing your keywords – or changing the site you use.

The Monster guide

to search agents

What happens if you're getting no results, or far too many? Search agent expert Ben Giddings of Monster.co.uk has the answers.

→ **Why aren't the matches more precise?**

Agents match jobseeker criteria with client information, and to get a nearperfect match, you need to be exceptionally prescriptive in terms of what information you allow either the employer or the jobseeker to put in. But no recruiter would accept such rigidity, so you have to try to get a balance between a tight search and giving the recruiters all the freedom and flexibility the internet offers them to talk about themselves.

→ **How do I get the best out of my keywords?**

My advice is not to be too specific. Better to get too many results than too few. You can use further keywords to refine your search from the results page on Monster. On Monster, our keyword search scans every word of a job advert, which means if you put in the keyword 'manager', your results will include every advert that contains the word 'manager'. So you could get an assistant or trainee position where the job 'reports to the Marketing **Manager**'. Keywords are best used if the user knows that keyword will be specific to the job they are looking for. For example, if you are after an accountancy position but your specific interest is retail, you can do a search on the Accounting/ Auditing category using the keyword 'retail'. That should narrow the search to retail-based accountancy positions.

→ **I've done all that, but strange things still happen. Is it me?**

Keywords are very good at defining and redefining searches. They are also very good at messing them up. Again it comes back to learning how to get the best out of the functionality. It also relies on recruiters putting useful information in their ads (so the keywords are picked up on searches) and putting their adverts in the right categories (recruiters often post their own jobs).

→ **And if absolutely nothing comes up?**

It could mean we don't have any relevant jobs for you. There will always be people who can find more relevant jobs elsewhere, and best of luck to them. It's far better to get a fulfilling career than to use a site that currently doesn't meet your needs.

Quickfire tips for search agents in general:

- refine your search once you've got some initial results;
- use Boolean operators such as AND and OR;
- rule out words you definitely don't want to appear (e.g. use 'NOT sales');
- think how employers phrase things;
- set up different agents with different combinations.

A final word from an expert at another of the popular sites, Edward Beesley of GoJob-site.co.uk: 'I would say that if you are entering the search string criteria that you feel are most accurate for you and your career aspirations and you are still receiving positions that are totally wide of the mark, then you need to contact the customer support department of the site you are using.'

Your shop window: online CVs

In your challenge to get the jobs to come to you, setting up agents is only one half of the deal. The other is to create an online CV, a term which itself can mean various things. We've already considered the fact that many sites proudly say how many CVs they have listed, but what exactly does that mean?

Essentially there are two poles, with various possibilities in between: at one end, you have a CV formatted and constructed by you, and at the other a situation where you are obliged to tailor your skills and experience into a format entirely determined by the site you're using. As ever, each has its own advantages.

One of the few downsides of the internet in this respect is that it takes away various possibilities in the creation of your CV. For a traditional paper CV, you have the option of choosing the fonts, the colour of paper, and all manner of other fancy options (although you're not recommended to take them). On line, the medium demands a little more consistency. This can work to your advantage: it should be your skills you are selling, not your ability to choose fancy stationery – unless you want to be a stationer.

Observing the proper form

Filling in online CVs is generally pretty straightforward, but there are various tricks that can help and a number of things to avoid:

→ to select a block of entries from a drop-down list, use [SHIFT-CLICK] on your PC to select the first and last, and those in between will be selected automatically;

→ to select a few entries in different places, use [CTRL-CLICK] on a PC or [SHIFT-CLICK] on a Mac;

→ press [TAB] on a PC or Mac to jump quickly from one field to the next: it saves your mouse wrist from extra work;

→ if you see options as little circles to click ('radio buttons'), you can select only one option from the list available;

→ with options in the form of squares with a cross in them when selected ('checkboxes'), you can choose as many as you want;

→ check everything through before you click 'Submit' – there's often a 'Reset' button if you've messed it all up, or you can go back through the fields with [ALT] + [TAB];

→ if an error occurs, read the message carefully: sometimes if you click the 'Back' button in your browser, your data will reappear, and you can try submitting it again;

→ if it doesn't reappear, you may have to start again, but check the homepage of this section (e.g. the My Monster page in the case of www.monster.co.uk) to make sure your information hasn't been saved after all;

→ don't spend time lining up your details in columns – it won't come out like that at the other end.

Let's look at the predetermined end of the spectrum first. Many of the better sites now have sophisticated CV-creation 'wizards' that help you format a complete, professional-looking CV, building an easy-to-use template to fill in on line full details of your past, present and hoped-for future. This process can take some time – Monster, for example, warns that half an hour or so is needed. Don't be put off, though: it offers the same advantages as setting up search agents, in that a one-off effort can reap rewards, with you barely lifting a finger to the mouse. Once you have created your online career profile, the effort is all on the part of the employers. They want to fill their vacancies quickly, so they will happily trawl through your details while you're busy doing something else.

Sending out speculative CVs by post is an infamously laborious – and costly – process. Here, you do it once, and you don't even have to decide which employers to target. They will come to you.

There are ways and means to go about doing all this, and the more carefully you approach it, the better hits you'll get. Make sure from the start that you have thought seriously not just about what you've done before but also about what you really want for the future. A good pro forma online CV will have spaces dedicated to just that.

It can take time and effort to do a CV, whatever the medium, but you should take it seriously. If you're doing it on line, think in particular about what title to give it, as this is what the employers will see first – there's more on this in the online CVs panel on the next page.

Not every jobsite is terribly sophisticated, and some will simply invite you to upload your present CV as an attachment. Most will accept a document in Microsoft Word format, and this does at least give you quite a bit of scope for being 'creative', but don't be tempted to overdo it. Like you, employers are in a hurry, and they too are using the internet for an easier life. Try to give it to them.

Other sites go for some kind of compromise between do-it-yourself and fill-in-a-form, usually employing a looser kind of form into which you can cut and paste various elements of the CV you've already got. This sounds like a helpful way to go, and can certainly save a lot of time, but you still need to think of who's going to be reading it. A little more time to reformat for the web will be to your advantage, although you don't have to go too far, as GoJobsite.co.uk content manager Edward Beesley points out: 'The best advice would be to keep your CV in the standard form and also keep an amended plain text version that can be easily pasted into an online form.'

What do they see in you?

It has been stressed that you need to think about the end viewer of your CV. So what do they actually see, and how do they find you? The way employers use a site such as *www.monster.co.uk* is very much the same as it is for you, except that they're coming from the other direction. For example, they too can set up search agents. Instead of trawling the vacancies, however, they trawl the CVs. They can enter keywords, too, and these will search the text that you have entered. This is why it is so

The Monster guide

to online CVs

→ **Think about the type of company that will invest in CV searches**

It's likely to be a large-scale operation with specific (often large-scale or regular) needs in a competitive sector, or a recruiter looking for someone with highly specialised skills. In some cases you're better off going to a niche site.

→ **Think carefully about the title you give your CV**

A CV title is the first thing an employer sees when presented with a list of potentially suitable CVs and your title has to say a lot about you in only a few words. 'Graphic design' says what field you work in, but the employer should know that already because they've just done a search for graphic designers. What about 'Senior Designer with International Agency', or even 'I did the Guinness ad' – they say much more.

→ **Don't overdo the attention-grabbing**

On the web, the words you choose to label yourself with count for a lot. Call your CV 'Slartybartfast the wonder Java guru' and no one will give you a second look. Give your CV the title 'Expert Java (3 yrs) & European Project Management' and people get interested. Recruiters want information, not slogans.

→ **Remember to renew**

Monster.co.uk gets around 1500–2000 new CVs a week posted on to the board. As more CVs are added, yours moves further down the list, making it less likely to be seen by an employer. To combat that, it's probably advisable to 'renew' your CV every month or so. This is normally a feature that you use to post your CV back on the board after one year (at which point it automatically becomes unsearchable). But if you renew every month or so, each time the database thinks you have posted a new CV and puts it back at the top of the most recent list, thereby keeping you up there with the newest ones. You can renew your CV just by clicking a link on 'My Monster' homepage.

→ **Remember your audience**

As well as thinking about what kind of employer is looking through the site you're using, think about the actual information they're looking for, and make sure you include it in the body of your CV. Include any technical aspects of your work – the employer might be looking for something precise such as 'C++'.

→ **Set up more than one CV**

Some jobsites will let you create more than one CV, each with its own title, just as you can with some search agents. Think of the different aspects of the work you are looking for, and employers sometimes target people like you in different ways. Put yourself in their field of vision in different ways – and again, remember to renew them all regularly to stay there.

important to put some thought into your online CV rather than just bashing it out. It's easy to think that it won't matter if you type in something hastily and then click a few buttons to submit it, but why be so cavalier? You have nothing to lose in creating an online CV, but you can always maximise your gain.

The main difference for the employer is that they are probably paying for the privilege of looking at your CV: they are likely to subscribe to various services provided by the site which enable them not just to look through CVs but also to append notes to them and store them for future reference in something similar to the online 'shopping baskets' you see on sites such as *www.amazon.co.uk*. Your challenge is to catch their eye – and reading the particular site's content on CV building, scanning its help pages and following the tips in this chapter can help you tailor your CV. It also means knowing how to sell yourself in more traditional ways.

> 'We try to screen all CVs we receive. Given certain skill/experience requirements we'll generally progress with a candidate if their CV radiates a personality compatible with our ethos: energy, enthusiasm and entrepreneurs.'
>
> *(Mark Whitehead, eLab)*

What recruiters are looking for

Filling in online CVs is generally pretty straightforward, but there are various tricks that can help and things to avoid:

Relevance: recruiters are deluged with hopeless applications, attracted by the money but not even addressing the basic job definition. Irrelevant applications never get anywhere. Recruiters are as professional at their job as you are at yours and they spot the wrong-uns within seconds. They do not even read naff-looking CVs containing the wrong information.

Information: your CV needs to be structured to give them the information that they are looking for. Usually they tell you what that is in the advertisement or online posting and if you don't understand what they are saying, you probably would not be right for the job.

Convergence: your covering letter and CV can be tweaked to pinpoint your case. Recruiters warm to candidates who show they have thought about the application and where possible have taken the trouble to find out about the job and company.

Corroboration: recruiters are looking for skills that match requirements and evidence of using those skills effectively. Unsubstantiated claims in the US style are hopeless – you need to establish and prove that you are the professional you say you are (e.g. 'good communication skills' makes you squirm but 'renegotiated and then continued ownership of a growing £3m business alliance that was previously failing' shows that you can communicate).

What more: sometimes people respond to expressions of vision and possibility that exceed their stated requirements. For jobs over £45k a year you aren't even starting to compete if you don't suggest that you have fresh ideas to bring to the interview. For big jobs they appoint big candidates who can offer something really positive.

© Steven Holmes and John Peters. This section is licensed for publication by Monster. You can contact them for advice and assistance on *www.cvservices.net*.

Other organisations

Career Advice

Alighn Ltd

✉ 12 Harley Street, W1G 9PG
☎ T 020 7323 4169
@ info@alighn.co.uk
Website www.alighn.co.uk

Army Careers Information Office

✉ 453-454 The Strand, WC2R 0RG
☎ T 020 7930 8603
Website www.army.mod.uk/careers/

C2 - The Graduate Careers Shop

✉ University of London Careers Service, 49-51 Gordon Square, WC1H 0PN
☎ T 020 7554 4555
@ careershop@careers.lon.ac.uk
Website www.careershop.co.uk

Career and Training Int. Ltd

✉ 143 Wembley Hill Road, HA9 8DT
☎ T 020 8795 0911
@ cti@careers-training.com
Website www.careers-training.com

Career Counselling

✉ 188 Albert Rd, N22 7AH
☎ T 020 8888 9706

Career Counselling Services

✉ 46 Ferry Rd, SW13 9PW
☎ T 020 8741 0335
@ careercs@dial.pipex.com
Website www.career-counselling-services.co.uk

Career Partnership

✉ 54 Skeena Hill, SW18 5PL
☎ T 020 8788 3795
@ ozten@red.net

Career Psychology

✉ 11 Waterloo Place, SW1Y 4AU
☎ T 020 7976 1010
@ info@career-psychology.co.uk
Website www.career-psychology.com

Careers and Training International Ltd

✉ 143 Wembley Hill Road, Wembley, HA9 8DT
☎ T 020 8795 0911
@ cti@careers-training.com
Website www.careers-training.com

Dickins and Co

✉ 150 Minories, EC3N
☎ T 020 7264 2261

Educational and Career Guidance

✉ 4 Cadogan Lane, SW1X 9EB
☎ T 020 7631 1209

Executive Action

✉ 6 Porter Street, W1U 6DD
☎ T 020 7299 2900
@ info@executive-action.com
Website www.careers-executive.com

Fairplace Consulting plc

✉ 36-38 Cornhill, EC3V 3PQ
☎ T 020 7816 0707
@ fairplace@fairplace.com

Gabbitas

✉ 126-130 Regent Street, W1B 5EE
☎ T 020 7734 0161
@ admin@gabbitas.co.uk
Website www.gabbitas.co.uk

Hogg Robinson Skillbase

✉ 3rd Floor, 110 Fenchurch Street, EC3M 5TT
☎ T 020 7379 7233
@ office.admin@hr.skillbase.com
Website www.skillbasecareers.com

ICM CareerCare

✉ 4 Brabant Court, Philpot Lane, EC3M 8AD
☎ T 020 7630 0155
@ icm@careersbp.co.uk
Website www.icmcareercare.com

Independent Schools Careers Organisation

✉ Regents College, Inner Circle, Regents Park, NW1 4NS
☎ T 020 7487 3660
@ jelkan@aol.com

InterExec

✉ 1st Floor, 16 St. Helens Place, EC3A 6DF
☎ T 020 7256 9972
@ city@interexec.co.uk
Website www.interexec.co.uk

Jo Ouston & Co

✉ Nelson House, Dolphin Square, SW1V 3NY
☎ T 020 7821 8299
Website www.joouston.co.uk

Lee Hecht Harrison

✉ 4th Floor, 25 Bucklersbury, EC4N 8DA
☎ T 020 7489 0700
@ lhhlondon@lhh.com
Website www.lhh.com

LifesWork Ltd

✉ 211 Piccadilly, W1J 9HG
☎ T 020 7917 2903
@ lifeswork@btinternet.com
Website www.lifework.ltd.uk

Meridian Consulting Ltd

✉ 7 Ludgate Broadway, EC4V 6DX
☎ T 020 7489 8070
@ pennameridian@e-penna.com
Website www.e-penna.com

Metropolitan Police Selection Centre

✉ 26 Aybrook St, W1U 4AN
☎ T 0845 727 2212
Website www.met.police.uk/recruitment

New Careers

✉ Wigham House, Wakering Rd, Barking, IG11 8QN
☎ T 020 8591 8400
@ enquiry@new-careers.co.uk
Website www.new-careers.co.uk

New Horizons (Careers) Ltd

✉ 3 Great James St, WC1N 3DB
☎ T 020 7831 9843
@ enquiries@nhcareers.co.uk
Website www.nhcareers.co.uk

Quantum Development and Outplacement Services Ltd

✉ 14 Ironmonger Lane, EC2V 8EY
☎ T 020 7726 2233
Website www.quantumdevelop.com

Royal Airforce Careers

✉ Room G146 MOD, St Christopher House, Southwark St, SE1 0TD
☎ T 020 7305 4278
Website www.raf-careers.com

Royal Navy and Royal Marines Careers Office

✉ 1a Iverna Gardens, Kensington, W8 6TN
☎ T 020 7938 4646
@ oclc.london@dnr.mod.uk
Website www.rnjob.co.uk

Sanders and Sidney plc

✉ Regent Arcade House, 19-25 Argyll Street, W1F 7TS
☎ T 020 7663 6633
Website www.pennasandersandsidney.com

Slesser Maclean

✉ 29 Needham Terrace, NW2 6QL
☎ T 020 8208 0751
@ slesser_mclean@msn.co.uk
Website www.slessermaclean.co.uk

Springboard UK

✉ 3 Denmark St, WC2H 8LP
☎ T 020 7497 8654
@ info.london@springboarduk.org.uk
Website www.springboard.org.uk

Tower Hamlets Graduate Forum

✉ 7-15 Greatorex St, E1 5NF
☎ T 020 7375 3010
@ info@careerslondon.com
Website www.careerslondon.com

Wheat

✉ 33 Throgmorton Street, EC2N 2BR
☎ T 020 7397 3340
@ jthomas@wheatsearch.com
Website www.wheatsearch.com

Image Consultants

Angela Bailey

✉ 24 Maida Avenue, W2 1ST
☎ T 020 7706 1010
@ abailey@zoo.co.uk

Color Me Beautiful

✉ 7 Stanhope Close, Rotherhite, SE16 6RQ
☎ T 020 7394 6191
@ normajgallagher@aol.com
Website www.cmb.co.uk

ImageCounts

✉ Jenny Cutler, ImageCounts, Suite 111 Caramom Building, 31 Shad Thames SE1 2YR
☎ T 020 7407 6764
@ enquiries@imagecounts.co.uk
Website www.imagecounts.co.uk

CV Writers

1-2-3 Express Services

✉ 35 Brompton Rd, Knightsbridge, SW3 1DE
☎ T 020 7823 9955
@ ksecservices@globalnet.co.uk
Website www.typingoverload.co.uk

Select CVs

✉ 138 Brompton Rd, Knightsbridge, SW3 1HY
☎ T 020 7581 8977
@ knightbridgecv@dilstart.net
Website www.selectcvs.co.uk

Focus CVs

✉ 109 Lupus Street/95 Wilton Rd, Pimlico, SW1V 3EN
☎ T 0845 090 0130
@ info@focuscvs.co.uk
Website www.focuscvs.co.uk

The CV Company

✉ 28A Lower Marsh, Southbank, SE1 7RG
☎ T 020 7401 7239
@ info@thecvcompany.net
Website www.thecvcompany.net

Jobsearchers.co.uk

✉ 1st Floor, The White House, Gerrards Cross, Bucks, SL9 9HF
☎ T 01753 890243
@ info@jobsearch.co.uk
Website www.jobsearchers.co.uk

Computer Training

Azlan Group

✉ Austin Friars House, 6 Austin Friars, EC2N 2HE
☎ T 020 7628 2300
Website www.aclan.com\uk\training

Camden Itec Ltd

✉ 7 Leighton Place, NW5 2QL
☎ T 020 7485 3324
Website www.camden-itec.co.uk

Banner Duncan Associates Ltd

✉ 1 Founders Court, Lothbury, EC2R 7DB
☎ T 020 7606 0700
@ info@bannerduncan.com
Website www.bannerduncan.com

Certified Computing Personnel

✉ 1 Olympic Way, HA9 0ND
☎ T 020 8903 6900
Website www.computingpersonnel.com

BigHand Ltd

✉ Westminster Business Square, 1-4 Durham St, SE11 5JH
☎ T 020 7793 8200
Website www.big-hand.co.uk

Computer Training Centre London Ltd

✉ 16-18 Whitechapel Rd, E1 1EW
☎ T 020 7377 6706
@ cpcll@msn.com
Website www.topqualitytraining.com

Computer Training Solutions

✉ 44 Welbeck St, W1G 8DY
☎ T 020 7486 9998
@ cts@it-uk.com
Website www.cts-uk.com

Computers and Training Centre

✉ 1a Evering Rd, Stoke Newington, N16 7QA
☎ T 020 7275 2705
@ info@computersandtraining.co.uk
Website www.computersandtraining.co.uk

DCT Resources Ltd

✉ Argyle House, 29 Euston Rd, NW1 2SD
☎ T 020 7837 4800
@ info@dct-tech.com
Website www.dct-tech.com

East London Advanced Technology Training (ELATT)

✉ 2nd Floor Arnold House, 36-41 Holywell Lane, Hackney, EC2P 2EQ
☎ T 020 7247 4682
@ enquiries@elatt.org.uk
Website www.elatt.org.uk

Gayleseen Ltd

✉ City Business Centre, Lower Rd, SE16 2BX
☎ T 020 7231 0404
Website www.gayleseen.co.uk

GHARWEG

✉ 5 Westminster Bridge Rd, SE16 7XW
☎ T 020 7620 1430
@ gharweg@aol.com

Happy Computers Ltd

✉ Cityside House, 40 Adler St, E1 1EE
☎ T 020 7375 7300
@ happy@happy.co.uk
Website www.happy.co.uk

Hoxton Bibliotech

✉ 24-33 Independent Place, The Forum, Shacklewell Lane, E8 2HD
☎ T 020 7275 8195
Website www.biblio-tech.net

Innovative E-Business Solutions

✉ Suite 15 Cannon Wharf, 35 Evelyn St, SE8 5TR
☎ T 020 7394 7961
@ Admin@iebsolutions.co.uk
Website www.iebsolutions.co.uk

Interquad Services Ltd

✉ 110 Middlesex St, E1 7HT
☎ T 020 7377 9585
@ info@interquad.com
Website www.interquad.co.uk

Intuition Computer Training

✉ Intuition House, 210 Borough High St, SE1 1JX
☎ T 020 7403 7259
@ frontdesk@intuition.co.uk
Website www.intuition.co.uk

IT Lab Training

✉ 13-25 Church Street, NW8 8DT
☎ T 0800 034 9697
@ info@itlab.co.uk
Website www.itlab.co.uk

287

IT-IQ

✉ 25 City Rd, EC1Y 1AA
☎ T 020 7670 3300
@ jeremywarren@it-iq.co.uk
Website www.it-iq.co.uk

Media Training

✉ Studio 14, Aberdeen Studios, 22 Highbury Grove, N5 2EA
☎ T 020 7359 9855
@ enquiries@mediatraining.ltd.uk
Website www.mediatraining.ltd.uk

Millennium Advanced Technology Training Ltd

✉ Whitechapel Technology Centre, Unit 2.35, 2nd floor, 75 Whitechapel Rd, E1 1DU
☎ T 020 7247 8684
@ abu@matt.ltd.co.uk

Optimum Technology Transfer Ltd

✉ 32 Sekforde St, Clerkenwell, EC1R 0HH
☎ T 020 7841 0101
@ info@optimum.co.uk
Website www.optimum.co.uk

Oxford House Computer Training

✉ 30 Market Place, W1W 8AW
☎ T 020 7436 4872
@ computing@oxfordhouse.co.uk
Website www.oxfordhouse.co.uk

Oxford Tutorial Services

✉ Unit 1, Spectrum House, 32-34 Gordon House, Kentish Town, NW5 1LP
☎ T 020 7485 4246

Parity Training Ltd

✉ 174-177 High Holborn, WC1V 7AA
☎ T 020 7632 8700
Website www.parity.net

Pass Training

✉ 100a Chalk Farm Rd, NW1 8EH
☎ T 020 7284 4995
@ info@pass.co.uk
Website www.pass.co.uk

Pathway Computer Training

✉ 6 Netherwood Rd, W14 0BJ
☎ T 0800 316 3393
@ info@pathwayuk.com
Website www.pathwayuk.com

Portable Training and Consultancy Services

✉ 113 Gloucester Place, W1U 6JR
☎ T 020 7935 9224
@ info@portablegroup.com
Website www.portablegroup.com

Premier Computer Solutions

✉ 4 Ravey Street, EC2A 4QP
☎ T 020 7729 1811
@ enquiries@premiercs.co.uk
Website www.premcs.com

Premier Computer Training

✉ Premier House, 150 Southampton Row, WC1B 5AL
☎ T 020 7837 2690
@ info@premierit.com
Website www.premierit.com

Pro & Pro Computer Training

✉ Brewmasters House, 91 Brick Lane, E1
☎ T 020 7375 3761
Website www.pro&pro.com

Spring IT Training Ltd

✉ Salisbury House, 30 Finsbury Circus, EC2M 7DT
☎ T 020 7452 7300
@ philippa_garsed@spring.com
Website www.spring.com

Stayahead Training Ltd

✉ 6-8 Long Lane, EC1A 9HF
☎ T 020 7600 6116
@ info@stayahead.com
Website www.stayahead.com

Stehle Associates

✉ 212 Piccadilly, W1J 9HG
☎ T 020 7917 9943
Website www.stehle.co.uk

Symmedia Ltd

✉ 1 Westbourne Rd, N7 8AR
☎ T 020 7928 1112
Website www.symmedia.co.uk

Systems Support

✉ Suites D & E, 5th Floor Diamond House, 36-38 Hatton Gardens, xxx
☎ T 020 7242 2926
Website www.system-support.co.uk

Training Prospects

✉ 45 Bloomsbury Square, WC1A 2RA
☎ T 020 7691 1939
@ enquiries@training-prospects.co.uk
Website www.prospect-us.co.uk

Online

Monster.co.uk

@ userservices@monster.co.uk
Website www.monster.co.uk
Description Monster.co.uk is the local content and language website for Monster.com, the leading global career portal on the Web. With over 1.3 million unique visits per month, Monster.co.uk connects the most progressive companies with the most qualified career-minded individuals, offering innovative technology and superior services that give them more control over the recruiting process. The Monster global network consists of 21 local sites, including the United Kingdom, France, the Netherlands, Sweden, Norway, Denmark, Finland, Belgium, Germany, Ireland, Spain, Italy, Luxembourg, Switzerland, the United States, New Zealand, Singapore, Australia, Canada, Hong Kong and India.

SecsintheCity.com

@ info@secsinthecity.com
Website www.SecsintheCity.com
Description SecsintheCity.com is a job noticeboard for secretarial and administration jobs in London. They have been going for 1 year and have most of the top agencies in London advertising vacancies on their site.

Workthing.com

Website www.workthing.com

www.doctorjob.com

@ gti@gti.co.uk
Website www.doctorjob.com
Description doctorjob.com, the No. 1 graduate careers website, is the place to be if you are at university or just graduated. The doctor's surgery is always open, providing job seekers with careers advice and hundreds of jobs.

www.e-job.net

@ www.e-job.com
Website www.e-job.net
Description e-job.com is the specialist job site for the 'e' professional. Covering e-Sales, New Media (design) and IT Technical, they allow job seekers to search for their future career.

www.firstpersonglobal.com

@ info@firstpersonglobal.com
Website www.firstpersonglobal.com
Description Career Management for business leaders in technology.

www.fish4jobs.co.uk

Website www.fish4jobs.co.uk
Description fish4jobs advertises around 40,000 job vacancies throughout Britain and is updated daily. With practical tips and advice on CVs and interviews the site also guides users through the whole process of getting a job. And with career advice from a resident life coach and free psychometric tests, fish4jobs will help to ensure users find the perfect job.

www.gisajob.com

@ sales@gisajob.com
Website www.gisajob.com

www.gradunet.co.uk

@ info@gradunet.co.uk
Website www.gradunet.co.uk
Description Gradunet is the UK's most established Graduate Recruitment Website. Since 1995, they have been pioneering on-line recruitment solutions for graduates and employers.

www.jobit.co.uk

@ support@jobit.com
Website www.jobit.co.uk
Description Jobit is a universal gateway to providing users with the ideal tools to create optimal matches between organisations and candidates. It's aim is to become the central resource centre for worldwide job markets with offices already located in the UK, USA and Australia.

www.jobs-at.com

@ Sales@Jobs-at.com
Website www.jobs-at.com

www.jobs.telegraph.co.uk

Website www.jobs.telegraph.co.uk/search.asp

www.jobsgopublic.co.uk

@ sales@jobsgopublic.com
Website www.jobsgopublic.com
Description The Jobsgopublic service is tailored for public sector recruitment and welcomes visitors interested in a career within the not for profit sector. Jobsgopublic was formed in 1998 and now works with hundreds of organisations in the UK to provide advertising and various technical solutions including career sites and career intranets.

www.jobshark.co.uk

Website www.jobshark.co.uk
Description Jobshark.com, founded originally in Canada in 1997, is one of the world's leading Internet Recruitment companies. JobShark now has operations in nine countries including Canada, the UK and Ireland, and across Latin America with offices in Chile, Argentina, Brazil, Venezuela, Peru, Colombia and Mexico. JobShark provides a sophisticated internet recruiting service for employers and job seekers interested in finding 'the right job' or the 'right candidate'. Through its proprietary matching technology, called JAWS, jobshark.com matches on skill sets and then notifies prosective candidates by email of matching job postings directly to qualified candidates

www.jobsite.co.uk

Website www.jobsite.co.uk
Description Every candidate is provided with his, or her, own 'My GoJobsite' home page that delivers all GoJobsite's services tailored specifically for their industry sectors. All services to job hunters are free of charge.

www.phdjobs.com

@ phdjobs@ecihumancapital.com
Website www.phdjobs.com
Description ECI Postgrad is a specialist recruitment consultancy that was established in 1998. Incorporating Phdjobs.com, ECI Postgrad is unique in the world of recruitment. Their aim is to be 'the world's leading provider of postgraduates to companies at the forefront of innovation.'

www.planetrecruit.com

@	feedback@planetrecruit.com
Website	www.planetrecruit.com
Description	PlanetRecruit was formed in 1999 to help candidates in their search for a new career. Since then, they've advertised over one million jobs and helped thousands of candidates find a new job in countries around the world. Their service is entirely free for job hunters – candidates can search for jobs, upload their CV/Resumé – making it available to hundreds of recruitment agencies across the world – and register for job alerts which will email the candidate with any new jobs that match their requirements

www.thisislondon.co.uk

Website	www.thisislondon.co.uk/dynamic/jobs/search/top.html
Description	Easy-to-use service lets job hunters search for vacancies at the click of a mouse. You can apply for jobs by email, be emailed vacancies that meet your needs, and complete a CV on line which is made available anonymously to potential employers. As well as vacancies covering all sectors, they carry lively, informative news and features.

www.topjobs.co.uk

@	topjobs@topjobs.co.uk
Website	www.topjobs.co.uk
Description	Launched in the UK in April 1996, TopJobs was one of the earliest brands within the Internet recruitment marketplace to focus on the potential of the Internet for recruitment advertising. Today, topjobs.co.uk is a well-established brand, specializing in targeting management, professional, technical and graduate job seekers.

www.totaljobs.com

@	andrew.griffin@totaljobs.com
Website	www.totaljobs.com

Index